RESEARCH HIGHLIGHTS IN SOCIAL WORK 48

Developments in Social Work
with Offenders

Research Highlights in Social Work

This topical series examines areas of particular interest to those in social and community work and related fields. Each book draws together different aspects of the subject, highlighting relevant research and drawing out implications for policy and practice. The project is under the editorial direction of Professor Joyce Lishman, Head of the School of Applied Social Studies at the Robert Gordon University.

Other books in the series

RESEARCH HIGHLIGHTS IN SOCIAL WORK 48

Developments in Social Work with Offenders

Edited by Gill McIvor and Peter Raynor

Jessica Kingsley Publishers
London and Philadelphia

First published in the United Kingdom in 2007 by
Jessica Kingsley Publishers
116 Pentonville Road
London N1 9JB, England
and
400 Market Street, Suite 400
Philadelphia, PA 19106, USA
www.jkp.com

Library of Congress Cataloging in Publication Data
A CIP catalog record for this book is available from the Library of Congress

British Library Cataloguing in Publication Data
A CIP catalogue record for this book is available from the British Library

ISBN 978 1 84310 538 1

Printed and Bound in Great Britain by
Athenaeum Press, Gateshead, Tyne and Wear

Contents

Part Two Assessment, Supervision and Intervention

Part Three Issues and Needs

Figures and Tables

CHAPTER 1

Introduction and Overview

Gill McIvor and Peter Raynor

Introduction

A previous volume in the Research Highlights Series entitled *Working with Offenders* was published over ten years ago (McIvor 1996). Since then there have been major organisational changes in probation and social work across the UK, including the creation in England and Wales of a National Probation Directorate, the National Offender Management Service and the Youth Justice Board. In Scotland major organisational changes have included local government reorganisation, the creation of local authority criminal justice partnerships and, more recently, the establishment of Community Justice Authorities. At the same time, there has been an unprecedented amount of legislative change that has resulted in the introduction of new court disposals, changes in sentencing powers and an increased focus upon 'seamless sentencing' and its implications for offender rehabilitation and resettlement. These developments need also to be set against an accumulating body of knowledge about what constitutes effective practice in the assessment, supervision and management of offenders in the community. Increasingly this knowledge base is shaping the focus and content of social work with offenders against an ever-changing organisational, legislative and policy background and against increasing levels of government expenditure aimed at reducing re-offending and enhancing community safety.

The landscape in which social workers and probation officers practise (both in the UK and internationally) is therefore almost unrecognisable in comparison with a decade ago. This volume brings together the contributions of authoritative commentators in this field to chart these changes and to discuss how they have impinged upon social work with offenders, providing a key contemporary synthesis and analysis of recent legislation, policy and research.

Developments in policy

The first section of this book focuses upon developments in policy and practice in social work with young and adult offenders in different parts of the UK. The primary concern of the book is with social work services to adult offenders (that is, those who would be the responsibility of the probation services in England and Wales, criminal justice social work services in Scotland or the Probation Board for Northern Ireland). However, it is instructive also to examine how juvenile justice policy has evolved over recent years, particularly in the light of devolution and other significant constitutional or political changes across the UK (not least of which has been the creation of a Labour Government in 1997) and pre-existing differences in philosophy and practice in its constituent jurisdictions. For example, what difference has a Labour Government made to the treatment of young people who commit offences in England and Wales? Has the devolution of legislative and policy-making powers to a Scottish Parliament amplified or attenuated within-UK differences in juvenile and criminal justice policy? And how have criminal justice policies in Ireland developed following in the aftermath of civil conflict and cessation of paramilitary violence? These and other issues are addressed in the following five chapters of the volume, beginning with Barry Goldson's critical analysis of New Labour's youth justice policies in Chapter 2. In this chapter Goldson argues that the unprecedented level of legislative and policy reform in youth justice in England and Wales has been directed principally at supporting the government's rhetoric of being 'tough on crime' (with little regard to the 'causes'). This has resulted in organisational changes, including the establishment of Youth Offending Teams accountable at the national level to the Home Office and Youth Justice Board and therefore institutionally separated from child welfare services; new modes of risk classification with net-widening tendencies; the intensification of responses to minor offending and the expansion of custodial sentencing of children and young people (with particularly notable increases in the use of detention with girls).

Scotland has its own separate judicial system and a distinctive approach to dealing with children and young people (in the main under 16 years of age) who offend. The Children's Hearings, introduced in 1971 following the publication of the Kilbrandon Report, enable young people who offend and those who require care and protection to be dealt with within a single, welfare-oriented system characterised by lay decision-making. However, as Bill Whyte demonstrates in Chapter 3, there have been significant developments in youth justice policy in recent years, aimed primarily at assuaging criticism that the system was unable to deal effectively with persistent young offenders (though it had not been adequately resourced to do so) and strengthening its capacity to respond more quickly and effectively to youth crime. Whyte argues that while some developments can be viewed as progressive and are to be welcomed (such as the introduction of specialist youth justice managers and practitioners in local authority children's services) other measures (such as the introduction of anti-social behaviour orders and youth courts for 16 and 17-year-olds) may serve to further criminalise young people for behaviour that might be more appropriately dealt with within an expanded (in terms of age) and well-resourced Children's Hearings System. Although a policy commitment to the principles of Kilbrandon has not been totally abandoned, the broad thrust of youth justice policy in Scotland has been in a punitive direction and this, coupled with the range of initiatives and measures that have been introduced, is indicative of what Whyte describes as a 'new and shared politicisation of youth justice' that is lessening differences in policy and practice across the UK.

Sam Lewis in Chapter 4 describes the rather different trajectory of policy and practice for adult offenders in England and Wales. (Although most public services are devolved to the Welsh Assembly Government, criminal justice is not, and Wales is obliged to implement Home Office policies.) She shows how social work approaches, albeit under other and more politically acceptable names, initially played a part in New Labour's 'evidence-based' approach, but have gradually been pushed into the background by an increasing focus on populist policy initiatives, punitive legislation and contestability. In particular, some serious attempts were made to correct the historical neglect of short-sentence prisoners, a risky and needy group for which virtually no resettlement provision was being made until the 'Pathfinder' projects of 1999–2003. These promising glimpses of 'joined-up' thinking were reflected in aspects of the 2003 Criminal Justice Act and in Patrick Carter's Correctional Services Review, but at the time of writing have been swamped by a rather depressing surge of populist initiatives: more prison places, a postponement of arrangements for the resettlement of short-sentence prisoners, and a preoccupation with breaking up the Probation Service to provide opportunities for the private and voluntary sectors to take over its work.

Significant and far-reaching organisational change has also featured prominently in Scotland over the last ten years. This has included local government reorganisation in 1996, followed by the creation of administrative groupings of local authorities to deliver criminal justice social work services and, most recently, the introduction of Community Justice Authorities (CJAs) with responsibility for the setting the strategic direction, resourcing and monitoring of services within their local area. These and other Scottish developments, including the introduction of a National Advisory Body on Offender Management and the establishment of a

Risk Management Authority (to provide national guidance on the effective assessment and management of risk among serious violent and sexual offenders), are discussed by Gill McIvor and Fergus McNeill in Chapter 5. As in England and Wales, more recent Scottish developments (including the CJAs) are seeking to better align practices in prisons and in the community. While agreeing that this is a laudable aim, McIvor and McNeill are concerned by the absence of an explicit commitment to custodial reductionism in recent policy documents. They are also, however, heartened by sustained policy reference to the importance of enhancing offenders' social inclusion which at least implicitly signifies a continued role for social work in the supervision of offenders in Scotland.

Partly as a result of its unique political circumstances (but also due to other distinctive characteristics such as a relatively low crime rate), certain aspects of probation practice in Northern Ireland have historically differed from other parts of the UK. As Gadd (1996) observed, for example, probation officers in Northern Ireland did not supervise parolees and, more generally, had no statutory role in the supervision and assessment of those involved in politically motivated crimes. An important feature of policy and practice has been the extensive involvement of part-nerships with community groups in the provision of services to offenders and their families. In Chapter 6, Tim Chapman and David O'Mahony indicate how post-conflict legislation has, as in other parts of the UK (and, indeed, more widely), placed a particular emphasis upon public protection and how the Probation Board for Northern Ireland's (PBNI) relationship with communities has weakened while its relationship with and accountability to government has been strengthened. (This has also been a marked feature of probation reorganisations in England and Wales.) With respect to youth justice, which is administered by the PBNI, significant devel-opments, especially since the easing of the troubles, have included the replacement of indeterminate residential training school orders with short determinate juvenile justice centre orders, the expansion of community supervision of juvenile offenders and creation of a Youth Justice Agency in 2003. The most fundamental changes have, however, arguably been brought about by the legislated introduction (via a newly established Youth Conference Service) of restorative justice as the primary method for dealing with young people in the criminal justice system.

Alongside major changes in the organisational arrangements for the supervision of offenders in different parts of the UK, the accreditation of probation programmes and programme providers represents a further mechanism for promoting greater uniformity of practice with increasingly centralised control and as such can be conceived to be a further form of governance of social work practice.

In Chapter 7 Susan Rex and Peter Raynor offer an appraisal of accreditation's positive contribution and its limitations. Susan Rex was part of the research team which carried out the pioneering evaluation of the Correctional Services Accreditation Panel in England and Wales for the Home Office, and Peter Raynor has been a member of accreditation panels both in England and Wales and Scotland. Again there have been contrasts in approach between these two jurisdictions, reflecting the different ways in which the shift towards evidence-based practice has been handled. The chapter aims to illustrate both the positive opportunities offered by accreditation processes and the difficulties which arise when it is combined with a top-down managerialist approach to practice development.

Assessment, Supervision and Intervention

Government concern with promoting evidence-based solutions to crime is reflected in its promotion of focused interventions (notably prison- and probation-based programmes) that are supported by research, in the development and evaluation of pathfinder initiatives and in the accreditation of services and interventions. The infrastructure and resources that are deemed necessary to support policy and practice developments such as these are being created through the increasing replacement of generic models of service delivery by more specialised and differentiated arrangements which support programme delivery. Traditional methods of supervision are being superseded by case management and service brokerage (e.g. Partridge 2004) while the range of community penalties has expanded, the aims of some disposals (for example, community service) have changed and increasing attention is being paid to issues such as compliance and attrition (e.g. Hedderman 2003; Kemshall and Canton 2002).

The second section of the book is concerned essentially with aspects of contemporary social work/probation practice. In this regard, one notable development in recent years has been the use of structured methods of assessment to identify the risks (of re-offending and of harm) posed by offenders and their needs, with the latter providing the focus for targeted interventions. In Chapter 8 Jim Bonta and Stephen Wormith, both from Canada, describe the approaches to risk and need assessment which have informed the development of the Level of Service Inventory (LSI) and its variants, which are the most wisely used and fully evaluated instruments for helping practitioners to carry out risk/need assessments as a regular part of their work. They outline an approach to integrated assessment and case management which should help practitioners to concentrate on those aspects of an offender's difficulties which contribute most to the risk of getting into trouble again. Recent research (Raynor 2007; Raynor *et al.* 2000) shows how repeated assessment can be used to measure changes in needs and risks, so that evidence of positive or negative responses to supervision can be gathered without necessarily waiting for a reconviction follow-up, thus putting a powerful evaluation tool into the hands of practitioners themselves.

The use of structured and targeted methods of intervention (usually involving cognitive behavioural methods and focusing upon changing offenders' attitudes and behaviour) has occupied an increasingly prominent position within the repertoire of techniques available to probation officers in their supervision of offenders. In addition to general programmes which aim to provide offenders with insight into their offending and to equip them with the skills to avoid engaging in similar behaviour in the future or programmes which address issues linked to offending (such as anger management) more specialised programmes have also been developed to addresses particular types of offending, such as domestic violence, drink driving and sexual offending. In Chapter 9, James McGuire provides a comprehensive overview of programmes that are being used by probation services across England and Wales (and, in some cases also in Scotland) and a summary of more recent programme evaluations, which have tended to produce somewhat mixed results. In acknowledging the criticisms that have been advanced regarding the use of offending behaviour programmes he nonetheless argues for interventions of this type as a means of reducing re-offending and promoting social inclusion, which would clearly be compatible with social work values and aims.

The widespread use of structured programmes in probation has resulted in revised arrangements for the supervision of offenders in the community. Whereas traditionally probation officers or social workers would assume responsibility for both supervising and enforcing orders and undertaking interventions aimed at reducing the likelihood of re-offending, these tasks have become increasingly differentiated (Robinson 2005) with a greater emphasis upon the role of case management in facilitating offenders' access to programmes and services and linking together diverse strands of an order. In Chapter 10 Frank Porporino and Elizabeth Fabiano, both internationally known as programme designers and pioneers of the movement towards evidence-based practice, discuss what motivates offenders to become active collaborators in the attempt to change their lives for the better. They outline an approach to the process and skills of case management which focuses particularly on motivation – arguably a neglected feature in the management of probation's offending behaviour programmes in England and

Wales, which have suffered from damagingly high levels of attrition, much of it due to offenders dropping out. Offenders cannot necessarily be coerced into choosing to change at the time that suits the system or the programme targets, but an approach which systematically presents the opportunities and possibilities of change could provide significant support for interventions offered at the right time.

While structured interventions are essentially concerned with addressing offenders' 'criminogenic' needs – increasingly within a framework of case management – *how* interventions are delivered is likely to have a considerable bearing upon how well offenders respond to them. Practitioners and academics alike have expressed concern that the 'what works' literature and policy interest in evidence-based practice have encouraged a somewhat technocratic approach to work with offenders which can be de-skilling for staff (Robinson 2005).[1] There is, however, a growing literature that highlights the importance of worker–client relationships in motivating offenders to change (for example, Burnett 2004; Burnett and McNeill 2005; Dowden and Andrews 2004; McNeill 2004) indicating, importantly, that there is still a place for traditional social work skills in offender supervision and case management. This is demonstrated in Chris Trotter's discussion, in Chapter 11, of pro-social modelling which has been shown to be associated with improved outcomes both in criminal justice and child protection settings (for the latter see Trotter 2004). Pro-social modelling, to use its broadest definition, involves demonstrating and re-inforcing pro-social values, expressions and behaviours (while confronting negative or pro-criminal attitudes and actions) and includes collaborative problem solving and role clarification. In this chapter Trotter addresses potential criticisms of pro-social modelling (including claims that it is superficial and symptom focused, potentially manipulative, judgemental and culturally insensitive) and highlights the importance of training for ensuring that practitioners have the appropriate skills both to engage with offenders pro-socially and to avoid undermining other aspects of intervention by inadvertently re-inforcing the behaviours they are attempting to change.

The significance of relationships is also reflected in Chapter 12 in which Fergus McNeill and Shadd Maruna examine the concept of desistance and suggest

---

1   It is also appropriate in this context to acknowledge the severing of qualifying probation training in England and Wales from social work training. In Scotland, by contrast, those involved in the provision of statutory social work services to the criminal justice system are still qualified social workers.

that generativity – caring for or helping others – may be a key factor in turning offenders away from crime. Emanating originally from the study of criminal careers, interest in the processes by which offenders cease offending has grown in recent years, supported by in-depth qualitative studies of offenders who have managed to desist (e.g. Maruna 2001; Jamieson *et al.* 1999; Farrell 2002). These studies point to the relevance of both structural factors and personal agency in facilitating desistance. McNeill and Maruna argue that a focus upon desistance and generativity can thus form the basis of strengths-based intervention that draws upon the individual's potential, in contrast to the emphasis upon deficits and risk reduction that underpins much cognitive-behavioural intervention.

One practical focus for generativity can be restorative justice, and in Chapter 13 Gwen Robinson outlines the origins and principles of restorative justice practices. These have been widely advocated since the 1970s, but have proved difficult to bring into large-scale use or full integration into official criminal justice systems which tend to be based on quite different principles. More recently restorative justice has enjoyed more political support as part of a process of making criminal justice more responsive to victims and communities. The chapter discusses potential and limitations, and whether the strong claims sometimes made for this approach are supported by the research. The principle of offenders doing something to restore their relational bonds with the rest of society also has much to contribute to our understanding of rehabilitation (Robinson and Raynor 2006).

The chapters in this section of the book are concerned with aspects of direct practice with offenders rather than examining the operation of different disposals. We therefore debated whether to include a separate chapter on community service but decided that it would be appropriate to do so in view of the important changes that have recently taken place in community service in England and Wales (currently referred to as 'community payback'), accompanied by underlying shifts in the ethos and perceived purpose of unpaid work. Chapter 14 on community service, by Gill McIvor, describes how the balance in emphasis has shifted between reintegration, rehabilitation and reparation, with the most recent policy objectives stressing enhanced community involvement in the identification of tasks for offenders to perform. While welcoming a renewed interest in the reparative/restorative contribution of unpaid work for the community (and, thus, according to McNeill and Maruna, its scope to encourage generativity), she also expresses concern at the potential for stigmatisation of offenders engaged in 'visible unpaid work'.

Issues and needs

The final section of the book addresses three areas of practice that have gained increasing prominence in recent years, beginning with Iain Crow's Chapter 15 on dealing with drug misusing offenders. In recent years services for offenders who engage in problematic drug use have increasingly been seen as part of the criminal justice agenda rather than the health agenda, and this chapter explores some of the consequences and implications of this. For example, while such a shift can improve access to services for some offenders, and the search for effective approaches has led to interesting new developments such as Drug Courts, the criminal justice context of treatment can also lead to an unhelpful overemphasis on enforcement and compliance. It is usually unrealistic to expect that drug misusing offenders will quickly become and remain drug free simply because they are subject to a court order. Moving away from drug misuse, like desistance from crime, is a process rather than an event, and services need to be provided in a way which recognises this.

A second area of practice that has been the focus of debate and discussion in recent years concerns the problem of how to ensure just and equal treatment to all groups in societies which are characterised by diversity and inequality, and in which much of the research that informs practice has been carried out primarily on white male offenders. In Chapter 16, Loraine Gelsthorpe explores how diversity can be addressed without undermining justice, fairness and equity in approach. In view of the paucity of relevant material in respect of several dimensions of diversity – for example, mental health, religious belief, age, disability and sexual orientation (see also Gelsthorpe and McIvor forthcoming) – the chapter focuses primarily upon issues relating to race and gender. She argues that attention to diversity is not only necessary to meet the 'equality criteria' that are enshrined in law, but also to maximise the effectiveness and perceived fairness of interventions with offenders. While it is critical that negative discrimination is avoided, in this chapter she makes a strong case for differentiated provision that promotes legitimacy and better meets offenders' needs.

The resettlement of prisoners following release from custody is a third area of practice that has received increasing policy attention across western jurisdictions with associated implications for organisational arrangements and for the nature and focus of probation practice. In Chapter 17 Maurice Vanstone discusses the origins and background of current initiatives and describes some of the recent work in England and Wales where resettlement work has recently been the focus of evaluated Pathfinder projects. Prisons and community-based services can work effectively together to join up services 'through the gate', but it is much more questionable whether they need to be merged in order to do so, as is being attempted in England and Wales. Arguably the different missions and different skills of custodial and non-custodial provision point to collaboration rather than merger. In Scotland the option of a single correctional agency was considered and rejected, partly on the basis of research which concluded that 'there is no evidence that particular organisational arrangements for the delivery of criminal justice provision in any one country lead to a higher or lower use of imprisonment or affect re-offending rates' (Coyle 2003, p.12). The way forward may be to concentrate on better practice rather than dramatic restructuring.

Concluding observations

It will be clear from the foregoing overview that the pace of change in probation policy and practice over the last decade has been unprecedented. While some developments may have sparked little comment or controversy (for example, most commentators have welcomed attempts to make resettlement services available to released short-sentence prisoners who previously had little or no access to them), the majority, by challenging long-established structures, practices or values have aroused considerable discussion and debate. For example, developments in technology have allowed for the introduction (and increasingly widespread use) of the electronic monitoring of offenders in the community which, especially initially, led to significant professional unease (Nellis 2003).

Should we then, on balance, be more or less optimistic about the future of social work with offenders in the UK (and beyond) than we were ten years ago? Some developments have been worrying: the widespread commitment to reducing the use of custodial punishment which was evident in the 1980s and early 1990s has been replaced by what sometimes looks like acquiescence in the face of rising prison numbers. Probation services in England and Wales no longer measure the extent to which they divert offenders from custody (Raynor 1998), with the result that they probably do so less than they did before. Also worrying, both in Britain and internationally, is a tendency to use actuarial risk assessments not to inform decisions about how to help people, but to simply to decide what degree of coercive control needs to be exercised over them (Feeley and Simon 1994). On the more positive side, some of the developments described in this book seem to point the way to a more humanistic, responsive and community-based style of work. Examples are the renewed interest in the supervisory relationship as a carrier of positive messages and assistance; the emerging focus on providing help in a way which encourages and reinforces the social and developmental processes revealed by research on desistance from offending and the continuing promise of restorative justice as a healing response to the harm caused by crime.

We conclude this introductory chapter by offering some brief reflection on the title of the book. We explicitly refer to social work with offenders – when this term has all but disappeared in probation policy and practice (and, indeed, training) in England and Wales – because we believe that social work skills remain central to effective engagement and intervention with offenders, however much the emphasis shifts towards rather narrowly defined and focused structured programmes. We would also argue that, despite overarching policy concerns with public protection, the supervision of offenders is ultimately unlikely to be effective unless it is able to locate interventions within the offender's social context. In other words, the supervision of offenders constitutes *social work* because of its need to reflect a commitment to *social justice and social inclusion*. We therefore repeat previous exhortations (e.g. Raynor, 1996) that criminal justice policy must be integrated with wider *social policy* concerns. In this regard it is disappointing that (despite some notable exceptions such as the report by the Social Exclusion Unit (2000) such policy articulation seems no nearer to being achieved; offenders tend still to be seen as a separate, less deserving group and are marginalised in discussions about how to meet the needs of the apparently more deserving. Peter Raynor's concluding chapter returns to this theme and attempts to weigh up the opportunities and threats which cluster around the future of effective social work with offenders. Is the glass half empty or half full? Read on and judge for yourselves; we hope you enjoy the book.

References

Burnett, R. (2004) 'One-to-One Ways of Promoting Desistance: In Search of an Evidence-Base.' In R. Burnett and C. Roberts (eds) *What Works in Probation and Youth Justice*. Cullompton: Willan.

Burnett, R. and McNeill, F. (2005) 'The Place of the Officer-Offender Relationship in Assisting Offenders to Desist from Crime.' *Probation Journal 52*, 3, 247–68.

Coyle, A. (2003) *Joining Up Criminal Justice Services: Scotland in an International Context*. London: International Centre for Prison Studies.

Dowden, C. and Andrews, D. (2004) 'The Importance of Staff Practice in Delivering Effective Correctional Treatment: A Meta-analysis'. *International Journal of Offender Therapy and Comparative Criminology 48*, 203–214.

Farrell, S. (2002) *Rethinking What Works with Offenders: Probation, Social Context and Desistance*. Cullompton: Willan Publishing.

Feeley, M. and Simon, J. (1994) 'Actuarial Justice: The Emerging New Criminal Law.' In D. Nelken (ed.) *The Futures of Criminology*. London: Sage.

Gadd, B. (1996) 'Probation in Northern Ireland.' In G. McIvor (ed.) *Working with Offenders: Research Highlights in Social Work 26*. London: Jessica Kingsley Publishers.

Gelsthorpe, L and McIvor, G. (2007) 'Dealing with Diversity.' In L. Gelsthorpe and R. Morgan (eds) *The Probation Handbook*. Cullompton: Willan Publishing.

Hedderman, C. (2003) 'Enforcing Supervision and Encouraging Compliance.' In W.H. Chui and M. Nellis (eds) *Moving Probation Forward: Theories, Practice and Research*. Harlow: Pearson Education.

Jamieson, J., McIvor, G. and Murray, C. (1999) *Understanding Offending Among Young People*. Edinburgh: The Stationery Office.

Kemshall, H. and Canton, R. (2002) *The Effective Management of Programme Attrition*. Report for the National Probation Service (Welsh Region). Leicester: De Montfort University.

Maruna, S. (2001) *Making Good: How Ex-convicts Reform and Rebuild their Lives*. Washington, DC: American Psychological Association.

McIvor, G. (1996) *Working With Offenders: Research Highlights in Social Work 26*. London: Jessica Kingsley Publishers.

McNeill, F. (2004) 'Supporting Desistance in Probation Practice.' *Probation Journal 51*, 3, 241–7.

Nellis, M. (2003) 'Electronic Monitoring and the Future of Probation.' In W.H. Chui and M. Nellis (eds) *Moving Probation Forward: Evidence, Arguments and Practice*. Harlow: Longman.

Partridge, S. (2004) *Examining Case Management Models for Community Sentences*. Online Report 17/04. London: Home Office.

Raynor, P. (1996) 'Effectiveness Now: A Personal and Selective Overview.' In G. McIvor (ed.) *Working with Offenders: Research Highlights in Social Work 26*. London: Jessica Kingsley Publishers.

Raynor, P. (1998) 'Reading Probation Statistics: a Critical Comment.' *VISTA 3*, 181–185.

Raynor, P. (2007) 'Risk and Need Assessment in British Probation: The Contribution of LSI-R.' *Psychology, Crime and Law*, 13, 2, 125–138.

Raynor, P., Kynch, J., Roberts, C. and Merrington, M. (2000) *Risk and Need Assessment in Probation Services: An Evaluation*. Research Study 211. London: Home Office.

Robinson, G. (2005) 'What Works in Offender Management?' *Howard Journal of Criminal Justice 44*, 3, 307–318.

Robinson, G. and Raynor, P. (2006) 'The Future of Rehabilitation: What Role for the Probation Service?' *Probation Journal 53*, 4, 335–347.

Social Exclusion Unit (2000) *Reducing Re-offending by Ex-prisoners*. London: Social Exclusion Unit.

Trotter, C. (2004) *Helping Abused Children and their Families*. Sydney: Allen and Unwin.

PART ONE

Developments in Policy

CHAPTER 2

New Labour's Youth Justice: A Critical Assessment of the First Two Terms

Barry Goldson

Introduction

The UK is the site of three separate legal jurisdictions: England and Wales, Northern Ireland, and Scotland. Each has produced, to a greater or lesser extent, quite distinctive youth justice systems, policies and practices. Since the election of the first New Labour Government in 1997, its pledge to be 'tough on crime' has characterised criminal justice policy in general, and youth justice policy in particular. If political devolution has served to neutralise, at least in part, the excesses of such 'toughness' in Northern Ireland and Scotland, the same cannot be said with regard to England and Wales, where both the pace and the content of youth justice policy reform has been extraordinary (Goldson 2004a). This chapter engages critically with key aspects of New Labour's youth justice policies in England and Wales during its first two terms of government (1997–2005). Owing to the usual limitations of a single chapter, it is not practical to cover all aspects of youth justice policy. Instead, emphasis will be upon the political context that frames contemporary policy formation; a schematic overview of the principal developments in legislation and an analysis of the primary consequences of this for youth justice policy and practice.

The origins of 'no more excuses'

Three days after returning from a visit to the US – as Shadow Home Secretary – in January 1993, Tony Blair coined what was to become a famous New Labour soundbite: 'tough on crime, tough on the causes of crime'. The timing of this was not a coincidence. Blair had been persuaded – by what he had seen and learnt in the US – to follow the example set by Bill Clinton's New Democratic Coalition. Clinton had repoliticised crime to positive electoral effect and Blair intended to do likewise (Tonry 2004). Whilst still in Opposition in the early mid-1990s, therefore, senior New Labour politicians increasingly adopted punitive rhetoric and symbolism with reference to their evolving criminal justice policies. In particular, responses to young offenders and youth crime in England and Wales were characterised by a consolidating 'institutionalised intolerance' (Muncie 1999), conceptually underpinned by demonic constructions of a childhood in 'crisis' (Scraton 1997). The 'Americanisation' of criminal justice in general, and youth justice in particular, operated *both* at the symbolic level of political rhetoric *and* at the material level of policy development (Jones and Newburn 2004; Muncie 2002; Pitts 2000, 2001).

Throughout this period, New Labour policy-makers published a range of documents focusing on youth justice and related matters, including: *Getting a Grip on Youth Crime* (Michael 1993a); *Cutting the Lifeline* (Michael 1993b); *Tackling Crime* (Michael 1993c); *Getting a Grip on Youth Crime: A Proposal for Earlier, Effective Action* (Michael 1993d); *Partners against Crime* (Labour Party 1994); *Access to Justice* (Labour Party 1995a); *Safer Communities, Safer Britain* (Labour Party 1995b); *Tackling Disorder, Insecurity and Crime* (Straw 1996); *Tackling Youth Crime, Reforming Youth Justice* (Labour Party 1996); *Tackling the Causes of Crime* (Straw and Michael 1996) and *Parenting* (Straw and Anderson 1996). The material content of what was to become New Labour's flagship criminal justice legislation, the Crime and Disorder Act 1998, therefore, had a lengthy period of pre-1997 general election gestation (D. Jones 2002).

It was not until the landslide election victory of the first New Labour Government in May 1997, however, that the full weight of its 'toughness' agenda was felt. Within months of coming to office, the newly elected government produced a raft of consultative documentation (Home Office 1997a, 1997b, 1997c), followed by a White Paper, ominously entitled *No More Excuses: A New Approach to Tackling Youth Crime in England and Wales* (Home Office 1997d). Clinton adopted and applied the notion of 'zero tolerance' in the US. Blair settled for 'no more excuses' in England and Wales.

Key milestones in law and policy

Taken together, developments in law and policy between 1997 and 2005 formulated the most radical overhaul of the youth justice system in England and

Wales since the inception of the first juvenile courts in 1908. It is not practical to engage with the detail of all of the legislation here, but even a schematic overview conveys the extent, reach and depth of policy reform.

Crime and Disorder Act 1998

The Crime and Disorder Bill commenced its passage through Parliament in December 1997 and it received Royal Assent on 31 July 1998. The Act served to completely restructure the youth justice system in England and Wales (see below). It also introduced a range of new interventionist powers and sentencing disposals including: Anti-Social Behaviour Orders (s.1); Parenting Orders (s.8); Local child curfew schemes (s.14); Reprimands and warnings (ss.65 and 66); Reparation Orders (s.67) Action Plan Orders (s.69); and the Detention and Training Order, a new custodial sentence (s.73) (Bell 1999). The Act further abolished the long-established principle of *doli incapax* that provided legal safeguards in respect of children aged 10–13 yrs (Bandalli 2000).

Youth Justice and Criminal Evidence Act 1999

Most notably, this Act introduced a new interventionist sentence, the Referral Order (s.1) for almost all children and young people appearing in court on first conviction, effectively making it a mandatory sentence (Goldson 2000; Haines 2000; Wonnacott 1999).

Criminal Justice and Court Services Act 2000

This Act (s.56) served to relax and extend the criteria relating to the imposition of Final Warnings (Home Office and Youth Justice Board 2001) – a further interventionist initiative – and it increased the courts' powers to penalise the parents of children who do not attend school regularly (s.72) (Goldson and Jamieson 2002).

Powers of the Criminal Courts (Sentencing) Act 2000

This Act (ss. 90 and 91) provided for the sentencing of children convicted of grave crimes and, according to Bateman (2002), when combined with specific sections of the Crime and Disorder Act 1998 it comprises a 'recipe for injustice'. The legislation also made provision for the electronic monitoring and surveillance of children (Nacro 2003a).

Criminal Justice and Police Act 2001

This Act extended both the application of child curfew schemes (s.48) and powers in respect of those eligible to impose child curfew schemes (s.49) (Walsh 2002). It also extended the powers of the courts to send children to prison and other locked institutions whilst on remand (s.130) (Goldson 2002a, pp.43–44), and it further applied the electronic surveillance of children (Nacro 2003a).

Police Reform Act 2002

This Act extended the range of people eligible to apply for Anti-Social Behaviour Orders and introduced interim Anti-Social Behaviour Orders that can be imposed prior to a full court hearing (ss.61–66) (Stone 2004).

Anti-Social Behaviour Act 2003

This Act was implemented following the publication in March 2003 of a White Paper entitled *Respect and Responsibility: Taking a Stand Against Anti-Social Behaviour.* The White Paper (Home Office 2003a, pp.1–2) set out a starkly authoritarian vision of a 'something for something society' where rights are reserved for the 're- sponsible...decent law abiding majority' whilst the so-called 'out of control minority' face a raft of new punishments and sanctions. The provisions of the legislation have been particularly targeted at children (Walsh 2003). Furthermore, the Anti-Social Behaviour Act, which received Royal Assent on 20 November 2003, also made the parents of children regarded as being 'disorderly', 'anti-social' or 'criminally inclined', eligible targets for formal statutory orders (Nacro 2004a).

Criminal Justice Act 2003

This Act also received Royal Assent on 20 November 2003. It extended powers to drug test children under the age of 16 (s.279), thus exposing them to 'highly intrusive and demanding' interventions (Nacro 2004b, p.8). Schedule 34 of the legislation further extended parenting orders to be used in conjunction with the Referral Order (as provided by the Youth Justice and Criminal Evidence Act 1999). Perhaps more significantly, these and other provisions of the Act opened up the 'potential to exacerbate already high levels of custody and increase the use of restrictive community sentences for those who might otherwise have received a lesser penalty' (Nacro 2004c, pp.7–8).

Cleaner Neighbourhood and Environment Act 2005

This Act covers a wide range of 'nuisance behaviours' and 'incivilities' together with 'environmental offences'. With specific regard to children and young people, provisions in relation to 'littering' (ss.18–27), 'graffiti' and 'other defacement' (ss.28–34), are the most likely to be invoked. In large part the legislation anticipates that such 'offences' will be disposed of by way of Fixed Penalty Notices, imposed by police officers and/or authorised officers of a relevant local authority. It is telling, however, that in issuing such a notice to a child the relevant authority is not required to consult with his/her parent/s or carer/s (Nacro 2005a, p.4)

Serious Organised Crime and Police Act 2005

This Act, as its title implies, is targeted at the 'heavy end'. Despite this, it contains a number of provisions that might well be applied to children, young people and/or parents in less 'serious' and not so 'organised' circumstances. In particular, extended stop and search powers (s.115), various provisions in respect of anti-social behaviour (ss.139–142) and the imposition of Parental Compensation Orders – whereby parents can be made liable for the payment of compensation imposed in relation to the behaviour of children under the age of ten (the age of criminal responsibility in England and Wales) – (s.144 and sch.10) are noteworthy (Nacro 2005a).

Inevitably, the consequences of such a wide-ranging corpus of youth justice law and policy are far reaching and multi-faceted and, as noted above, the limits of space prohibit a comprehensive analysis here. In the remainder of this chapter, therefore, four key issues are reviewed: first, the radical restructuring and expansion of the youth justice apparatus itself; second, the conflation of crime, disorder and anti-social behaviour, and the concomitant emphasis on 'risk' and pre-emptive or pre-offence intervention; third, the intensification of early post-offence intervention; fourth, the expansion and diversification of custodial sanctions.

System restructure, welfare contraction and correctional distension

The Crime and Disorder Act 1998 served to radically restructure the youth justice apparatus in England and Wales by establishing a new national and local infrastructure. At the national level the legislation ushered in a new executive non-departmental public body: the Youth Justice Board for England and Wales (YJB). The Board's responsibilities include advising the Home Secretary on the operation of the youth justice system; monitoring performance; establishing national standards and supporting new practice initiatives. The *Introductory Guide to the Crime and Disorder Act 1998* (Home Office 1998, p.1) provides that: 'the purpose of the youth justice system is to cut offending [and] action must be taken quickly to nip youth offending in the bud'. Moreover, section 37(1) of the Act itself states: 'it shall be the principal aim of the youth justice system to prevent offending by children and young people'. An overtly correctional emphasis was evident from the outset therefore, and, in an early public statement, the YJB declared its intent to promote: 'a culture in which it is a matter of shame to appear in a youth court' (Youth Justice Board 1999, pp.1–2).

At the local level the 1998 Act served to impose new duties on local authorities requiring them to prepare an annual youth justice plan, and to provide and co-ordinate services to 'tackle' youth offending in their area. Equally, the police, the Probation Service and the Regional Health Authorities are statutorily obliged to contribute to, and co-operate with, such arrangements. From April 2000 such locally based plans for 'tackling' youth crime were operationalised primarily by multi-agency 'Youth *Offending* Teams' (YOTs) in all areas of England and Wales. The emphasis on 'offending' in the very title of these teams, together with their composition, organisational location and newly defined lines of accountability (within both local and national government structures), is highly significant in signalling the diminution of welfare imperatives and the cementing of correctional priorities. Two points are particularly significant.

First, the 'Youth *Offending* Teams' replaced 'Youth *Justice* Teams'. Here the substitution of the term *justice* by *offending* is symbolically vital. Such a shift institutionalised a process whereby children in trouble are increasingly cast primarily as 'offenders' as distinct from 'children in need'. To put it another way, the child as 'threat' conceptualisation has become more prevalent, whilst the child as 'victim' identity has receded further to the margins (Goldson 2004b).

Second, and of more tangible significance, is the creation and organisational location of the YOTs, which mark a fundamental shift in youth justice policy and practice away from the statutory child-care operations of Social Services Departments at both the local and the national level. Locally the YOTs were distanced from social care and child welfare services and managed instead under the umbrella of multi-agency 'steering groups.' Chief Executive's Departments and corporate 'crime and disorder reduction' and 'community safety' 'partnerships'. Nationally youth justice no longer falls within the Department of Health's (or more latterly the Department for Education and Skills portfolio) rather YOTs are ultimately accountable to the YJB and, through it, to the Home Office. In other words, youth justice services in England and Wales have been systematically and in-stitutionally distanced (locally and nationally) from mainstream child welfare services.

For Muncie and Hughes (2002) such restructuring impulses are symptomatic of broader reconfigurations within which new modes of governance have emerged and solidified, characterised, at least in part, by 'responsibilising' and 'remoralising' strategies'. In this way processes of responsibilisation serve to legitimise the contraction of conventional child welfare services and the partial withdrawal of social care agencies (Goldson 2002b), whereas the remoralisation imperative galvanises the expansion of surveillant, correctional and ultimately punitive inter-ventions (Garrett 2004; Goldson 2002c; Goldson and Jamieson 2002). Thus, on the one hand eligibility criteria for statutory child welfare are heightened and social services are accordingly more tightly rationed (C. Jones 2002), whilst on the other hand the youth offending apparatus has expanded on an almost industrial scale. The 155 YOTs in England and Wales are substantially sized organisations and, in the financial year 2003–4 alone, their combined statutory funding amounted to more than £217,788 million. Furthermore, this figure took no account of the significant funding for YOTs provided by the Single Regeneration Budget (SRB), European funding, the Neighbourhood Renewal Fund, the Children's Fund or the Quality Protects initiative. Nor did it include the £24.3 million that the YJB invested in the Intensive Supervision and Surveillance Programme (ISSP), the £10 million investment in 'prevention programmes' or the £6.5 million committed by way of ancillary 'grants' (Youth Justice Board for England and Wales 2005).

Net widening, 'risk' and pre-offence intervention

The expanded youth justice apparatus in England and Wales, perhaps inevitably, has embraced a wider population of children. Underpinned by constructions of 'risk' and tilted towards 'anti-social' and 'disorderly' children – whatever such terms are taken to mean – in *addition* to child 'offenders' interventions are more broadly applied and net-widening processes are evident. Children (and in some cases their parents too) who are deemed to have 'failed' or be 'failing', to be 'posing risk' and/or to be 'threatening' (either actually or potentially), are increasingly drawn into the formal youth justice/youth offending nexus. In this way, the age of criminal responsibility becomes more fluid as interventions target not only the 'criminal' but also the 'near criminal', the 'possibly criminal', the 'sub-criminal', the 'anti-social', the 'disorderly' or the 'potentially problematic' in some way or another.

The logic of pre-emptive initiatives such as 'Youth Inclusion and Support Panels' (YISPs) that seek to 'identify' the 'most *at risk* 7–13 year olds' in 92 local authority areas of England and Wales and engage them in 'programmes' (Home Office 2004, p.41, emphasis added), means that *guilt* is no longer the only founding principle of youth justice intervention in England and Wales. Instead, formal intervention can be triggered without an 'offence' being committed, premised instead upon a 'condition.' a 'character' or a 'mode of life' that is adjudged to be 'failing' or posing 'risk'. These new modes of risk classification and pre-emptive intervention are unencumbered by such legal principles as 'the burden of proof', 'beyond reasonable doubt' and 'due legal process'. Instead, intervention is triggered by assessment, discretion and the spurious logic of prediction and actuarialism. Children thus face judgement, and are exposed to criminalising modes of state intervention, not only on the basis of what they have done, but what they might do, who they are or who they are thought to be.

Such processes give rise to a range of concerns with regard to natural justice, human rights, criminal justice and criminological rationality (Goldson 2005; Kempf-Leonard and Peterson 2000). More immediately, they are fundamentally flawed and Sutton, Utting and Farrington (2004), paradoxically amongst the keenest and most prominent advocates of the early intervention 'risk factor' paradigm, have cautioned:

> In particular, any notion that better screening can enable policy makers to identify young children destined to join the 5 per cent of offenders responsible for 50–60 per cent of crime is fanciful. Even if there were no ethical objections to putting 'potential delinquent' labels round the necks of young children, there would continue to be statistical barriers. Research into the continuity of anti-social behaviour shows substantial flows out of – as well as in to – the pool of children who develop chronic conduct problems. This demonstrates the dangers of assuming that anti-social five year olds are the criminals or drug abusers of tomorrow. (p.5)

The intensification of early post-offence intervention

It will have become apparent that youth justice policy formation (in England and Wales) under the first two New Labour administrations, was characterised by an interventionist emphasis. From the outset the *No More Excuses* White Paper stated:

> The trouble with the current cautioning system is that…too often a caution does not result in any follow up action, so the opportunity is lost for *early intervention* to turn youngsters away from crime… The Government feels that more radical action is now needed… The Crime and Disorder Bill will *abolish cautioning* and replace it

with a statutory police reprimand and Final Warning scheme... When a Final Warning is given, this will usually be followed by a community *intervention programme*... (Home Office 1997d, paras 5.10–5.12, emphases added)

As noted above, sections 65 and 66 of the Crime and Disorder Act 1998 abolished the diversionary practice of cautioning and established instead, on a statutory basis, the system of reprimands and Final Warnings. The reprimand applies to children who have not previously been convicted of an offence (s.65(1)(d)), whilst the Final Warning (a 'one-off' disposal unless at least two years have elapsed from the date of an earlier warning) is reserved for 'second-time' offenders, and those who are alleged to have committed an offence which is not considered so serious that a charge must result (s.65(3)(b)). A Final Warning may be issued instead of a reprimand for the child's *first offence* where 'the constable...considers the offence to be so serious as to require a warning' (s.65(4)). When a Final Warning is administered by a police officer s/he is required to refer the child to the local Youth Offending Team for a 'rehabilitation programme' assessment (s.66(1)).

Reprimands and Final Warnings have been subjected to wide-ranging critique. At the level of practice it has been argued that they have substituted the diversionary latitude and case-specific flexibility that the system of cautioning provided, with a mechanistic and doctrinaire 'three tier approach'. In other words 'a first offence generally results in a reprimand; a second offence will receive a warning; a third offence automatically gives rise to prosecution...irrespective of the nature of the offending' (Pragnell 2005, p.77). At a more theoretical or conceptual level, this pays scant regard to the principle of proportionality and negates the jurisprudential and human rights contexts within which it is located (Bell 1999; Cadman 2005; Goldson 2000). Similarly, at the level of evidence and outcome the interventionist thrust runs counter to the proven effectiveness of some diversionary and decriminalising strategies for child offenders (Bateman 2003). Conversely, as Pragnell (2005, p.80) has observed, although the 'Youth Justice Board has hailed the final warning scheme a great success in helping to prevent offending...the available evidence indicates that the picture is more complicated than the Board's pronouncements suggest'. Whilst it might well be the case that 70 per cent of children do not re-offend following a reprimand or warning intervention, therefore (Hine and Celnick 2001), the reality is such that the same children would be just as unlikely to re-offend following a first arrest in any event, with or without formal intervention (Kemp *et al.* 2002). At best, therefore, it seems fair to conclude that such interventions are outcome neutral. At worst, they invoke, at least potentially, the counter-productive consequences that criminal labelling, stigmatisation, net-widening and tariff-shortening can induce (Goldson 2000). In short, more

methodologically sophisticated research and more considered and judicious interpretation of evidence is required. In the meantime, perhaps policy-makers should
refrain from 'overstating apparently positive research results' (Bottoms 2005, p.12).

In the same way that the Crime and Disorder Act 1998 provided for more
focused intervention at the pre-court stage, the Youth Justice and Criminal Evidence
Act 1999 did likewise at the post-court stage by introducing the Referral Order.
During the passage of the legislation through Parliament, Paul Boateng, Home
Office Minister of State, described the Referral Order as: 'a fundamentally different
way of considering how to intervene most productively and effectively in the life of
a young person to stop crime and offending' (cited in Wonnacott 1999, p.271).

Part 1 of the 1999 Act provides that the Referral Order is the standard
sentence imposed by the Youth Court, or other Magistrates Court, for children who
have been convicted of an offence or offences for the *first time*. Such children are
normally referred by the Court to a Youth Offender Panel, principally comprising
volunteer 'community panel members.' who establish a 'programme of behaviour'
that the child is obliged to observe. The principal aim of the programme is the
prevention of re-offending by the child (s.8(1)). Section 8 of the Youth Justice and
Criminal Evidence Act identifies typical components of such an interventionist
programme, which include financial or other forms of reparation to the victim/s of
the offence/s; mediation sessions with the victim/s; unpaid work as a service to the
community; conditions that require the child to be at home at specified times and
attend school or work; specified activities to 'address offending behaviour' and/or
to serve rehabilitative purposes with respect to drug and/or alcohol misuse;
reporting conditions to persons and/or places; prohibition from association with
specified persons and/or places; and compliance with the supervision and
recording requirements of the programme. The terms of the programme form the
basis of the 'youth offender contract' (s.8(6)) that the child is required to sign
(s.8(5)(b). Once a 'programme of behaviour' has been established and a 'youth
offender contract' has been signed, the child's 'progress' in complying with its
terms is subject to review by the Youth Offender Panel which convenes further
meetings for this purpose (s.11).

In many respects the Referral Order, effectively a mandatory sentence, is the
flagship of early intervention. Not unlike reprimands and Final Warnings, however,
the Order has attracted critical attention. It has been argued that in many important
respects it runs counter to the provisions of international human rights standards,
treaties, conventions and rules (Goldson 2000), and that it distorts the principles of
restorative justice (Haines 2000). The early empirical research conveys mixed
messages and more time is probably required before conclusive evidence is available

(Crawford and Newburn 2003). What is clear, however, is that in providing for earlier and more intensive intervention within the youth justice system in England and Wales, the Referral Order precipitated 'massive' system expansion whereby 27,000 children each year attend Youth Offender Panels staffed by 5000 newly recruited volunteers (Earle 2005, p.105).

The expansion and diversification of custodial sanctions

An increasing reliance on penal detention is the most conspicuous element of New Labour's 'toughness' agenda (Goldson 2000c). The cumulative effect of developments in youth justice law and policy in England and Wales between 1997 and 2005, has been to substantially expand and diversify custody. Whilst it is true to say that such trends were initiated prior to the election of the first New Labour administration, they simply consolidated afterwards. The total annual number of custodial sentences imposed upon children rose from approximately 4000 per annum in 1992 to 7600 in 2001, a 90 per cent increase (Nacro 2003b and 2005b). During the same period the child remand population grew by 142 per cent (Goldson 2002a). In March 2004 alone there were 3251 children (10–17 years inclusive) in penal custody in England and Wales: 2772 in Prison Service Young Offender Institutions; 290 in Local Authority Secure Children's Homes and 189 in privately managed Secure Training Centres (Youth Justice Board 2005, p.78).

Furthermore, within the general trend of custodial expansion and diversification (where the private sector plays an increasingly significant role) a range of critical observations might be made. First, whilst comparative analyses of youth justice systems in general, and rates of child imprisonment in particular, are extraordinarily difficult (Muncie 2003 and 2005; Muncie and Goldson 2006), it appears that by 2004 greater use of penal custody for children was being made in England and Wales than in most other industrialised democratic countries in the world (Youth Justice Board for England and Wales 2004). Second, in addition to substantial increases in the numbers of children sent to custody, sentences also increased in length (Home Office 2003b), and proportionately more children were sentenced to long-term detention (Graham and Moore 2004). Third, law and policy has provided for the detention of younger children and Nacro (2003b, p.12) has observed that 'as a result the detention of children under the age of 15 years has become routine'. Fourth, the expansionist drift has been disproportionately applied in terms of gender and the rate of growth is higher for girls than boys (Nacro 2003b). Furthermore, girls are regularly detained alongside adult prisoners, a practice seriously questioned by penal reform organisations (Howard League for

Penal Reform 2004) and Her Majesty's Chief Inspector of Prisons (2004, p.3) alike. Fifth, racism continues to pervade youth justice sentencing processes and custodial regimes. For example, black boys are 6.7 times more likely than their white counterparts to have custodial sentences in excess of 12 months imposed upon them in the Crown Court (Feilzer and Hood 2004), and black child prisoners are more likely than white detainees to encounter additional adversity within custodial institutions owing to racist practices (Cowan 2005). Sixth, for all child prisoners the jailhouse, however it is configured, remains a dangerous place. The emotional and psychological well-being of many child prisoners is routinely damaged (Goldson 2002a), literally thousands are physically harmed and, at the extremes, child deaths in penal custody continue to occur with distressing regularity (Goldson and Coles 2005). Seventh, the failings of penal custody to prevent children from re-offending are well established. In October 2004, for example, a Parliamentary Select Committee reported that reconviction rates stand at 80 per cent with regard to released child prisoners (House of Commons Committee of Public Accounts 2004) and, despite substantial investment in new sentences, regimes and custodial institutions in England and Wales such failure continues to apply.

Conclusion

In order to comprehend modern youth justice policy in England and Wales at least some historical contextualisation is necessary. Indeed, since the 'invention' of 'juvenile delinquency' in the nineteenth century, and the subsequent inception of a specific corpus of legislation, court structures, policies, procedures and practices for the processing of 'young offenders' at the beginning of the twentieth, youth justice policy has been beset by tension and complexity. In this way, Muncie and Hughes (2002, p.1) explain that: 'youth justice is a history of conflict, contradictions, ambiguity and compromise...[it] tends to act on an amalgam of rationales, oscillating around and beyond the caring ethos of social services and the neo-liberal legalistic ethos of responsibility and punishment'. There can be little doubt, however, that 'toughness' imperatives are currently prevalent and they are consistently expressed at the symbolic level of political rhetoric and the institutional level of law and policy. In this sense neo-liberal priorities are in the ascendancy and, despite the many internal tensions between the inclusionary and exclusionary elements of New Labour policy, there are no immediate signs of reverse 'oscillation' with specific regard to youth justice.

Postscript

In 2005, the year that this chapter was written, the general election result returned New Labour for a third successive term. Since that time, the government has continued to advance correctional and, ultimately, punitive policy imperatives through a distorted discourse of 'respect' (Home Office 2006). Paradoxically, however, previous adherents to New Labour's youth justice in England and Wales appear to be losing 'respect' for the direction that law, policy and practice is taking.

In 2006 Rob Allen completed eight years' service as a senior member of the Youth Justice Board by reflecting that a 'fundamental shift is needed in the way that we respond to young people in conflict with the law' (Allen 2006, p.6). Furthermore, on 26 January 2007, Professor Rod Morgan resigned as Chairperson of the YJB. In an open letter distributed widely to non-governmental organisations, Morgan (2007) explained that the youth justice system in England and Wales is being 'swamped' by 'the growth of the number of children and young people in custody and the substantial increase in the numbers of children and young people being criminalized and/or prosecuted'. Finally, on 14 February 2007, John Fayle, a former head of policy at the YJB, became the third ex-senior official in less than six months to make public his profound concerns about New Labour's youth justice programme. Fayle (2007, p.1) stated that 'the rising number of children in custody in England and Wales is little short of a national scandal'.

Informed by rigorous research and compelling evidence, a number of academic experts, youth justice policy analysts, children's human rights agencies and penal reform organisations have been offering similar observations since 1997. Perhaps most recently, a collaborative partnership – comprising more than 30 national and international scholars and policy analysts engaging a detailed scrutiny of youth justice systems in 13 different jurisdictions – has aimed to establish the contours of a 'youth justice with integrity' or a 'principled youth justice' (Goldson and Muncie 2006; Muncie and Goldson 2006). The approach adds depth and authority to some of the concerns that have been recently expressed by Allen, Morgan, Fayle and others. If the New Labour government is even remotely interested in evidence-based policy, it must take account of such reasoned critique.

References

Allen, R. (2006) *From Punishment to Problem Solving: A New Approach to Children in Trouble.* London: Centre for Crime and Justice Studies.

Bandalli, S. (2000) 'Children, Responsibility and the New Youth Justice.' In B. Goldson (ed.) *The New Youth Justice.* Dorset: Russell House Publishing.

Bateman, T. (2002) 'A Note on the Relationship between the Detention and Training Order and Section 91 of the Powers of the Criminal Courts (Sentencing) Act 2000: A Recipe for Injustice.' *Youth Justice 1*, 3, 36–41.

Bateman, T. (2003) 'Living with Final Warnings: Making the Best of a Bad Job?' *Youth Justice 2*, 3, 131-140.

Bell, C. (1999) 'Appealing for Justice for Children and Young People: A Critical Analysis of the Crime and Disorder Bill.' In B. Goldson (ed.) *Youth Justice: Contemporary Policy and Practice.* Aldershot: Ashgate.

Bottoms, A. (2005) 'Methodology Matters.' *Safer Society 25*, 10–12.

Cadman, S. (2005) 'Proportionality in the Youth Justice System.' In T. Bateman and J. Pitts (eds) *The RHP Companion to Youth Justice.* Dorset: Russell House Publishing.

Cowan, R. (2005) 'Juvenile Jail Staff Accused of Racism.' *Guardian*, June 14.

Crawford, A, and Newburn, T. (2003) *Youth Offending and Restorative Justice: Implementing Reform in Youth Justice.* Cullompton: Willan.

Earle, R. (2005) 'The Referral Order.' In T. Bateman and J. Pitts (eds) *The RHP Companion to Youth Justice.* Dorset: Russell House Publishing.

Fayle, J. (2007) 'Locked in Battle.' *Society Guardian*, February 14.

Feilzer, M. and Hood, R. (2004) *Differences or Discrimination?* London: Youth Justice Board for England and Wales.

Garrett, P. (2004) 'The Electronic Eye: Emerging Surveillant Practices in Social Work with Children and Families.' *European Journal of Social Work 7*, 1, 57–71.

Goldson, B. (2000) 'Whither Diversion? Interventionism and the New Youth Justice.' In B. Goldson (ed.) *The New Youth Justice.* Dorset: Russell House Publishing.

Goldson, B. (2002a) *Vulnerable Inside: Children in Secure and Penal Settings.* London: The Children's Society.

Goldson, B. (2002b) 'New Labour, Social Justice and Children: Political Calculation and the Deserving–Undeserving Schism.' *The British Journal of Social Work 32*, 6, 683–695.

Goldson, B. (2002c) 'New Punitiveness: The Politics of Child Incarceration.' In J. Muncie, G. Hughes and E. McLaughlin (eds) *Youth Justice: Critical Readings.* London: Sage.

Goldson, B. (2004a) 'Differential Justice? A Critical Introduction to Youth Justice Policy in UK Jurisdictions.' In J. McGhee, M. Mellon and B. Whyte (eds) *Meeting Needs Addressing Deeds: Working with Young People who Offend.* Glasgow: NCH, pp.27–45.

Goldson, B. (2004b) 'Victims or Threats? Children, Care and Control.' In J. Fink (ed.) *Care: Personal Lives and Social Policy.* Bristol: The Policy Press in association with The Open University.

Goldson, B. (2005) 'Taking Liberties: Policy and the Punitive Turn.' In H. Hendrick (ed.) *Child Welfare and Social Policy.* Bristol: The Policy Press.

Goldson, B. and Coles, D. (2005) *In the Care of the State? Child Deaths in Penal Custody in England and Wales.* London: INQUEST.

Goldson, B. and Jamieson, J. (2002) 'Youth Crime, the "Parenting Deficit" and State Intervention: A Contextual Critique.' *Youth Justice 2*, 2, 82–99.

Goldson, B. and Muncie, J. (2006) (eds) *Youth Crime and Justice: Critical Issues.* London: Sage.

Graham, J. and Moore, C. (2004) *Trend Report on Juvenile Justice in England and Wales.* European Society of Criminology Thematic Group on Juvenile Justice, Accessed on 24/08/06 at http://www.esc-eurocrim.org/workgroups.shtml#juvenile_justice

Haines, K. (2000) 'Referral Orders and Youth Offender Panels: Restorative Approaches and the New Youth Justice.' In B. Goldson (ed.) *The New Youth Justice.* Dorset: Russell House Publishing.

Her Majesty's Chief Inspector of Prisons (2004) *Report on an Announced Inspection of HMP Eastwood Park 22–26 September 2003 by HM Chief Inspector of Prisons.* London: Home Office.

Hine, J. and Celnick, A. (2001) *A One Year Reconviction Study of Final Warnings.* Sheffield: The University of Sheffield.

Home Office (1997a) *Tackling Youth Crime: A Consultation Paper.* London: Home Office.

Home Office (1997b) *Tackling Delays in the Youth Justice System: A Consultation Paper.* London: Home Office.

Home Office (1997c) *New National and Local Focus on Youth Crime: A Consultation Paper.* London: Home Office.

Home Office (1997d) *No More Excuses – A New Approach to Tackling Youth Crime in England and Wales.* London: Stationery Office.

Home Office (1998) *Crime and Disorder Act 1998: Introductory Guide.* London: Home Office.

Home Office and Youth Justice Board (2001) *Final Warning Scheme: Further Guidance for the Police and Youth Offending Teams.* London: Home Office and Youth Justice Board.

Home Office (2003a) *Respect and Responsibility – Taking a Stand Against Anti-Social Behaviour.* London: The Stationery Office.

Home Office (2003b) *Prison Statistics England and Wales.* London: The Stationery Office.

Home Office (2004) *Confident Communities in a Secure Britain: The Home Office Strategic Plan 2004–08,* London: The Stationery Office.

Home Office (2006) *Respect Action Plan.* London: Home Office.

House of Commons Committee of Public Accounts (2004) *Youth Offending: The Delivery of Community and Custodial Sentences.* Fortieth Report of Session 2003–04, London: The Stationery Office.

Howard League for Penal Reform (2004) 'Girls Held in Adult Prisons against their "Best Interests".' Press Release 20 January. London: Howard League for Penal Reform.

Jones, C. (2002) 'Voices From the Front Line: State Social Workers and New Labour.' *British Journal of Social Work 31,* 547–562.

Jones, D. (2002) 'Questioning New Labour's Youth Justice Strategy: A Review Article.' *Youth Justice 1,* 3, 14–26.

Jones, T. and Newburn, T. (2004) 'The Convergence of US and UK Crime Control Policy: Exploring Substance and Process.' In T. Newburn and R. Sparks (eds) *Criminal Justice and Political Cultures: National and International Dimensions of Crime Control.* Cullompton: Willan.

Kemp, V., Sorsby, A., Liddle, M. and Merrington, S. (2002) 'Assessing Responses to Youth Offending in Northamptonshire.' *Research Briefing 2,* London: Nacro.

Kempf-Leonard, K. and Peterson, E. (2000) 'Expanding Realms of the New Penology: The Advent of Actuarial Justice for Juveniles.' *Punishment and Society 2,* 1, 66–97.

Labour Party (1994) *Partners against Crime: Labour's New Approach to Tackling Crime and Creating Safer Communities* Labour Party document B/040/94. London: Labour Party.

Labour Party (1995a) *Access to Justice.* Labour Party Conference 95 paper. London: Labour Party.

Labour Party (1995b) *Safer Communities, Safer Britain: Labour's Proposals for Tough Action on Crime.* Labour Party document B/045/95 and Conference 95 paper. London: Labour Party.

Labour Party (1996) *Tackling Youth Crime, Reforming Youth Justice. A Consultation Paper on an Agenda for Change.* London: Labour Party.

Michael, A. (1993a) *Getting a Grip on Youth Crime.* London: Labour Party.

Michael, A. (1993b) *Cutting the Lifeline.* London: Labour Party.

Michael, A. (1993c) *Tackling Crime.* London: Labour Party.

Michael, A. (1993d) *Getting a Grip on Youth Crime: A Proposal for Earlier, Effective Action.* London: Labour Party.

Morgan, R. (2007) 'Open Letter Distributed to Children's Charities and Non-Governmental Organisations'26 January, 2007.

Muncie, J. (1999) 'Institutionalised Intolerance: Youth Justice and the 1998 Crime and Disorder Act.' *Critical Social Policy 19*, 2, 147–175.

Muncie, J. (2002) 'Policy Transfers and What Works: Some Reflections on Comparative Youth Justice.' *Youth Justice 1*, 3, 27–35.

Muncie, J. (2003) 'Juvenile justice in Europe: Some Conceptual, Analytical and Statistical Comparisons.' *Childright 202*, 14–17.

Muncie, J. (2005) 'The Globalization of Crime Control – The Case of Youth and Juvenile Justice: Neo-Liberalism, Policy Convergence and International Conventions.' *Theoretical Criminology 9*, 1, 35–64.

Muncie, J. and Goldson, B. (eds) (2006) *Comparative Youth Justice: Critical Issues.* London: Sage.

Muncie, J. and Hughes, G. (2002) 'Modes of Youth Governance: Political Rationalities, Criminalization and Resistance.' In J. Muncie, G. Hughes and E. McLaughlin (eds) *Youth Justice: Critical Readings.* London: Sage.

Nacro (2003a) *Detention and Training Order Early Release – The Revised Guidance and Use of Electronic Monitoring.*Youth Crime Briefing, March. London: Nacro.

Nacro (2003b) *A Failure of Justice: Reducing Child Imprisonment.* London: Nacro.

Nacro (2004a) *Parenting Provision in a Youth Justice Context* Youth Crime Briefing, June. London: Nacro.

Nacro (2004b) *Some Facts about Young People who Offend – 2002*, Youth Crime Briefing, March. London: Nacro.

Nacro (2004c) *New Legislation – Impact on Sentencing.* Youth Crime Briefing, March. London: Nacro.

Nacro (2005a) *Recent Youth Justice Legislation.* Youth Crime Briefing, June. London: Nacro.

Nacro (2005b) *A Better Alternative: Reducing Child Imprisonment.* London: Nacro.

Pitts, J. (2000) 'The New Youth Justice and the Politics of Electoral Anxiety.' In B. Goldson (ed.) *The New Youth Justice.* Dorset: Russell House Publishing.

Pitts, J. (2001) *The New Politics of Youth Crime: Discipline or Solidarity.* Basingstoke: Palgrave.

Pragnell, S. (2005) 'Reprimands and Final Warnings.' In T. Bateman and J. Pitts (eds) *The RHP Companion to Youth Justice.* Dorset: Russell House Publishing.

Scraton, P. (ed.) (1997) *'Childhood' in 'Crisis'?* London: UCL Press.

Straw, J. (1996) *Tackling Disorder, Insecurity and Crime.* London: Labour Party.

Straw, J. and Anderson, J. (1996) *Parenting.* London: Labour Party.

Straw, J. and Michael, A. (1996) *Tackling the Causes of Crime: Labour's Proposals to Prevent Crime and Criminality.* London: Labour Party.

Stone, N. (2004) 'Orders in Respect of Anti-Social Behaviour: Recent Judicial Developments.' *Youth Justice 4*, 1, 46–54.

Sutton, C., Utting, D. and Farrington, D. (2004) *Support from the Start: Working with Young Children and their Families to Reduce the Risks of Crime and Anti-Social Behaviour.* Research Brief 524, March. London: Department for Education and Skills.

Tonry, M. (2004) *Punishment and Politics: Evidence and Emulation in the Making of English Crime Control Policy.* Cullompton: Willan.

Walsh, C. (2002) 'Curfews: No More Hanging Around.' *Youth Justice 2*, 2, 70–81.

Walsh, C. (2003) 'Dispersal of Rights: A Critical Comment on Specified Provisions of the Anti-Social Behaviour Bill.' *Youth Justice 3*, 2, 104–111.

Wonnacott, C. (1999) 'New Legislation. The counterfeit contract – reform, pretence and muddled principles in the new referral order.' *Child and Family Law Quarterly 11*, 3, 271–287.

Youth Justice Board for England and Wales (1999) *Policy Statement.* Accessed on 19/07/2000 at http://www.youth-justice-board.gov.uk.

Youth Justice Board for England and Wales (2004) *Strategy for the Secure Estate for Juveniles: Building on the Foundations.* London: Youth Justice Board for England and Wales.

Youth Justice Board for England and Wales (2005) *Youth Justice Annual Statistics 2003/04.* London: Youth Justice Board for England and Wales.

CHAPTER 3

Youth Justice: Developments in Scotland for the Twenty-first Century

Bill Whyte

Introduction

UK systems of youth justice share a commitment to common goals including prevention, early intervention and better integrated and co-ordinated provision for young people involved in crime, but have pursued them in contrasting and distinctive ways in the different legal jurisdictions. Since the Act of Union 1701 which created the UK, Scotland has retained its own separate legal system. The re-establishment of a parliament in Scotland in 1998 formally devolved law and policy in this area to the Scottish government.

One immediate effect of political devolution has been a new and shared politicisation of youth justice which seems to be lessening some of the differences between UK jurisdictions (Bottoms and Dignan 2004). A greater political emphasis on legal rights, individual responsibility and accountability, due process and just deserts, often associated with a retreat from welfare, sits in tension alongside the Scottish use of non-criminal and extra-judicial processes recommended by the United Nations Convention on the Rights of the Child (UNCRC) (1989) and its associated guidance (see Beijing Rules (United Nation 1985); Guiding Principles of Riyadh (United Nations 1990a); Havana Rules (United Nations 1990b)). Like all western jurisdictions, Scotland is reviewing the nature and balance in its youth justice provision. The combination of two concepts, special responses to children and young people and equal rights under the law create tension, in practice, on how best to reconcile the competing claims of the law, judicial process and punishment with the need to consider the best interests and the rights of the child or young person while effectively reducing offending in politically acceptable ways.

In principle the Children's Hearing system sits comfortably within the UN Convention on the Rights of the Child (CRC) framework. The Social Work (Scotland) Act 1968 introduced a distinctive approach to youth justice in Scotland which has lasted for over 30 years (Lockyer and Stone 1998). Scottish youth courts were disbanded and replaced by a lay decision-making tribunal – Children's Hearings – which deals with children at risk and children who offend within a unified welfare-based system. This removed the centrality of the courts from decision-making, so that for most young people under 16 issues of disposal are dealt with by Hearings while matters of adjudication of legal issue remain matters for the courts.

The Children (Scotland) Act 1995 provided an updated statutory framework for the system in the light of the UN CRC but did not fundamentally change the principles or institutions with one important departure. Section 16(5) of the Act introduced for the first time provision for a hearing (or court) to make a decision not consistent with the 'best interests' principle, if they consider it necessary to protect the public from serous harm. Legislation currently places a statutory duty on local authorities to promote social welfare and the whole authority is responsible for children 'looked after' because of offending (Kearney 2000; Moore and Whyte 1998).

Ongoing Reviews – Back to the Future?

The shape of youth justice provision in the early part of the twenty-first century in Scotland is still being moulded and developed and most aspects of social policy have been subject to review. What began as a review of youth crime, ongoing since 2000, has now extended to a full review of the Children's Hearings system as a whole. The Scottish Executive launched a review of the Children's Hearings System in April 2004 with the publication of *Getting it Right for Every Child* (Scottish Executive 2004b) following a commitment made in the Coalition Partnership Agreement, the basis for establishing a new government in 2004.

The consultation sought views on the principles and objectives of the Children's Hearings System, expected outcomes, scope for specialisation, links with child protection, monitoring and evaluation, influence over parents and community involvement; and how best to achieve the principles and outcomes. At the same time a national review of social work and workforce issues was under way (Scottish Executive 2005b) following the establishment of the Scottish Social Services Council, which is responsible for the registration of social workers.

One reason for the wide-ranging review of the Hearings system has been the changes in volume and balance of cases over the last decade. In 2003 and 2004 the largest number of children (45,000) were referred since the system began in 1971, with more than two-thirds of these referrals based on care and welfare grounds. The number referred on non-offence grounds has more than doubled since 1992. While the number of children referred on offence grounds has remained relatively static over a number of years, there has been an increase in the number of young people involved in persistent offending. In 2002–3 the average number of alleged offences referred to the Reporter was 3.15 compared with 2.86 in 2001–2. Between 2002 and 2003 there was a 13 per cent increase in the number of children referred with ten or more alleged offences (Scottish Children's Reporter Administration (SCRA) 2004).

Research and responses to the Executive's consultations have indicated strong support for the welfare-orientated principles of the Hearings system (the 'Kilbrandon principles'). Similarly a recent inquiry into Children's Hearings found that:

> Judging by the evidence the inquiry heard, the Scottish children's hearings system is highly esteemed in other countries… The general view is that Scotland was right to make the break from the 19th century adjudication and punishment model of youth justice. (NCH 2004, p.6)

Widespread concern, however, was been raised about the low levels of resourcing and staffing available to support the process. An essential ingredient in casting children who offend as children in need was the establishment of unified local authority services to provide early multi-agency and multi-disciplinary responses to individual, family and community concerns. Despite support for the vision, in reality local authorities have not been particularly effective at delivering better integrated provision. Audit Scotland (2002) noted that around 400 children were not getting the services they needed, mainly because of staff shortages. The system was seen to be struggling to deal with young people persistent in offending, mainly because of the lack of specialist services and social workers.

Youth Justice Policy in Scotland

It's a Criminal Waste: Stop Youth Crime Now, Scotland's youth crime review report (Scottish Executive 2000) provided the basis for a re-examination of youth justice provision. It concluded that while the principles underpinning the Hearings system were fundamentally sound, practices and the resources to support them had fallen behind the times and that change was overdue. These conclusions were reinforced by the Audit Scotland report (2002) which expressed concern that around 64 per cent of financial resources were being used up in legal and administrative processes rather than on direct provision for young people involved in crime.

Scottish research had highlighted that some of the most difficult and disadvantaged young people were discharged from the Hearings system at the recommendation of child-care social work only to reappear in criminal proceedings within a matter of months. Many of the most difficult 'graduates' had experienced custody by age the age of 18 (Waterhouse *et al.* 2000; Whyte 2004). Hallett *et al.* (1998) had identified a degree of ambivalence among Children's Panel members and professionals about dealing with persistent offenders within the Hearings system. Young people heavily caught up in crime seemed, in effect, to be being transferred out or up to the adult criminal system.

The review recognised that a range of responses were required to improve:

- prevention: to increase effective universal provision for all children and their families to reduce or compensate for conditions which expose children to harmful behaviours of all kinds; paying particular attention to drugs and alcohol related risks for those under 16 and to the issue of school exclusion

- early intervention: quick response and targeted assistance for individual children whose behaviour or family circumstances indicate vulnerability towards offending and other problems

- diversion: from both Children's Hearings and criminal courts to allow immediate action to address problems and re-equip children and young people for more positive citizenship

- structured intervention: only when necessary and at the right time and right level

- participation: of young people and families; more joint action between voluntary and statutory agencies, communities and the commercial and business sectors to create safer communities in which individual needs, responsibilities and rights are respected and in which restorative justice features; better information on factors which contribute to youth crime and its reduction.

The review's conclusions restated the importance of dealing with young people persistent in their offending as children in need and in the context of better integrated services for children, of which specialist youth justice services should continue to be part. This signalled support, in principle, for the continuation of the 'Kilbrandon approach' to youth crime, while at the same time updating policy, practice, structures and procedures to be more effective in reducing offending.

On the basis of the review's recommendation, an ambitious Action Programme to Reduce Youth Crime was announced in 2002 under a range of key headings:

- increasing public confidence in Scotland's Youth Justice System

- giving victims an appropriate place in the youth justice process

- encouraging all children and young people to thrive

- easing the transition between the youth justice and adult criminal justice systems

- effective early intervention.

Later in that year an ad hoc ministerial group chaired by Scotland's First Minister produced a revised '10 point Action Plan' (Scottish Executive 2002a) setting out areas of improvement required to tackle the problem of persistent offending, to enhance community safety, and to improve the effectiveness of Scotland's youth justice services. It included:

- establishing well resourced Children's Hearings to fast-track persistent offenders under 16

- a Youth Court feasibility project for persistent offenders aged 16 and 17, with flexibility to deal with 15-year-olds

- reviewing the use of restriction of Liberty Orders, and Community Service orders

- a Safer Scotland police campaign on high visibility policing, covering youth disorder

- spreading best practice, and establishing firm standards, for community-based projects

- consideration of a Scottish-wide application of a system of police warnings, and a detailed exploration of restorative cautions

- reconfiguration of secure accommodation available nationally, with increased specialist provision for girls

- development of national standards to operate between local authorities, the Criminal Justice system and Children's Hearings, covering reporting, timescales, outcomes and follow-up

- promoting parental responsibility including compulsory parenting orders

- measures to increase the speed of referral to the courts.

The amended action points were broadly in line with the original Action Programme with some notable developments, in particular the establishment of 'fast track' Children's Hearings, and re-establishment of a youth court for 15–18s as part of the summary jurisdiction of the adult criminal court.

The latter replaced a proposal to establish a bridging pilot to deal with more 16 and 17-year-olds in Hearings, which would have given procurators fiscal powers to refer directly to the Hearings system thus resolving a long-standing anomaly in the continuity of the youth justice process between Children's Hearings and criminal justice. The establishment of a youth criminal court, instead, seems to reflect the growing punitive rhetoric dominating all UK jurisdictions, driven by politicians under pressure to be seen to be tough on crime (Pitts 1992).

The associated focus on anti-social behaviour was responded to by updating the action plan to include early trailing of proposals, subsequently laid out in the consultation document *Putting the Community First* (Scottish Executive 2004b) and implemented by the Anti-Social Behaviour etc. (Scotland) Act 2004. This introduced a raft of new measures for addressing anti-social behaviour and youth disorder aimed particularly at young people under the age of 16. While the subsequent guidance does its best to cast these measures as child care measures within the context of Children's Hearings, they reflect the political commitment to 'toughen up' the Children's Hearings system. The measures, which are broadly similar to those introduced in England and Wales, include acceptable behaviour contracts (ABCs), anti-social behaviour orders (ASBOs), community reparation orders (CROs), parenting orders (POs) and the introduction of electronic monitoring when included as part of a programme of intensive support as an alternative to secure accommodation (ISMS). These measures are all available for young people under the age of 16 either as part of a programme of supervision within the Hearings system or as alternatives through court-based routes.

A programme for action

National Standards for Youth Justice Services were introduced in 2002, setting a target of 2006 for full implementation. They are intended to reinforce the legal and corporate responsibilities of local authorities for planning integrated children services of which youth justice services are part. By April 2006 all local authorities, as part of their integrated children services plan, should have established an inter-agency strategy group for youth justice services to drive more effective co-ordination and establish shared protocols for implementing better integrated screening, assessment and associated action planning at varying points in the youth justice process. The developments are similar to those proposed for children services as a whole (Department for Education and Skills 2004; Scottish Executive 2005a).

The service standards incorporate six core objectives towards which most current developments are focused:

1. to improve the quality of the youth justice process

2. to improve the range and availability of programmes to stop youth offending

3. to reduce the time taken to reach and implement hearing decisions

4. to improve information on youth justice services to victims and local communities

5. to target the use of secure accommodation appropriately and ensure it is effective in reducing offending behaviour

6. to improve the strategic direction and co-ordination of youth justice services by local youth justice strategy teams.

The priority group are those persistent in their offending. The Standards define 'persistence' as five episodes of offending within a six-month period. A baseline figure was established and each local authority set a target of a 10 per cent reduction of young people who are persistently offending by April 2006 and a further 10 per cent reduction by 2008. For all young people meeting the definition of persistence, local authorities are required to carry out an initial assessment and for those where compulsion is being considered, a structured comprehensive assessment using either ASSET or YLS/CMI (Youth Level of Service/Case Management Inventory) is required before a Children's Hearing meets.

The intention of having a low threshold for initial assessment should, in principle, ensure that children's needs and deeds are not ignored until problems become severe – a problem identified by the review. It should also allow the opportunity for positive early preventive intervention on a voluntary basis consistent with the principles of the Hearings system. However in defining this threshold as one of persistence, the Executive ignored the messages from previous research (Hagell and Newburn 1994) about the risks of adopting a one-dimensional definition of persistence, which might on one hand net-widen, and on the other miss more serious and risky young people. Anecdotal evidence suggests that this development has resulted in greater police reporting of very minor offences so that by June 2005 the numbers of young people meeting the criteria for persistence had risen from 1201 in November 2004 to 1260, further fuelling the political demand for tougher responses. The response of the conservative opposition to the rise in numbers has been to demand that young people of 14 and 15 should be dealt with by the newly established criminal youth courts rather than by the Hearings system.

Despite this turbulence in the system, signs of positive progress are apparent. Each local authority has been required to appoint a 'senior officer' to co-ordinate the delivery of youth justice services and dedicated and specialist staffing, in some cases multi-disciplinary, has been appointed as part of children service staffing in every local authority. Multi-disciplinary strategic planning groups now exist in all authorities and are actively meeting the new requirements to audit youth crime annually and to measure change against established baseline data, mapping service provision and monitoring outcomes. The identified priorities in the action programme include young people involved in violent offences, young women, drug misuse and offending, and the involvement and support for parents and families with a view to reducing secure accommodation. These changes, if implemented effectively, will reflect a 'step' change in youth justice practice in Scotland.

Giving victims and communities an appropriate place in youth justice

The action programme placed a strong emphasis on giving victims and communities a greater stake in the Hearings system, particularly by improving information and services to victims and by developing a communication strategy to inform communities of its activities. The plan reflected the findings of the Scottish Crime Survey (Scottish Executive 2002b) which showed young people who admitted to committing offences were themselves more likely to be a victim of crime (65%) than non-offenders (41%). Early findings from the Edinburgh Study of Youth Transitions, similarly, found a marked tendency for children who have been in public care to have high rates of delinquency, trauma and victimisation and concluded that being a victim of crime and abuse may be one of the most important predictors of delinquency by age 12 (Smith 2004).

Substantial investment has been provided to support the extension of restorative justice approaches across Scotland. Restorative practices have captured world wide attention and have been a major omission from contemporary Scottish practice. To think that it is not in the best interests of children and young people to understand the consequences of their criminal behaviour, to appreciate the harm done and, where possible, to have the positive experience that can be gained from making good with the support of family or other positive social networks, is to fail to recognise important elements of moral and social development. Yet this has seldom been a priority in Scottish practice since the 1970s, when some restorative work was done in youth justice. Restorative police cautions and restorative conferencing are now available across the country.

However, in the absence of a clear policy direction for service development, there are risks that the value of restorative practices can be overstated and that scarce resources can be poorly targeted to uses that have limited impact on those most risky and needy. There is some evidence that police restorative cautioning has been focused on relatively minor first offences without providing families first with an opportunity or assistance to resolve the matter. Police restorative cautions with this group has shown no better results than other forms of diversion (Dutton and Whyte 2006). The Scottish Executive is reviewing restorative practices with a view to establishing policy and the Scottish Children's Reporters Administration, in partnership with local authorities, has developed professional practice principles for the use of restorative measures within the Hearings system nationally.

One new disposal intended to add to the range of restorative measures, which highlights the tension between Children's Hearings and criminal justice is the Community Reparation Order introduced by the Anti-Social Behaviour, etc. (Scotland) Act 2004 (s.120). The measure is available as a low-tariff order for those involved in antisocial behaviour. It is a criminal conviction and is intended, as a fine on time, to involve a programme of between 10 and 100 hours of 'prescribed activities' to enable reparation either specifically to the victim or more generally to the community. The order, which is being piloted from 2005 in Sheriff and District courts in three areas in summary criminal proceedings, does not require the consent of the individual nor a social work assessment (SER). The disposal is available for young people aged 12 to 16 and national guidance requires local authorities to make special provision to meet the needs of this age group, in particular that they are kept apart from activities involving those over 16 years of age. The guidance makes no comment on how this order should operate, if at all, within the context of the Children's Hearings system, which would normally deal with all such offences within its non-criminal process and could, with existing powers, require reparation as part of a supervision requirement. It is to be assumed that such young people will become 'jointly reported' to both systems and decisions taken on how to proceed. Two complementary approaches may emerge to avoid relatively minor offences being dealt with through criminal processes. Equally, new anti-social behaviour measures may see more children appearing in court.

Children's Hearings, youth justice and the wider community

Scottish Executive consultation on anti-social behaviour suggested that there is a relatively low awareness of the Children's Hearing system in local communities, despite the fact that panel members are recruited locally and have links with the community they serve. The *Where's Kilbrandon Now?* inquiry (NCH 2004) concluded that more information about children's circumstances and the interventions that are made on their behalf should be made public as a way of meeting government requirement for greater accountability and to increase support for the system.

Commentators suggest that when community members are asked to help, plan and become involved in an intervention, they develop a sense of ownership (Graham 1998). Involving the community can also make it easier to obtain resources and volunteers to carry out long-term support. However there is very little research on how best to assist neighbourhoods to take responsibility for their difficult young people without excluding these young people further. Developments through Communities that Care in Scotland (Bannister and Dillane 2005) and community projects, such as FARE in Glasgow, may provide models for the future. Community Safety panels and other mechanisms for engaging community members have been set up and a large investment in street wardens is underway as part of measures to tackle anti-social behaviour. Whether such measures will increase community participation in assisting young people and reassure the public or simply increase and fuel punitive attitudes and fear remains to be seen.

The 2004 Act extended ASBOs to 12–15-year-olds. Sheriff civil courts can grant an ASBO or interim ASBO against a young person 'persistently' engaged in anti-social behaviour, for whom alternative approaches have not been effective in protecting the community. National guidance expects sheriffs will consider the views and advice of the Principal Reporter to the Children's Hearing, before making the decision on whether to grant a full ASBO. While an ASBO is a civil order, any breach is a criminal offence and will be reported to the Procurator Fiscal to decide on what action should be taken. For the first time, in Scotland, this provides a breach mechanism with the potential of criminal conviction built into a child-care measure and another example of the increase in dual pathways for young people.

Early voluntary agreements are also provided for by the 2004 Act and are encouraged by national guidance to prevent the need for legal remedies. Voluntary agreements have been available under social work legislation since 1968 but seldom used. Guidance stresses that written agreements should be considered on an inter-agency basis, setting out the behaviour that the young person has agreed to stop and the support they can expect to receive to change their behaviour. If resources are made available, these will provide a sensible response to anti-social behaviour and to other difficulties experienced by young people. However, guidance on acceptable behaviour contracts or agreements (ABA) as they have come to be known, pays scant attention to the Scottish child-care context and reads as if it has been lifted from another jurisdiction. ABAs can be used with or without referral to the Reporter although contact with social work is encouraged. The guidance seems to assume a lead role for police and housing staff. Young people persistently in trouble are likely to have a range of difficulties and will almost certainly be children in need under s.22 of the Children (Scotland) Act 1995. For the police and housing to take a lead role without clear protocols for communication with children's services could lead to major difficulties.

A major challenge facing community safety initiatives in Scotland is to find effective non-criminalising mechanisms to promote neighbourhood safety. As yet there is limited evidence to suggest that the Social Inclusion Partnership programmes, funded through the Better Neighbourhood Services Fund, have reached out in a determined way to the most difficult and challenging young people and their families, who ought to be, in terms of the 1995 Act, the highest priority for all such providers. Some local authorities have decided to be more imaginative and, rather than simply deploying street wardens, are considering replicating the Danish SSP (School, Social Agencies and Police) community safety programmes, which deploy trained street youth workers in schools and in neighbourhoods. They are normally on call 24/7 to link speedily with young people and families where concerns over youth crime are identified, to respond speedily to the concerns of local residents and to report regularly to SSP co-ordination groups to assist targeting help and support. These programmes also provide resources for youth clubs to do outreach and street work in their local communities in an attempt to engage with young people in the streets rather than simply move them on as new powers of dispersal seem intended to do.

Speedy welfare and justice

Fifteen Time Interval Standards were established in 1 April 1999 to cover every stage of action by each agency involved in Children's Hearings including the Police, SCRA and local authorities. The time intervals overall standard indicates that the maximum time interval from offence to reporter decision or Children's Hearing should be between 80–120 working days depending on the complexity of the case. In 2002–3 the average time taken in dealing with offence cases was 125 days compared with 134 in 2001–2. If use of compulsion is to be a last resort, then speeding up this process in itself may not result in greater effectiveness in reducing youth crime. Possibly a more meaningful measure would be the time between an offence and direct contact with families offering assistance to resolve difficulties. The absence of staff able to respond quickly, such as the flexible SSP workers discussed above, could result in speedier processes to draw young people unnecessarily into formal processes as a means of ensuring intervention.

The demand for speedy and more effective responses to young people persistent in their offending resulted in the development of a two-year pilot of 'fast track' Children's Hearings, established in February 2003. The Scottish Executive allocated just under £1.5 million to 'fast track' for 2002–3 and £3.4 million for 2003–4. The pilots took place in six local authorities (Hill *et al.* 2005). They targeted young people under the age of 16 (or over 16 and already subject to supervision) defined as 'persistent' in their offending. It was intended that 'fast track' would:

- reduce re-offending through implementing more effective interventions and offer guaranteed places on programmes focused on tackling offending behaviour

- be faster – up to one third quicker from charge to disposal

- be better informed – with an agreed assessment and reporting process and better information on the range of available programmes

- help prevent re-offending through more effective monitoring of supervision requirements.

(Scottish Executive 2003, p.1)

While the fast track sites were running, all other local authorities were charged with similar objectives under national standards. Scottish Executive evaluation (Hill *et al.* 2005) found that in the first 18 months just over 300 young people defined as 'persistent' were included in fast track. The comparison sites, expected to have similar numbers, had about 20 per cent fewer young people defined as persistent in the same period and were experiencing smaller increases in numbers of offence referrals (8% versus 42%). As a consequence they were able to concentrate their resources on fewer cases, which partly explains the fact that comparison sites actually spent more on those defined as 'persistent' than the specially designated fast track sites. The evaluation concluded that the approach was successful in speeding up the process for dealing with those defined as persistent. Mixed results were achieved with regard to the effects of fast tracking on young people. Offending by young people in fast track did decrease but the reduction in comparison sites was greater. The researchers recognised that differences might be accounted for by the samples and limitation of data, but indicate that a major factor was that comparison sites had well-resourced strategies in place, already producing reductions in offending. A clear message from the research is that the Hearings system can have a positive effect on reducing offending among young people. It is less clear what impact 'fast tracking' in itself has.

Children's Hearings and parents

A fundamental principle in dealing with young people who offend through the Hearings system is the concept of working in partnership with parents. For this reason Kilbrandon did not recommend that Hearings should have direct compulsory powers over parents. Hearings have powers to attach conditions under a supervision requirement to influence and direct parents to engage with the development of their child. A focus of the Scottish Executive review, however, has been the extent to which control over parents should be increased and extended over and above current measures. While there was a general consensus amongst consultation responses over the need for good parental support and for the Hearings system to articulate more clearly their expectations of parents, views were very mixed on the extent to which Hearings should have direct powers over parents. The dominant view was that this will not address the fundamental issue of the lack of provision for family support and the need for well-resourced multi-agency intervention and prevention strategies. Other more practical issues about how to enforce such action were also raised. The consultation also sought views on a more radical option of whether 'family hearings' should be established but this received little positive support as most respondents were keen to ensure that the child or young person, and not the parents, should still be at the centre of the system and that the welfare of the children involved in offending should remain paramount. Greater use of family group conferencing is already being developed to engage families in key decision-making processes.

Nonetheless the Anti-Social Behaviour, etc. (Scotland) Act 2004 (Part 9) extended powers available to the Children's Reporter and to Hearings in relation to parents. For the first time, the Principal Reporter has power to ask civil courts to introduce a parenting order for those parents whose actions, or failure to exercise their responsibilities, contribute to anti-social, or offending, behaviour for children under 16. An application for a parenting order may also be made where the parents are failing to protect the child or act in a way that puts the child's welfare at risk. This greater political emphasis on the personal responsibility of children and parents has been matched with powers to meet the argument that equal leverage should be placed on service providers to guarantee the quality of assistance. It is the responsibility of local co-ordination to ensure that mainstream services are directed by principles of effectiveness and are subject to meaningful quality assurance measures. The establishment of strategic planning groups in each local authority and the appointment of youth justice co-ordinators in Scotland are intended to achieve this. The legislation now provides Hearings with powers to direct the Principal Reporter to take court action against local authorities should they fail to give effect to supervision requirements.

Intensive supervision and secure accommodation

The Anti-Social Behaviour etc. (Scotland) Act 2004 also introduced new powers into the Children (Scotland) Act 1995 (s.36) to provide Intensive Support and Monitoring Services (ISMS). The provision allows Hearings to impose a supervision requirement with a special condition (ISMS) as an alternative to secure accommodation for those meeting the legal criteria, whether by reason of offending or for other care reasons. Scottish Executive estimates that numbers will be small. Recent research found that between July and December 2003 a total of 104 young people received a secure authorisation and 79 were placed in a secure setting. The remaining 25 were maintained in the community or were accommodated in open residential units (Walker and Moodie 2004).

Electronic monitoring of young people under 16 will be a key element of ISMS as part of a package of measures and will allow, for the first time, conditions of movement restriction. The package of services will include a minimum of 30 hours direct contact, 24/7 support, a health and education programme and an aftercare plan. The maximum time for which a young person can be tagged is six months. Hearings retain the power to review the provisions at any time and a statutory review is required within three months. The impact of tagging on young people is a contentious issue and its effectiveness open to debate. However the opportunity to develop 'wrap around' provision and supervision in the community for the most troubled and troublesome children is long overdue and may have very positive spin offs for the provision of graduated programmes of supervision for young people without tagging, particularly for those heavily involved in offending. These young people were often discharged from Hearings around the age of 15 only to find themselves quickly in the adult criminal system.

Interface between youth justice and the adult criminal justice system

A major commitment of the action programme was to create a more integrated welfare and justice system for 16 and 17-year-olds. The government has been under considerable pressure in recent years as Scotland is the only country in the UK routinely dealing with 16 and 17-year-olds in adult criminal courts. The Scottish Executive decided to establish a criminal youth court to deal with persistent offenders. Persistent was defined as three offences – a lower threshold than for 'persistence' in the Hearings system. Guidance stresses that no young person should be dealt with by the youth court who could otherwise, be dealt with by a Children's Hearing. The distinctive characteristics of the youth court include:

- fast tracking of young persons to and through the Youth Court

- dedicated Youth Court staff to support and service the court (e.g. Fiscal, Clerk, social work) with four of the nine Sheriffs from Hamilton Sheriff Court presiding over the Youth Court

- fast track breach procedures

- additional resources across agencies to enable provision of a quality and consistent service

- formation of a multi-agency Implementation Group, chaired by a Youth Court Sheriff, to review the working and operation of the court

- appointment of a full-time Youth Court Co-ordinator to service the Implementation Group and co-ordinate practice

- ability to electronically monitor as a condition of bail

- external research and evaluation of the Youth Court's operation and programmes.

The development includes some very positive modifications to adult proceedings. The youth court has dedicated youth court sheriffs and provides continuity of judicial oversight in dealing with issues relating to community supervision; regular judicial reviews; the capacity to take into account additional outstanding charges in a single court hearing; and 'fast track' breach procedures. More notably, substantial additional resources have been committed to ensure that new and extended supervisory programmes are available as a matter of routine. These are all welcomed developments as is the appointment of a youth court co-ordinator to improve multi-disciplinary co-operation. However, it is questionable if the youth courts are directed by any coherent guiding principles or philosophy, equivalent to the Kilbrandon principles, that makes them a distinctly 'youth' process in the terms of the Beijing rules requirement to be 'different from adult proceedings'. The pilot youth court has the same range of powers of disposal as the adult sheriff summary court, including the power to refer young people to a Children's Hearing or to impose an adult conviction. The main vehicle for community supervision through the youth court is a probation order which attracts an adult criminal conviction under existing legislation although it remains an order of the court made 'instead of sentencing' (s.228).

Scottish Executive evaluation (Popham *et al.* 2005) found that the Youth Court proceedings were more likely to result in detention or community based social work disposals than were those in the normal summary (para.1). Professionals were cautiously optimistic that the Youth Court would be effective in reducing re-offending, at least with some young people who appeared before it. Six-month reconviction rates among young people sentenced in the Youth Court did compare favourably with the comparator courts, especially given that the Youth Court specifically targeted 'persistent' offenders whose reconviction rate might have been expected to be higher (para.19). However, the number of cases available for analysis was relatively low. The study concluded that there was a broad consensus that the Youth Court represented an improvement over previous arrangements of dealing with youth crime in adult summary courts and that youth courts should be rolled out more widely. The study and pilot had no remit to indicate whether young people in this age group might have been just as effectively dealt with in a well-resourced Hearings system without the criminalising implications. Scotland currently has a situation where some young people involved in serious or persistent offending may be dealt with by the Hearings system at 16 or 17; young people of a similar age not involved in the Hearings system will be dealt with in a youth criminal court, possibly for less serious offending. Young people under the age of 16 committing very serious offences will continue to appear in the adult criminal court, subject to the Lord Advocate's guidance.

Scottish Executive policy developments show a determination to improve youth justice services. The re-establishment of a Youth Court may provide a welcomed complement to the existing Children's Hearings system and may be a substantial improvement on adult criminal courts. If new resources result in more young people being retained in the Hearings system until the age of 18, the role of the Youth Court should remain limited for this age group. It would be a much more positive step to see youth courts extended to more serious offenders appearing on indictment and to older youth up to 21, as in some European countries, rather than to see them extended downwards, as has been called for by some politicians. Despite a clear policy statement that there is no intention to net-widen, a major challenge for a well-resourced Youth Court is to ensure it does not unintentionally draw young people more readily into its criminal jurisdiction rather than divert them.

Getting it right for every child

The first phase of the Children's Hearings review raised fundamental questions about services and the system. The second phase consultation (Scottish Executive 2005a), still underway at the time of writing, is seeking views on proposed developments and changes. Proposals include a unified approach to children's services, a single integrated assessment framework for all children, information sharing and record keeping. No change in the boundaries between the Children's Hearings system and the criminal justice system are proposed. The stated rationale for change is 'to allow professionals to spend less time processing children and their families through systems such as child protection, youth justice or Children's Hearings and more time tackling family and child concerns (section 1). Proposals include new statutory duties on all agencies:

- to identify children who are in need

- to seek and record the child's views

- to co-operate so that agreed action happens

- to act on Children's Hearings decisions

- to appoint a lead professional to plan and coordinate activity where a child requires multi-agency input

- to be accountable for their actions.

More specific proposals include:

- a duty to co-operate with each other in meeting the needs of children and to establish local co-ordination and monitoring

- a single integrated assessment, planning and recording tool

- an action plan must be agreed by all agencies where a child's needs are complex, serious, require multi-agency input or are likely to require compulsory measures

- a lead professional from among the agencies must be appointed

- a referral to the children's hearings system should meet two tests – significant needs and a need for compulsion

- any plan endorsed by a hearing as a condition of supervision can only be amended by a hearing

- hearings to be held outside school hours, so children do not miss classes

- place for community representatives or victims to sit in on the hearing when appropriate

- children's hearings should provide information to communities about the nature of decisions made and their outcomes

- greater continuity of panel members from one children's hearing to another

- duty on the SCRA to ensure the provision of legal representation for children, where this is necessary

- agencies to keep the public and communities informed

- grounds for referral to the reporter and the Children's Hearings system to be based on two traditional tests that have seldom operated – significant need and the likely need for compulsion. it is proposed that if a referral does not meet the criteria for a hearing, the principal reporter will be given the authority to send the child's case back to the agencies to fulfil their duties towards the child.

These are ambitious and very positive objectives but significant developments in these areas have still to be delivered. It remains to be seen, for example, if the recommendation to have a designated member of school staff take day time responsibility for the care, welfare and tracking of progress of 'looked after' children will equally apply to young people 'looked after' because of their offending.

Early intervention

Of all the proposed developments, it is the promotion of effective early intervention that presents the greatest opportunities, challenges and risks. Entry to the Children's Hearings system was always intended to be premised on the possibility of early intervention. The legal test for entry is the need for 'compulsory' measures. It is difficult to justify the need for compulsion if no relevant provision has been previously offered or refused; if young people have not failed to co-operate or comply; if their situation does not present such high risk that only compulsion can safeguard others or themselves. Anecdotal evidence suggests that few young people have, in the past, been offered well-structured multi-disciplinary provision of any sort before being made subject to compulsory measures.

Generally speaking the practice model on offer in Scotland for many years seems to have been one dominated by diversion without service – in effect radical non-intervention (Schur 1973). While there continues to be a place for diverting many young people on the assumption they will simply 'grow out' of crime with minimal intervention, others simply will not. Doing nothing may well be a missed opportunity to provide positive help at an early stage. This, of course, has to be weighed against the unintended consequences of early intervention.

For some young people, personal difficulties combined with early involvement in offending may be a stepping stone in a pathway to more serious, violent and persistent offending (Loeber and Farrington 1998). Studies have suggested that the risk of becoming involved in persistent offending is two to three times higher for a child aged under 12 than for a young person whose onset of delinquency is later (McGarrell 2001). However, because children tend not to commit particularly serious or violent offences, and because they usually have not acquired an extended pattern of criminal behaviour, they often receive limited appropriate attention for this behaviour (Snyder and Sickmund 1995).

It is the arena of early intervention, in particular, that has highlighted tensions in current government policy. The evidence of high levels of disadvantage among young people who offend is well established. Labour-led administrations, north and south of the border, have expressed a commitment to tackling child poverty 'within a generation'. A substantial investment has been made on child poverty measures in what essentially has to be a long-term strategy. In the shorter term, anti-social behaviour is a major concern for communities and needs to be taken seriously. However in the context of increasingly punitive rhetoric there is a risk of creating parallel pathways for young people in trouble and of separating early prevention strategies for youth crime from strategies for better integrated social and educational provision for children and families and from any framework of children's rights. To date, in Scotland's dual system, criminal pathways are seldom used for under 16s. The introduction of anti-social measures will test the capacity of local authorities to co-ordinate provision and operate in a multi-systemic way across the 'whole authority' as required by child-care legislation, and maintain non-criminal responses.

There is some promising evidence from England and Wales that early voluntary intervention approaches can be implemented positively (Greater London Community Safety Partnership 2007). In the Scottish context, to spend large amounts of money to see a reduction in minor offences, important though that may be, but to fail to halt the progression to custody or secure accommodation of those at risk of serious and persistent offending will, in the long run, provide communities with limited comfort, particularly as early criminalisation and detention of young people is as good an indicator for progression of criminality and the associated harm to future victims as is available. One US review concluded:

> If there is one clear finding to be gleaned from the research on juvenile justice pro-gramming in recent decades, it is that removing youthful offenders from their homes is often not a winning strategy for reducing long-term delinquency. Most juvenile...facilities...suffer very high recidivism rates. Intensive commu-nity-based supervision programs typically produce recidivism rates as low or lower than out-of-home placement (at a fraction of the cost), while intensive family-focused or multi-dimensional intervention programs have produced the lowest recidivism rates of all. (Mendel 2000, p.16)

Concluding comments

The developments in youth justice in recent years in Scotland have been significant and have been backed by substantial resources. More has been done in the last few years than in the previous 20 to take youth crime seriously. The initial recommenda-tions of the government review and the action programme represent a very positive development in youth justice policy and practice in Scotland and gives optimism that a quality service suited to the twenty-first century and consistent with the principles of CRC (Convention on the Rights of the Child) can be established.

The landscape is changing fast and it is too early yet to judge the outcomes of changes and proposed changes. More recent proposals, creating parallel legal processes, whether civil or criminal, have the capacity to increase criminalisation and undermine effectiveness unless they are part of a coherent system of youth justice and child protection. There is little debate that Scottish practices and provision in the area of youth crime need to be and are being brought up to date. Much has been achieved or is being put in place. But some up dating may require a revisit of original concepts and philosophies to ensure that Scotland does not lose as much as is gained in the process of change.

References

Audit Scotland (2002) *Dealing with Offending by Young People.* Edinburgh: Auditor General Accounts Commission.

Bannister, J. and Dillane, J. (2005) *Communities that Care: An Evaluation of the Scottish Pilot Programme.* Edinburgh: Scottish Executive.

Bottoms, A. and Dignan, J. (2004) 'Youth Justice in Great Britain.' In M. Tonry and A. Doob (eds) *Youth Crime and Youth Justice: Comparative and Cross-National Perspectives in Crime and Justice A Review of Research 2.* Chicago: University of Chicago.

Department for Education and Skills (2004) *Every Child Matters: Change for Children.* London: DfES.

Dutton, K. and Whyte, B. (2006) *Restoring Justice and Welfare.* Briefing Paper No. 8. Edinburgh: CJSWDC.

Graham, J. (1998) *Schools, Disruptive Behaviour and Delinquency: A Review of Research.* London: Home Office.

Greater London Community Safety Partnership (2004) *Mayor of London Community Safety Quarterly* Issue 1. London: GLC.

Hallett, C. Murray, C. with Jamieson, J and Veitch, B. (1998) *The Evaluation of Children's Hearings in Scotland, Volume 1: Deciding in Children's Interests.* Edinburgh: Scottish Executive Central Research Unit.

Hagell, A. and Newburn, T. (1994) *Persistent Young Offenders.* London: Policy Studies Institute.

Hill, M., Walker, M., Moodie, K., Wallace, B., Bannister, J., Khan, F., McIvor, G. and Kendrick, A. (2005) *Fast Track Children's Hearings Pilot.* Edinburgh: Scottish Executive.

Kearney, B. (2000) *Children's Hearings and the Sheriff Court.* London: Butterworths

Lockyer, A. and Stone, F. (eds) (1998) *Juvenile Justice in Scotland: Twenty Five Years of the Welfare Approach.* Edinburgh: T&T Clark.

Loeber, R. and Farrington, D. (1998) *Serious and Violent Juvenile Offenders: Risk Factors and Successful Interventions.* Thousand Oaks: Sage.

McGarrell, E. (2001) 'Restorative Justice Conferences as an Early Response to Young Offenders.' *OJJDP Juvenile Justice Bulletin.* August. Washington, DC: US Department of Justice.

Mendel, R. (2000) *Less Hype More Help. Reducing Youth Crime: What Works and What Doesn't?.* Washington, DC: American Youth Policy Forum.

Moore, G. and Whyte, B. (1998) *Social Work and Criminal Law in Scotland.* Edinburgh: Mercat Press.

NCH (2004) *Where's Kilbrandon Now?* Glasgow: NCH Scotland.

Pitts, J. (1992) 'Juvenile Justice Policy in England and Wales.' In J. Coleman and C. Warrant-Adamson (eds) *Youth Policy in the 1990s : The Way Forward.* London: Routledge.

Popham, F., McIvor, G., Brown, A., Eley, S., Malloch, M., Murray, C., Piacentini, L. and Walters, R. (2005) *Evaluation of the Hamilton Youth Court Pilot.* Edinburgh: Scottish Executive.

Schur, E. (1973) *Radical Non-Intervention: Rethinking the Delinquency Proble.* Englewood Cliff, NJ : Prentice Hall.

Scottish Children's Report Administration (2004) *Annual Report 2003–2004.* Stirling: Scottish Children's Reporter Administration.

Scottish Executive (2000) *It's a Criminal Waste: Stop Youth Crime Now.* Edinburgh: Scottish Executive.

Scottish Executive (2002a) *Scotland's Action Programme to Reduce Youth Crime*. Edinburgh: Scottish Executive.

Scottish Executive (2002b) *The 2000 Scottish Crime Survey*. Edinburgh: Scottish Executive CRU.

Scottish Executive (2004a) *Getting it Right for Every Child*. Edinburgh: Scottish Executive.

Scottish Executive (2004b) *Putting the Community First*. Edinburgh: Scottish Executive.

Scottish Executive (2005a) *Getting it Right for Every Child: Proposals for Action*. Edinburgh: Scottish Executive.

Scottish Executive (2005b) *21st Century Social Work Review*. Edinburgh: Scottish Executive.

Smith, D. (2004) *The Links between Victimization and Offending. Edinburgh Study of Youth Transitions Number 5*. Edinburgh: University of Edinburgh.

Snyder, H.N. and Sickmund, M. (1995) *Juvenile Offenders and Victims: A National Report*. Pittsburgh, PA: National Center for Juvenile Justice.

United Nations (1985) *Standard Minimum Rules for the Administration of Juvenile Justice* [The Beijing Rules]. Geneva: United Nations.

United Nations (1990a) *Guidelines for the Prevention of Juvenile Delinquency* [The Riyadh Guidelines]. Geneva: United Nations.

United Nations (1990b) *Minima Rules for the Prevention of Minor Deprived of Liberty* [Havana Rules]. Geneva: United Nations.

Walker, M. and Moodie, K. (2004) 'Survey of Secure Accommodation.' Unpublished report for the Scottish Executive.

Waterhouse, L., McGhee, J., Whyte, B., Loucks, N., Kay, H. and Stewart, R. (2000) *The Evaluation of Children's Hearings in Scotland, Volume 3: Children in Focus*. Edinburgh: Scottish Executive Central Research Unit.

Whyte, B. (2004) 'Responding to Youth Crime in Scotland.' *British Journal of Social Work 34*, 395–411.

CHAPTER 4

Adult Offenders: Policy Developments in England and Wales

Sam Lewis

Introduction

The casual observer might wonder whether a desire to do 'social work' has had any influence on New Labour's approach to dealing with adult offenders. Recent policy documents make no mention of social work. The desire to help and assist appears to have been lost in the drive to 'punish' and 'manage' the offending population. Nevertheless, some of what is done with offenders would still be called 'social work' in other countries. This chapter explores the competing influences that have shaped New Labour's criminal justice policies for adult offenders in England and Wales, and provides a critical appraisal of recent key policy developments.

Putting New Labour's criminal justice policies in context

Before considering the specific criminal justice policies advanced by New Labour, it is necessary to put the Government's criminal justice strategy in context. Ideological 'drivers', practical considerations, evidence as to 'What Works', and an increased emphasis on resettlement have all influenced their criminal justice agenda.

Ideological drivers

There are three ideological 'drivers' that have affected both the tone and content of New Labour's criminal justice agenda. The first 'driver' is their commitment to being 'tough on crime'. One aspect of the relaunching of Labour as 'New Labour' involved revoking the damaging claim, made by the Conservative Party during the 1992 general election, that Labour was 'soft on crime' (Downes and Morgan 2002). During the 1997 election campaign the Labour Party endeavoured to 'steal back' (Brownlee 1998, p.315) the subject of law and order from their political opponents. Their election manifesto claimed that under the Conservative Government crime had doubled whilst police numbers fell (Labour Party 1997, pp.22–3). They promised to 'be tough on crime and tough on the causes of crime' (p.22), placing particular emphasis on their commitment to the first half of Blair's now-famous 'couplet' (Young and Matthews 2003).[1] Whilst it is widely acknowledged that this rebranding exercise succeeded, it effectively 'locked both parties into unreflective toughness' (Tonry 2003, p.6). Tonry (2003) suggests that as a result, (tough) style has at times won out over (evidence-based) substance. The Government's recently stated intention to 'toughen up every aspect of the criminal justice system' (Home Office 2004b, p.6) suggests that it remains wedded to this 'tough' stance.

The second 'driver' is 'the new managerialist penology' (Brownlee 1998). Brownlee suggests that the last 40 years have seen a 'globalized' shift away from welfarism and interventionism and towards cost-cutting, managerialist strategies. In this situation, '[t]he maintenance of the criminal justice system itself and the continual striving for ever greater efficiency of operation become *the* inherent values which are to be pursued' (Brownlee 1998, p.323, emphasis in original). Others have criticised New Labour for their 'punitive managerialist' stance (Cavadino and Dignan 2002; Lewis 2005), and noted the conflict between efforts to 'manage' law and order on the one hand, and the pursuit of policies informed by a humanistic concern for the rights and needs of offenders on the other (Lewis 2005). The effect of this 'new managerialism' is considered further below.

Third, New Labour's criminal justice policies should also be seen in light of the demise of the 'just deserts' approach, and the Government's search for a rational and politically saleable alternative set of principles. Calls for a 'just deserts' approach were first heard in the 1970s, which saw growing pessimism about both the efficacy (Brody 1976; Martinson 1974) and the morality (American Friends Service Committee 1971; von Hirsch 1976) of the dominant rehabilitative model. The new

---

1   This famous slogan first appeared in an article by Tony Blair, entitled 'Crime is a Socialist Issue', which was published in the *New Statesman* in 1993.

system, which called for punishments to be proportionate to the seriousness of the current offence, was intended to produce 'better justice through a more consistent approach to sentencing, so that convicted criminals get their "just deserts"' (Home Office 1990, p.2). The principle of 'just deserts' was enshrined in the Criminal Justice Act 1991, making it the guiding principle of sentencing and officially marking the end of the rehabilitative era.

As noted by Cavadino *et al.* (1999), however, '[t]he Act became caught up in a period of media attention and political controversy that was quite unprecedented for criminal justice legislation' (p.21), much of which focused on the limited extent to which courts were able to take previous convictions into account when passing sentence. In May 1993, as a result of the unexpected furore, the then Home Secretary, Kenneth Clarke, announced that this controversial aspect of the Act would be repealed. Provisions contained in the Criminal Justice Act 1993 stated that '[i]n considering the seriousness of any offence, the court may take into account any previous convictions of the offender or any failure of his to respond to previous sentences' (s.66). Thus began the gradual erosion of the 'just deserts' principle.

In 2000 the Government announced that the desert-based sentencing system created by the 1991 Act was unsatisfactory, affording 'little opportunity to take into account how offenders respond to measures taken during their sentence which are designed to reduce their re-offending, nor the need for some form of reparation to society' (Home Office 2000, p.1). It commissioned a review of the sentencing framework, which was led by John Halliday. The resulting report (Halliday 2001), officially entitled *Making Punishments Work* but widely referred to as the Halliday Report, advanced a new sentencing framework that is discussed in detail below.

Practical considerations

Practical considerations have also had an impact. The latest monthly prison population figures available at the time of writing state that on 30 November 2004 the prison population stood at 75,740, an increase of 2 per cent on a year earlier.[2] Projected trends in the prison population to 2011 present ten possible scenarios, with the projected figures ranging from a 'low' of 76,000 to a 'high' of 87,500.[3] A desire to curb the burgeoning prison population without appearing 'soft' is evident in recent policy proposals.

2   Available at http://www.homeoffice.gov.uk/rds/pdfs04/prisnov04.pdf

3   Available at http://www.homeoffice.gov.uk/rds/pdfs05/hosb0105.pdf

Critics have also drawn attention to the 'down-tariff drift' in both custodial and non-custodial sentencing:

> Offenders who ten years ago would have been put on probation or given community service [are] now being sent to prison, generally for sentences of less than 12 months. And many offenders who ten years ago would have been fined [are] now getting community service or even being made subject to Community Punishment and Rehabilitation Orders... (Morgan 2002/03, p.30)

That custodial sentences are being given to offenders who previously would have received community penalties is cited by Hough *et al.* (2003) as one of two main factors driving up the prison population.[4] That community penalties are being imposed on offenders who previously would have been fined means that 'Probation Service caseloads [are] silting up with low level, low risk offenders many of whom arguably did not warrant the Service's ministrations' (Morgan 2002/3, p.30), presenting a major problem for the already overstretched Probation Service (Morgan 2003). Efforts to arrest this 'down-tariff drift' are also apparent in the Government's criminal justice agenda.

Evidence as to 'What Works'

In the late 1990s the Government launched a programme of research known as the 'What Works' initiative:

> It is a programme which aims to ensure **all** probation practice is based on evidence of success. *What Works* is part of the Crime Reduction Strategy launched by the Home Secretary in July 1998 ... £21m has been earmarked for *What Works* in the next three years (1999–2002). The funds will be used to develop high-quality programmes for the prison and probation services, based on what is known to reduce re-offending. (Home Office 1999, p.3, emphasis in original)

Four priority areas were identified for research and development: the resettlement of short-term prisoners (Lewis *et al.* 2003); offending behaviour programmes (Hollin *et al.* 2002); basic skills programmes (McMahon *et al.* 2004), and community punishment schemes (Rex and Gelsthorpe 2002; Rex *et al.* 2004). In theory at least, the findings from these 'Pathfinders' were intended to inform policy decisions. It has been suggested, however, that the Government has not always paid

---

4   The other factor cited by the authors is that offenders who would previously have been sent to custody are receiving longer sentences.

heed to the evidence, resulting in policies that range 'from sensible and substantive through muddled and bound-to-fail to cynical and disingenuous' (Tonry 2003, p.6).

The focus on resettlement

In Autumn 2001 the Prisons and Probation Inspectorates published *Through the Prison Gate*, their joint thematic review of resettlement services for ex-prisoners. Similar assessments were conducted, and reports produced, by the National Audit Office (2002) and the Social Exclusion Unit (2002). All of the reports reached similarly gloomy conclusions. Short-term prisoners have the highest levels of need, are the most likely group to be reconvicted, and yet receive the least help. A significant majority of all prisoners have severe problems in areas such as housing, education and employment, substance misuse, and mental and physical health, which are often exacerbated by being in prison. Resettlement plans for those on licence may be undermined by a lack of joined up working 'through the prison gate' and between different service providers.

In theory at least, the Government has taken on board the message that 'improving the process of ex-prisoner resettlement is an urgent and overdue priority' (Maruna 2004, p.6). Provisions contained in recent policy documents and legislation are designed to provide a more efficient and effective system of resettlement. They have also attracted criticism, however (see, for example, Maruna 2004; Morgan 2004). These provisions, and the potential problems associated with them, are discussed in detail below.

Key policy developments

Since gaining office in 1997 New Labour has taken significant steps towards transforming the way in which offenders are dealt with. This discussion will focus on provisions contained in the most recent and relevant policy documents and legislation, namely: the Halliday Report (Halliday 2001); the White Paper *Justice for All* (Home Office 2002); the Criminal Justice Act 2003; the Carter Review (Carter 2004) and the Government's response (Home Office 2004a), and the Management of Offenders and Sentencing Bill (2005).

The purposes and principles of sentencing

The Halliday Report (Halliday 2001) responded to the Government's concerns about the existing desert-led sentencing system by advocating a 'hybrid' (p.164) model, which combines desert and utilitarian principles. Under this model, desert will set the outer limits of punishment, within which sentencers may pursue utilitarian aims such as crime reduction and reparation. In addition, it is argued that '[t]he existing "just deserts" philosophy should be modified by incorporating a new presumption that severity of sentence should increase when an offender has sufficiently recent and relevant previous convictions' (p.21). On this formulation, then, repeat offenders will receive more punishment on account of their previous convictions. The justification for this is said to be two-fold: it would better reflect what recidivists deserve whilst increasing opportunities for reform.

These recommendations informed measures contained in the subsequent White Paper, *Justice for All* (Home Office 2002), and are enshrined in the Criminal Justice Act 2003. The purposes of sentencing are set out, for the first time in legislation (Home Office 2002, p.87), as: punishment; crime reduction; reform and rehabilitation; public protection and reparation (s.142). There is no indication in the Act, however, which, if any, of these purposes should be prioritised. According to the new principles of sentencing, sentence severity should reflect the seriousness of the offence. This is calculated according to 'the offender's culpability in committing the offence and any harm which the offence caused, was intended to cause or might forseeably have caused'. In addition, there is a presumption that sufficiently recent and relevant previous convictions will have an aggravating effect on sentence (s.143).

The Halliday Report noted that, without clear and detailed guidelines on how previous convictions should affect sentence, the new presumption of increased punishment for repeat offenders will be unpredictable and may lead to disproportionately severe sentences (2001, p.iii). This point has subsequently been made by others (Jones 2002; Roberts 2002; von Hirsch 2002). As Hutton notes (2003, p.134), there is nothing in the Criminal Justice Act 2003 that will prevent this inconsistency.

Some commentators have condemned the new presumption without reservation. Von Hirsch, for example, rejects the justifications advanced in the Halliday Report for the new system of record-enhanced sentencing, whilst arguing that such an approach could incur 'unacceptable human and financial costs' by, for example: raising the prison population, thus incurring obvious financial costs, and human costs 'in terms of the added suffering inflicted on those involved'; and imposing longer sentences on repeat offenders for rehabilitative purposes, the rehabilitative benefits of which 'would be marginal at best' (2002, p.211). He concludes:

> These manifest human and social costs and doubtful benefits would be achieved at a very substantial sacrifice of justice. No sentencing system that relies heavily on

previous offending instead of on the degree of blameworthiness of the current offence can claim to be a fair and proportionate one... There should be no place in England and Wales for a sentencing philosophy of incarcerating up [sic] the usual suspects. (pp.211–212)

The new community order

The Halliday Report notes that over the past decade there has been a proliferation of new community sentences (2001, p.38). This development, it argues, is 'not helpful to understanding sentencing. The present law...is complex and should be simplified and made more understandable to the community, sentencers and offenders' (p.38). The Report recommends replacing the existing 'alphabet soup' (Travis 2001, p.4) of penalties with a single sentence which, as stated in the subsequent White Paper *Justice for All*, will provide the courts with 'a menu of options which can be combined to form a single sentence' (Home Office 2002, p.92) tailored to the needs of the individual. The White Paper also suggests that these 'tough community sentences' will provide 'a credible alternative to custody' (p.86).

The Criminal Justice Act 2003 provides the legislative platform for the new community order. An order may comprise one or more of 12 different elements: an unpaid work requirement; an activity requirement; a programme requirement; a prohibited activity requirement; a curfew requirement; an exclusion requirement; a residence requirement; a mental health treatment requirement; a drug rehabilitation requirement; an alcohol treatment requirement; a supervision requirement, and, for offenders under the age of 25, an attendance centre requirement (s.177). In line with the new principles of sentencing, the severity of the combined elements of the order should be commensurate with the seriousness of the offence (s.148).

It is difficult to see, at this stage, how sentencers will go about calculating the overall severity of an order comprising several different elements with multiple aims. It is also hard to imagine how the newly created Sentencing Guidelines Council, originally recommended by Halliday and established by virtue of provisions contained in the Criminal Justice Act 2003 to promote consistency in sentencing (s.167–173), could provide guidance that would ensure consistency of approach (see Hutton 2003). There is at least the potential, therefore, for inconsistency. Further, in the absence of clear guidelines, 'a system of smorgasbord sentencing...might result in the piling-on of conditions that taken in aggregate are sometimes too burdensome relative to the seriousness of the offence' (Tonry 2003, p.9).

Will the new community order do anything to arrest the 'down-tariff drift' in community sentences? It is possible, in theory at least, that the combined efforts of the Government and the Sentencing Guidelines Council will convince the judiciary that the new unified sentence is 'tough enough' to be moved 'up tariff' and imposed on those people who currently receive a short prison sentence, thus complying with the Government's wish to control prison numbers. It is also possible, however, that any reduction in the use of custody will be overshadowed by the 'net-widening' effects of the proposals, if the new sentence is regularly imposed on offenders who previously would have got a community sentence but the combined elements of the new order are more intrusive than the sentences formerly imposed. More conditions provide increased scope for breach, which can result in more onerous requirements being imposed, or a prison sentence of up to 51 weeks (Criminal Justice Act 2003, Schedule 8). Wasik also raises the prospect that '[s]entencers may in future tend to use the "community sentence" only once in a criminal career…rather than, as at present, trying two or three different *forms* of community sentences before deciding that custody has become inevitable' (2004, p.305, emphasis in original). Rather than reducing the prison population, then, the new community order may contribute to its continued rise.

The reform of short-term prison sentences

Prisoners serving sentences of less than 12 months account for the majority of those released each year: 62 per cent of all adult prisoners discharged from determinate sentences in 2002 had served such a sentence (Home Office 2003, Table 4.11). Research has shown (Maguire *et al.* 1997), and subsequent reports have confirmed (Her Majesty's Inspectorates of Prison and Probation 2001; National Audit Office 2002; Social Exclusion Unit 2002), that such prisoners have the greatest levels of need, are the most likely group to be reconvicted, and yet receive the least help. The Halliday Report argued that such sentences also lack utility, as 'only half of such sentences are served…and the second half is subject to no conditions whatsoever'. affording Prison Staff 'little opportunity to work on the factors which underlie the criminality' (2001, p.iv). The Report opined that 'a more effective recipe for failure could hardly be conceived' (p.22).

The Halliday Report recommended replacing the short-term sentence with a new sentence of 'custody plus', which was endorsed by the White Paper, *Justice for All*, and is established by virtue of provisions contained in the Criminal Justice Act 2003 (s.181). The new sentence will comprise an initial custodial period of between 2 and 13 weeks, and a post-release period of supervision to be served in full and lasting from 26 to a maximum of whatever period would take the sentence as a whole to 51 weeks. Anyone who breaches the terms of their licence may be returned to custody for some or all of the remainder of their sentence (s.254 and s.256). The content of the licence period would be tailored to the individual, comprising one or more conditions taken from a menu of options, as with the new community order. According to Halliday (2001, p.22), this will allow 'pioneering work' conducted as part of the Government's 'What Works' programme (see Lewis *et al.* 2003) to be carried out on a wider scale.

Roberts and Smith describe the rationale behind the new sentence, and the 'plus' part in particular, thus:

> to provide…resettlement assistance, to monitor offenders' progress (or lack of it) on licence, to require or prohibit specific activities to reduce the risk manifested individually by each offender in his circumstances, and to require offenders' participation in cognitive-behavioural programmes tailored to deal effectively with their offending behaviour. (2003, p.188)

That the new sentence effectively removes the possibility of an offender spending between three and six months in custody is also noteworthy.[5] This, coupled with the statement that 'prison must be reserved for serious, dangerous and seriously persistent offenders, and for those who have consistently breached community sentences' (Home Office 2002, p.86), and the recognition of the difficulties caused by high prison numbers (p.106), suggests that the controlled use of custody plus is also intended to curtail the rising prison population.

This raises (at least) two questions: how effective will 'custody plus' be in aiding resettlement, and how likely is 'custody plus' to temper the rising tide of prisoners? With regard to the former question, Roberts and Smith are not hopeful:

> [A]ttaching demanding and intrusive requirements to the licence period is not what has been meant by resettlement and conflicts with its original premise. Of course, there are likely to be gains for the offenders and for the rest of us when licence requirements are suited to the offender's needs – and the offender complies. But the benefit is likely to be confounded by hasty and inaccurate targeting of the

5　　Offenders can spend a maximum of three months in custody under 'custody plus'. Prisoners serving custodial sentences of between 12 months and less than 4 years will still automatically be released at the half-way stage, to serve the remainder of their sentence on licence. Thus someone given a 12-month sentence will spend 6 months in custody.

programmes, by indiscriminate use of other licence requirements, and by excessively punitive responses to failures to comply. (2003, p.199)

The authors' concerns about overly punitive responses to breach highlight the potential conflict between key ideological drivers (in particular 'being tough' and 'managing' criminal justice) on the one hand, and affording resettlement on the other. For example, what will happen when an ex-prisoner with (for the sake of argument) a well-tailored post-release package, that has the potential to facilitate resettlement, breaches a condition of her licence? Will a desire to 'manage' the offender population and a need to 'be tough' coupled with strict enforcement rules mean that she is swiftly returned to prison? Or will a commitment to resettlement coupled with professional discretion enable her to remain in the community? Maruna cites Harry Fletcher, an Assistant General Secretary for the National Association of Probation Staff (NAPOfficers), as saying that '[F]or the last four years, probation staff have been obliged to follow strict national standards on enforcement. Previously there was greater professional discretion' (2004, p.7). If current trends continue, then the prognosis looks poor.

There are numerous other reasons to fear for the success of custody plus. The negative effects of the short period of incarceration might actually reduce or negate the positive effects of rehabilitative work (Roberts and Smith 2003); the ability of the various 'What Works' cognitive-behavioural programmes to reduce re-offending and promote resettlement, attendance at which may be a requirement, remain unproven (Roberts and Smith 2003); and if, as some writers have predicted (see Roberts and Smith 2003), custody plus is a popular sentencing choice, will the resources be available to meet the demand for resettlement services? The Government must find some way to avoid these potential pitfalls if it is to achieve its stated aims with regard to resettlement via custody plus.

This brings the discussion back to the second question: how likely is 'custody plus' to moderate the growing prison population? This is difficult to predict, not least because it is dependent on so many factors. Will the judiciary be tempted to use custody plus with offenders who would previously have received a community sentence? Will strict enforcement procedures be applied? Will prisoners who would previously have spent between three and six months in prison receive longer prison terms in future? If the answer to any of these questions is 'yes', the effect of the new sentence may be to *exacerbate* the problem of prison population.

The Halliday Report also advocated a new 'suspended sentence plus', described as a 'sentence of suspended imprisonment combined with (in effect) a community sentence' (2001, p.36). The White Paper, *Justice for All*, named the new sentence 'custody minus' and stated that this would be more rigorous than the existing suspended sentence that it would replace (Home Office 2002, pp.93–4). The new 'suspended sentence order', without the 'custody minus' label, was introduced by virtue of provisions contained in the Criminal Justice Act 2003 (see s.189–194). Suspended terms of imprisonment will be for between 28 and 51 weeks, whilst the community-based supervision period may last for between six months and two years. When dealing with offenders who are in breach of a suspended sentence order the court has several options: allowing the order to continue as before; requiring the offender *either* to complete the prison term previously specified *or* a lesser prison term; and amending the original order by imposing more onerous requirements, extending the supervision period, or extending the operational period (Schedule 12).[6]

Justice for All brushed aside concerns raised in the Halliday Report about introducing a new sentence of intermittent custody:

> We will legislate for a new sentence of Intermittent Custody, where offenders will serve their custodial sentence at weekends or during the week with the rest of their sentence in the community. The sentence will enable an offender to continue in regular employment, maintain caring responsibilities, or follow a court specified educational or reparative programme in the community. (Home Office 2002, p.94)

The Criminal Justice Act 2003 laid the legislative foundations for this new sentence (s.183–186). An intermittent custody pilot scheme began in January 2004, allowing designated courts in 11 probation areas to use the new sentence. The courts are in the catchment areas for two purpose-built intermittent custody centres located at prisons in Preston and Lincoln.[7]

The new sentence has much to offer in terms of reducing the negative impact of a prison sentence by helping prisoners to maintain their accommodation, employment, and community and family ties. The success of the provisions depends, in large part, on whether sufficient intermittent custody centres can be built to meet the demand. The Act makes it clear that '[a] court may not make an

---

6   The operational period is defined as the period within which, upon breach of the conditions of the community aspect of an order, a court may require the prison sentence to take effect (see S.189[1][b][ii]).

7   The information about intermittent custody came from:
     http://www.homeoffice.gov.uk/n_story.asp?item_id=781;
     http://www.hmprisonservice.gov.uk/prisoninformation/prisonservicemag
     azine/index.asp?id=1031,18,3,18,0,0; http://news.bbc.co.uk/
     2/hi/uk-news/3427031.stm (accessed on 17/01/05).

intermittent custody order unless…arrangements for implementing such orders are available in the area proposed to be specified in the intermittent custody order' (s.184[1]). Given the current punitive climate, there is also a risk that courts will use intermittent custody for offenders who would previously have received a community penalty, thereby increasing the prison population.

The National Offender Management Service

In March 2003 the Government asked Patrick Carter to conduct a review of correctional services in England and Wales. His findings were published in a report entitled *Managing Offenders, Reducing Crime: A New Approach* (Carter 2003), known colloquially as the Carter Report. The Report recommended 'far reaching reforms, which build on…the new sentencing framework set out in the Criminal Justice Act (2003)' (p.1).

The Report stated:

> The use of prison and probation has increased by over a quarter since 1996, even though the number of people arrested and sentenced has remained broadly constant. The growth is due to the increased severity of sentences, which is linked to the fall in the use of fines. (p.9)

It went on to note that '[t]he increased use of prison and probation has only had a limited impact on crime' (p.17), and '[s]entencing remains poorly targeted', as '[t]oo much of the increased use of prison and probation has been focused on those offenders with no previous convictions' (p.18). Further:

> The system remains dominated by the need to manage [the Prison and Probation Services] rather than having a focus on the offender and reducing re-offending… [T]he services remain largely detached from one another and the structure of the system encourages concentration on the day-to-day operation of the services. A more strategic approach to the end-to-end management of offenders across their sentence is needed. (p.23)

The Report called for a new National Offender Management Service (NOMS), combining the existing Prison and Probation Services. NOMS would be led by a single Chief Executive, who would be supported by a National Offender Manager and who, in turn, would be supported by Regional Offender Managers (see Chapter 7). The Report claimed that '[t]his new structure would break down the silos of the [Prison and Probation] services. It would ensure the end-to-end management of offenders, regardless of whether they were given a custodial or community sentence' (p.33). The Report also argued that fines should be 'rebuilt as a credible punishment', stating that 'a Day Fine system should be introduced in England and Wales' (p.27). It also emphasised the crucial role of the new Sentencing Guidelines Council (discussed above) in ensuring greater consistency and effectiveness in sentencing practice.

It is also important to note that the Report advocated greater use of competitive tendering in the provision of correctional services. Indeed, some writers have suggested that 'contestability' was the dominant concept in the Report, and the 'logical outworking of managerialist principles, though one that was not fully supported...by empirical evidence' (Bottoms, Rex and Robinson 2004, p.7). This provoked strong opposition, not least from the Probation Service which feared losing out to private companies and voluntary sector organisations. Critics also pointed to possible discontinuities in the supervision of individual offenders if services were to be fragmented into 'purchasing' and 'providing' sections.

The predicted benefits of the proposals, as stated in the Report, include suppressing the rising prison population to below 80,000 by 2009, and 'increasing the effectiveness of offender management. This would be achieved through preventing further sentencing drift, increasing the use of fines and intensive community sentences and marginal reductions in sentence length' (p.39). The Report states, however, that 'the package is crucially dependent on the Sentencing Guidelines Council managing sentencing practice and in particular rebuilding the use of fines' (p.39).

In his foreword to the Government's response to the Carter Report, entitled *Reducing Crime – Changing Lives* (Home Office 2004a), the then Home Secretary, David Blunkett, stated that '[t]he Report has been developed closely with the Home Office and I fully support the approach he describes' (p.2). The Government's response endorsed many of the Report's recommendations, including the establishment of NOMS, and promised to 'explore further' the possibility of a day fine system (p.12). It also endorsed the principle of 'contestability.' and vowed to encourage greater involvement of the private and voluntary sector in the provision of criminal justice services (p.14).

After a national consultation exercise on the proposed design of NOMS, the Home Office announced a significant rethink regarding their plans for greater contestability. In July 2004 the then Minister for Correctional Services, Paul Goggins, said that the plans had been put on hold temporarily.[8] This situation was

8   See the statement by Paul Goggins, accessed on 18/01/05 at:
     http://www.probation.homeoffice.gov.uk/print/page239.asp.

short-lived, however. In November 2004 the Prime Minister, Tony Blair, told the Chief Executive of NOMS, Martin Narey, that contestability should be introduced to community penalties promptly, whilst asserting a pressing need for the prompt 'market testing' of several prisons (Fletcher 2004/5, p.2). NAPO expressed dismay at the renewed plans, which were seen as paving the way for privatisation, heralding the 'effective abolition' of the Probation Service (McNight 2004/5, p.1).

The *Management of Offenders and Sentencing Bill* (2005) provided the legislative response to the Carter Report. It established the aims of NOMS as the protection of the public; the reduction of offending; the proper punishment of offenders; ensuring offenders' awareness of the effects of crime on victims and the public and the rehabilitation of offenders (s.1). It also afforded the Home Secretary greater power to direct local probation boards to commission services from specified providers (s.2). This 'confirmed NAPO's worst fears' about their traditional role being usurped by the private sector (Fletcher 2005, p.1). The Bill introduced a new day fine scheme (s.43), and extended the remit of the Sentencing Guidelines Council to include consideration of 'the resources that are, or are in future likely to be, available for giving effect to sentences' when issuing guidelines (s.37).[9]

In spite of widespread scepticism, the proposals in the 2005 Bill cannot be dismissed as all bad. If custody plus is to operate as planned, offenders must be afforded a smooth transition between custody and community. The overarching management strategy for and the improved joined-up working between the Prison and Probation Services that NOMS provides should, in theory, make this possible. The reintroduction of day fines has long been advocated by academic commentators (see, for example, Morgan 2003). If they are used as intended, very low level offenders who currently receive community orders will in future be fined, resulting in the welcome 'up-tariffing' of community sentences. Further, sentencing guidelines that took into account the (lack of) prison capacity had the potential to suppress the rising prison population and to give effect to Carter's proposal to limit it to 80,000. However, it was widely recognised that much would depend on the precise form the proposals eventually took, and the most recent developments outlined in the final section of this chapter are not encouraging.

9   See also the Home Office press release, accessed on 18/01/05 at: http://www.homeoffice.gov.uk/pageprint.asp?item_id=1208

Other significant developments

Several other notable policy documents were published in 2004. In particular, July 2004 saw the publication of *Confident Communities in a Secure Britain: The Home Office Strategic Plan 2004-08* (Home Office 2004b), alongside *Cutting Crime, Delivering Justice: The Criminal Justice Strategic Plan 2004–08* (Office for Criminal Justice Reform 2004). The Home Office also published their *Reducing Re-offending National Action Plan* (Home Office 2004c), their long-awaited response to the Social Exclusion Unit's report on resettlement (Social Exclusion Unit 2002), which has both been welcomed as 'providing a real starting point for taking rehabilitation forward' (see Dalkin and Padel 2004, p.17), and lampooned by a co-author of the original Social Exclusion Unit report as a series of 60 'inaction points' that comprise a 'catalogue of indifference' (Corner 2004). Space constraints prohibit a detailed discussion of these documents, but together they add to the considerable body of evidence that underlines New Labour's determination to be seen as taking an activist stance in relation to criminal justice.

Conclusion

At the time of the last General Election in 2005 it was still difficult to tell what form the new criminal justice landscape would take. Some of the new provisions had the potential to achieve a more humanitarian criminal justice system, but their success depended largely on the extent to which politicians were prepared to promote (or at least not undermine and denigrate) such measures. Would New Labour politicians be able to resist the temptation to sabotage their own more progressive strategies for the sake of a tough soundbite? Developments since the election (won by Labour with a reduced majority) have been less than reassuring, and illustrate yet again the volatility and populism which have characterised policy-making in this field (see also Raynor in this volume). Later in 2005 Charles Clarke replaced David Blunkett as Home Secretary, and quietly abandoned the target of limiting prison numbers to 80,000 as well as the proposal to take resources into account when issuing sentencing guidelines. Clarke was in turn replaced in May 2006 by John Reid following media revelations concerning foreign national prisoners who had been released without being considered for deportation. Also in 2006 a series of high-profile cases received widespread media coverage and fuelled concerns about sentencing practice, the adequacy of risk assessments conducted on prisoners before release and the supervision of dangerous offenders in the community.[10] In July 2006 Reid revealed plans to reform the Home Office (Home Office 2006a, 2006b; Home Office Immigration and Nationality Directorate 2006) which were intended to restore the reputation of the Home Office and rebuild public confidence (Home Office 2006b, p.5). This drive to appease the public has prompted a series of 'tough' proposals which undermine some of the more progressive policies outlined above.

Substantial sections of the Criminal Justice Act 2003 were brought into force in 2004 including those regarding the purposes of sentencing; the new community order; the Sentencing Guidelines Council; the suspended sentence order, and intermittent custody. The custody plus provisions were not brought into force, however, and the Home Office has stated that because of 'the need to prioritise prison and probation resources on more serious offenders, we will not now implement the new sentence of Custody Plus…in autumn 2006' as previously planned (2006b, p.34). The shelving of custody plus has left a huge hole in plans for the resettlement of short-term prisoners (see Lewis *et al.* 2007).

The Management of Offenders and Sentencing Bill (2005) ran out of time at the end of the 2004/05 Parliamentary session. Plans to increase the use of competitive tendering in the provision of correctional services continue apace, however. In October 2005 the Home Office published a consultation document entitled *Restructuring Probation to Reduce Re-offending* which provided details of plans to introduce contestability into the Probation Service (NOMS 2005). In April 2006 the Home Office published a summary of responses to the consultation document, entitled *Working with Probation to Protect the Public and Reduce Re-offending*, which confirmed the Government's intention to 'introduce legislation to restructure the Probation Service as soon as Parliamentary time allows' (NOMS 2006a, p.8). This was in spite of the fact that most responses to the consultation were negative, including a detailed academic critique (Hough, Allen and Padel 2006). In August 2006, in *Improving Prison and Probation Services: Public Value Partnerships*, further information was provided:

10   See, for example, the cases of Craig Sweeney
      (http://www.guardian.co.uk/print/0,,329526199-104770,00.html),
      Damien Hanson (http://www.guardian.co.uk/crime/article/
      0,,1701789,00.html and http://www.guardian.co.uk/crime/article/
      0,,1867305,00.html) and Anthony Rice
      (http://www.guardian.co.uk/crime/article/0,,1771610,00.html).
      All accessed on 21/09/06.

> This year and next year we are requiring local probation areas, on a voluntary basis, to double and then double again the proportion of services they contract out. From April 2008, legislation permitting, we will go further and compete a much larger proportion of the interventions they provide – up to £250m worth of services a year. (NOMS 2006b, p.2)

At the time of writing this, in late 2006, NOMS commissioning plans with further details of the contestability programme are due to be published shortly (NOMS 2006b, p.4) and a new Offender Management Bill giving effect to the probation 'reforms' is making its way through Parliament. In July 2006 the Government published a review of the criminal justice system entitled *Rebalancing the Criminal Justice System in Favour of the Law-abiding Majority* (Home Office 2006b), which includes further proposals for reform. A key theme is the need to restore public faith in the criminal justice system. Taking steps to address public misperceptions about crime and sentencing practice would be a good place to start (Home Office 2006c; Hough and Roberts 1999). However, longer and tougher sentences and the introduction of a National Enforcement Service to deal with those who do not pay fines or comply with court orders are proposed. In order to deal with the inevitable increased demand for prison places 8000 new places are to be built in addition to 900 places currently under construction (Home Office 2006b).

Overall, then, it appears that potentially progressive policies designed to aid resettlement, arrest the rising prison population, and reverse the down-tariff drift in sentencing have been abandoned or at best indefinitely postponed. More prisons, more populism and more contestability are the order of the day. Unless and until steps are taken to challenge the media and public imaginary of 'the crime problem' that is fuelling this 'tough' agenda the goal of achieving a more humanitarian criminal justice system in England and Wales is likely to remain out of reach.

References

American Friends Service Committee (1971) *Struggle for Justice*. New York: Hill and Wang.

Bottoms, A., Rex, S. and Robinson, G. (2004) 'How Did We Get Here?' In A. Bottoms, S. Rex and G. Robinson (eds) *Alternatives to Prison: Options for an Insecure Society*. Cullompton: Willan.

Brody, S. (1976) *The Effectiveness of Sentencing*. Home Office Research Study No. 35. London: HMSO.

Brownlee, I. (1998) 'New Labour – New Penology? Punitive Rhetoric and the Limits of Managerialism in Criminal Justice Policy.' *Journal of Law and Society 25*, 3, 313–335.

Carter, P. (2003) *Managing Offenders, Reducing Crime: A New Approach*. London: Home Office Strategy Unit.

Cavadino, M., Crow, I. and Dignan, J. (1999) *Criminal Justice 2000: Strategies for a New Century.* Winchester: Waterside Press.

Cavadino, M. and Dignan, J. (2002) *The Penal System: An Introduction.* London: Sage.

Corner, J. (2004) 'Viewpoint: Inaction Plan.' In *Safer Society, 22, Winter 2004.* London: NACRO. Available online at http://www. nacro.org.uk/safersociety/backissues.htm (accessed 31/08/07).

Dalkin, J. and Padel, U. (2004) 'The Reducing Re-offending Action Plan and Prisoner Resettlement.' In *Criminal Justice Matters 56*, 16–17.

Downes, D. and Morgan, R. (2002) 'The Skeletons in the Cupboard: The Politics of Law and Order at the Turn of the Millennium.' In M. Maguire, R. Morgan and R. Reiner (eds) *The Oxford Handbook of Criminology* (3rd edn) Oxford: Oxford University Press.

Fletcher, H. (2004/5) 'Blair Demands that Private Sector Runs Community Penalties.' *NAPO News 165.* London: NAPO.

Fletcher, H. (2005) 'Contracting Out and Sentencing Bill Published.' *NAPO News 166.* London: NAPO.

Halliday, J. (2001) *Making Punishments Work: Report of a Review of the Sentencing Framework for England and Wales.* London: Home Office.

Her Majesty's Inspectorates of Prison and Probation (2001) *Through the Prison Gate: A Joint Thematic Review.* London: Home Office.

Hollin, C., McGuire, J., Palmer, E., Bilby, C., Hatcher, R. and Holmes, A. (2002) *Introducing Pathfinder Programmes into the Probation Service: An Interim Report* Home Office Research Study No. 247. London: Home Office.

Home Office (1990) *Crime, Justice and Protecting the Public.* Cm 965. London: Home Office.

Home Office (1999) *What Works. Reducing Re-offending: Evidence-based Practice.* London: Home Office.

Home Office (2000) *A Review of the Sentencing Framework: Publicity Leaflet.* London: Home Office.

Home Office (2002) *Justice for All*, Cm 5563. London: Home Office.

Home Office (2003) *Prison Statistics for England and Wales 2002*, Cm 5996. London: Stationery Office.

Home Office (2004a) *Reducing Crime – Changing Lives: The Government's Plans for Transforming the Management of Offenders.* (The Government's response to the Carter Report). London: Home Office.

Home Office (2004b) *Confident Communities in a Secure Britain: The Home Office Strategic Plan 2004-08*, Cmd 6287. London: Stationery Office.

Home Office (2004c) *Reducing Re-offending: National Action Plan.* London: Home Office.

Home Office (2006a) *From Improvement to Transformation: An Action Plan to Reform the Home Office so it Meets Public Expectations and Delivers its Core Purpose of Protecting the Public.* London: Home Office.

Home Office (2006b) *Rebalancing the Criminal Justice System in Favour of the Law-abiding Majority: Cutting Crime, Reducing Reoffending and Protecting the Public.* London: Home Office.

Home Office (2006c) *Crime in England and Wales 2005/06*, Chapter 3. London: Home Office.

Home Office Immigration and Nationality Directorate (2006) *Fair, Effective, Transparent and Trusted: Rebuilding Confidence in our Immigration System.* London: Home Office.

Hough, M., Allen, R. and Padel, U. (eds.) (2006) *Reshaping Probation and Prisons.* Bristol: Policy Press.

Hough, M., Jacobson, J. and Millie, A. (2003) *The Decision to Imprison: Sentencing and the Prison Population.* London: Prison Reform Trust.

Hough, M. and Roberts, J.V. (1999) 'Sentencing Trends in Britaln Public Knowledge and Public Opinion.' *Punishment and Society 1*, 1, 11–26.

Hutton, N. (2003) 'Sentencing Guidelines.' In M. Tonry (ed.) *Confronting Crime: Crime Control Policy under New Labour.* Cullompton: Willan.

Jones, P. (2002) 'The Halliday Report and Persistent Offenders.' In S. Rex and M. Tonry (eds) *Reform and Punishment: The Future of Sentencing.* Cullompton: Willan.

Labour Party (1997) *New Labour – Because Britain Deserves Better.* London: Labour Party.

Lewis, S. (2005) 'Rehabilitation: Headline or Footnote in the New Penal Policy?' *Probation Journal 52*, 2, 117–133.

Lewis, S., Maguire, M., Raynor, P., Vanstone, M. and Vennard, J. (2007) 'What Works in Resettlement? Findings from Seven Pathfinders for Short-term Prisoners in England and Wales.' *Criminology and Criminal Justice 7*, 1, 33–53.

Lewis, S., Vennard, J., Maguire, M., Raynor, P., Vanstone, M., Raybould, S. and Rix, A. (2003) *The Resettlement of Short-term Prisoners: An Evaluation of Seven Pathfinders.* RDS Occasional Paper No. 83. London: Home Office.

Maguire, M., Raynor, P., Vanstone, M. and Kynch, J. (1997) *Voluntary After-Care.* Report to the Home Office. Cardiff: Michael and Associates.

Martinson, R. (1974) 'What Works? – Questions and Answers about Prison Reform.' *The Public Interest 35*, 22–54.

Maruna, S. (2004) '"California Dreamin"': Are we Heading toward a National "Waste Management" Service?' *Criminal Justice Matters, 56*, 6–7.

McMahon, G., Hall, A., Hayward, G., Hudson, C. (2004) *Basic Skills Programmes in the Probation Service: an Evaluation of the Basic Skills Pathfinder.* Home Office Research Findings 203. London: Home Office.

McNight, J. (2004/5) 'Probation Service to be Dismantled.' *NAPO News 165.* London: NAPO.

Morgan, R. (2002/3) 'Probation: Cutting Through the Silt.' *Criminal Justice Matters 50*, Winter 30–31.

Morgan, R. (2003) 'Thinking about the Demand for Probation Services.' *Probation Journal 50*, 1, 7–19.

Morgan, R. (2004) 'Resettlement, the *Criminal Justice Act 2003* and NOMS: Prospects and Problems.' *Criminal Justice Matters 56*, 4–5.

National Audit Office (2002) *Reducing Prisoner Reoffending.* London: Stationery Office.

NOMS (2005) *Restructuring Probation to Reduce Re-Offending.* London: Home Office.

NOMS (2006a) *Working with Probation to Protect the Public and Reduce Re-offending: Summary of Responses to Restructuring Probation to Reduce Re-Offending.* London: Home Office.

NOMS (2006b) *Improving Prison and Probation Services: Public Value Partnerships.* London: Home Office.

Office for Criminal Justice Reform (2004) *Cutting Crime, Delivering Justice: The Criminal Justice Strategic Plan 2004-08*, Cmd. 6288. London: OCJR.

Rex, S. and Gelsthorpe, L. (2002) 'The Role of Community Service in Reducing Offending: Evaluating Pathfinder Projects in the UK.' *Howard Journal 41*, 4, 311–325.

Rex, S., Gelsthorpe, L., Roberts, C. and Jordan, P. (2004) *What's Promising in Community Service: Implementation of Seven Pathfinder Projects.* Home Office Research Findings 231. London: Home Office.

Roberts, J. (2002) 'Alchemy in Sentencing: An Analysis of Sentencing Reform Proposals in England and Wales.' *Punishment and Society 4*, 4, 425–442.

Roberts, J. and Smith, M.E. (2003) 'Custody Plus, Custody Minus.' In M. Tonry (Ed.) *Confronting Crime: Crime Control Policy under New Labour.* Cullompton: Willan.

Social Exclusion Unit (2002) *Reducing Re-offending by Ex-prisoners.* London: Office of the Deputy Prime Minister.

Tonry, M. (2003) 'Evidence, Elections and Ideology in the Making of Criminal Justice Policy.' In M. Tonry (Ed.) *Confronting Crime: Crime Control Policy under New Labour.* Cullompton: Willan.

Travis, A. (2001) 'Blunkett Reforms: Focus Shifts to Repeat Criminals.' *The Guardian,* 6 July.

von Hirsch, A. (1976) *Doing Justice: The Choice of Punishments.* New York: Hill and Wang.

von Hirsch, A. (2002) 'Record-enhanced Sentencing in England and Wales.' In S. Rex and M. Tonry (eds) *Reform and Punishment: The future of sentencing.* Cullompton: Willan.

Wasik, M. (2004) 'What Guides Sentencing Decisions?' In A. Bottoms, S. Rex and G. Robinson (eds) *Alternatives to Prison: Options for an Insecure Society.* Cullompton: Willan.

Young, J. and Matthews, R. (2003) 'New Labour, Crime Control and Social Exclusion.' In R. Matthews and J. Young (eds) *The New Politics of Crime and Punishment.* Cullompton: Willan.

CHAPTER 5

Developments in Probation in Scotland

Gill McIvor and Fergus McNeill

Introduction

This chapter offers an account of the distinctive features of criminal justice social work in Scotland, with a focus upon developments that have taken place over the last ten years and, in particular, the changes in policy, legislation and practice that have occurred since devolution in 1999. Scotland has its own judicial system and separate legislation from other parts of the UK and responsibility for the provision of social work services to the criminal justice system remains with local authority social work departments. This renders distinctive both the form and underpinning philosophy of community-based services to offenders in Scotland. However, as the following discussion will indicate, Scottish policy has not been immune to the wider developments that have characterised western jurisdictions over the last decade, such as the growing emphasis upon the use of structured interventions and upon the assessment and management of risk. It could, moreover, be argued that since devolution the Scottish criminal justice system has come under an increasingly intensive political gaze, resulting in unprecedented developments in legislation, policy and practice. Although it appears that being governed by New Labour in London and Edinburgh between 1999 and 2007 produced some predictable convergences of penal ideologies and related policy and organisational changes north and south of the border, the influence of 'correctionalism' in Scotland has been somewhat more attenuated than in England and Wales (McNeill, 2004; Robinson and McNeill 2004).

Regulation and governance

It is now more than a decade since the publication of a previous volume in this series that examined developments in social work with offenders in the UK (McIvor 1996a). In Scotland the policy and practice landscape has changed almost beyond recognition in the intervening time. When the earlier volume was published, national objectives and standards for social work services to the criminal justice system (with associated ring-fenced funding from central government) had been in operation in Scotland for five years and local authorities were poised for a major reorganisation that would result in the creation of 32 unitary (single-tier) authorities (McIvor 1996b). The practical constraints upon service delivery and development that arose from local government reorganisation quickly became apparent, resulting in the publication of the *Tough Option* consultation paper in 1998 that set out three options for the future provision of criminal justice social work services: the status quo, a single centralised service or the creation of 'groupings' of local authorities with shared responsibility for service delivery (Scottish Office 1998). Following the consultation, local authorities were invited to come forward with proposals for the restructuring of criminal justice social work to enable a smaller number of inter-authority groupings to be established (Scottish Executive 1999). The resultant 'Tough Options Groupings', consisting of eight partnership groupings, three unitary authorities and three island authorities, came into effect in April 2002.

The 2003 election campaign, however, signalled further significant changes to the organisational context of criminal justice social work services in Scotland when the Scottish Labour Party's Manifesto for the Scottish Parliamentary election campaign promised the creation of a single agency or 'Correctional Service for Scotland' (Scottish Labour 2003). The Partnership Agreement between Scottish Labour and the Scottish Liberal Democrats, published following the elections, moderated this position slightly by undertaking to 'publish proposals for consultation for a single agency to deliver custodial and non-custodial sentences in Scotland with the aim of reducing reoffending rates' (Scottish Executive 2003, p.36 (emphasis added)).

The analysis of responses to the *Reducing Reoffending* consultation (Scottish Executive 2004a) highlighted widespread lack of support for the bringing together of the Scottish Prison Service and criminal justice social work services under a single correctional agency structure (Scottish Executive 2004b) and, in the face of strong opposition to the establishment of a single agency, the *Criminal Justice Plan*, published in December 2004, set out proposals for the creation, instead, of Community Justice Authorities (CJAs) (Scottish Executive 2004c). Following a consultation which sought views on their functions, structure and constitution and the role of partner organisations (Scottish Executive 2005), eight CJAs were established in April 2006 to facilitate strategic planning across areas and between partner agencies, with some agencies (including the police, courts, prosecution, prisons, Victim Support Scotland, Health Boards and relevant voluntary agencies) becoming statutory partners within the CJAs. Established through the Community Justice Authorities (Establishment, Constitutions and Proceedings (Scotland) Order, contained in the Management of Offenders (Scotland) Act 2005), in the first year of operation 2006–2006 their primary responsibility will be to produce a strategic plan for their area in consultation with statutory and non-statutory partner bodies. Thereafter their responsibilities will include the allocation of resources across and monitoring of criminal justice social work services within the area. It is intended that the CJAs will redesign services around the following offender groups: less serious/first-time offenders; offenders with mental health problems; offenders with substance misuse problems; persistent offenders, including young offenders coming through from the youth system; prisoners needing resettlement and rehabilitation services; violent, serious and sex offenders and women offenders (Scottish Executive 2006a).

A National Advisory Body on Offender Management, chaired by the Justice Minister, was established in March 2006. Described as a 'new body to tackle Scotland's high re-offending rates' (Scottish Executive 2006b) and with a membership consisting of representatives from the Convention of Scottish Local Authorities, Association of Directors of Social Work, voluntary sector, Victim Support Scotland, ACPOS, Parole Board, Risk Management Authority and a range of experts, its roles are to develop and review the national strategy for managing offenders, provide advice to enhance offender management practice and support the work of the new Community Justice Authorities. The first National Strategy for the Management of Offenders (Scottish Executive 2006a) was published in May 2006, aimed at encouraging 'a set of common aims and expected outcomes centred on increased public protection and delivering a consistent approach to managing offenders in prison and in the community' (Scottish Executive 2006c).

Rehabilitation and correctionalism

A concern to stress the responsibilisation of the offender but to balance it explicitly (though usually more quietly and discreetly) with notions of tolerance and inclusion has been evident in Scottish penal policy since the introduction of national objectives and standards in 1991. Paterson and Tombs, for example, describe the 'responsibility model' of practice initiated by the standards as recognising 'both that offenders make active choices in their behaviour and that choice is always situated within a person's particular social and personal context'

(1998, p.xii). By the late 1990s, although there was evidence of a hardening of the rhetoric around community penalties, the link between crime and social exclusion continued to be recognised: 'Criminal justice social work services are often dealing with the consequences of exclusion and it follows that…offenders…should be able to access services and resources which can assist in their reintegration' (Scottish Office 1998; section 2.2.1). Similar sentiments were expressed by the First Minister in 2003 when he outlined his vision for the future of criminal justice in Scotland (McConnell 2003, p.11): 'There is a balance to be struck. A balance between protection and punishment – and the chance for those who have done wrong to change their behaviour and re-engage with the community as full and productive members.'

The same theme underpinned the third of the *Criminal Justice Social Work Services: National Priorities for 2001–2002 and Onwards*, which was to 'Promote the social inclusion of offenders through rehabilitation, so reducing the level of offending' (Justice Department 2001, p.3). In this context, rehabilitation was cast as the means of progressing towards two compatible and interdependent ends: not only the reduction of re-offending but also the social inclusion of offenders. This reading of rehabilitation remained entirely consistent with the social welfare philosophy underlying the Social Work (Scotland) Act 1968. South of the border, by contrast, there has been little evidence to be found in similar strategic documents to indicate that the promotion of offenders' welfare or social inclusion is regarded as a laudable end in its own right. Indeed, where 'rehabilitation' has been articulated as an aim in official documentation, it is 'rehabilitation-as-treatment' or 'correctionalism' which is inferred: that is, the reduction of reoffending risk via the application of accredited, 'rehabilitative' programmes of intervention (see National Probation Service 2001, p.7; Robinson and McNeill 2004).

Although the recent National Strategy for the Management of Offenders (Scottish Executive 2006a) makes no explicit reference to reducing the use of custody, there has been evidence of a continuing commitment to the penal reductionism or 'anti-custodialism' (Nellis 1995) that was evident in the original national standards (Social Work Services Group 1991). This was reflected, for example, in the second of the National Priorities which is to 'Reduce the use of unnecessary custody by providing effective community disposals' (Justice Department 2001, p.3) and in recent enquiries by the Scottish Parliament's cross-party Justice 1 Committee into the use of alternatives to custody (Eley *et al.* 2005).

Over the last decade there has also been a commitment in Scotland, as in the rest of the UK, to the development of 'evidence-based' probation practice. The National Objectives and Standards introduced in 1991 provided a framework aimed at raising minimum standards of practice but they did not, in themselves, provide detailed guidance on the methods and approaches that might be adopted to increase the likelihood that supervision might impact positively upon offenders' behaviour. Subsequent initiatives have been more directly concerned with increasing the effectiveness of work undertaken with offenders in the community or on release from prison (McIvor 2004a). These include the convening in 1998 of the Getting Best Results (GBR) Steering Group which brought together representatives from central government, local authorities, the independent sector and academics to provide leadership, direction and co-ordination in the development of effective practice in the community supervision of offenders[1]; and, most recently, the establishment of an Effective Practice Unit in the Community Justice Division of the Justice Department.

A key task for the GBR Steering Group was the development of a framework for the accreditation of community-based programmes and providers. Accreditation was originally introduced in Scotland by the Scottish Prison Service in 1996. A separate Community Justice Accreditation Panel was established in 2003[2], based on the work undertaken by the GBR accreditation sub-group, with the first programme (a sex offender programme) receiving accreditation in 2005. The Prison and Community Justice Panels were formally merged in 2006 (as the Scottish Accreditation Panel for Offender Programmes) and the new panel has been tasked with devising a common framework for accreditation across the prison and community settings.

1   Specific areas addressed by this initiative included the revision of National Standards, staff development and training, quality assurance and the development of a national framework for monitoring and evaluation. Additionally, a Pathfinder Provider Initiative was launched in 2000, adopting a different focus to the programme-based approach that had been introduced in England and Wales. Instead the Scottish Pathfinders were tasked with developing mechanisms to support the pursuit of effective practice at all levels of the organisation.

2   There was an overlap of membership with the Scottish Prison Service panel to encourage the development of a consistent approach to accreditation and to ease the proposed transition to a joint panel. It was also anticipated that the Community Justice Accreditation Panel would in due course also assume responsibility for the accreditation of youth justice programmes, though this would require a slightly differing approach that recognised the more systemic and holistic approach to supervision on this context.

The expansion of non-custodial options

Following the introduction of 100 per cent funding and national standards the use of both probation and community service in Scotland rose markedly, though the prison population and proportionate use of imprisonment also continued to rise (McIvor 1996b) and has generally continued on a steady upward trajectory to this day (Scottish Executive 2006d). It appears that during the late 1990s confidence in the ability of probation and community service alone to halt or even reverse rising prisoner numbers began to erode. Most of the key initiatives that have been subsequently introduced have been aimed at enabling the courts to deal more effectively with particular 'problems' or groups of offenders; in general, the intention has been both to reduce the courts' apparent over-reliance on custody and to reduce offending.

Regarded as particularly appropriate for those facing a custodial sentence or to contain the behaviour of persistent offenders who posed a nuisance to their communities, electronically monitored Restriction of Liberty Orders (RLOs) have been rolled out across Scotland since May 2002 after being piloted in three sites (Lobley and Smith 2000). Introduced under Section 245A of the Criminal Procedure (Scotland) Act 1995, RLOs require offenders to be restricted to a particular location for up to 12 hours a day for a period of up to 12 months or to avoid a particular location for up to 12 months. The use of electronically monitored bail is currently being piloted and proposals in the Criminal Justice Plan (Scottish Executive 2004c) for the introduction of Home Detention Curfews for prisoners serving sentences of more than three months gained legislative expression in the Management of Offenders (Scotland) Act 2005.

The introduction of two pilot Youth Courts in 2003 and 2004 was also aimed at addressing the behaviour of 'persistent' 16 and 17-year-old offenders (persistent being defined as three or more 'episodes' of offending within a period of six months) or those of the same age whose circumstances or offending suggested that such intervention might be necessary. The Youth Courts are characterised by fast track processing of cases, the availability of a wider range of age-appropriate services and resources and ongoing judicial overview. Evaluation of the first pilot site suggested that target time scales were generally being met, however it was still too soon to assess the impact of participation in the Youth Court on young people's offending behaviour (Popham *et al.* 2005). A parallel scheme to fast track younger offenders to and through children's hearings was abandoned following the initial pilot phase when it became apparent that outcomes were no better for young people who took part in Fast Track in comparison with similar young people dealt with under existing procedures in comparison areas (Hill *et al.* 2005).

Dealing with drug-related offending has been a priority issue in recent years and Scotland, in common with other western jurisdictions, has sought to develop more effective ways of responding to drug-related crime. Drug Treatment and Testing Orders (DTTOs) were introduced in two pilot sites in Scotland (under the UK-wide Crime and Disorder Act (1998)) and have subsequently been subject to national roll-out. DTTOs differed from existing community penalties in a number of important respects. First, they allowed for the regular drug testing of offenders as a requirement of the court. Second, they emphasised the case management role of the supervising officer, who would be responsible for co-ordinating service provision rather than directly providing services. Third, and perhaps most signifi-cantly, they included provision for sentencers to take an active role in reviewing the progress of offenders on orders by bringing them back to court on a regular basis (or, alternatively, scrutinising progress through paper-based reviews).

The pilot DTTO schemes that had previously been introduced in England had met with varying degrees of success (Turnbull *et al.* 2000). However, results from the Scottish pilots were more encouraging, with evidence of reductions in self-reported drug use (Eley et al 2002) and reconviction (McIvor 2004b). DTTOs drew upon the Drug Court model that had evolved during the 1990s in the US but have been criticised for representing a 'watered down' version of that model, insofar as they do not allow for the development of the co-ordinated multi-professional team approach which characterises Drug Courts in other jurisdictions (Bean 2002). Alert to the shortcomings of DTTOs in this respect, and following a review of interna-tional developments in Drug Courts (Walker 2001), the Scottish Executive decided to build upon the experience of the DTTO pilot sites by introducing pilot Drug Courts in Glasgow and Fife. The Glasgow Drug Court became operational in November 2001 and the Fife Drug Court made its first orders in September 2002. A further three-year period of pilot funding was granted in March 2006 following an evaluation of their first two years of operation (McIvor *et al.* 2006). The Scottish Executive's interest in problem-solving courts was extended in 2004 with the intro-duction of a pilot Domestic Abuse Court in Glasgow.

The pilot Drug Courts had succeeded in engaging effectively with offenders with lengthy histories of drug misuse and drug-related crime and linking them into treatment and other services. However, professionals had expressed concern that they were less effective in engaging with women. Encouraging the use of community-based alternatives to imprisonment for women had been a priority policy area since the late 1990s following the suicide of seven women in Scotland's only dedicated female prison. Despite this, as in other jurisdictions, the rate of female imprisonment has continued to rise at an unprecedented rate to an all-time high (Scottish Consortium on Crime and Criminal Justice 2006). The drug testing of prisoners had revealed that most women received into Scottish prisons were drug users (Scottish Prison Service 2000) yet imprisonment did not appear to break the cycle of drug use and drug-related crime. In 2003 the 218 Time Out Centre was established in Glasgow with a view to providing the courts with a residential and non-residential alternative to custody for women and offering a resource for women whose offending might place them at risk of imprisonment in the future. Initial evaluation of the Time Out Centre suggested that it is a resource that has been broadly welcomed by professionals and service users alike (Loucks *et al.* 2006), though more time will be required for its impact upon recidivism to be assessed. It is unlikely that the resource-intensive, holistic approach that has been developed at 218 could be replicated across Scotland. However, it is probable that elements of practice developed by the Time Out Centre – and, indeed by criminal justice social workers in other locations – could be adapted for use in other parts of the country.

Risk and public protection

In Scotland the focus and purpose of probation has changed over the last hundred years from supervision to treatment to welfare to responsibility and, more recently, to public protection (McNeill 2005). As in England and Wales, this has had an important influence on the content and purpose of Social Enquiry Reports (SERs). For example, although the most recent National Standards for Social Enquiry Reports describe the purpose of reports as being to 'provide the court with information and advice they need in deciding on the most appropriate way to deal with offenders' (Social Work Services Group 2000, para. 1.5) this includes 'assessing the risk of re-offending, and in more serious cases the risk of possible harm to others…(and) requires an investigation of offending behaviour and of the offender's circumstances, attitudes and motivation to change' (para. 1.6). Here, then, as in the rest of the UK, assessment practice is increasingly driven by concerns about risk and, as in England and Wales, this has had important implications for the focus of assessments and manner in which they are undertaken. The increasing use of structured approaches to assessment – and, in particular, the use of actuarial methods for the assessment of risk – reflected the growing influence of managerialism and 'actuarial justice' (Feeley and Simon 1992) upon probation practice in Scotland and in the rest of the UK.

The initial focus of actuarial tools – reflecting the anti-custodial objectives of criminal justice social work practice at the time – was on predicting the likelihood of a custodial sentence being imposed by the courts; the intention being to assist practitioners to identify those offenders for whom alternatives to imprisonment should be considered. In Scotland the national standards (Social Work Services Group 1991) provided detailed guidance on the appropriate content of reports and encouraged social workers to target community-based social work disposals upon offenders who would otherwise be at risk of receiving a sentence of imprisonment. A standardised instrument for measuring risk of custody – the Dunscore – developed in the early 1990s for use in the Scottish context (Creamer, Ennis and Williams 1993) was widely used by social workers to assist in identifying those offenders for whom probation or community service might be recommended as an alternative to custody.

During the 1990s, however, with an increasing emphasis upon effective practice and increasing policy preoccupation with public protection, the emphasis shifted from assessing risk of custody to assessing the risk of reconviction and the risk of harm. Early tools – such as the Offender Group Reconviction Score (OGRS) (Copas 1995) that predicted the percentage likelihood of being reconvicted in England and Wales – were based purely upon static historical data (such as sex, age, number of previous convictions). Subsequent tools have become more sophisticated and include a structured assessment of the offender's circumstances and needs. The first tool of this kind to be widely used in Scotland (as in England and Wales) was the Level of Service Inventory – Revised (LSI-R) (Andrews and Bonta 1995). The Social Work Services Inspectorate subsequently developed the Risk Assessment Guidance and Framework (RAGF), which was a structured tool combining actuarial indicators with clinical or professional judgements. It incorporated assessments of risk of re-offending, criminogenic need and risk of harm. The RAGF used the same predictive factors as OGRS but there was no algorithm to determine precise levels of risk and judgements were made using 'high', 'medium', or 'low' descriptions (Social Work Services Inspectorate 2000). Practitioners who had used the RAGF regarded its ability to identify risk of harm, its ease of use, its compatibility with other risk assessment procedures and its ability to predict violent offending as strengths. It was also viewed by social workers as assisting professional judgements of risk and encouraging a more structured approach to assessment and case planning (McIvor and Kemshall 2002).

By the mid-to-late 1990s the growing emphasis on public protection across the UK coincided with the introduction of significantly higher risk populations of offenders to probation caseloads. In Scotland, legislative changes in the early 1990s required all prisoners serving sentences in excess of four years to undertake community supervision on release either on parole or on (compulsory) non-parole licences (Prisoners and Criminal Proceedings (Scotland) Act 1993). Subsequently, advances in both the rhetoric and the practice of public protection were rapid. Although it did not appear as an objective in the original standards (Social Work Services Group 1991), by the time of the publication of *The Tough Option* (Scottish Office 1998) the minister responsible was declaring both that 'our paramount aim is public safety' (section 1.2) and that the pursuit of reductions in the use of custody 'must be consistent with the wider objective of promoting public and community safety' (section 1.2.3). Revisions to the Scottish Standards on throughcare services (Social Work Services Group 1996) and court reports (Social Work Services Group 2000), as well as other central reports and guidance (Social Work Services Inspectorate 1997, 1998) both presaged and reflected this shift in emphasis (for a more detailed discussion of the emergence and pre-eminence of public protection in official discourses and in practitioners' accounts on both sides of the border, see Robinson and McNeill 2004).

This concern with enhancing public protection has focused in particular upon serious violent and sexual offenders who are regarded as posing a significant risk of harm. Policy interest in the risks posed by sexual and violent offenders can be traced to *A Commitment to Protect* (Social Work Services Inspectorate 1997) followed by the MacLean Report in 2000 and the Cosgrove Report in 2001. In terms of shaping further legislation and policy, the MacLean Report was particularly influential insofar as two of its main recommendations – the introduction of an Order for Lifelong Restriction (OLR) and the establishment of a new body for ensuring the effective assessment and management of risk (the Risk Management Authority) – gained expression in the Criminal Justice (Scotland) Act 2003. The Risk Management Authority was established as a non-departmental public body in the autumn of 2004. Its roles include policy advice, identifying best practice, commissioning and undertaking research, standard setting for risk assessment and management, accreditation of risk assessors and risk assessment methods and approving offender risk management plans.

The Risk Management Authority is concerned essentially with those offenders who are deemed to pose the greatest risk, however other recent legislative and policy changes in Scotland have had a broader focus upon managing the transition of prisoners between prison and the community. Since the revision of early release arrangements in 1993, the majority of short sentence prisoners have not been subject to statutory supervision on leaving prison[3], though most have been entitled to voluntary assistance from the social work department in the 12 month post-custody period. Throughcare has long been acknowledged to be one of the most poorly developed of the criminal justice social work services, not least because of the practical difficulties involved in providing a consistent service to prisoners located across the prison estate (McIvor and Barry 1998). The Tripartite Group that was established in 2001 and comprised representatives from the Scottish Executive, local authority social work departments and the Scottish Prison Service identified three priority groups for voluntary post-release support – sexual offenders and those who committed offences against children, young offenders and offenders with drug problems[4] – and recommended the establishment of specialist local authority throughcare services to better engage with prisoners during their sentences and after release (Scottish Executive 2002).

More far reaching proposals were, however, heralded by a review of early release arrangements by the Sentencing Commission for Scotland (2006). The proposals, which at the time of writing are subject to consultation (Scottish Executive 2006e), are that prisoners sentenced to more than 14 days will serve at least one half of the sentence in prison and will be subject to supervision on licence in the community for the remainder of the sentence. Some of the Commission's proposals found expression in the Custodial Sentences and Weapons Act (2007) which will require that all prisoners sentenced to more than 14 days are subject to some form of risk assessment prior to release and some form of supervision licence when released. Evidently, these provisions, if implemented, will have significant implications for criminal justice social work, where the workload is likely to shift towards resettlement work and away from community disposals. Indeed, a growing emphasis upon prisoner resettlement/re-integration can also be discerned from the creation, structure and objectives of the new Community Justice Authorities and the in the National Strategy for the

3   Only prisoners serving sentences of four years or more were eligible to apply for parole and only those with shorter sentences who were made subject to specific requirements by the courts were supervised for a period following their return to the community.

4   A Transitional Care Initiative had been introduced by the Scottish Prison Service and Cranstoun Drug Services to provide short-term prisoners with drug problems with support during the first 12 weeks following release. The Transitional Care initiative formally ended in July 2005 with the introduction of a new national Throughcare Addiction Service (TAS) for prisoners with drug problems in Scotland (MacRae *et al.* 2006).

Management of Offenders (Scottish Executive 2006a) where ex-prisoners are identified as one of the priority groups around whom services should be developed.

The future of criminal justice social work

Recent analysis of historical records has led one of the authors to conclude that, although penal politics, public sensibilities and sentencing practices have all changed in various ways over the last hundred years, the problem of securing reductions in the financial and human costs associated with imprisonment endures (McNeill 2005). In this historical context, the more recent story of the development of criminal justice social work is centrally concerned with the pursuit of quality and effectiveness and with it the credibility on which the success of these services as a force for penal reductionism was thought to depend. An optimistic reading would suggest that the last century's evolving organisational arrangements, legislative bases and constructions of practice represent shifting attempts to realise new and better penal practices, but that they are essentially reinventions of the same core purposes around sponsoring constructive changes both in individual offenders and in the system of justice itself.

With respect to the future of criminal justice social work, the evidence points towards both continuity and change. Since Rifkind's (1989) decision to embark on a penal reductionist path, Scottish policy has been characterised by its focus on reducing the use of custody, enhancing the social inclusion of offenders and, latterly, protecting the public by reducing re-offending. Though the policy emphasis has shifted at times in the degree of emphasis given to each of these aims, Ministers and civil servants have tended to recognise their interdependence. Against this backdrop, perhaps the most significant and worrying contemporary change is the absence of any explicit commitment to reducing the use of custody in the new national strategy (Scottish Executive 2006a). When set alongside the introduction of the dehumanising discourse of 'offender management'[5] and the currently proposed changes to prisoner release arrangements, the apparent abandonment of penal reductionism could signal the emergence of a service focused much more narrowly than hitherto on protecting the public by working with prison service

5   It is interesting to note that the impact of the discourse of 'offender management' in Scotland (to describe the national policy focus) has been offset by the contemporaneous introduction of the term 'community justice' (to describe the bodies responsible at the local level for strategy and service delivery).

colleagues to develop better resettlement policies and practices. While this attention to working with those *exiting* Scottish prisons is both necessary and overdue, with the use of imprisonment and the duration of sentences rising in Scotland, it hardly seems to be the time to be distracted from the question of inappropriate *entry* to prison.

In terms of continuity, the new national strategy confirms the ongoing direction of Scottish policy since the *Tough Options* paper (Scottish Office 1998) in that the overarching 'shared aim' of offender management services is 'to reduce both the amount of offending and the amount of serious harm caused by those already known to the criminal justice system' (Scottish Executive 2006a, p.3). Moreover, the specific target for such services is defined as a 2 per cent reduction in reconviction rates in all types of sentence by March 2008. Interestingly, the strategy sets out to explain its focus on re-offending in some detail and it is worth quoting the relevant section in full here:

> All offending matters. But the community has a specific right to expect public agencies to use their contact with know offenders to reduce the risk that they will offend again, particularly in those cases which raise the most serious concerns about public protection. At the moment, most offending is reoffending. Of those convicted of a crime or offence in 2002, two-thirds had at least one previous conviction.
>
> This has an impact not only on individual victims and hard-pressed communities but also on offenders and their families. This is why a central theme of the overall strategy and a key component of our drive to reduce reoffending is Closing the Opportunity Gap and tackling social exclusion and poverty. The strategy will therefore depend for much of its success on helping offenders and their families access the services they need, such as advice on financial services, benefits and sustainable support, and also for these services to recognise offenders and their families as groups who should have equal access to their services. (pp.3–4)

While the first paragraph in this excerpt emphasises the importance, in the public interest, of reducing re-offending, the second paragraph helpfully and unequivocally re-asserts the importance of enhancing the social inclusion of (ex-) offenders. Admittedly, this is primarily cast as an instrumental necessity in the pursuit of the over-arching goal of reducing re-offending, but in places the tone of the strategy comes close to advancing the notion of rights-based rehabilitation (see Lewis 2005). Though this commitment to social inclusion is somewhat ironic, given the exclusionary impact of imprisonment (Social Exclusion Unit 2002) and the plan's silence on reducing the use of imprisonment, it leaves open (and perhaps even requires) the continuation of probation's long-standing association with social work in Scotland.

There is no doubt that the character of probation work in Scotland has been and continues to be profoundly influenced by this association. Robinson and McNeill (2004), for example, note that Scottish criminal justice social workers, whilst accepting public protection as their overarching aim, typically insist that protecting communities *requires* helping offenders; that the social work relationship is their primary vehicle for change and that both offending behaviour and their efforts to bring about change have to be located in their wider social contexts. That similar messages have emerged recently from desistance research may account in part for its developing influence on Scottish policy and practice (McNeill 2004; McNeill *et al.* 2005).

In this sense then, there is perhaps some evidence in Scotland that traditional 'welfare' practices, rather than being eclipsed, have been reinscribed and relegitimated in and through the new discourses of risk and protection associated with the 'Culture of Control' (Feeley and Simon 1992; Garland 2001; O'Malley 2004). Of course, this kind of hybridisation of welfare and risk is far from benign and unproblematic (Hannah-Moffat 2005). Necessarily, it will be some time before we can say whether the process of reinscription and relegitimation, set within the context of the new socio-political settlement that has followed devolution, will lead to a fundamental adulteration of the humanitarianism that has shaped probation's history in Scotland, as elsewhere. It does seem clear, however, that criminal justice social work is at a critical stage in its evolution during which, as well as changes in its political and organisational contexts, fundamental questions arise about its purposes, values and practices. Given that the last decade (a decade of *declining* crime rates) has seen both considerable expansion in the range and use of community penalties *and* an increase in the use of custody, there are perhaps danger signs that the hybridisation of welfare and risk in Scotland may be resulting in an expansion in the 'carceral reach' of the state. There is certainly strong evidence that this extending reach is particularly evident in Scotland's most deprived communities (Houchin 2005). One key test for the current reforms, therefore, will be whether they avoid the danger that 'offender management' services in Scotland conspire to reinforce and exacerbate the social exclusion that is implicated in the genesis of offending and re-offending.

Acknowledgement

This chapter draws heavily on material contained in a chapter prepared by the authors for the *Probation Handbook* edited by Loraine Gelsthorpe and Rod Morgan and published in 2007 by Willan Publishing. We are grateful to the editors of that book for permission to use the material here.

References

Andrews, D.A. and Bonta, J. (1995) *The Level of Service Inventory – Revised Manual.* Toronto: Multi-Health Systems Inc.

Bean, P. (2002) *Drugs and Crime.* Cullompton: Willan.

Copas, J. (1995) 'On Using Crime Statistics for Prediction.' In M. Walker (ed.) *Interpreting Crime Statistics.* Oxford: Clarendon Press.

Cosgrove, Lady. (2001) *Reducing the Risk: Improving the Response to Sex Offending. Report of the Expert Panel on Sex Offending.* Edinburgh: Scottish Executive.

Creamer, A., Ennis, E. and Williams, B. (1993) *The Dunscore: A Method for Predicting Risk of Custody within the Scottish Context and its Use in Social Enquiry Practice.* Dundee: University of Dundee Department of Social Work.

Eley, S., Gallop, K., McIvor, G., Morgan, K. and Yates, R. (2002) *Drug Treatment and Testing Orders: Evaluation of The Scottish Pilots.* Edinburgh: Scottish Executive Social Research.

Eley, S., McIvor, G., Malloch, M. and Munro, B. (2005) *A Comparative Review of Alternatives To Custody: Lessons From Finland, Sweden And Western Australia.* Scottish Parliament Justice 1 Committee. Accessed on 18/04/07 at http://www.scottish.parliament.uk/business/committees/justice1/reports-05/j1r05-custody-01.htm.

Feeley, M. and Simon, J. (1992) 'The New Penology: Notes on the Emerging Strategy of Corrections and its Implications.' *Criminology 30,* 4, 449–74.

Garland, D. (2001) *The Culture of Control: Crime and Social Order in Contemporary Society.* Oxford: Oxford University Press.

Hannah-Moffat, K. (2005) 'Criminogenic Needs and the Transformative Risk Subject: Hybridizations of Risk/need in Penality.' *Punishment and Society 7,* 1, 29–51.

Hill, M., Walker, M., Moodie, K., Wallace, B. *et al.* (2005) *Fast Track Children's Hearings Pilot.* Edinburgh: Scottish Executive Social Research.

Houchin, R. (2005) *Social Exclusion and Imprisonment in Scotland.* Glasgow: Glasgow Caledonian University.

Justice Department (2001) *Criminal Justice Social Work Services: National Priorities for 2001–2002 and Onwards.* Edinburgh: The Scottish Executive.

Lewis, S. (2005) 'Rehabilitation: Headline or Footnote in the New Penal Policy?' *Probation Journal 52,* 2, 119–135.

Lobley, D. and Smith, D. (2000) *Evaluation of Electronically Monitored Restriction of Liberty Orders.* Edinburgh: Scottish Executive Central Research Unit.

Loucks, N., Malloch, M., McIvor, G. and Gelsthorpe, L. (2006) *Evaluation of the 218 Centre.* Edinburgh: Scottish Executive Social Research.

McConnell, J. (2003) 'Respect, Responsibility and Rehabilitation in Modern Scotland.' Apex Lecture 1, September 2003, Edinburgh: Scottish Executive.

MacLean Report (2000) *A Report on the Committee on Serious Violent and Sexual Offenders.* Edinburgh: Scottish Executive.

MacRae, R., McIvor, G., Malloch, M., Barry, M. and Murray, L. (2006) *Evaluation of the Scottish Prison Service Transitional Care Initiative.* Edinburgh: Scottish Executive Social Research.

McIvor, G. (1996a) *Working with Offenders: Research Highlights in Social Work 26.* London, Jessica Kingsley Publishers.

McIvor, G. (1996b) 'Recent Developments in Scotland.' In G. McIvor (ed.) *Working with Offenders: Research Highlights in Social Work 26.* London, Jessica Kingsley Publishers.

McIvor, G. (2004a) 'Getting personal: Developments in Policy, Practice and Research in Scotland.' In G. Mair (ed.) *What Matters in Probation.* Cullompton: Willan.

McIvor, G. (2004b) *Reconviction Following Drug Treatment and Testing Orders.* Edinburgh: Scottish Executive Social Research.

McIvor, G., Barnsdale, L. Malloch, M., Eley, S. and Yates, R. (2006) *The Operation and Effectiveness of the Scottish Drug Court Pilots.* Edinburgh: Scottish Executive Social Research.

McIvor, G. and Barry, M. (1998) *Social Work and Criminal Justice Volume 7: Community-based Throughcare.* Edinburgh: The Stationery Office.

McIvor, G. and Kemshall, H. (2002) *Serious Violent and Sexual Offenders: The Use of Risk Assessment Tools in Scotland.* Edinburgh: Scottish Executive Social Research.

McNeill, F. (2004) 'Desistance, Rehabilitation and Correctionalism: Prospects and Developments in Scotland.' *Howard Journal of Criminal Justice 43*, 4, 420–436.

McNeill, F. (2005) 'Remembering Probation in Scotland.' *Probation Journal 52*, 1, 23–38.

McNeill, F., Batchelor, S., Burnett, R. and Knox, J. (2005) *21st Century Social Work Reducing Reoffending: Key Skills.* Edinburgh: Scottish Executive.

National Probation Service (2001) *A New Choreography.* London: Home Office.

Nellis, M. (1995) 'Probation Values for the 1990s.' *Howard Journal of Criminal Justice 34*, 1, 19–44.

O'Malley, P. (2004) 'The Uncertain Promise of Risk.' *Australian and New Zealand Journal of Criminology 37*, 3, 323–343.

Paterson. F. and Tombs, J. (1998) *Social Work and Criminal Justice Volume 1: The Policy Context.* Edinburgh: Stationery Office.

Popham, F., McIvor, G., Brown, A,. Eley, S., Malloch, M., Piacentini, L. and Walters, R. (2005) *Evaluation of the Hamilton Sheriff Youth Court.* Edinburgh: Scottish Executive Social Research.

Rifkind, M. (1989) 'Penal Policy: The way ahead.' *Howard Journal of Criminal Justice 28*, 81–90.

Robinson, G. and McNeill F. (2004) 'Purposes Matter: The Ends of Probation.' In G. Mair (ed.) *What Matters in Probation.* Cullompton: Willan.

Scottish Consortium on Crime and Criminal Justice (2006) *Women in Prison in Scotland: An Unmet Commitment.* Edinburgh: Scottish Consortium on Crime and Criminal Justice.

Scottish Executive (1999) *Minister Outlines Way Forward For Criminal Justice Social Work.* Scottish Executive News Release: SE1070/1999.

Scottish Executive (2002) *Tripartite Group Report Throughcare: Developing the Service.* Edinburgh: Scottish Executive.

Scottish Executive (2003) *A Partnership for a Better Scotland.* Accessed on 31/08/07 at http://www.scotland.gov.uk/library5/government/pfbs.pdf.

Scottish Executive (2004a) *Reduce, Rehabilitate, Reform: A Consultation on Reducing Reoffending in Scotland.* Edinburgh: Scottish Executive.

Scottish Executive (2004b) *Consultation on Reducing Reoffending in Scotland: Analysis of Responses.* Edinburgh: Scottish Executive.

Scottish Executive (2004c) *Scotland's Criminal Justice Plan.* Edinburgh: Scottish Executive.

Scottish Executive (2005) *Supporting Safer, Stronger Communities: Consultation on Community Justice Authorities.* Edinburgh: Scottish Executive.

Scottish Executive (2006a) *Reducing Reoffending: National Strategy for the Management of Offenders.* Edinburgh: Scottish Executive.

Scottish Executive (2006b) *National Advisory Body on Offender Management.* Accessed on 18/04/07 at http://www.scotland.gov.uk/News/Releases/2006/03/20150733.

Scottish Executive (2006c) *National Strategy of Offender Management.* Accessed on 18/04/07 at http://www.scotland.gov.uk/News/Releases/2006/05/22104805.

Scottish Executive (2006d) *Statistical Bulletin Criminal Justice Series: CrJ/2006/3: Criminal Proceedings In Scottish Courts, 2004/05.* Edinburgh: Scottish Executive.

Scottish Executive (2006e) *Release and Post Custody Management of Offenders.* Edinburgh: Scottish Executive.

Scottish Labour (2003) *Scottish Labour Manifesto 2003: On Your Side.* Accessed on 18/04/07 at http://www.scottishlabour.org.uk/manifesto/

Scottish Office (1998) *Community Sentencing: The Tough Option: Review of Criminal Justice Social Work Services.* Edinburgh: Scottish Office Home Department.

Scottish Prison Service (2000) *Partnership and Co-ordination: SPS Action on Drugs.* Edinburgh: Scottish Prison Service.

Sentencing Commission for Scotland (2006) *Early Release from Prison and Supervision of Prisoners on their Release.* Edinburgh: The Sentencing Commission for Scotland.

Social Exclusion Unit (2002) *Reducing Re-offending by Ex-prisoners.* London: Social Exclusion Unit.

Social Work Services Group (1991) *National Objectives and Standards for Social Work Services in the Criminal Justice System.* Edinburgh: Social Work Services Group.

Social Work Services Group (1996) *Part 2 – Service Standards: Throughcare.* Edinburgh: Social Work Services Group.

Social Work Services Group (2000) *National Standards for Social Enquiry and Related Reports and Court Based Social Work Services.* Edinburgh: Social Work Services Group.

Social Work Services Inspectorate (1997) *A Commitment to Protect. Supervising Sex Offenders: Proposals for More Effective Practice.* Edinburgh: Scottish Office.

Social Work Services Inspectorate (1998) *Management and Assessment of Risk in Social Work Services.* Edinburgh: Scottish Office.

Social Work Services Inspectorate (2000) *Risk Assessment Guidance and Framework.* Edinburgh: Scottish Executive.

Turnbull, P.J., McSweeney, T., Webster, R., Edmunds, M. and Hough, M. (2000) *Drug Treatment and Testing Orders: Final Evaluation Report.* Home Office Research Study 212. London: Home Office.

Walker, J. (2001) *International Experience of Drug Courts.* Edinburgh: Scottish Executive Central Research Unit.

CHAPTER 6

Youth and Criminal Justice in Northern Ireland

Tim Chapman and David O'Mahony

Introduction

To understand policy and practice issues relating to how young offenders (10–16-year-olds, increased to 10–17-year-olds in 2006) are dealt with in Northern Ireland it is necessary to know something of its history over the past 35 years. This history has two distinct phases – conflict and post conflict (McGarry and O'Leary 1995). The story of youth policy with offenders reflects the changing relationships of power between the statutory sector and local communities. This turbulent and complex history has challenged work with offenders and has created more than one social work model for Northern Ireland. This chapter will explain and describe four key paradigms that have emerged within policy and practice with offenders:

1. an inclusive model of intervention

2. a public protection model

3. a multi-disciplinary therapeutic model

4. a restorative justice model.

In attempting to achieve this in one chapter we will inevitably simplify or omit some significant developments and themes.

Work with offenders during conflict

The primary statutory agency for rehabilitative work with both adults and young people who offend throughout the 30 or more years of the Troubles was the

Probation Service or, as it came to be called in 1982, the Probation Board. Not only did it have statutory duties to provide court reports on and supervise adults and young people on Probation Orders and Community Service Orders and to provide a welfare and after care service to prisoners, it also had a substantial budget to fund services provided by voluntary and community organisations.

For most of this period the Northern Ireland Office was preoccupied by security issues arising from a highly volatile and often violent political conflict much of which centred on the criminal justice system – the police, courts and prisons (McEvoy 2001). Traditional law and order politics were overshadowed by more pressing concerns. Thus, except for occasional legislation and negotiations over budgets, Northern Ireland did not experience regular government intervention in the management of offenders during the conflict. This created a space in which the Probation Board in partnership with the voluntary sector and the community could create a range of interventions with people who offend. While some of the interventions were innovative and unique to Northern Ireland, the underlying motivation, similar to that of many individuals, communities and organisations, was to create some sense of normality and safety in abnormal and often dangerous circumstances.

The first major challenge of the Troubles to the Probation Service was the introduction of mandatory custodial sentences for any young person convicted of rioting. The provision of individualised assessment in the form of reports to the juvenile court became an absurd exercise. There was a clear contradiction between rehabilitation and the realities of political conflict. In 1975 the National Association of Probation Officers (NAPO) developed a policy on politically motivated offenders which enabled officers to resist preparing court reports on people who had committed offences for political purposes and supervising them on statutory orders. This contributed to the Service's capacity to operate within the most militant communities while protecting staff from the threat of violence. While every other agency in the criminal justice system has struggled to recruit Catholics, the Probation Service has always had a mixed-religion workforce. The Probation Service, in common with other statutory social work agencies and voluntary organisations, had in essence adopted a politically neutral and non-sectarian stance in relation to the conflict.

A second similar challenge arose from paramilitary prisoners who resisted the state's policy of criminalisation (Crawford 2003). They did not see themselves as in need of rehabilitation. Probation officers recognised that offending or other therapeutic programmes were inappropriate. Prisoners did, however, acknowledge that they had basic welfare needs, mostly in relation to communicating with families and legal representatives (McEvoy 2001). In spite of continuous tension and periods of intense conflict, often violent, over the years probation officers achieved respect for their role from both paramilitary sides. The Probation Board also funded a range of organisations to provide services to prisoners and their families.

These two examples illustrate how the Probation Service created space for relevant practice by depoliticising their work within a highly political environment. This strategy was common to many other statutory agencies in Northern Ireland as Pinkerton observes:

> During the early period of the present round of the Troubles, the longest and most vicious in Northern Ireland's history, the British government attempted to manage the crisis by depoliticising it. The crisis of legitimacy was reset as a series of technical security, economic and social problems to be solved by apolitical, professional experts. (1998, p.18)

While in England and Wales work with offenders was actively addressing discriminatory and oppressive practice, in Northern Ireland the practice's commitment to being non-sectarian inhibited it from challenging sectarianism in the community and in the criminal justice system in spite of clear evidence of inequality and oppressive behaviour. Furthermore, the lack of local law and order politics, while avoiding the excesses of populist criminal justice policies, resulted in a lower level of transparency and accountability than the general public has a right to expect.

The voluntary and community sectors

The Probation Board for Northern Ireland's community development funds amounted to almost 20 per cent of its total budget. Much of it was spent on hostels for homeless and high risk offenders, vocational training workshops and services for prisoners' families. Most of these services were delivered by two major voluntary organisations specialising in crime prevention and the rehabilitation of offenders, Extern and NIACRO (Northern Ireland Association for the Care and Ressetlement of Offenders). A further significant proportion of funds was invested in partnerships with local community groups committed to crime prevention.

Political marginalisation, antagonism towards the state and deprivation in Northern Ireland have resulted in the growth of a very strong network of community and voluntary organisations delivering services to the unemployed, to women, to the elderly and to youth (McGarry and O'Leary 1995). Many community groups sought to divert young people from offending. They were motivated by the perception that the criminal justice system had failed to protect them and to contain youth crime. They were also concerned about the vicious punishments being inflicted on young people by paramilitary organisations for anti-social behaviour. While these draconian measures were supported by many beleaguered members of local communities, they proved no more effective in reducing offending than the state's system of punishments. This community activism had a significant effect upon practice with young people involved in offending.

Chapman and Pinkerton (1987) described how car crime or 'joyriding' in west Belfast created a fundamental change in probation practice. Probation officers were faced with clear evidence of the ineffectiveness of traditional social work methods and had to adopt a community-based approach which entailed close working relationships with community-run projects.

In the early 1980s the west Belfast Auto Project, modelled on a similar project in London, engaged young people involved in car crime. While it was managed by Extern, a voluntary organisation, it had been set up and staffed by local people concerned with the problem. It was funded by the Probation Board and the Department of Health and Social Services. Although it was evaluated as effective in reducing re-offending, it was closed due to its high costs. In the late 1980s the West Belfast Parents and Youth Support Groups (WBPYSG) and the Probation Board chose to form an alliance to deliver a new approach, the Turas project.

This partnership involved a team of probation officers and local community workers employed by two very different organisations working together. This not only created management challenges for both organisations, but also generated some very innovative practice (Chapman 1995). Turas was basically an outreach project appealing to the concerns of mothers and the community for someone to take young people engaged in dangerous activities off the streets at times when they were at most risk – late at night, particularly at weekends. After three years the contract was completed to the satisfaction of all parties. Consultations with the community revealed that local people were more concerned about drug use among young people than car crime. Consequently the Probation Board funded a drug outreach project.

These innovations in practice challenged the traditional social work base of the Probation Service. This was reflected in staffing. The Probation Board recruited staff with youth and community work qualifications and ex-offenders through a New Careers project. Activities and programmes, usually delivered in the evenings and weekends when offenders are most at risk, became the norm.

The development of effective practice

The Report of the Children and Young Person's Review Group (the Black Report) published in 1979 outlined a policy aimed at 'a realistic balance between welfare and justice' (Para. 5.58) which maintained the Probation Service as the lead agency for juvenile offenders and placed it clearly within the justice framework. This corresponded to the Chief Probation Officer's vision of punishment in the community (Griffiths 1982). The challenge of the Black Report to the Probation Service was assessed by Chapman:

> The Service needs to develop more sophisticated methods of assessment and a variety of effective programmes which help the young person and the scapegoating group to change their way of interacting. The potential for doing this exists within present practice but to be fully realised it demands changes in the internal management structure, the development of specialisms within community oriented teams, greater liaison with other statutory agencies and voluntary organisations, and a commitment to research into *what works* in helping young people. (1983, p.108)

This vision of an effective practice within a community context took some time to come to fruition. As Northern Ireland moved towards a peace process in the early 1990s, the Probation Board like other Probation Services became increasingly influenced by research into effective practice. The Northern Ireland Treatment of Offenders Order 1989 introduced statutory provision for day centres and specified activities. The Corporate Plan for 1992 to 1997 committed the Probation Board to deliver an increased intensity and improved quality of intervention in response to levels of risk of offending. A range of cognitive behavioural programmes were designed to suit local culture and styles of delivery. These addressed anger management, alcohol and drug use, and car crime (joyriding) and disqualified drivers. The most intensive programme was targeted at the most high risk offender. This programme was called Stop Think And Change (STAC). It was evaluated as having a measurable positive impact on criminogenic needs such as motivation to change, victim awareness, personal responsibility, moral attitude, impulsivity and empathy. A limited reconviction study also reported promising results in reducing re-offending (Chapman and Doran 1998).

Other innovative approaches included a residential cognitive behavioural programme, the Ramoan programme, which enabled intensive group and individual work on offending. This was particularly useful for high risk offenders from rural communities. The ineffectiveness of the criminal justice system to protect women from domestic violence led to a close working relationship with Women's

Aid and the delivery of a programme for perpetrators. Similarly the Probation Board pioneered a day centre dedicated to the provision of structured supervision programmes for sex offenders.

In relation to youth offending the Board developed a range of interventions ranging from diversionary adventure learning activities through the Duke of Edinburgh Award to intensive supervision of persistent offenders through the Watershed programme which provided an intensive programme of assessment, restorative justice, residential work, learning activities and personal coaching over a nine-month period.

In conclusion, during around 25 years of violent, political conflict in Northern Ireland the Probation Board had been the dominant force in work with offenders both through its statutory duties and its capacity to fund community initiatives and enter into partnerships with voluntary and community organisations. The interventions that emerged were shaped by the challenges that the 'troubles' generated. At its best it combined the energy of community activism and the professionalism of probation officers.

This distinctive practice has been described as inclusive (Chapman 1998). This is an approach which:

- is responsive to community concerns over crime

- bypasses, when necessary, the institutional systems of accessing services, e.g. through court orders

- is based upon partnership with those closest to the problem

- reaches out to the most marginalised by delivering services at the most appropriate times and places

- is delivered by a flexible and multi-skilled staff group.

Post-conflict work with offenders

One of the outcomes of the Good Friday Agreement was a fundamental review of the criminal justice system in Northern Ireland (Criminal Justice Review Group 2000). This Review signalled the intention of government to take a stronger lead in criminal justice policy than previously. Freed of the security priorities of the civil conflict the Northern Ireland Office now directed its attention to the management of ordinary offenders. This included inspecting the practice of the Probation Board. This had not occurred throughout the Troubles. The impact of inspection was to direct attention inwards towards the importance of conforming to and monitoring standards of practice agreed with government and the courts. This marked a fundamental change in the internal culture of the Probation Board.

Post-conflict legislation relating to probation has emphasised public protection. The Criminal Justice (Northern Ireland) Order 1996 provided for custody probation orders and licences for sex offenders. The Criminal Justice (Northern Ireland) Order 1998 arranged for the monitoring and multi-agency risk management of sex offenders.

The Criminal Justice Review Implementation Plan will drive the development of a closer relationship between the Probation Board and the Prison Service. The two organisations have agreed a common assessment system and adopted offending behaviour programmes from England and Wales. A Programme Approval Group has been set up to assure the quality of programmes delivered, to make arrangements for accreditation and to ensure that programmes are evaluated.

As the Probation Board's relationship with government has become stronger, other developments have weakened its relationship with the community. Peace brought the so-called "Peace Dividend". Significant funds were invested by the European Union in supporting the peace process. This meant that many community groups who previously depended upon Probation Board funding were receiving much higher sums from a variety of other sources.

The government has established a community safety strategy which requires local authorities to form community safety partnerships that will develop and implement local plans to prevent crime and the fear of crime. The Probation Board will no longer be such a big player in supporting community-based crime prevention. Furthermore, in many areas of high crime community restorative justice schemes began to assume responsibility for dealing with offenders using restorative processes. These schemes originated as an alternative to paramilitary punishments – 'kneecappings', etc. (McEvoy and Mika 2002). Particularly in republican areas these schemes refused to co-operate with the police. Consequently statutory agencies including the Probation Board were put under pressure by government to avoid working closely with them.

We describe below how changes in the legislation and structure of the youth justice system has affected the Probation Board's work with young people. These developments further reinforce the emerging probation model of work with offenders, one which has changed significantly from its inclusive practice during the period of conflict. The emerging practice is:

- more responsive to government policy and public concerns over crime, emphasising public protection through risk management

- firmly based upon statutory authority and compliance with government standards

- concerned with the social inclusion of offenders through accredited programmes in partnership with the Prison Service

- concerned with the enforcement of offenders' compliance with statutory requirements

- increasingly focused on adult offenders (see next section).

Youth justice

In 1979 the Young Persons Review Group published their recommendations. The 'Black Report', as it became known, was a fundamental review of the whole system of youth justice and made a number of significant recommendations. The report recognised that that a completely different approach would be necessary in Northern Ireland. This was a time when there had been over ten years of violent civil unrest and Northern Ireland was also facing severe social and economic problems. There were deep concerns regarding the impact of the violent conflict on a whole generation of young people and a recognition that the conflict had driven communities into isolation and undermined the legitimacy of the criminal justice system.

The Report stressed the importance of developing a whole range of preventative and diversionary work in the community. This would have to involve the family, schools and community, all working together. It emphasised the need to divert offenders away from the criminal justice system and that only cases that posed a real or serious threat to society should be brought before the courts. The report recommended that young people who offend and children facing care or protection proceedings should be managed and treated completely separately. The lead agency for youth justice would continue to be the Probation Service administered by a Board. The resulting legislation, the Probation Board (Northern Ireland) Order 1982, brought into existence the modern Probation Board.

Other than establishing the Probation Board, very few of the recommendations of the Black report were implemented by government until nearly 20 years later (O'Mahony and Deazley 2000). As stated above, the peace process enabled the Northern Ireland Office (NIO) to focus its attention on the reform of the criminal justice system. They returned to the core idea in the Black Report – the separation of systems addressing youth offending from those administering child care. With this in mind the NIO adopted a proactive approach to the management of the training school system which had been used to accommodate both young people who had offended persistently and those whom residential child-care services could not manage. This latter group had been increasing partly due to Social

Services Trusts' policy of closing children's homes. The training schools were funded by the NIO and costs were increasing rapidly.

The use of custody for young offenders was dramatically reduced through the Criminal Justice (Children) (Northern Ireland) Order 1998 (O'Mahony 2002). Lengthy indeterminate training school orders were replaced by short determinate juvenile justice centre orders which are served partly in juvenile justice centres and partly through supervision in the community by the Probation Board (Chapman 1997).

The other part of the NIO strategy was to develop 'Whitefield' (Dawson *et al.* 2004). Whitefield was established in 1977 as a day assessment centre and was administered within the training school system. Whitefield had been a significant but limited player in social work with young people who offend or are at risk. It employed social workers and teachers and developed a reputation for high quality and innovative work with vulnerable young people. It tended to receive more referrals to address family and educational needs than offending, which remained the Probation Service's remit.

Once again it was in the early 1990s, as the Troubles eased, that the NIO began to focus on Whitefield and invest in its expansion. In 1990 Whitefield was one centre in Belfast. There are now centres throughout Northern Ireland. It is envisaged that this will increase to 24 centres in the next few years. These centres provide a range of services to children at risk of offending or already involved in crime. The approach is systemic, involving counselling, cognitive skills training and family support (Dawson *et al.* 2004).

In 2003 the Youth Justice Agency was established and the Whitefield network became Community Services. Thirty-six per cent of these were referred by court order or the Youth Conference Service, 27 per cent were referred by other justice agencies and 37 per cent were referred by social services and education. Community Services have statutory responsibility for attendance centre orders, and orders provided for by the Justice (NI) Act 2002 – community responsibility orders, through which young people are required to participate in citizenship training, and reparation orders, through which young people make an act of reparation to their victims. Community Services also operate a bail supervision and information scheme. In spite of the increase in statutory work staff in Community Services have expressed a strong ambivalence towards enforcement, preferring their previous voluntary relationship with young people.

The Community Services approach to social work with offenders:

- is responsive to the needs of other agencies working with young people at risk

- is based upon a voluntary relationship in most cases

- is based upon partnership primarily with those who deliver child-care and therapeutic services

- is ambivalent about the enforcement of offenders' compliance with statutory requirements

- is multi-modal and delivered by multi-disciplinary teams or partnerships.

Youth justice and restorative justice

As mentioned earlier, community restorative justice projects have been set up in number of mainly loyalist and republican areas to deal with neighbourhood disputes, local crime problems and as an alternative to the brutal punishment beatings inflicted on young people by paramilitaries (McEvoy and Mika 2002). However, restorative justice has recently become a central element of the way the formal criminal justice system works with young offenders in Northern Ireland.

The police were one of the first criminal justice agencies to embrace restorative justice practices in Northern Ireland. They replaced their traditional method of cautioning juveniles in 2001 and all cautions (for young people) are now delivered by specially trained youth diversion officers using a restorative justice framework. The restorative cautions emphasise the importance of the young person taking responsibility for their actions and encourage empathy for the victim, as well as giving victims the opportunity to move towards forgiveness and healing.

Research (O'Mahony, Chapman and Doak 2002) found that the scheme has been successful in securing some of the aims of restorative justice, in that reintegration was achieved through avoidance of prosecution and through a process which emphasised the young person was not bad. There were drawbacks, such as that the process was often found to be used for young and relative minor offenders who had not been in trouble with the police before and there were low levels of victim participation. But it was also found that the scheme was successful for offenders in highlighting the impact of offending on the victim, participants were generally very satisfied with the process and it was regarded as a significant improvement over traditional caution practice.

Restorative justice and youth conferencing

The most recent and fundamental changes to youth justice in Northern Ireland have taken place following the enactment of the Justice (Northern Ireland) Act 2002 which provided for the introduction of the Youth Conference Service. The legislation reflects a key recommendation from the Criminal Justice Review Group (2000) which called for restorative justice to be used as the primary approach for young offenders in the criminal justice system. This Service provides restorative youth conferences for virtually all young people who commit offences other than low risk offenders who are cautioned in a restorative manner by the police (O'Mahony, Chapman and Doak 2002) and the most serious offenders. The Service takes referrals from the Public Prosecution Service directly (diversionary conferences) or from the Youth Court (court-ordered conferences). Diversionary conferences result in voluntary agreements made by young people to make reparation and to prevent re-offending. Court ordered conferences result in similar agreements enforced through a Youth Conference Order. The Youth Conference Service's duty is to facilitate restorative processes (known as Youth Conferences) which challenge young people who have committed offences to make amends to their victims and to undertake actions which will prevent their further offending. Youth Conference co-ordinators must have a professional qualification that equips them to work with young people. They are not necessarily trained in social work and include youth workers, probation officers and social workers.

Restorative justice is based upon the belief that those most affected by the harm caused by a crime (victims and those close to them and perpetrators and those close to them) should determine what should be done to repair the harm and ensure that it is not repeated. The role of the professional is to facilitate this decision-making process. Given that restorative justice has become mainstream in Northern Ireland and not a marginal method, the professional community who make a living out of the youth justice system has found this core idea very challenging and there has been some resistance to it from every part of the system including probation officers, police officers and magistrates.

The Youth Conference Service has adopted a model which balances the rights, needs and interests of the victim with those of the young person. It has been very successful in engaging victims in conferences (62% according to the evaluation by Beckett *et al.* 2004). While most of the agreements made through a youth conference have the statutory authority of a youth conference order, compliance is addressed through restorative processes rather than a standardised 'three strikes' approach. Remarkably few orders have been returned to the youth court due to non-compliance. Practice is governed by a few clear statutory rules and by detailed practice guidelines (Youth Conference Service 2002) rather than standards. The Service has negotiated service level agreements with a range of organisations in the community and voluntary sector to deliver programmes and services to support action plans agreed at conferences. These programmes are designed to make sense to victims. The most recent evaluation of the Youth Conferencing Scheme (Campbell *et al.* 2006) has shown it to be largely successful in meeting its objectives. It managed to attract relatively high levels of victim participation (69 per cent of conferences were attended by a victim, or victim representative) and the majority of victims and offenders who participated were satisfied or very satisfied with the process and agreed outcomes. Interestingly, many of the victims said they partici-pated in order to help the offender and offenders generally found the experience challenging, but welcomed the opportunity to apologise directly for what they had done. Over 2,500 youth conferences have now been completed throughout Northern Ireland.

The restorative approach adopted by the Youth Conference Service:

- is responsive to the needs of both victim and young person who committed the crime

- is based upon both statutory authority and voluntary commitment

- is based upon partnerships with victims, young people, families and supporters and providers of services to reduce re-offending

- gains compliance through restorative processes

- develops agreements between young people and their victims which are delivered by a range of people, from the community, voluntary and statutory sectors.

Once the Youth Conference Service covers the whole of Northern Ireland, the primary community-based court order for young people who offend will be the Youth Conference Order. This new development combined with the expansion of Community Services as the Youth Justice Agency's means of delivering community-based programmes will restrict the Probation Board's role within the youth justice system. It is still unclear how the Probation Board will respond to this challenge. Several options are possible including: to focus exclusively on adult offenders; building on its core competencies, to specialise in the intensive supervision of serious and persistent young offenders; to second probation officers into a Northern Irish version of Youth Offending Teams under the authority of the Youth Justice Agency.

Whatever shape these developments take, the Criminal Justice Review also recommended that restorative justice should be found a place within the current sentencing framework for adults. This offers the Probation Board an opportunity to develop its work in this area.

Conclusions

Youth justice policy and practice in Northern Ireland has undergone considerable change over the past 35 years and in many respects these changes have occurred out of the difficulties and opportunities that have arisen over its recent history. Specifically youth justice has been shaped by the tensions between local communities and the state. One way of working that emerged from this tension was an inclusive practice which depended upon partnership between statutory agencies and the community. It generated a great deal of innovative and effective practice. However, as the peace process progressed, the state reasserted its place at the centre of the management of youth crime. This has resulted in an uneasy mix of public protection and rehabilitation. As these statutory approaches were being consolidated, the community sector was developing a network of restorative justice programmes. Most recently, with the mainstreaming of restorative justice within the statutory Youth Justice Agency, the very approach to delivering justice formally to young people has been completely transformed.

A political settlement in Northern Ireland has created the opportunity to develop protocols for cooperation between the statutory and community restorative justice programmes. When these issues are resolved Northern Ireland has the opportunity once again to integrate the community and state systems of managing youth crime. A unique form of youth justice could emerge. For this to happen government, the Youth Justice Agency and the community will be required to be ambitious in their vision, generous in their relationships with each other and rigorous in their strategic thinking.

References

Beckett, H. Campbell, C. O'Mahony, D. Jackson, J. and Doak, J. (2004) *Interim Evaluation of the Northern Ireland Youth Conferencing Scheme.* Belfast: Northern Ireland Office (also available at www.nio.gov.uk).

Black Report (1979) *Report of the Children and Young Persons Review Group* Belfast: HMSO.

Campbell, C. Devlin, R. O'Mahony, D. Doak, J., Jackson, J. Corrigan, T. and McEvoy, K. (2006) *Evaluation of the Northern Ireland Youth Conference Service.* NIO Research and Statistical Series: Report No. 12. Belfast: Northern Ireland Office.

Chapman, T. (1983) 'The Black Report and Probation Practice.' In B. Caul, J. Pinkerton and F. Powell (eds) *The Juvenile Justice System in Northern Ireland.* Belfast: Ulster Polytechnic.

Chapman, T. (1995) 'Creating a Culture of Change: A Case Study of a Car Crime Project in Belfast.' In J. Maguire (ed.) *What Works: Reducing Re-Offending.* Chichester: Wiley.

Chapman, T. (1997) 'The Criminal Justice (Children) (Northern Ireland) Order: A Long Time Coming – Was it Worth the Wait?' *Child Care in Practice 4,* 2, 130–137

Chapman, T. (1998) 'The Same but Different: Probation Practice in Northern Ireland.' In *Social Work and Social Change in Northern Ireland.* London: CCETSW (NI).

Chapman, T. and Doran, P. (1998) 'Working with High Risk Offenders.' In *Challenge and Change: Celebrating Good Practice in Social Work in Northern Ireland.* London: CCETSW (NI).

Chapman, T. and Pinkerton, J. (1987) 'Contradictions in Community.' *Probation Journal 34,* 1, 13–16.

Crawford, C. (2003) *Inside the UDA: Volunteers and Violence.* London: Pluto Press.

Criminal Justice Review Group (2000) *Review of the Criminal Justice System in Northern Ireland.* Belfast: HMSO.

Dawson, H., Dunn, S., Morgan, V. and Hayes, A. (2004) *Evaluation of the Youth Justice Agency Community Services.* Belfast: Statistics and Research Branch, NIO.

Griffiths, W.A. (1982) 'Supervision in the community.' *Justice of the Peace August 21,* 514–515.

McEvoy, K. (2001) *Paramilitary Imprisonment in Northern Ireland: Resistance, Management and Release.* Oxford: Oxford University Press.

McEvoy, K. and Mika, H. (2002) 'Restorative Justice and the Critique of Informalism in Northern Ireland.' *British Journal of Criminology 42,* 3, 469–475.

McGarry, J. and O'Leary, B. (1995) *Explaining Northern Ireland: Broken Images.* Oxford: Blackwell.

O'Mahony, D. (2002) 'Juvenile Crime and Justice in Northern Ireland.' In N. Bala, J. Hornick, H. Snyder and J. Paetsch (eds) *Juvenile Justice Systems: An International Comparison of Problems and Solutions.* Toronto: Thompson Educational Publishing.

O'Mahony, D. and Deazley, R. (2000) *Juvenile Crime and Justice.* Criminal Justice Review Group Research Report 17. Belfast: HMSO.

O'Mahony, D., Chapman, T. and Doak, J. (2002) *Restorative Cautioning: A Study of Police Based Restorative Cautioning Pilots in Northern Ireland.* Research and Statistical Series No. 4. Belfast: Northern Ireland Office.

Pinkerton, J. (1998) *Social Work and the Troubles: New Opportunities for Engagement in Social Work and Social Change in Northern Ireland.* London: CCETSW (NI).

Youth Conference Service (2002) *Practice Guidelines.* Belfast: Youth Conference Service.

CHAPTER 7

Accreditation

Sue Rex and Peter Raynor

Introduction

One innovative and unusual feature of the movement towards evidence-based practice with offenders in Britain has been the use of accreditation panels as a form of quality control for the design of programmes. This chapter draws heavily, particularly in the first half, on a process-based evaluation of the Correctional Services Accreditation Panel (CSAP) in which one of the authors was involved (Rex *et al.* 2003). It also draws, particularly in the second half, on the experience of the other author as an appointed member of CSAP and its predecessor, the Joint Accreditation Panel (JAP), and of the Scottish Community Justice Accreditation Panel (CJAP). Both authors' views are given in a personal capacity and not on behalf of the Home Office or any other official body.

The history of accrediting offender programmes

England and Wales is something of a pioneer in accrediting programmes for offenders, having started to use accreditation in the Prison Service over a decade ago. Accreditation panels for prisons-based general offender and sex offender treatment programmes were originally established in 1996 (for an account of this early period see Lipton *et al.* 2000). Their work was subsumed within the work of the Joint Prison/Probation Services Accreditation Panel (or JAP) when it was set up in July 1999 as part of the Government's Crime Reduction Programme. This new body was tasked with assisting the Prison and Probation Services to achieve their aim of using 'What Works' principles to reduce re-offending through accredited offender programmes. This was an important remit, given the Home Office's target, agreed with the Treasury as part of the Crime Reduction funding package, to reduce re-offending by 5 per cent.

The second part of 2002 saw significant changes in the composition, remit and working methods of the Accreditation Panel. A new renamed Panel under the continuing chairmanship of Sir Duncan Nichol was recruited and met for the first time in March 2003. Ministers approved new terms of reference for the new Panel, largely marking a natural evolution in its business. One important change was to expand its work into so-called 'integrated systems' covering offender assessment, referral, case management, and through-care, in recognition of the need to ensure that the surrounding conditions support effective programmes with offenders[1]. Accordingly, a new set of integrated systems criteria – as well as revised programme accreditation criteria – were produced in time for the Panel's meeting in September 2002, which it used to award 'Recognised' status to Enhanced Community Punishment[2]. This marked a radical development for the Panel, whose previous focus had been exclusively on the accreditation of offender programmes.

Evaluating the evaluators

It was while the new Panel was being formed during 2002 that a process-based evaluation was undertaken to look at the performance of the existing Panel in its central functions of accrediting programmes and monitoring their subsequent delivery. The evaluation covered the following: composition and working arrangements; the process of accreditation and the accreditation criteria; the Panel's role in developing programmes; its contribution to a culture of effectiveness and the costs of the accreditation process. The methods adopted for the evaluation have been written up elsewhere (Rex and Bottoms 2003; Rex *et al.* 2003); it drew on observation of panel meetings as well as interviews and questionnaires with those

1   There is an analogy in the health care setting, where the success of a patient's recovery from an operation will depend in part upon the adequacy of the arrangements for post-operative care and rehabilitation. One criminal justice example is the 'through the gate' proposals by the Social Exclusion Unit for a continuous model of case management spanning imprisonment and release into the community (Social Exclusion Unit 2002; see also Chapter 17 in this volume).

2   The Enhanced Community Punishment scheme was developed by the National Probation Directorate in the light of the Community Service Pathfinder projects conducted under the Crime Reduction Programme. Its title reflects the renaming of the Community Service Order as the Community Punishment Order under the Criminal Justice and Court Services Act 2000.

involved with or affected by the work of the Panel, including panel members, prison and probation staff and sentencers. Its findings were limited both by the fact that the evaluation formed a snapshot of the Panel's work at a time of flux and by the fact that varying proportions of different groups of people responded to the invitation to participate in the research. Whilst the policy and panel perspectives were well represented, relatively little could be learnt about understandings and views of the Panel's work held by prison and probation staff not managing or delivering offender programmes.

A review of the available literature showed that the Scottish and Canadian systems for accrediting offender programmes had incorporated some aspects of the English model. This limited what could be learnt through comparison. Elsewhere (for example, Sweden), offender programme accreditation was at the time of the evaluation at too early a stage for useful comparative analysis. The differing contexts (for example, education or health) in which other public services are accredited also made direct comparisons with offender programme accreditation quite difficult[3].

Panel membership

The Chair of the Panel, Sir Duncan Nichol, formerly Chief Executive of the National Health Service, was reappointed for a further three years (until May 2005) while the evaluation was underway. There are two types of panel member: 'appointed' (independent experts) and 'nominated' (holding official positions connected to the prison and probation services). In 2002 there were 12 appointed members and 7 nominated members. In addition, four individuals (two further representatives from the prison and probation services, a diversity adviser and an adviser on drugs programmes) regularly participated in panel meetings, so that their role came to resemble that of panel members. This changed the apparent balance between participants who had been appointed following a competitive process (12, plus an independent chairman) and those brought in because of their position as officials within the relevant agencies (11).

The Panel's independence as a non-departmental public body was regarded as an asset, and one that those interviewed for the evaluation thought it important to

3   To date, accreditation has been most prevalent in health care and education settings in the US and often directed at individuals and facilities rather than programmes (see Pickering 1996; Scrivens 1995).

preserve. In Scotland, the Prison Accreditation Panel was chaired by a member of the Prison Service Board, and the Canadian Correctional Service panel by an Assistant Commissioner of the Correctional Service. The Scottish Community Justice Accreditation Panel set up in April 2003 was chaired by Alan Finlayson, who was appointed as a Sheriff following his retirement from the post of Reporter to Children's Panels.

In addition to maintaining the academic strength of the Panel, interviewees identified a need for broader expertise (for example, in substance misuse programmes and operational delivery) and a more ethnically diverse membership[4]. The general consensus about these matters was reflected in the 2002 recruitment exercise for new Panel members. The plan was to reduce the permanent nominated membership to three, and to co-opt other participants as required by the agenda. As regards the new appointed members, experts were sought in a wider range of fields (with fewer specialists in sex offender programmes) and candidates encouraged from ethnic minority backgrounds.

One source of potential tension identified during the evaluation was the presence on the Panel of people who had been involved in developing programmes. Their contribution in judging programme content was seen as crucial. Nonetheless, concerns were raised about a possible indirect conflict of interest when a programme for which a panel member had acted as a consultant or developer was being considered (even though he or she was excluded from discussion of that programme). This issue was particularly contentious for programme developers and programme staff, from whom one suggestion was that a panel member who had acted as consultant should withdraw from membership of the Panel for a period. (In Canada, Subject Panel members are prohibited from having a previous or current connection with the management or development of a Correctional Services programme.) In the interests of transparent propriety, the report of the evaluation recommended that where a panel member had acted as a consultant for a programme, he or she should be required to withdraw from the entire Panel week in which the relevant programme was being considered. (This recommendation was not in fact adopted, and the panel continued to deal with possible or notional

4   At the time of the evaluation, there were five specialists in sex offender
       programmes (plus three specialists in the drugs field and four generalists).
       Panel members thought that the Panel's future involvement in sex offender
       programmes would be diminished and that this change called for a
       reassessment of the balance between areas of expertise.

conflicts of interest in its original manner.) It also recommended that there should be a clear distinction between full panel members and co-opted participants to avoid the latter, over time and with frequent attendance, acquiring the de facto status of panel membership.

Accrediting programmes

At the time of the evaluation, the Panel had accredited fifteen programmes in six meetings (up to and including its meeting in February/March 2002): six programmes for sex offenders; five addressing general offending behaviour; two tackling aggression and violence; a drink impaired driving programme and a substance misuse programme. Most had achieved accreditation at their first or second formal submission, nine having been submitted earlier for 'advice' from the Panel. This compared with 15 accredited programmes and 22 accredited sites by the Scottish Prison Accreditation Panel, and 6 accredited programmes (42 sites) in Canada. The estimated costs of the English process were relatively modest; the cost of a Panel Day in 2001/2 was just over £14,000 (£10,000 to assemble the relevant people) and accreditation of a typical in-service programme cost between £25,000 and £30,000[5]. Unfortunately, it was not possible to collect comparable data for Scotland or Canada.

Both panel members and applicants described the Panel as working in a collaborative constructive spirit, although applicants sometimes saw academic debate as overshadowing the provision of practical 'What Works' advice on their submissions. A point of common agreement was the need for high standards to maintain the credibility of accredited programmes, without making accreditation a virtually insurmountable hurdle. Applicants sometimes perceived real practical difficulties in producing adequate research evidence to support submissions for

5   In estimating these costs, we have included the following personnel: appointed and nominated Panel members; secretariat and letter writers; and advisers and ex-officio participants. We have also included a cost for accommodation, but not travel as it was not possible to separate the cost of travel specifically to JAP meetings from other expenses. Programme submission costs included local costs (preparing submission documents, responding to Panel comments and meeting its requirements) and the costs of the Headquarters element in providing advice and support for the submission up to the point of application. We then added an estimate of the direct JAP costs, based on the amount of time committed by the Panel to consideration of the submission.

accreditation, especially in new or emerging areas of practice. Some thought that programme models had been dismissed prematurely because they did not fit within a cognitive behavioural framework, but it was also recognised that the Panel had become more open to different approaches. (In fact the Panel did accredit programmes which were not cognitive behavioural, including a 12-step substance misuse programme and a therapeutic community.)

In their experience of submitting programmes, some programme developers identified a need for more specific guidance about what was required through pro-formas or examples of what had been found helpful in earlier submissions, and for clearer feedback on whether changes were essential to gain accreditation. They also expressed a wish for fuller consultation with panel members about the Panel's requirements, perhaps in the context of site visits by panel members to see how a programme ran in practice. The sheer volume of submission material (five manuals plus appendices) presented difficulties for panel members, who generally received programme submissions as they convened for JAP meetings rather than in advance. Programme developers were aware of these constraints, and understandably frustrated if they thought insufficient attention had been given to the fruits of their hard work.

As well as suggesting that clearer guidance should be provided on the structure of programme submission and the contents of the different manuals, the evaluation report proposed that the submission process might be improved by appointing panel members as previewers of submission material. In practice, a system not unlike this emerged, as Chairs of sub-panels became responsible for reviewing all the material submitted and for asking sub-panel members to give particular attention to different parts of the submission, depending on individual expertise.

Diversity

In the absence of clear evidence relating to diversity, people have formed strong opinions.[6] Programme developers and evaluators, and staff delivering programmes,

---

6   Reporting the paucity of female samples in the primary studies on which
        'What Works' knowledge is based, and the failure consistently to code
        ethnicity either in the studies or in meta-analyses, McGuire concludes that:
        'There is a requirement for more careful study of the kind of variations
        that might need to be made in programmes to accommodate diversity
        amongst participants. This needs to take account of variations in age,
        gender, ethnicity or other cultural differences. It also needs to focus on the

all expressed doubts about whether the range of accredited programmes met the needs of ethnic minorities, female offenders, and offenders with learning difficulties. Panel members and programme developers both saw diversity as presenting a challenge with which the accreditation process had been slow to engage. Views were divided on whether to include a specific accreditation criterion on diversity or whether the solution lay in monitoring how diversity was addressed in the design and delivery of programmes.

This area has been the subject of a variety of recent initiatives, some of which had attracted little attention: the appointment of a diversity adviser to the Panel; the Prisons/Probation Diversity Review; and research on the literacy requirements for offenders attending accredited programmes (Davies *et al.* 2004) and on the criminogenic needs of black and Asian offenders (Lewis *et al.* 2006). The new terms of reference for the Panel approved in 2002 envisaged that it would ensure that diversity was taken into account in accredited programmes. From what could be discovered about how the Canadian and Scottish panels addressed diversity, and about relevant developments in health care accreditation, these issues did not seem to have been taken further in those other settings. In relation to health, it seemed that very similar issues had arisen to those faced by the Panel: how to include the consumer perspective; and whether to have special 'diversity' standards or to ensure that all standards accommodate diversity.

A culture of effectiveness?

One important question is the extent to which CSAP contributes to a culture of effectiveness in the prison and probation services. On this, the evidence from programme staff for the evaluation was encouraging (unfortunately, the attempt to collect views from other prison and probation staff was largely unsuccessful, which in itself might be taken as a discouraging indication of their interest in the Panel's work). Overall, programme staff endorsed the 'What Works' project to which the Panel was contributing, were strongly committed to accredited programmes and demonstrated a reasonable understanding of the role performed by the Panel. Over 40 per cent saw the Panel's role as about 'quality control' and nearly 80 per cent agreed that the accreditation criteria 'set high standards that increase the likelihood of effectiveness' (Rex *et al.* 2003, p.79). However, actual knowledge of

adaptation of materials for people with literacy problems, communication problems or learning disabilities' (2002, p.30).

accreditation decisions was limited, with only a quarter claiming detailed knowledge or a reasonable overview. Perhaps as a result, nearly half of programme staff registered neutral views when asked to rate the decisions of the Panel (although only six rated them as poor or very poor).

Interviewed programme staff saw their information about the Panel's activities as limited. This impinged on their faith in accredited programmes, as did their perception of a poor response from Headquarters (taken as evidence of a 'controlling' stance by the Panel itself) to requests for advice about or proposed modifications to programme content or delivery. There were signs that in the long run these matters could damage the Panel's legitimacy and the credibility of its decisions. In Autumn 2002 a joint change control mechanism was launched so that practitioners' concerns about particular programmes could be transmitted to the Panel, and programmes reviewed in the light of that feedback.[7]

At the time of the evaluation, panel members had begun undertaking visits to programme sites, and this contact between the Panel and the field seemed helpful in raising awareness of each others' work. Indeed, the revised terms of reference for the Panel recognised the need to raise its profile with correctional staff. The profile of the Panel and transparency of its decisions would, it was thought, be helped by further site visits and contributions to conferences, training events and seminars for programme staff to debate important questions such as diversity and programme integrity. In practice, a number of these activities were undertaken, but proved hard to maintain on the necessary scale. So, for example, most members were able to make only a very limited number of site visits, and even this limited commitment proved unsustainable.

The perceived legitimacy of the Panel

Overall, the evaluation suggested, the Panel could claim significant achievements in its first three years, mainly in accrediting high quality programmes and in providing advice to programme developers. However, a number of structural issues

7   The 'Change Control System', developed by the National Probation Directorate (NPD), was approved by the Panel in September 2002. Under this system, the Joint Change Control Panel (comprising panel members amongst others) received reports from NPD and Prison Service Headquarters (based on feedback collected from the field) and submitted an annual report to JAP proposing possible changes in both prisons and probation programmes.

were raised that impinged on its perceived legitimacy. Given the implications of its decisions for programmes or integrated systems whose future viability is reliant upon its approval, and its symbiotic relationship with the Correctional Services (and now the National Offender Management Service), questions are likely to continue to be raised about the independence of the Panel.

One issue concerned access to the Panel. Headquarters personnel in the Prison and Probation Services acting as 'gatekeepers' between their services and the Panel were seen as performing an important role, but were not always seen as effective in managing submissions and communicating Panel expectations to applicants. The existence of 'gatekeepers' had undoubtedly been beneficial, both in promoting professional programme development and in using the Panel's time efficiently. However, there was a need to guard against the possibility that gatekeeping might stifle innovation by blocking access for a particular kind of programme. Cases were observed where the gatekeeping function was undermined by private sector providers (for example, contracted out prisons) who applied to the Panel direct. To avoid premature applications coming before the Panel (which is not an efficient use of its resources), some sort of filtering mechanism might be desirable that retains fairness and parity of treatment.

Another issue was the Panel's oversight of audit, carried out in the respective services by Prison Service Headquarters and HM Inspectorate of Probation. There was some disquiet about the organisational disparity in audit arrangements and the apparent application of tougher standards in probation than in prison audits, with implications for achievement of performance targets.[8] Progress had been slow in meeting the Panel's wish to move towards a unified system of audit for both correctional services, in spite of considerable efforts by some panel members to promote this.

---

8   For the purposes of assessing agency performance against Key Performance Indicator (KPI) targets, the number of offenders actually completing a specific programme is multiplied by the percentage IQR (Implementation Quality Rating) score awarded by the audit process for the quality of delivery at that site. Whilst IQR scores awarded within the Prison Service had averaged 95 per cent, those awarded by HM Probation Inspectorate had mostly fallen below 70 per cent, at the time of the evaluation. This meant that almost all completions counted towards prison service targets, but just over two-thirds of completions towards probation targets.

After the evaluation

The Home Office evaluation pointed to a number of possible developments in the role of the CSAP: in contributing to curriculum development, reviewing accredited programmes in the light of research and practitioner feedback and in accrediting integrated systems. The revised terms of reference in 2002 envisaged that it would take a more proactive stance on curriculum development. Indeed, some of the interviewees pointed to a need for the Panel to move beyond considering individual applications to provide greater input into policy and strategic questions relating to programme development. It was argued that the Panel could draw on its considerable collective experience in the correctional field to contribute more broadly to curriculum development and decisions about piloting new approaches. A likely area for future development appeared to be reviewing programmes in the light of feedback from practitioners, and of audit and evaluation findings. In time, this would inevitably lead to questions such as whether to withdraw a particular accreditation, or to approve changes in design and content.

Concerning the move into integrated systems, some Panel members expressed considerable enthusiasm for this kind of development, which they saw as a logical extension of their work, responding, for example, to the need to provide continuity of services. Others doubted the susceptibility of these broader approaches to the accreditation process, arguing that the Panel should stick to its 'core business' rather than overstretch itself by attempting to accredit everything. They perceived dangers in the Panel's adopting too wide a role in accrediting prison or probation activities: bureaucratic costs, dilution of treatment programmes and a risk of creating confusion over what exactly was being accredited. Recent developments, reviewed in the final part of this chapter, certainly suggest that what were seen as natural developments by some panel members at the time have not retained their attraction in the face of radical changes in the way the Home Office proposes to mange the penal system.

Strengths and weaknesses of accreditation in the British context

The accreditation of rehabilitative programmes has now been a feature of work with offenders in Britain for over ten years, and it is possible to undertake some further assessment of its impact so far. Its strengths were well illustrated in the Home Office study in England and Wales, which, as we have seen, concluded that it could improve quality control in structured work with offenders and could contribute to the use of new methods with greater confidence and consistency than would otherwise have been the case. Experience in Scotland, up to the time of writing, has been similar, bearing in mind the more dispersed management there of services for offenders in the community and the preference for a more gradual and consensual development process. At one point the *Sunday Herald* reported with some relish that a programme which had been funded by the Scottish Executive had failed to secure accreditation on its first referral to the Panel – a clear indicator of the Panel's independence (*Sunday Herald* 2004). However, the picture in England and Wales is now more complex, and calls for some comment on what accreditation can and cannot be expected to achieve.

First, it is important to recognise that the role of accreditation is limited: it can support moves towards more effective practice in systems which are already committed to move in that direction, but it cannot drive this movement itself, and it does not *guarantee* the effectiveness of programmes in all times and places. What it does is to put programme designs through an assessment process based on international research on effective programmes, in order to avoid obvious threats to effectiveness and to allow reasonable confidence that, given consistent implementation and support, they *can* work. If accreditation is seen as a guarantee, it becomes vulnerable to the criticism that it is insensitive to the variety and unpredictability of the particular circumstances in which it will be put to use, and to the general unpredictability of human behaviour (Smith 2004); if, on the other hand, it is seen more realistically as one of a number of ways in which we can try to increase the *probability* that something will work, this may not be enough to satisfy can-do managers under pressure from politicians to 'deliver'. For example, a key criterion for accreditation in England and Wales is that a programme should be subject to continuing monitoring and evaluation, but the Panel's proposal to revisit programmes and look again at accreditation in the light of evaluation results was never implemented. In general, evaluation results from the roll-out of programmes in England and Wales have been inconclusive, reflecting considerable problems of implementation (Raynor 2004).

In addition, accreditation was sometimes treated almost as a substitute for evaluation. A clear illustration of this risk is provided by the history of Enhanced Community Punishment in England and Wales. This very ambitious and complex scheme aimed to enhance the rehabilitative potential of Community Punishment (the English name for Community Service) through the systematic use of pro-social supervision (influenced by Trotter 1993) and of approved work placements designed to train offenders in useful skills. It was the subject of a huge development effort and many referrals to the Panel, because it was needed to deliver half the Probation Service's programme completion target. This essential role was made very clear to the Panel. A new form of accreditation (of 'integrated systems') was devised to deal with it, and it was eventually accredited subject to strong advice that it should be implemented gradually, and an explicit requirement that it should be fully evaluated. In the event it was rolled out as quickly as areas could manage to design schemes, and no evaluation was carried out. The recent report by Her Majesty's Inspectorate of Probation (2006) rightly praises the substantial achievement of getting ECP into place, but identifies a range of implementation problems, suggesting a falling-off of quality since the original roll-out. In addition there are new arrangements and priorities arising from the new unpaid work requirement (introduced in the 2003 Criminal Justice Act) and Community Payback (which involves members of the community in the choice of work to be undertaken by offenders). These developments must have implications for accredited ECP, none of which have been reported to or discussed with the Panel.

Second, it is clear that the role and contribution of accreditation panels is affected by the nature of their relationships with the bodies which set them up. For example, the development of evidence-based offender management in Scotland has differed from the policies pursued in England and Wales, and this has affected the panels in both jurisdictions. In Scotland, where criminal justice social work services have been provided by local authority social work departments, the Scottish Executive has had to work in partnership with them (McIvor 2004) and with the new co-ordinating Community Justice Authorities, and the Community Justice Accreditation Panel had a significant development role in addition to its consideration of programme designs. Far fewer programmes were accredited from 2003 to 2005 by CJAP in Scotland than during the equivalent period by CSAP in England, but each one involved a significant amount of dialogue with programme developers, local authorities and the Scottish Executive. In England and Wales the more centralised approach of the Home Office, which controlled both the Prison Service and, since 2001, the National Probation Service, has led to a more limited and focused view of the role of a panel, with a strong emphasis on the accrediting of programmes as a core function.

As well as differences in their approach to community-based programme development, the British panels have been connected in different ways to their respective Prison Services. In Scotland the pre-existing Prison Service accreditation arrangements were amalgamated with the Community Justice Accreditation Panel after this had been running for two years with a focus on criminal justice social work. In England and Wales the joint panel set up in 1999 incorporated from the start the roles and many of the practices of the earlier Prison Service panels, and ways of dealing with community-based programmes had to be developed in this context. For prison services, the development of offending behaviour programmes is only one of many activities, and arguably the establishment of accreditation panels has helped to strengthen the credibility and influence of the quite small psychology units which have promoted programmes within the prisons.

The future of accreditation in England and Wales

It is also becoming clear, at least in England and Wales, that the role of accreditation panels needs to be renegotiated as policies change. In England and Wales the establishment of the National Offender Management Service (a protracted process which began in 2004 and is still not complete at the time of writing – see Chapter 4 in this volume) has led to new proposals about accreditation which reflect the desire of NOMS managers to exercise more control over the process. The 2003 Criminal Justice Act provides a continuing legal basis for accreditation, with attendance on an accredited programme listed as one of the requirements available for inclusion in the new generic community order. Current indications are that programmes will continue to be the main intervention for many offenders; however, figures for 2004–5 suggest that referrals for programmes may have reached a plateau at just under 44,000 per year (National Probation Directorate 2005). The regional strategies for reducing re-offending which have been prepared as the basis of planning by Regional Offender Managers are designed around seven 'pathways' into offending, or areas of criminogenic need on which services should be targeted. These are accommodation; education, training and employment; mental and physical health; drugs and alcohol; finance, benefits and debt; children and families of offenders; and attitudes, thinking and behaviour. Only two of these 'pathways' are covered by the current range of accredited programmes. It seems likely that programmes will retain their place as one of a range of approaches which can be tried with offenders under supervision, which should also include or be underpinned by a consistently supportive, pro-social and problem-solving approach to personal supervision.

The other major determinant of the future of accreditation will be the precise form taken by the restructuring of the Probation Service to fit the National Offender Management Service (NOMS), and the intention to commission a substantial proportion of 'interventions', including programmes, from the private and voluntary sectors. At the time of writing the details of these arrangements remain unclear, as they have been ever since NOMS was announced. However, some private and voluntary sector representatives have indicated that they regard existing accreditation arrangements as too complex and burdensome. The Home Office has also announced that the Correctional Services Accreditation Panel will lose its independent status as soon as the legislative timetable allows, and that final decisions about accreditation will then be made within NOMS. At the same time, panel members will be encouraged to become more involved in giving advice to programme developers and to Home Office researchers. It remains to be seen exactly how these developments will impact on the work of the CSAP, and more importantly on the design and quality of accredited programmes. So far there is little doubt that accreditation has had a positive influence on the quality of programmes for offenders. At the same time, it is important to remember that effective practice with offenders cannot be built solely on programmes (Morgan 2003).

References

Davies, K., Lewis, J., Byatt, J., Purvis, E. and Cole, B. (2004) *An Evaluation of the Literacy Demands of General Offending Behaviour Programmes.* Findings 233. London: Home Office.

Her Majesty's Inspectorate of Probation (2006) *Working to Make Amends.* Inspection Findings 1/06. London: HMIP.

Lewis, S., Raynor, P., Smith, D. and Wardak, A. eds (2006) *Race and Probation.* Cullompton: Willan.

Lipton, D., Thornton, D., McGuire, J., Porprino, F. and Hollin, C. (2000) 'Program Accreditation and Correctional Treatment.' *Substance Use and Misuse 35*, 2–14, 1705–1734.

McGuire, J. (2002) 'Integrating Findings from Research Reviews.' In J. McGuire (ed.) *Offender Rehabilitation and Treatment: Effective Programmes and Policies to Reduce Re-offending.* Chichester: Wiley.

McIvor, G. (2004) 'Getting Personal: Developments in Policy and Practice in Scotland.' In G. Mair (ed.) *What Matters in Probation.* Cullompton: Willan.

Morgan, R. (2003) 'Foreword.' *Her Majesty's Inspectorate of Probation Annual Report 2002/2003.* London: Home Office.

National Probation Directorate (2005) *Annual Report for Accredited Programmes 2004–2005.* London: National Offender Management Service.

Pickering, E. (1996) 'Evaluating the Benefits and Limitations of an Accreditation System'. *World Hospital 31*, 1, 31–5.

Raynor, P. (2004) 'The Probation Service "Pathfinders": Finding the Path and Losing the Way?' *Criminal Justice 4*, 3, 309–325.

Rex, S.A. and Bottoms, A.E. (2003) 'Evaluating the Evaluators: Researching the Accreditation of Offender Programmes.' *Probation Journal 50*, 4, 359–368.

Rex, S.A., Lieb, R., Bottoms, A.E. and Goodwin, L. (2003) *Accrediting Offender Programmes: A Process-based Evaluation of the Joint Prison/Probation Services Accreditation Panel.* Home Office Research Study No. 273. London: Home Office.

Scrivens, E. (1995) *Accreditation: Protecting the Professional or the Consumer.* Buckingham: Open University Press.

Smith, D. (2004) 'The Uses and Abuses of Positivism'. In G. Mair (ed.) *What Matters in Probation.* Cullompton: Willan.

Social Exclusion Unit (2002) *Reducing Re-offending by Ex-Prisoners.* London: Social Exclusion Unit.

Sunday Herald (2004) 'Airborne's successor "not good enough".' Sunday Herald 11 April 2004.

Trotter, C. (1993) *The Supervision of Offenders – What Works? A Study Undertaken in Community-based Corrections, Victoria.* Melbourne: Social Work Department, Monash University and Victoria Department of Justice.

PART TWO

Assessment, Supervision and Intervention

CHAPTER 8

Risk and Need Assessment

James Bonta and Stephen Wormith

Offender assessment lies at the heart of most correctional practices. The placement of offenders into different levels of security and supervision, the release of offenders from prisons and the allocation of treatment resources all depend upon accurate and reliable assessments. How well we have conducted offender assessment in the past and today is the focus of this chapter. We begin with a brief review of the history of risk and need assessments and end with a presentation of state-of-the-art risk/need assessment. Throughout the chapter we hope to demonstrate to the reader that there is a movement towards more comprehensive assessments that are strongly rooted in theory and evidence.

The early years of risk assessment

Actuarial, evidence-based risk assessments are highly structured assessment instruments where the individual items are assigned numerical weights, combined in some mechanical way, and the scores related to criminal behaviour. These instruments have a long history. In 1928 Burgess demonstrated that 22 'facts' could differentiate parole successes from parole failures. These 22 variables are summarised in Table 8.1 along with the risk factors found in other 'second generation' risk scales (Bonta 1996). Second generation risk scales are evidence-based offender instruments that consist mainly of static factors. In terms of predictive accuracy they consistently outperform 'first generation' subjective and clinical judgments of offender risk (Grove *et al.* 2000).

The list of risk factors constructed by Burgess is a mix of criminal history and socio-demographic variables, court processes and psychiatric evaluation. Some items are crudely described (e.g. 'Hobohemia', 'inferior' intelligence) and one item is clearly racist (nationality of father). It is noteworthy that the vast majority of items are static in nature and only a few measure potential offender needs (e.g. egocentrism).

Following Burgess, there were a number of other evidence-based offender risk formulas. For example, Glueck and Glueck (1950) presented three prediction tables based on:

1.   social factors (e.g. supervision by mother)

2.   character traits as measured by the Rorschach (e.g. defiance)

3.   psychiatric personality traits (e.g. extroversion).

Of particular interest is that the Glueck prediction tables (and their research) had an underlying theoretical framework which was quite in contrast to the 'dustbowl empiricism' evident in the Burgess risk prediction scheme and in many of the risk assessment instruments that followed. The theory guiding the work by the Gluecks was psychodynamic and holds little sway today. With respect to treatment much of the empirical risk factors delineated by them, however, are as important today as they were then.

The Burgess and Glueck predictions schemes never enjoyed much popularity and it was not until the 1970s that second generation risk scales became firmly established in correctional practice. Leading the widespread introduction of risk scales was the Salient Factor Score (SFS). The original SFS (Hoffman and Beck 1974) was a nine-item scale, which was gradually reduced to six items by 1981 (Hoffman 1983). This actuarial risk scale was developed to assist in the selection of parole releases from US federal prisons. Introduced in 1973, the US Parole Commission used the scale for all parole applicants until sentencing guidelines were introduced and federal parole was phased out for offenders sentenced after 1987 (Hoffman 1994). The last version of the SFS (Table 8.1) consists almost exclusively of criminal history variables (heroin/opium dependence is the exception). Earlier versions had items such as employment, education and release plans but they were later deleted to keep congruent with the 'just deserts' model that was sweeping the US. Research on the SFS did, however, provide good evidence of its predictive validity with both male (Hoffman 1994; Hoffman and Beck 1976; Hoffman, StoneMeierhoefer and Beck 1978) and female inmates (Hoffman 1982).

A decade later, Canada followed with a similar risk scale called the Statistical Information on Recidivism scale (SIR; Nuffield 1982). Like the SFS, the SIR is also comprised mostly of criminal history items but it was not as closely tied to the just deserts model. In addition to criminal history risk factors, the SIR had a few dynamic items (i.e. dependents, employment and marital status; see Table 8.1). However, the dynamic items of the SIR could hardly be of much use for treatment planning unless

Table 8.1: Early to present actuarial risk assessment

Actuarial risk scales (indicator of risk)

Burgess	Glueck	SFS	SIR	OGRS
Offence (fraud, burglary)	Social factors: Discipline (strict, erratic)	Offence (auto theft)	Offence (theft, break and enter)	Offence (burglary)
Co-offenders (4 or more)	Supervision (unsuitable)	Age (young)	Age (young)	Age (young)
Nationality of father (Irish, British, German)	Affection of father (hostile, indifferent)	Prior incarcerations (one or more)	Prior incarceration (3 or more)	Prior youth custody (no.)
Parental status ('broken home')	Affection of mother	Prior convictions (1 or more)	Dependents (3 or more)	Court appearances (no.)
Marital status (single)	Family cohesiveness (unintegrated)	Prior parole failure, escape (yes)	Marital status (single)	
Type of offender (habitual)	*Rorschach:* Social assertion ('marked')	Heroin/opiate dependency · Prior parole failure	Gender (male)	

Continued on next page

Table 8.1 *continued*

Actuarial risk scales (indicator of risk)

Burgess	Glueck	SFS	SIR	OGRS
Social type ('ne'er do well')	Defiance			
County (Cook)	Suspicion			
Community size (urban)	Destructiveness			
Residence (transient)	Emotional Lability			
Neighborhood ('Hobohemia')	*Psychiatric:* Adventurous			
Recommendation for leniency (no)	Extroverted			
Plea bargain (yes)	Suggestible			
Sentence length (determinate)	Stubborn		Sentence (6 or more years)	

Time served before parole	Emotionally unstable	Time since last offence (6 months or less)	Time since first conviction
Prior criminal history (yes)		Prior convictions (no.)	
Employment (unemployed)		Employment (unemployed)	
Prison misconduct (2 or more)		Prision security (maximum)	
Age paroled (young)			
Intelligence ('inferior')			
Egocentric			
Psychiatric prognosis ('unfavourable')			

plans were limited to finding work, a partner and raising children. Nevertheless, studies of the SIR have shown the scale to be quite robust in the prediction of criminal behaviour (Bonta *et al.* 1996; Cormier 1997; Nafekh and Motiuk 2002). The SIR remains in use today in the Canadian federal correctional system, along with other assessment tools, as part of the general inmate assessment process.

More recently, the UK developed the Offender Group Reconviction Scale or OGRS (Copas and Marshall 1998). Derived in part from the Risk of Reconviction score (Copas, Marshall and Tarling 1996), the OGRS is a six-item scale with four of the items being criminal history items (see Table 8.1). As with the other second generation risk scales described in this section, the OGRS has demonstrated impressive predictive validity in both general male offender populations (Copas *et al.* 1996), young offenders (Taylor 1999) and mentally disordered offenders (Gray *et al.* 2004).

In summary, the 1970s saw the widespread use of offender risk assessment scales. However, these risk scales were comprised mostly of static risk factors (e.g. criminal history, past substance abuse, age). Although correctional staff were able to differentiate offenders according to risk they were minimally served in terms with what to do with that risk. For that task, an assessment of dynamic risk factors was required but the concept of dynamic risk was not formally described until 1990. In the meantime, corrections struggled with the role of offender needs in the management of risk.

Towards the concept of criminogenic needs

Despite the use of evidence-based offender risk scales stretching back to the 1920s, most of these scales were limited to decisions concerning levels of custody and supervision. The notion of using risk assessments to guide interventions to reduce risk was foreign to most correctional agencies. This is not to say that there was no interest in reducing recidivism. Most correctional agencies then, as well as today, saw one of their goals as reducing recidivistic crime. From the 1950s to the publication of Martinson's (1974) negative review of offender treatment programmes, the promise of offender rehabilitation was widely embraced.

One of the consequences of the 'Nothing Works' pessimism generated by Martinson's report was that clinicians and researchers were beginning to recognise that not all treatment programmes were equally effective. A corollary to this conclusion was the realisation that some of the goals of the wide array of treatment programmes operating at the time were not relevant to offender behaviour.

Most of the clinical researchers and practitioners who provided treatment programmes to inmates and probationers were psychologists. Naturally, the programmes offered were heavily influenced by the theoretical models and techniques that were popular during the mid-twentieth century. The programmes were an eclectic mix of psychodynamic, client-centred and behaviour modification techniques. In these early days of offender rehabilitation research the evidence as to what approaches worked best with offenders was only beginning to appear. Offenders were exposed to a wide and diverse range of interventions that sometimes focused on the bizarre (e.g. nude encounter groups run by psychopaths: Rice, Harris and Cormier 1992). The offender assessment strategies prevalent at the time reflected an abysmal understanding of the needs of offenders that must be addressed if recidivism is to be reduced (the benefits of hindsight are marvellous).

Part of the problem was the tremendous influence of psychopathological perspectives of criminal behaviour. These perspectives had at their core the assumption that the psychological problems presented by offenders were indeed risk factors or predictors of criminal conduct. A mental disorder or some other emotional-cognitive deficit was seen to be at the root of criminal conduct and therefore we needed to assess these factors and then eliminate or diminish their influence (Andrews and Bonta 2003).

Armed with a psychopathological model of criminal behaviour, psychologists went about administering to offenders general personality tests such as the Minnesota Multiphasic Personality Inventory (MMPI) and the Rorschach and also specific measures tapping anxiety, self-esteem, depression and the like.

The assessment of a wide range and emotional and personality variables was attractive because it provided targets for treatment. You are neurotically anxious? We'll teach you relaxation exercises. Feeling depressed? We'll teach you how to cope better. Poor self-esteem? We can make you feel better about yourself. In the glory days of rehabilitation (1950 to the early 1970s) any assessment approach that promised an objective way of assessing the treatment needs of offenders was too much to resist. The assessment of emotional and psychological problems, and the acceptance of the psychopathological model of criminal behaviour, are fine, if the research is supportive. Although evidence did exist for some time on the importance of certain personality traits (i.e. anti-social personality) most of the evidence rested on cross-sectional methodologies that simply compared offenders with non-offenders (Schuessler and Cressey 1950; Tennenbaum 1977; Waldo and Dinitz 1967). The type of support needed to convince us of the value of emotional and psychopathological factors in criminal behaviour requires prospective methodologies to establish the predictive validity of these variables. Except for assessments of anti-social personality, evidence of this type is either weak or non-existent.

Gendreau, Little and Goggin (1996) conducted a comprehensive meta-analysis on the predictors of recidivism among adult offenders. The predictors were placed into eight categories and measures of self-esteem, anxiety, depression, and the like were categorized as 'personal distress'. The average effect size was 0.05 based on 66 studies involving over 19,000 offenders. Of the eight categories of risk predictors, personal distress was one of the poorest sets of predictors. In a meta-analysis of the predictors of recidivism among mentally disordered offenders, Bonta, Law and Hanson (1998) found that clinical factors (e.g. psychosis, mood disorder) were unrelated to general recidivism ($r = -.02$, N = 11,156) and violent recidivism ($r = -.03$, N = 7552).

Efforts to specifically tailor general personality tests to correctional populations or to create new personality-based measures for offender risk and need assessment has also met with limited success. Megargee and Bohn (1979) constructed a typology of offenders based on the MMPI but this produced weak evidence as to predictive validity (Motiuk, Bonta and Andrews 1986). Other personality-based assessment tools specifically developed for use with offenders were the Adult Internal Management System (AIMS) developed by Quay (1984) and the I-Level (Sullivan, Grant and Grant 1957) and Conceptual Level (Hunt and Hardt 1965) systems originally developed for youth but also applied to adults (Van Voorhis 1994). All of these general personality-based assessment systems classified offenders into different types requiring different management strategies. For example, the Neurotic-Anxious type of offender in the AIMS system may require isolation from more predatory inmates who would victimise these offenders. Note that these personality-based systems dealt with the style of management rather than suggesting highly focused treatment targets. For example, in the stage-based personality classification systems (i.e., I-Level and Conceptual Level) it was a more of a matter of waiting for youth to develop to a higher stage of cognitive-emotional function, sometimes with some gentle challenging of thinking styles, than providing a treatment programme with clearly defined and measurable goals. Once again, we find that the *general* personality-based assessments, as opposed to assessments of antisocial personality specifically, demonstrated relatively poor predictions of criminal behaviour (Andrews and Bonta 2003) the importance of anti-social personality will be discussed shortly.

Despite the evidence that variables based upon psychopathological models of crime were not strong risk factors, offender need assessments continued to focus on indicators of emotional distress or general personality traits. A 1986 review of offender need assessment practices in 38 states found health, psychological and vic-timization needs were the top three ranked areas from a total of ten potential needs (Clements 1986). Boothby and Clements (2000) surveyed correctional psychologists and found that 87 per cent were using the MMPI and 20 per cent the Rorschach.

Evidence-based actuarial risk scales, specifically developed to predict the risk of re-offending, were used by 12 per cent of reporting correctional psychologists.

Even the most widely used offender classification system in the US during the 1980s included need factors that were not predictive of recidivism. The Wisconsin classification system consisted of two instruments: a risk scale and a need scale. Both are scorable instruments but only the risk scale was evaluated with respect to predictive validity in the original validation research (Baird, Heinz and Bemus 1979). The need scale consists of 12 items ranging from employment to health. In a later study (Bonta *et al.* 1994) the needs scale showed lower predictive validity than the risk scale and some items (e.g. health, mental ability) showed absolutely no relationship with recidivism. A true offender risk-need scale did not appear until the formulation of the concept of criminogenic needs and the subsequent development of the Level of Service Inventory (LSI).

The assessment of criminogenic needs

In the late 1970s, Don Andrews began to formulate the concept of criminogenic needs. Criminogenic needs are *dynamic* risk factors and they are distinguishable from offender needs that are minimally related to criminal behaviour (Andrews, Bonta and Hoge 1990). Examples of criminogenic needs are anti-social attitudes and criminal associates; examples of non-criminogenic needs are self-esteem and feelings of emotional discomfort such as anxiety and loneliness (factors deemed important in psychopathological models of crime). In addition, dynamic risk factors demonstrate equivalent predictive validities found for static risk factors (Gendreau *et al.* 1996). The important implication from the concept of criminogenic needs is that these needs could serve as targets for treatment intervention that would reduce recidivism. Risk assessment no longer meant enhancing or loosening of correctional control but now provided an opportunity to purposely intervene and change offender risk levels.

The Level of Service Inventory (LSI: Andrews 1982) was a natural outgrowth of the criminogenic need principle and it included both static (e.g. criminal history, past substance abuse) and dynamic risk items (e.g. procriminal attitudes, current alcohol/drug problems). This integration of static risk factors with criminogenic needs represents the third generation of offender risk assessment (Bonta 1996). The dynamic risk items describe the criminogenic needs of the offender and can serve as targets for intervention. The best-known version of the LSI, the Level of Service Inventory-Revised (LSI-R: Andrews and Bonta 1995) consists of 54 static and dynamic items organized around 10 general domains. Over two-thirds of the items are dynamic.

Numerous studies have demonstrated the predictive validity of the LSI-R related instruments (for reviews, see Andrews and Bonta 1995, 2003; Gendreau, Goggin and Smith 2002). In the UK, the Offender Assessment System (OASys) (Howard, Clark and Garnham 2004) has been developed with many features similar to the LSI-R and recently, the fourth generation Level of Service/Case Management Inventory has been published (LS/CMI: Andrews, Bonta and Wormith 2004). There are, however, two features of the LSI-R that set this instrument apart from OASys and other similar offender assessment instruments. They are evidence of dynamic predictive validity and a theoretical basis.

Dynamic predictive validity refers to changes in risk/need scores being associated with changes in the probability of recidivism. From a risk and need assessment perspective it is expected that an offender's overall level of risk to re-offend would be influenced by changes in the dynamic risk items. Evaluating the predictive validity of a risk-need instrument requires an initial assessment followed by a re-assessment later in time. The change scores are then correlated with future recidivism. This research methodology is rarely used in offender assessment research and the LSI-R is the only instrument with *any* evidence of its dynamic predictive validity and even with the LSI-R there are only four studies (Andrews and Robinson 1984; Motiuk, Bonta and Andrews 1990; Raynor 2007; Raynor *et al.* 2000).

The studies by Peter Raynor and his colleagues (Raynor 2007; Raynor *et al.* 2000) are the largest evaluations of the dynamic validity of the LSI-R. Two samples of probationers (N = 157 and N = 203) were assessed and reassessed six months later and recidivism was measured one year after the reassessment. The results are shown in Table 8.2. When LSI-R scores increased upon retest (i.e. offenders moved from low risk at intake to high risk at retest), higher reconvictions rates were found, when scores decreased, reconvictions rates decreased.

Table 8.2: Dynamic validity of the LSI-R (% recidivated)

Reassessment		
Intake	*Low risk*	*High risk*
Sample 1: Low risk	26.2	54.8
High risk	55.3	78.4
Sample 2: Low risk	29.0	59.0
High risk	54.0	76.0

Notes: Sample 1 from Raynor *et al.* 2000; Sample 2 from Raynor 2007.

Evidence of the dynamic predictive validity of the LSI-R is extremely important for case management. Approximately two-thirds of the items on the LSI-R are dynamic or changeable. Thus for total LSI-R scores to decrease there must be changes on the dynamic items. These items, and on a more general level most of the subcomponents, serve as treatment targets for criminogenic needs. The correctional worker can focus on areas identified by the LSI-R as problematic and be encouraged by the dynamic predictive validity research that successfully addressing these needs would reduce recidivism.

The second feature of the LSI-R is its theoretical basis. The LSI-R is one of the few offender risk instruments that have a theoretical basis (the Psychopathy Checklist-Revised is another: Hare 1990). The general personality and social psychological theory of criminal behaviour presented by Andrews and Bonta (2003) is a social learning perspective that is congruent with the research on offender assessment and treatment. The theory assumes that criminal behaviour is learned within various social contexts. The reward-punishment contingencies that operate in a range of social settings (e.g. work, school, family, recreation) interact with person factors (e.g. impulsivity, sensation seeking, poor self-control, callousness) to produce behaviour. Social support for the behaviour and cognitions conducive to criminal behaviour are central factors as well as criminal history and a constellation of personality factors (e.g. impulsiveness, thrill-seeking, egocentrism) that some call an anti-social personality. Note that the theory is highly specific with respect to the personality characteristics that are relevant to criminal behaviour. It is anti-social personality traits and not the generalised emotional discomfort characteristics posited by psychopatho-logical perspectives of criminal conduct. Other factors of moderate relevance include family/marital functioning, substance abuse and indicators of social achievement (e.g. education and employment).

All ten subcomponents of the LSI-R can be derived from this general theory of behaviour (see Table 8.3). The theory assumes that behaviour is learned and therefore, can be modified through planned human service intervention. The theory also assumes that there are many aspects to an individual's circumstances that are dynamic and changeable. In other words, the general personality and social learning theory is supportive of offender rehabilitation.

There is some empirical evidence indicating that similar assessment and treatment techniques could be applied to specific offender populations. The major predictors of recidivism are very similar for mentally disordered offenders (Bonta *et al.* 1998) and sex offenders (Hanson and Bussire 1998; Hanson and Morton-Bourgon 2005). The evidence for the wide applicability of the LSI-R is impressive. The LSI-R has demonstrated predictive validity with female offenders

Table 8.3: The LSI-R Subcomponents in order of their theoretical importance (number of items)

Criminal History (10)	Financial (2)
Companions (5)	Accommodation (3)
Attitude/Orientation (4)	Family/Marital (4)
Emotional/Personal (5)	Alcohol/Drug Problem (9)
Education/Employment (10)	Leisure/Recreation (2)

Note: The Emotional/Personal subcomponent pays special attention to anti-social personality characteristics. In the LS/CMI this subcomponent is subsumed under the subcomponent Anti-social Pattern.

both in the community and in residential and custodial settings (Andrews 1982; Coulson *et al.* 1996; Cumberland and Boyle 1997; Lowenkamp, Holsinger and Latessa 2001; Raynor *et al.* 2000; Rettinger 1998; Washington State Institute for Public Policy 2003). Similarly, LSI-R scores predicted recidivism for Aboriginal offenders and other racial groups (Bonta 1989; Lowenkamp *et al.* 2001; Rettinger 1998; Washington State Institute for Public Policy 2003), young adults (ages 16 to 18: Andrews, Dowden and Rettinger 2001) and mentally disordered offenders (Harris, Rice and Quinsey 1993).

Fourth generation risk/need assessment

With the formal implementation of risk/need assessment protocols across many correctional jurisdictions, questions arise about the complete utilization of the assessment results in case supervision and intervention. Although the third generation LSI-R may set the stage for treatment planning, there is no guarantee that correctional workers actually formulate and implement plans based on a risk/need assessment. Consequently, a number of recent studies have examined the extent to which correctional case management practices reflect, on an individual case level, the findings of a detailed risk/needs assessment.

One example is a study of case management in a Canadian province (Bonta *et al.* 2004). Probation officers conducted risk/need assessments and researchers evaluated whether the results from the assessments made their way into case management plans and whether probation officers targeted identified criminogenic needs in their supervision sessions with probationers. The results showed: 1) many criminogenic needs identified during assessment were not present in the intervention plan, and 2) during supervision the identified criminogenic needs were infrequently addressed. In other words, probation staff was not taking full advantage of the risk/need assessment, which in this case was a validatd modification of the Wisconsin Risk and Needs instrument (Bonta *et al.* 1994).

In another Canadian province, Girard, Miller and Mazaheri (2004) examined the application of risk/need assessments, in this case a version of the Level of Service Inventory (Andrews, Bonta and Wormith 1995), to the practices of probation officers as illustrated in their client case files. In a review of more than 1800 files, the mean percentage score (73%) on a series of assessment criteria fell in the predetermined 'satisfactory range' (i.e. 66% to 80%), while the mean percentage score on a series of case management planning criteria (64%) failed to meet this standard. Interestingly, the distribution of scores in the case management plan category was quite bimodal. Many probation officers either did very well or failed miserably. Specifically, more than half of the cases were rated as very satisfactory (a score of more than 80%), with plans to address criminogenic factors that included specific tasks, goals and timelines for interventions, while more than one-third of the cases showed very little such evidence. Moreover, there was no evidence that client motivational issues were even being considered in 60 per cent of the cases. In the same vein, Harris, Gingerich and Whittaker (2004) demonstrated in a US study that probation officers, who conducted risk/need assessments based on the Client Management Classification System (CMC: Lerner, Arling and Baird, 1986), often failed to follow the guidelines emanating from these assessments in the supervision of their adult probationers. Overall, the recidivism rates of offenders who were supervised by staff trained in CMC was lower than the recidivism rates of offenders who were supervised by probation officers who were not trained in CMC. However, the recidivism rate of the former group was negatively correlated with the extent to which staff trained in CMC used the techniques. These results suggest that a more thorough usage of CMC by trained staff would have reduced the recidivism rates of their clients even further.

Clearly, it is naïve to expect that correctional workers will automatically extrapolate and apply their risk/needs assessments to their case management practice (e.g. Andrews *et al.* 1990). Without specific guidelines to designate risk level in accordance with risk score, or to establish supervision standards in accordance with risk level, the application of risk to practice by correctional workers will either not occur or will be inconsistent. Consequently, most tools provide cut-off scores to identify risk levels and correctional agencies provide policies to identify standards of supervision (if they are not already provided by the instrument itself). Similarly, mechanisms must be established to link the needs portion of risk/need assessment with correctional practice. This may be done by the agency, by means of policy and administrative review procedures (Girard *et al.* 2004) or by the instrument itself. The Level of Service/Case Management Inventory (LS/CMI: Andrews, Bonta and Wormith 2004), along with the Correctional Assessment and Intervention System (CAIS: National Council on Crime and Delinquency 2003) are examples of the latter approach, what may be called the 'fourth generation' of risk assessment (Andrews, Bonta and Wormith 2006).

The LS/CMI was planned with three principal objectives in mind. First, it was designed to streamline the LSI-R with as little expense to validity as possible, or none. Second, it was intended to extend the traditional risk/need assessment to a more comprehensive assessment of the many and diverse offender characteristics that are relevant to good case management and supervision (e.g., the assessment of strengths and responsivity factors). Third, it was to integrate the assessment process with offender case management. As such, it constitutes the next generation in the evolution of offender risk assessment scales (see Box 8.2 for a summary of the major components of the LS/CMI).

Concerning the first objective, the LS/CMI consists of fewer (43) items and fewer (8) domains than its predecessors, as a number of low frequency and statistically redundant items were eliminated. The validity of this version has been established by reanalysis of previous LSI research (Andrews 1995; Simourd 2004), concurrent analyses of multiple versions of the LSI (Rettinger 1998; Rowe 1999) and original analyses in prospective recidivism studies (Girard and Wormith 2004; Nowicka-Sroga 2004). Although the predictive validity correlations vary considerably, most are in the 0.26 to 0.40 range for a variety of outcome measures and various offender groups, including youth, women, long-term offenders, sexual offenders, domestic violence offenders and mentally disordered offenders (Andrews 1995; Andrews *et al.* 2004; Girard and Wormith 2004; Nowicka-Sroga 2004; Rettinger 1998; Rowe 1999; Simourd 2004). These validities are similar to those from the LSI-R research, which is hardly surprising since the correlation between the two versions of the LSI is very high ($r = .97$: Andrews *et al.* 2004).

The second objective of the LS/CMI, its expansion to include a number of other client characteristics, represents a significant departure from traditional risk and risk/needs assessment. This includes what are described as æspecific' risk need factors, institutional factors, other client issues such as social, health and mental health concerns, and responsivity factors. Specific risk/need factors are those offender characteristics that are not routinely included in the assessment of general risk/need, but when they do occur, they may be of such importance that they

Table 8.4: The major components of the LS/CMI (number of items)

A. General Risk/Need Factors (43)

Criminal History (8)	Companions (4)
Education/Employment (9)	Alcohol/Drug problem (8)
Family/Marital (4)	Procriminal attitude/Orientation (4)
Leisure/Recreation (2)	Anti-social pattern (4)

B. Specific Risk/Need Factors (35)

Personal problems with criminogenic potential (14)

History of perpetration (21)

Sexual assault (7)

Other forms of violence (7)

Other forms of anti-social behaviour (7)

C. Prison experience: institutional factors (14)

D. Other client issues (21)

    Social, health, and mental health (21)

E. Special responsivity (11)

F. Case management plan

    Programme targets and intervention plan

    Criminogenic needs/other client needs/responsivity considerations

G. Progress record

    Criminogenic needs/non-criminogenic needs

H. Discharge summary

    Type of discharge/discharge summary narrative

'override' the quantitatively derived risk level that is derived from the general/need score. These items are particularly important in the identification of potentially violent individuals and include personal or idiosyncratic problems with criminogenic potential and a history of perpetration, particularly violence. A section on prison experience that documents past institutional behaviour and previous classifications is particularly relevant to institutional workers and the demands on them for speedy and safe placements. Similarly, other client issues constitute a list of primarily non-criminogenic needs that may, nonetheless, require attention by the correctional agency, be it institutional or community based.

A section on special responsivity issues itemises client characteristics that are likely to affect the impact of various approaches to service delivery and, as such, constitute important considerations in the programme planning process. Finally, positive attributes of the offender, client strengths, or those characteristics that mitigate or protect against the influence of otherwise negative risk/need factors, are recorded.

To a committed risk/need enthusiast it might seem heretical to confound the assessment process with seemingly irrelevant components. As noted previously, it has been a long and arduous journey to arrive at the stage whereby standardised risk/needs assessment enjoys its standing in many, although not all, correctional jurisdictions. Consequently, expanding the scope of offender assessment beyond predetermined, fixed lists of risk and criminogenic need items may appear to be a regressive step. But to adhere rigidly to the simplistic risk/need notion is both unrealistic and misguided as it ignores the decades of experience with countless case workers and a vast diversity of client issues.

It is also a disservice to the offender and the community to simplify the complexity of good offender assessment and case management. Case workers cannot ignore idiosyncratic, case-specific criminogenic needs. The context of services and the setting in which they are offered (e.g. prison or community) must be considered. Even interventions that address appropriate criminogenic targets can amount to a waste of time and resources when delivered in a manner that is not suitable for the offender. Basic health care and humanitarian needs are fundamental rights of offenders and a moral responsibility of correctional agencies to address. Ironically, schemes that ignore these needs in their efforts to be more efficient by focusing exclusively on identified criminogenic needs may lose out in the end. Although targeting non-criminogenic needs alone will not, by definition, alter client risk, it can have such an impact on some of the most problematic responsivity factors, such as motivation, that the best criminogenic treatment, on its own, may be ineffectual and a waste of valuable resources. Similarly, drawing on a client's area of strength does not directly address the offender's criminogenic needs. However, it can prepare the offender and contribute to a greater sense of æresilience' (Masten 2001). It is, in fact, all of these additions to the LSI that set the stage for its next and perhaps most important innovation.

The third objective extends the LS/CMI into the case management process. By formalising the link between risk/need assessment and the process of offender case management into a single document, the prospects for a case management process that is driven by risk/need assessment are maximised. In establishing such a framework, it must be acknowledged that there are numerous definitions of case management and various models of its delivery (Partridge 2004). For our purposes, case management includes a full range of supervision practices, direct intervention and service delivery to the client, and indirect referral to a third party for individual counselling, therapy or group programmes. Models of case management can include sole responsibility/generalist (from admission to discharge), functional specialisation (assessment, supervision, treatment), client type specialization (sexual offenders, violent offenders, mentally disordered offenders) and multi-disciplinary teams (concurrent responsibilities). Each of these models presents advantages and disadvantages concerning the ease with which it is likely to adhere to the need principle by addressing the criminogenic needs of individual offenders (Andrews and Bonta 2003). The LS/CMI is designed in a sufficiently generic fashion so as to accommodate these differences. However, a theme that runs throughout the LS/CMI case management documentation is that all case management plans, client activities, client behaviour and client outcome are consistently linked back, or related, to the principles of risk, need and responsivity.

The case management portion of the LS/CMI begins with a summary of administrative decisions that have already been made in accordance with the current risk/need assessment. It then documents a critical step in the supervision of any offender, the action plan. This includes the identification of targets (both criminogenic and non-criminogenic needs), the plans to address them (interventions) and the approaches taken to do so (as suggested by responsivity considerations). The next section (Section G in Table 8.4), the progress record, records client activities. But it does so by relating noteworthy developments to the previously established criminogenic and non-criminogenic needs, and documenting the extent to which change has occurred, either positively or negatively. Finally the discharge summary provides an overview of the offender status upon completion or termination of supervision, in particular, the extent to which legal conditions have been fulfilled and programme objectives have been met. There are a number of advantages to this kind of integrated assessment and case management approach, some of which are more obvious than others. First, by design, such integration facilitates the application of client assessment to client intervention and programming efforts. The LS/CMI, with its risk/needs/ responsivity focus throughout the process, ensures that this is done in a sound, theoretical and empirically supported manner. Second, an integrated assessment and case management scheme is generalisable and portable. It may be applied regardless of the case management or service delivery model and as long as case workers are familiar with the tool, cases can be transferred with relative ease.

It may be implicitly understood, but it should also be pointed out that an integrated system of risk/need assessment and case management requires implementation at the agency or systemic level (Bonta *et al.* 2001; Lowenkamp, Latessa and Holsinger 2004). Consequently, all case workers must operate from a common ground in that the language and theoretical underpinnings remain the same even though individual case flexibility is allowed, or encouraged, within the LS/CMI process. However, it should be noted that case management practices with the CAIS are formula based, with various offender profiles directing the case management process to a specific strategy and approach to case supervision (National Council on Crime and Delinquency 2003).

A third advantage to an integrated assessment and case management scheme is that it monitors the integrity of case management on an individual basis by documenting events and the delivery of services in relation to the identified needs (i.e. the case plan). Fourth, recoding at this level allows for some pretty straightforward, but important research. As Motiuk (1997, p.22) asked: 'What needs to be done next? We need to study how well our correctional plans and interventions work.' Finally, an integrated instrument and case management system, whose components have been planned and designed concurrently, lends itself much more readily to automation than schemes that are theoretically, functionally and technologically unrelated and are forced together after the fact. Of course, assessment and case management schemes that are integrated at the electronic level also provide further assistance in research and evaluation.

Future directions

The last 25 years have shown significant developments in the area of offender assessment. We are now moving beyond simple risk and need assessment to include a more comprehensive assessment of client characteristics that are attentive to responsivity, strengths, idiosyncratic risk factors and their integration into case management strategies. These fourth generation assessment tools are just beginning to make their way into use and we expect that future research on these instruments will outline their strengths but, more importantly, their limitations. Undoubtedly, research will investigate the generalisability of the new instruments to different offender groups and to the prediction of different types of offending behaviour. There is already some evidence that these instruments may be surprisingly robust in their applicability to different offender groups and to different outcomes (Andrews *et al.* 2004, 2006; Bourgon and Bonta 2004; Hanson and Morton-Bourgon 2005). However, research will certainly find some limits to fourth generation assessment but this will take us to the next steps in improving offender assessment strategies.

References

Andrews, D.A. (1982) *The Level of Supervision Inventory (LSI): The First Followup.* Toronto: Ontario Ministry of Correctional Services.

Andrews, D.A. (1995) *Current Knowledge Regarding the LSI.* Unpublished report to the Ontario Ministry of Correctional Services. Ottawa, ON: Carleton University.

Andrews, D.A. and Bonta, J. (1995) *The Level of Service Inventory – Revised.* Toronto: Multi-Health Systems.

Andrews, D.A. and Bonta, J. (2003) *The Psychology of Criminal Conduct* (3rd edn). Cincinnati, OH: Anderson Publishing Company.

Andrews, D.A., Bonta, J. and Hoge, R.D. (1990) 'Classification for Effective Rehabilitation: Rediscovering Psychology.' *Criminal Justice and Behavior 17,* 19–52.

Andrews, D.A., Bonta, J. and Wormith, J.S. (2004) *Level of Service/Case Management Inventory (LS/CMI): An Offender Assessment System. User's Manual.* Toronto, ON: Multi-Health Systems.

Andrews, D.A., J. Bonta and Wormith, J.S. (2006) 'The Recent Past and Near Future of Risk and/or Need Assessment.' *Crime and Delinquency 52,* 7–27.

Andrews, D.A., Dowden, C. and Rettinger, J.L. (2001) 'Special Populations within Canada.' In J.A. Winterdyck (ed.) *Corrections in Canada: Social Reactions to Crime.* Toronto, Ontario: Prentice Hall.

Andrews, D.A., Hoge, R.D., Robinson, D. and Andrews, F. J. (1990) *Case Management Strategies Survey.* Research Report No. R-08. Ottawa, ON: Correctional Service of Canada.

Andrews, D.A. and Robinson, D. (1984) *The Level of Supervision Inventory: Second Report.* Report to Research Services (Toronto) of the Ontario Ministry of Correctional Services.

Baird, S.C., Heinz, R.C. and Bemus, B.J. (1979) *Project Report #14: A Two Year Followup.* Wisconsin: Department of Health and Social Services, Case Classification/Staff Deployment Project, Bureau of Community Corrections.

Bonta, J. (1989) 'Native Inmates: Institutional Response, Risk, and Needs.' *Canadian Journal of Criminology 31,* 49–62.

Bonta, J. (1996) 'Risk-needs Assessment and Treatment.' In A.T. Harland (ed.) *Choosing Correctional Options that Work: Defining the Demand and Evaluating the Supply.* Thousand Oaks, CA: Sage.

Bonta, J., Bogue, B., Crowley, M. and Motiuk, L. (2001) 'Implementing Offender Classification Systems: Lessons Learned.' In G.A. Bernfeld, D.P. Farrington and A.W. Leschied (eds) *Offender Rehabilitation in Practice: Implementing and Evaluating Effective Programs.* Chichester: Wiley.

Bonta, J., Harman, W.G., Hann, R. G. and Cormier, R.B. (1996) 'The Prediction of Recidivism among Federally Sentenced Offenders: A Re-validation of the SIR Scale.' *Canadian Journal of Criminology 38,* 61–79.

Bonta, J., Law, M. and Hanson, R.K. (1998) 'The Prediction of Criminal and Violent Recidivism among Mentally Disordered Offenders: A Meta-analysis.' *Psychological Bulletin 123*, 123–142.

Bonta, J., Parkinson, R., Pang, B., Barkwell, L. and Wallace-Capretta, S. (1994) *The Revised Manitoba Classification System.* Ottawa, ON: Solicitor General Canada.

Bonta, J., Rugge, T., Sedo, B. and Coles, R. (2004) *Case Management in Manitoba Probation (2004–01).* Ottawa, ON: Public Safety and Emergency Preparedness Canada.

Boothby, J.L. and Clements, C.B. (2000) 'A National Survey of Correctional Psychologists.' *Criminal Justice and Behavior 27*, 716–732.

Bourgon, G. and Bonta, J. (2004) *Risk Assessment for General Assault and Partner Abusers (2004–04).* Ottawa, ON: Public Safety and Emergency Preparedness Canada.

Burgess, E.W. (1928) 'Factors Determining Success or Failure on Parole.' In A.A. Bruce, A.J. Harno, E.W. Burgess, and J. Landesco (eds) *The Workings of the Indeterminatesentence Law and the Parole System in Illinois.* Springfield, IL: State Board of Parole.

Clements, C.B. (1986) *Offender Needs Assessment.* College Park, MD: American Correctional Association.

Copas, J. and Marshall, P. (1998) 'The Offender Group Reconviction Scale: A Statistical Reconviction Score for Use by Probation Officers'. *Journal of the Royal Statistical Society 47*, 159–171.

Copas, J., Marshall, P. and Tarling, R. (1996) *Predicting Reoffending for Discretionary Conditional Release.* Home Office Research Study 150. London: Home Office.

Cormier, R.B. (1997) 'Yes, SIR! A stable risk prediction tool.' *Forum on Corrections Research 9*, 1, 3–7.

Coulson, G., Ilacqua, G., Nutbrown, V., Giulekas, D. and Cudjoe, F. (1996) 'Predictive utility of the LSI for Incarcerated Female Offenders.' *Criminal Justice and Behavior 23*, 427–439.

Cumberland, A.K. and Boyle, G.J. (1997) 'Psychometric Prediction of Recidivism: Utility of the Risk Needs Inventory.' *Australian and New Zealand Journal of Criminology 30*, 72–86.

Gendreau, P., Goggin, C. and Smith, P. (2002) 'Is the PCL-R Really the "Unparalleled" Measure of Offender Risk? A Lesson in Knowledge Cumulation.' *Criminal Justice and Behavior 29*, 397–426.

Gendreau, P., Little, T. and Goggin, C. (1996) 'A Meta-analysis of the Predictors of Adult Offender Recidivism: What Works!' *Criminology 34*, 575–607.

Girard, L. and Wormith, J.S. (2004) 'The predictive validity of the Level of Service Inventory-Ontario Revision on general and violent recidivism among various offender groups.' *Criminal Justice and Behavior 31*, 150–181.

Girard, L., Miller, C. and Mazaheri, N. (2004) *Collaborative Evaluation Process, Aggregate Report II: Lessons Learned.* North Bay, ON: Ministry of Community Safety and Correctional Services.

Glueck, S. and Glueck, E.T. (1950) *Unraveling Juvenile Delinquency.* Cambridge, MA: Harvard University Press.

Gray, N.S., Taylor, J., Snowden, R.J., MacCulloch, S., Phillips, H. and MacCulloch, M.J. (2004) 'Relative Efficacy of Criminological, Clinical, and Personality Measures of Future Risk of Offending in Mentally Disordered Offenders: A Comparative Study of HCR-20, PCL-SV, and OGRS.' *Journal of Consulting and Clinical Psychology 72*, 3, 523–531.

Grove, W.M., Zald, D.H., Lebow, B.S., Snitz, B.E. and Nelson, C. (2000) 'Clinical versus mechanical prediction: A meta-analysis.' *Psychological Assessment 12*, 19–30.

Hanson, R.K. and Bussire, M.T. (1998) 'Predicting Relapse: A Meta-analysis of Sexual Offender Recidivism Studies.' *Journal of Consulting and Clinical Psychology 66*, 348–362.

Hanson, R.K. and Morton-Bourgon, K. (2005) 'The characteristics of persistent sexual offenders: A meta-analysis of recidivism studies.' *Journal of Consulting and Clinical Psychology 73*, 1154–1163.

Hare, R. D. (1990) *The Hare Psychopathy Checklist-Revised*. Toronto: Multi-Health Systems.

Harris, P.M., Gingerich, R., and Whittaker, T.A. (2004) 'The "effectiveness" of delinquency supervision.' *Crime and Delinquency 50*, 235–271.

Harris, G.T., Rice, M.E. and Quinsey, V.L. (1993) 'Violent Recidivism of Mentally Disordered Offenders: The Development of a Statistical Prediction Instrument.' *Criminal Justice and Behavior 20*, 315–335.

Hoffman, P.B. (1982) 'Females, Recidivism, and Salient Factor Score: A Research Note.' *Criminal Justice and Behavior 9*, 121–125.

Hoffman, P.B. (1983) 'Screening for risk: A revised salient factor score (SFS 81)' *Journal of Criminal Justice 9*, 539–547.

Hoffman, P.B. (1994) 'Twenty Years of Operational Use of a Risk Prediction Instrument: The United States Parole Commission's Salient Factor Score.' *Journal of Criminal Justice 22*, 477–494.

Hoffman, P.B. and Beck, J.L. (1974) 'Parole decision-making: A Salient Factor Score' *Journal of Criminal Justice 2*, 195–206.

Hoffman, P.B. and Beck, J.L. (1976) 'Salient Factor Score validation – A 1972 release cohort.' *Journal of Criminal Justice 4*, 69–76.

Hoffman, P.B., Stone-Meierhoefer, B. and Beck, J.L. (1978) 'Salient Factor Score and Release Behavior: Three Validational Samples.' *Law and Human Behavior 2*, 47–63.

Howard, P., Clark, D.A. and Garnham, N. (2004) *An Evaluation and Validation of the Offender Assessment System (OASys)*. London: Home Office.

Hunt, D.E. and Hardt, R.H. (1965) 'Developmental Stage, Delinquency, and Differential Treatment.' *Journal of Research in Crime and Delinquency 2*, 20–31.

Lerner, K., Arling, G. and Baird, S.C. (1986) 'Client Management Classification Strategies for Case Supervision.' *Crime and Delinquency 32*, 254–271.

Lowenkamp, C.T., Holsinger, A.M. and Latessa, E.J. (2001) 'Risk/need Assessment, Offender Classification and the Role of Child Abuse.' *Criminal Justice and Behavior 28*, 543–563.

Lowenkamp, C.T., Latessa, E.J. and Holsinger, A.M. (2004) 'Empirical evidence on the importance of training and experience in using the Level of Service Inventory-Revised.' *Topics in Community Corrections* Annual Issue, 49–53.

Martinson, R. (1974) 'What Works? – Questions and Answers about Prison Reform.' *The Public Interest 35*, 22–54.

Masten, A.S. (2001) 'Ordinary Magic: Resilience Processes in Development.' *American Psychologist 56*, 227–238.

Megargee, E.I. and Bohn, M.J., Jr (1979) *Classifying Criminal Offenders: A New System Based on the MMPI*. Beverly Hills, CA: Sage.

Motiuk, L.L. (1997) 'Classification for Correctional Programming: The Offender Intake Assessment (OIA) Process.' *Forum on Corrections Research 9*, 1, 18–22.

Motiuk, L.L., Bonta, J. and Andrews, D.A. (1986) 'Classification in Correctional Halfway Houses: The Relative and Incremental Predictive Criterion Validities of the Megargee-MMPI and LSI systems.' *Criminal Justice and Behavior 13*, 33–46.

Motiuk, L.L., Bonta, J. and Andrews, D.A. (1990) 'Dynamic Predictive Criterion Validity in Offender Assessment.' Paper presented at the Canadian Psychological Association Annual Convention, June, Ottawa.

Nafekh, M. and Motiuk, L.L. (2002) *The Statistical Information on Recidivism – Revised 1 (SIR-R1) Scale: A Psychometric Examination.* Ottawa, ON: Correctional Service of Canada.

National Council on Crime and Delinquency (2003) *Correctional Assessment and Intervention System (CAIS).* Madison, WI: NCCD.

Nowicka-Sroga, M. (2004) 'The Level of Service Inventory – Ontario Revision: A Recidivism Follow-up Study within a Sample of Male Young Offenders.' Unpublished doctoral dissertation, University of Ottawa. Ottawa, ON.

Nuffield, J. (1982) *Parole Decision-Making in Canada. Research Towards Decision Guidelines.* Ottawa: Ministry of Supply and Services, Canada.

Partridge, S. (2004) *Examining Case Management Models for Community Sentences.* Online Report 17/04. London: Home Office.

Quay, H.C. (1984) *Managing Adult Inmates: Classification for Housing and Program Assignments.* College Park, MD: American Correctional Association.

Raynor, P. (2007) 'Risk and Need Assessment in British Probation: The Contribution of the LSI-R.' *Psychology, Crime, and Law* 13, 2, 125–138.

Raynor, P., Kynch, J., Roberts, C. and Merrington, S. (2000) *Risk and Need Assessment in Probation Services: An Evaluation.* Home Office Research Study No. 211. London: Home Office.

Rettinger, J. (1998) 'A Recidivism Follow-up Study to Investigate Risk and Need within a Sample of Provincially Sentenced Women.' Unpublished doctoral dissertation, Carleton University, Ottawa, ON.

Rice, M.E., Harris, G.T. and Cormier, C.A. (1992) 'An Evaluation of a Maximum Security Therapeutic Community for Psychopaths and Other Mentally Disordered Offenders.' *Law and Human Behavior 16,* 399–412.

Rowe, R.C. (1999) 'The Prediction of Recidivism in a Parole Sample: An Examination of Two Versions of the Level of Service Inventory.' Unpublished report. Ottawa, ON: Carleton University.

Schuessler, K.F. and Cressy, D.R. (1950) 'Personality Characteristics of Criminals.' *American Journal of Sociology 55,* 476–484.

Simourd, D.J. (2004) 'Use of Dynamic Risk/need Assessment Instruments Among Long Term Incarcerated Offenders.' *Criminal Justice and Behavior 31,* 306–323.

Sullivan, C., Grant, M.Q. and Grant, J.D. (1957) 'The Development of Interpersonal Maturity: Applications to Delinquency.' *Psychiatry 20,* 373–385.

Taylor, R. (1999) *Predicting Reconvictions for Sexual and Violent Offences using the Revised Offender Group Reconviction Scale. Research Findings No. 104.* London: Home Office Research, Development and Statistics Directorate.

Tennenbaum, D.J. (1977) 'Personality and Criminality: A Summary and Implications of the Literature.' *Journal of Criminal Justice 5,* 225–235.

Van Voorhis, P. (1994) *Psychological Classification of the Adult Male Prison Inmate.* Albany, NY: State University of New York Press.

Waldo, G.P. and Dinitz, S. (1967) 'Personality Attributes of the Criminal: An Analysis of Research Studies, 1950–1965.' *Journal of Research in Crime and Delinquency 4,* 185–202.

Washington State Institute for Public Policy (2003) *Washington's Offender Accountability Act: An Analysis of the Department of Corrections' Risk Assessment.* Document number 03-12-1202, December. Olympia, WA: WSI.

CHAPTER 9

Programmes for Probationers

James McGuire

Introduction

Probation and social work agencies in many parts of the UK and elsewhere have now accumulated several years of experience of delivering the structured forms of interventions known as *offending behaviour programmes*. The present chapter focuses on this development, and has three main objectives. One is to outline the rationale for having embarked on such an activity to begin with. The second is to describe the nature and variety of some of the programmes currently in operation. The third is to review current and emerging evidence concerning their usefulness, with respect to the key outcome of reducing re-offending, which was a principal objective in embarking on programmes-based work

Rationale: Background research

The impetus to devise and deliver the kinds of specially designed packages or programmes now in regular use was driven by the emergence of large-scale evidence concerning their potential effectiveness in reducing criminal recidivism. For two or three decades in the second half of the last century, sometimes colloquially alluded to as the era of 'nothing works', the prospects of changing the behaviour of individuals who had committed a series of offences were regarded as slim. Social workers, probation officers, criminologists and others were aware of the "age-crime curve": that at some stage in their lives, the majority of even the most persistent offenders become gradually less involved in crime (Laub and Sampson 2001). The question facing criminal justice professionals was whether that could be induced to occur earlier, a process sometimes referred to as 'tertiary prevention' – reducing crime rates of adjudicated offenders. This is contrasted with primary and secondary prevention which focus on developmental, environmental or other initiatives to decrease opportunities for or propensities towards crime in the first place (McGuire 2004).

Evidence-based practice

In drawing and acting on the findings of research reviews, probation services have been portrayed as having recently entered a stage of 'evidence-based practice' (EBP) (Raynor 2004a) in common with, though perhaps somewhat later than, a number of other public services, notably healthcare and education. That process has been welcomed in some quarters and many practitioners have been enthusiastic about drawing on the findings of empirical studies, using outcome evaluations to drive the design of services, and fostering closer links with research, even integrating it into everyday practice (McIvor 1995).

Others, however, have considered EBP a sinister development. It has often been linked to the growth of 'managerialism' which in turn is associated with cost-cutting initiatives and increased top-down control – not just of offenders in the community, but of practitioners themselves, through the implementation of detailed monitoring and accountability procedures. Undoubtedly, the ethos of criminal justice agencies has altered considerably over approximately the last ten years. Within this, the arrival of programmes has even been cast as an element in a perceived greater 'repressiveness'. Needless to say, those involved in advocating the use of programmes have disavowed such an outcome as having been any part of their aims.

From the moment back in the 1970s when the 'nothing works' conclusion was first pronounced, there were already those who dissented from what rapidly became an orthodox position. Encouraging results existed that ran counter to the penal pessimism of the time. Gendreau and Ross (1980) launched their pointedly titled 'bibliotherapy for cynics' and marshalled a set of positive findings in an edited volume just one year after Robert Martinson published a withdrawal of his initial negative conclusions (see Martinson 1974, 1979). The field has been radically transformed since then, to an extent that there are now several volumes containing examples and reviews of successful outcomes (Hollin 2001; Hollin and Palmer 2006; McGuire 2002; McMurran and McGuire 2005; Sherman *et al.* 2002).

The major departure that probably had most influence on this reversal was the application of the method of statistical review of research literature known as meta-analysis. First employed within social science in studies of aspects of education and the impact of psychological therapy, meta-analysis was used by Garrett (1985) in a review of the effectiveness of psychosocial interventions in young offender institutions. Garrett surveyed 111 studies conducted in the period 1960–83, evaluating residential treatment programmes. The studies described work with a cumulative sample of 8076 individuals in experimental groups, and 4979 in comparison/control groups. She found positive effects of interventions across a wide range of outcome variables including recidivism. Cooper and Rosenthal (1980) had previously shown that meta-analysis produced less bias in the research review process than the traditional 'narrative' format. Garrett's (1985) review exemplified its power for synthesising data from a large array of primary research studies.

Other meta-analytic reviews followed, examining different segments of the research literature. Although there were overlaps in the studies subsumed in different reviews, the number of basic or 'primary' studies in this area has now exceeded 2000, and up to late 2006 a total of 60 meta-analyses had been published with direct reference to psychosocial interventions with offenders. (This excludes reviews of substance abuse treatment which are carried out predominantly in healthcare settings; other systematic reviews of sentencing that did not employ meta-analysis; and several reviews focused primarily on 'cost–benefit' analysis.) A summary of the main areas covered in the meta-analyses and the number of reviews pertaining to each is shown in Table 9.1.

Table 9.1 Meta-analytic reviews of interventions with offenders

Young offenders 10	Drunk-driving 1
Sex offenders 6	Skills training 1
Deterrence/Sanctions 5	Educational/Vocational services 2
European studies 5	'Principles of Human Service' 1
Cognitive-behavioural methods 5	School-based interventions 1
Family interventions 4	Relapse prevention 1
Substance-abuse 3	Age as moderator 1
CDATE Project (all studies) 2	Gender as moderator 1
Restorative Justice / Mediation 4	Ethnicity as moderator 1
Therapeutic communities 1	Personality disorder 1
Cognitive versus non-cognitive 1	Staff skills and practice 1
Violence/Domestic violence 1	Treatment integrity 1

Apart from the broad generalisation that tertiary prevention works, the firmest trend that can be extracted from the accumulated data set is that an applied framework grounded in *cognitive social learning theory* (Bandura 2001; Ross and Fabiano 1985) has generated the strongest and most consistent findings with respect to effect sizes in reducing recidivism. Structured, programmatic interventions founded on principles derived from this theory (Andrews 2001; McGuire 2005a) have provided the basis for most of the methods now familiar in accredited offending behaviour work. Before examining the composition of these programmes in more detail, let us look first at the theoretical model that underpins them.

Rationale: Conceptual model

It is difficult to separate the process of working directly with offenders, and attempting to engender change, from the wider issue of how society responds to the presence of crime within it and of how justice is 'dispensed'. The latter is usually considered to be a matter of criminal law and of penal and social policy, but it inevitably sets the framework for the ways in which offenders are managed inside the criminal justice system.

Historically, there have been several main approaches that have influenced how communities react to offenders: retribution, deterrence, incapacitation and rehabilitation. The first three generally entail restrictions on liberty or other punitive sanctions and an assumption that the infliction of pain or discomfort is either justified in itself (retribution), will remove offenders' opportunities for committing crime (incapacitation) or will somehow teach them a lesson (deterrence). Of these three approaches, the last is by far the most widely deployed. In respect of its utilitarian function, from the standpoint of behavioural psychology deterrence doctrine can be classified as 'eliminative' or 'pathological' in its orientation. That is, it seeks to reduce the likelihood of criminal activity by increasing the chances that those who engage in it will suffer unpleasant consequences as a result (specific deterrence). Further, the expectation of this happening will similarly influence anyone tempted to offend (general deterrence).

The usage of offending behaviour programmes, by contrast, is a fundamentally rehabilitative activity. As such, in behavioural terminology its purpose is 'constructional' and emphasises the learning of new behaviours, attitudes and capacities; the acquisition of skills and the expansion of an individual's repertoire for solving the problems with which he or she is faced. This is linked to the hypothesis that acts of crime are in many cases attempts to accomplish goals or solve problems in ways that society has deemed unacceptable; which frequently cause harm to others and often to individuals themselves.

This is a more specific focus than what has been called the 'penal welfarism' of earlier approaches to understanding 'the causes of crime' (Bottoms, Rex and Robinson 2004). Within that framework the burden of explanation is placed on social conditions, structural inequalities, relative deprivation, and related factors. These are undoubtedly important contributory factors in generating the activities labelled as criminal. But differential reactions to them produce a further layer of complexity: family socialisation and individual/personal factors also contribute to the occurrence of crime events.

Developmentally, these factors interact with one another within an ongoing, dynamic, transactional progression. Many contemporary theories of crime recognise the multi-directionality of causal links through various phases within this. Social learning theory rests on an assumption of *reciprocal determinism* concerning how individual and situational factors inter-relate. In common with many other intricacies of human behaviour, patterns of repetitive criminality are acquired through behavioural and cognitive learning processes and become established via the interplay of numerous individual, familial and other environmental variables.

In essence then, the model posits that in conjunction with environmental influences and crime opportunities, a range of psychosocial factors is associated with involvement in persistent offending behaviour. Systematic research has shown that the most prominent factors include the presence of and attachment to criminal associates; adherence to anti-social attitudes and beliefs; and a pattern of deficits in social-interactive, problem-solving and self-management skills (Andrews and Bonta 2003; McGuire 2004, 2005a). The theoretical model elaborated upon this basis entails a number of propositions. Essentially it suggests that there is predictable variation between people in their likelihood of becoming involved in crime, and of continuing that involvement (Andrews 1989). Such patterns are a function of the interaction between environmental and personal variables within their individual histories. This furnishes a basis for allocating offenders according to risk levels and criminogenic needs, and employing selected methods of working that will address and reduce these accordingly.

Possibly the most influential of the meta-analyses so far published was conducted by Andrews *et al.* (1990). These authors tested a series of hypotheses derived from the above model of 'human service principles', with the concepts of *risk, need* and *responsivity* at its core (for definitions and fuller discussion, see McGuire 2004). They proposed that interventions applying those principles would yield higher effect sizes than other types of work. Andrews and his colleagues used this theoretical model heuristically to formulate a set of hypotheses regarding elements of interventions that were most likely to contribute to reducing recidivism. To test the model, they subdivided a set of 154 outcome studies into four groups according to the extent to which they possessed those elements. The observed effect sizes differed systematically between the groups in the manner predicted by the model. These findings provided a compelling demonstration of the possibility of delineating a cluster of factors that could be shown to increase the likelihood of success in reducing recidivism (Andrews, Bonta and Hoge 1990).

Policy and practice: The crime reduction programme

The process of assembling ideas and exercises for working with offenders, and structuring them into the coherent sequences now called programmes is not entirely new. Such activities have been employed in probation work for many years, within some forms of individual casework but more often in 'groupwork', which formed a gradually more influential aspect of practice some time before the episode now collectively constructed as that of 'what works' (Vanstone 2000).

But the exponential take-off in usage of structured programmes in recent years almost entirely reflects the impact of the Crime Reduction Programme (CRP), a multi-faceted policy development instigated by the Labour government in the late 1990s. The CRP involved the investment of approximately £400 million, with a wide span of ramifications pertaining to the philosophy, objectives, management, organisation and delivery of the entire gamut of criminal justice services.

With reference to probation, the shape that the CRP took was much influenced by the accumulating findings on effective methods of reducing criminal recidivism; by a review of research conducted internally by the Home Office (Vennard, Sugg and Hedderman 1997) and by a review of practice commissioned by the Inspectorate of Probation (Underdown 1998). The decision to identify, develop, validate and disseminate a series of structured offending behaviour programmes, to be known during their pilot phase as Pathfinders, flowed from the findings of these reviews (Ellis and Winstone 2002).

The nature of programmes

McGuire (2001, 2004) has defined programmes as essentially consisting of a planned sequence of learning opportunities. The typical programme incorporates a pre-arranged set of activities, with clearly stated objectives, so entailing a number of elements interconnected in a suitable design. The closest parallel to this in other settings is that of a curriculum in a school or college. The way this is done is also documented so that it can be reproduced on other occasions, enabling practitioners at other sites to deliver it in more or less the same way – or to modify it to suit varying recipients or different circumstances.

Programme manuals

Hence a key feature of most programmes currently in use is the provision of a manual or collection of materials informing or directing how the programme should be used. There is a widespread view that the presence of a manual means that programme contents become ossified and their delivery deteriorates into a dull, rigid and potentially sterile activity. However, as McMurran and Duggan (2005) have noted, manuals can be of various types with different levels of specification contained within them. Some are very prescriptive, to the extent of providing tutors with exact textual instruction to be read at specific points during sessions. Others are more flexible and allow for varying amounts of adaptation and innovation by practitioners; for example, to adjust materials to the needs of different user groups, an important aspect of responsivity. In mental health, Kendall *et al.* (1998) illustrated how there can be intrinsic creativity within a therapeutic manual in the amelioration of anxiety problems amongst children. Duncan, Nicol and Ager (2004) used Delphi technique to survey practitioners on their perceptions of the features of good intervention manuals. Among the most highly rated 'essential' characteristics were that the manual be appropriate for the problem addressed; that its content be coherent and focused, that it should provide illustrations of difficult points and that it should be based on a clear theoretical model.

Hollin (2006) has forwarded several reasons why programmatic or manual-based interventions have become widely propagated, and reviews the advantages that probably led to this. First, the availability of a structured manual provides an invaluable resource for staff training, including that of non-specialist 'front-line' staff. This in turn affords a second, economic advantage, in allowing a larger number of service users or participants to be accessed; especially through using group programmes. Third, by clarifying the nature of the work to be done, a 'manualised' approach allows opportunities to monitor integrity of delivery and treatment adherence. Fourth, the preceding reasons then make the process of evaluation considerably easier. Overall, the presence of a manual clarifies the kind of activity in which participants are being engaged, and facilitates communication concerning it.

Programme accreditation

In England and Wales, Scotland, Canada and elsewhere, criminal justice agencies have set up processes for the validation or *accreditation* of intervention programmes – much as similar bodies exist to ensure quality control and other features of training schemes in industry, or degree programmes in higher education.

The Correctional Services Accreditation Panel in England and Wales and the Accreditation Panel for Offender Programmes in Scotland are specialist advisory groups of independent experts whose role is to scrutinise programme proposals and judge their suitability for use in probation or other settings. A key procedure for doing this is the publication of criteria for accreditation, evolved through practice, feedback and review. Those applicable to probation programmes in England and Wales are summarised in Table 9.2. Within the systems of accreditation that have been established in some jurisdictions, the manualisation referred to above is an indispensable element in gaining programme approval. The availability of a manual makes explicit what a programme involves (at least it ought to!), and greatly facilitates decision-making over its quality and suitability for use.

Table 9.2: Correctional Services Accreditation Panel: Accreditation criteria

1. The programme is based on a clear, explicit model of change

2. There are clear and appropriate selection criteria

3. Materials and methods target a range of dynamic risk factors

4. The programme entails use of demonstrably effective methods of intervention

5. Methods focus on the acquisition and development of relevant skills

6. There are clear, explicit links between sequencing, intensity, and duration of components

7. Methods used will engage and motivate participants

8. The programme is integrated with other aspects of service provision

9. Provision is made for monitoring integrity

10. Provision is made for ongoing and outcome evaluation

At the time of writing, several programmes for probationers have been success-fully endorsed through this format. The National Probation Service *Interventions News* published in April 2005 refers to 'a suite of 19 high quality accredited programmes' (Home Office 2005a, p.1). These programmes are conventionally divided into two groups. The first comprises 'general' programmes designed to address a range of standard types of offence, where participants are likely to have exhibited versatility in their criminal records with no type of offence predominat-ing. Others are focused on 'specific' offences such as substance abuse, drunk driving, acquisitive crime, violence, domestic violence, racially motivated offending and sexual offending. Several programmes have also been accredited for use in prisons (for a full list, see Lewis 2005).

To provide a brief overview, the compilation of programmes available for pro-bationers as of August 2006 is presented in Table 9.2. In what follows, each programme will be briefly described; the information has been collated from various sources including published reports, programme manuals in some instances, and web pages of the National Offenders Management Service.

General programmes

Most of the general offending behaviour programmes in current use were initially accredited for use in prisons, as formal arrangements were first established in that setting (Lipton *et al.* 2000). All of these programmes are considered suitable for both male and female offenders.

REASONING AND REHABILITATION (RANDR)

The forerunner of many other programmes, RandR was developed in Canada and originally piloted in a probation-based experiment in Ontario, where participants had a lower reconviction rate and a lower re-incarceration rate than comparable groups, one attending life skills training, the other a "no-treatment" condition, at nine months follow-up (Ross, Fabiano and Ewles 1988). The programme was introduced to the UK via the STOP probation experiment in Mid Glamorgan in the early 1990s (Raynor and Vanstone 1996). RandR has reportedly since been used with more than 50,000 offenders in 17 countries and there are numerous outcome studies in both community and prison settings (Antonowicz 2005; Robinson and Porporino 2001). Indeed the volume of data is sufficient for the effects of RandR to have been incorporated in two meta-analytic reviews (Tong and Farrington 2006; Wilson, Bouffard and MacKenzie 2005). Further evaluative data will be presented below.

Table 9.3: Accredited offending behaviour programmes in current use (2006)

General programmes	Specific programmes

• Reasoning and Rehabilitation
• Enhanced Thinking Skills
• Think First
• One-to-One
• Black and Asian Offenders Module
• Cognitive Skills Booster
	• Drink-Impaired Drivers Programme
	• Addressing Substance-Related Offending
	• Programme for Reducing Individual Substance Misuse
	• Offender Substance Abuse Programme
	• Aggression Replacement Training
	• Cognitive Self-Change Programme
	• Integrated Domestic Abuse Programme
	• Community Domestic Violence Programme
	• Women's Acquisitive Offending
	• Racially Motivated Offending
	• Programmes for sex offenders:
	  – Thames Valley
	  – West Midlands
	  – Northumbria

While the exact format of RandR has evolved over the years, at present it consists of 38 two-hour sessions (Porporino and Fabiano 2000). There are several intervention targets, including interpersonal problem-solving, social skills, emotional self-management, creative thinking, critical reasoning and negotiation (Antonowicz 2005; McGuire 2006). The programme employs a mixture of different types of activity, including brief instruction, self-assessments, modelling, role-play, structured games, discussion and feedback; and each session comprises a balanced variety of exercises designed to sustain the interest of group participants. This format, which is central to achieving responsivity, has been emulated in many other programmes.

ENHANCED THINKING SKILLS (ETS)

This programme was developed as a shorter, modified version of RandR with fewer 'targets of change' and condensing materials into 20 two-hour sessions (Clark 2000). Since its inception it has become the most widely used programme in prisons in England and Wales; for example, during 2003–4 it was run in 89 prisons (Cann *et al.* 2003) and it is also implemented in many probation areas. There are several outcomes studies of prison samples, usually jointly with RandR, with respect to both psychometric change (Blud and Travers 2001) and post-release recidivism (see below). Evaluation data for probation settings remains more limited but ETS has been included in the Pathfinder evaluation to be described below.

THINK FIRST

This programme was initially developed for use by probation teams providing alternatives to custody, though later a parallel version was designed for use inside prisons. The community version entails a combination of individual and group formats (McGuire 2000). There are four initial one-to-one sessions each lasting an hour, followed by 22 two-hour group sessions, and a subsequent series of six individual hour-long sessions focused on self-risk management, amounting to a total of 54 hours of contact time. The programme differs from most others described here in containing sessions and exercises in which participants explicitly analyse their own criminal acts, first individually and then collectively in the group, using an adapted form of functional analysis (McGuire and Priestley 1985). After accreditation in 2000 the programme was 'rolled out' to 31 probation areas and it has been the most widely used of the general group programmes within community sentences; outside the UK it is employed in four Australian states. There have been short-term psychometric evaluations in both prisons and probation (McGuire 2005b; McGuire and Hatcher 2001) and effects on recidivism have been evaluated in probation settings (Roberts 2004a; Steele 2002 and see below).

ONE-TO-ONE

As its title suggests, the programme has a unique status as the first manualised general intervention designed explicitly for use on an individual basis (Priestley

2000). The materials were designed for use in providing a highly structured form of face-to-face supervision, taking participants through a sequence of exercises designed to impart skills (problem-solving, social interaction, self-control) similar to those targeted by the group programmes, but located in the context of the case manager-probationer dyad. There is one pre-programme session followed by 20 sessions each lasting 1–1½ hours. The programme places a greater emphasis on the use of 'homework' assignments and application of self-monitoring procedures. Outside the UK it is extensively used in Scandinavian countries. To date the completion rate of the programme has shown wide variability and it has proved difficult to conduct a thorough evaluation of a cohort sufficient to draw conclusions regarding its recidivism outcomes.

BLACK AND ASIAN MODULE PATHFINDER PROGRAMME

Recognising that within community sentences specific issues may arise for black and Asian offenders, including personal histories of discrimination and racism that may be linked to offending, an additional module has been designed for use prior to participation in other general offending programmes. This consists of four sessions that enable participants to explore issues of cultural identity and experiences within the criminal justice system. Stephens, Coombs and Debidin (2004) have reported on the implementation of these sessions used as a preparatory module for Think First, but the findings of their study were in many respects inconclusive and the authors made several recommendations for further data collection. To date, no further specific information is available on the extent of implementation of this module or evaluation of how it is perceived by participants.

COGNITIVE SKILLS BOOSTER

This programme possesses another kind of uniqueness: it is exclusively designed as a follow-up for the four basic general offending programmes just described, simul-taneously acting as a kind of refresher course and morale-raiser while serving relapse prevention purposes. The rationale derives from evidence that 'booster' sessions can preserve therapeutic effects beyond a period when they might otherwise have dissipated. A process evaluation of its delivery in 14 probation areas (and 12 prisons) found that the programme was valued by probationers, though they noted that the materials were more suited to those who had attended ETS than the other three programmes (Dawson, Walmsley and Debidin 2005). These authors have advocated fuller evaluation using a randomised controlled trial, though in doing so it may prove difficult to avoid multiple-treatment interference effects (Cook and Campbell 1979).

Specific programmes

In addition to the materials just outlined, the current portfolio also includes a range of accredited programmes for individuals whose criminal histories show a preponderance of one specific type of offence. While most of the programmes are suitable for both women and men, few are designed for male or female offenders only, according to the prevalence of certain types of offending.

ADDRESSING SUBSTANCE-RELATED OFFENDING (ASRO)

There are three programmes focused on substance abuse, of which at present ASRO is the most widely disseminated. It consists of 20 sessions of 2½ hours duration each, which address an inter-related series of issues including motivation to change, identification of personal risk factors, self-monitoring and management of moods, and relapse prevention through development of a non-drug lifestyle. The programme combines general cognitive-behavioural methods with those that have been specifically developed for work in the addictions field (McMurran and Priestley 2004).

PROGRAMME FOR REDUCING INDIVIDUAL SUBSTANCE MISUSE (PRISM)

PRISM is an individualised variant of ASRO, containing similar materials but employing design elements akin to those used in the One-to-One programme, with which it is also closely associated. The programme applies a problem-solving model to enable individuals to analyse difficulties they are facing that may be linked to their offending. They then set targets for self-change, and develop skills required for achieving them with particular reference to the reduction of substance misuse and of offending. The length of the programme may vary from 10 to 20 sessions depending on individuals' needs.

OFFENDER SUBSTANCE ABUSE PROGRAMME (OSAP)

More recently, a third programme has been devised for work on drug-related offending. OSAP comprises a series of five modules, totalling 26 2½ hour sessions, and employs methods broadly similar to those applied in ASRO and PRISM, with additional material on social skills. No formal evaluation has been reported to date.

DRINK-IMPAIRED DRIVERS PROGRAMME (DIDS)

DIDS is distinctive in that it was the first accredited programme to be developed internally by probation practitioners (from the South Yorkshire Probation Service).

To date, it is also the one that has invariably achieved the highest completion rates (for 2004–5: 89%); however, participants generally have discernibly lower risk of reconviction scores than those allocated to other programmes. DIDS is designed for men aged 17 and over with a current offence of drink-driving, particularly where there have been previous similar offences, and there are aggravating features such as involvement in an accident or a particularly high blood alcohol level. The programme consists of 14 sessions each lasting 2½ hours and is based partly on an educational model, though it also includes exercises focused on problem-solving skills and on attitude change.

WOMEN'S ACQUISITIVE CRIME (WAC)

Designed for female offenders with a pattern of acquisitive offending, this programme applies motivational interviewing techniques to issues associated with emotional self-management and interpersonal relationships. It consists of 31 two-hour sessions delivered over a period of between 11 and 16 weeks. No outcome evaluation has been reported to date.

AGGRESSION REPLACEMENT TRAINING (ART)

Initially developed in the US for work with young offenders (Goldstein, Glick and Gibbs 1998), this programme has been adapted into a number of formats and disseminated in a wide range of locations in many countries (Goldstein, Nensén, Daleflod and Kalt 2004). In its probation-based version adapted by practitioners in Wiltshire Probation Service it comprises five individual sessions run by case managers, followed by 18 two-hour group sessions distributed over a period of 6–12 weeks. Its content consists of four intercalated modules respectively focused on attitudes and beliefs, perspective taking, interpersonal skills and self-control. There is initially positive outcome evidence from a 12-month follow-up of the Wiltshire programme (Sugg 2000; and see McGuire and Clark 2005), and in other probation areas as part of the Pathfinder Evaluation Project (Hatcher *et al.* submitted 2007).

CONTROLLING ANGER AND LEARNING TO MANAGE IT (CALM)

This is a variant form of anger management programme, designed for individuals with a pattern of reactive (angry or emotional) aggression (as contrasted with instrumental aggression, where the behaviour is intended to accomplish other goals). There is substantial evidence in favour of the effectiveness of these types of interventions with a wide range of groups (see McGuire 2004 for a brief overview).

However in the light of some disappointing outcomes with adult prisoners, other authors (e.g. Howells and Day 2003) have argued for careful modulation of assessment and selection procedures, taking account of 'readiness to change'. CALM entails 24 sessions of 2–2½ hours delivered over a flexible period that may vary from 8 to 24 weeks.

The prison-based version of the programme unfortunately became engulfed in adverse publicity when it emerged that Damien Hanson, a man with a considerable history of violence who had attended CALM and reportedly gained from it while in prison, subsequently committed a particularly brutal murder in the course of an armed robbery, while under parole supervision. These events caused enormous alarm and controversy, and a report by the Inspector of Probation was highly critical of the arrangements made for Mr Hanson's discharge and supervision (HM Inspectorate of Probation 2006). Despite ensuing press reports that all such programming had been 'axed', CALM has however been maintained in prisons. Its continued use has been vigorously defended by one of the Canadian psychologists who developed it (Winogron 2006), on the grounds that it was not intended or expected to reduce the type of aggression that Damien Hanson displayed.

COGNITIVE SELF-CHANGE PROGRAMME

This is a very intensive programme designed for work with high-risk offenders who have committed serious assaults. The programme follows a modular format and the larger proportion of it, Blocks 1 to 5, is delivered in prison, with group sessions covering a lengthy period of potentially up to 17 months, followed by individual sessions until the end of sentence. Then, depending on the outcomes of risk assessment, Block 6 may be provided to individuals supervised on parole licence by the probation service. This is focused on skills practice and application of a relapse prevention plan. The programme is based on the work of Bush (1995) in prisons in Vermont, which was evaluated by Henning and Frueh (1996) who found significant reductions in re-offending on a two-year follow-up.

DOMESTIC VIOLENCE PROGRAMMES

Two principal intervention are now used to address this type of offending; they are respectively the Integrated Domestic Abuse Programme (IDAP) and the Community Domestic Violence Programme (CDVP). Both are intended for use with heterosexual male domestic violence offenders. The former was developed as a successor to earlier programmes such as the Duluth model, and allied approaches that applied a conjunction of feminist and cognitive-behavioural principles, also addressing masculine self-concepts. Evaluation of these programmes produced very encouraging outcomes (Dobash *et al.* 2000; Scourfield and Dobash 1999). IDAP involves 27 two-hour sessions run at weekly intervals followed by 13 individual sessions, with a range of intervention targets that include the develop- ment of respect and trust; establishment of non-violent and non-threatening behaviour; work on responsible parenting and training in negotiation skills. CDVP is a slightly shorter programme that was imported to the UK from Correctional Services Canada; the core elements comprise 25 group and 9 individual sessions. The direct delivery of both these programmes is supplemented by co-ordinated inter-agency work focused on risk assessment and management, and contact with and monitoring the safety of spouses who have been victimised.

Bilby and Hatcher (2004) have reported a process evaluation of the transition between the earlier and later models. Initially, the Duluth programme was site-tested in two probation areas only (London and West Yorkshire). IDAP was awarded full accreditation in 2004, and as of mid-2005 was reportedly being used in 34 probation areas, and CDVP at the same time-point used in eight areas. While a recent meta-analytic review suggests that on average only modest effects have been obtained from interventions for domestic violence (Babcock, Green and Robie 2004) those described are nevertheless clinically meaningful and valuable.

PROGRAMMES FOR SEX OFFENDERS

Given the complexity of risk factors associated with sexual offending, the perceived intractability of the behaviour and the extreme concern to which this type of offending gives rise, these programmes are more intensive than those used for most other offence 'specialisms'. They typically require at least a hundred hours of contact, and often far more, corresponding to an offender's assessed level of risk. Research on sexual offending has shown the necessity of addressing a wide range of treatment targets. Moreover, such work places additional demands on therapists and tutors (Marshall *et al.* 2006). Hence, alongside the greater time commitment, the structure and contents of these programmes are more elaborate than most of the others described in this chapter and, like domestic violence programmes, may include adjunctive work with offenders' partners.

There are three programme variants used in different regions of England and Wales. Working from south to north, they are respectively the Thames Valley, West Midlands and Northumbria programmes. The decision to retain and develop all three was based on an assumption that comparative evaluation would at some stage allow a choice to be made between them (Home Office 2002), but this no longer appears to be expected. A recent meta-analysis has confirmed earlier positive findings on the effects of treatment in reducing this type of offending (Lösel and Schmucker 2005). At the time of writing a further programme is in development for internet-related offending (National Offender Management Service 2006).

RACIALLY MOTIVATED OFFENDING

While this programme has been under discussion for some time and is understood to be at an advanced planning stage, no specific information concerning its contents or methods, or planned implementation, was available at the time of writing.

Selection, participation, attrition, completion

Allocation to offending behaviour programmes is based on assessment of suitability which focuses on both risk levels and on criminogenic needs. Levels of risk have customarily been assessed using the *Offender Group Reconviction Scale* (Version 2: OGRS-2; Copas and Marshall 1998), an instrument developed by the Home Office Research, Development and Statistics Directorate. The scale was derived from analysis of patterns of conviction and sentencing among a large sample of offenders serving a range of both custodial and community penalties. The OGRS-2 has demonstrated a high level of predictive validity over a period of two years with sizeable offender populations (Lloyd, Mair and Hough 1996). It also compares favourably with other prediction methods in follow-up of offenders with mental disorders (Gray *et al.* 2004).

In addition to risk levels, there is also assessment of factors influencing an individual's pattern of offending, using semi-structured interviews and psychometrics. The overriding objective of assessment is to examine the extent to which an individual exhibits a cluster of criminogenic needs which alongside his or her offence history indicates suitability for a particular accredited programme. Progress on programmes and the extent to which such dynamic risk factors have changed during participation is subsequently evaluated by means of a set of parallel measures (National Probation Service 2004).

All of this information is now consolidated in a formal appraisal process entitled the *Offender Assessment System* (OASys: National Probation Service 2002), which is also electronically based, and as from March 2006 secured connectivity between all probation areas, and also with the Prison Service. The assessment procedure is based on extensive survey work with offenders and analysis of risk/needs profiles (Howard 2006) and in addition to providing the information necessary for programme allocation, OASys also yields predictions of the risk of serious harm. From a different perspective, O'Beirne, Denney and Gabe (2004) have suggested that the use of OASys has exposed the degree to which probation staff may themselves be at risk in conducting assessments with some offenders.

Both the numbers of referrals and the numbers of probationers successfully completing offending behaviour programmes have steadily increased since their arrival as potential additional requirements in probation orders. Their growth has been charted in successive Annual Reports on Accredited Programmes and other documents, which show 19,868 completions during the year 2006–7 (National Probation Service 2006a). Although the target figures have been rising robustly, they are still low compared to numbers on Unpaid Work (previously Enhanced Community Punishment, Community Service Orders, now 're-badged' as Community Payback) which during 2005–6 stood at 55,437 (National Probation Service 2007). According to a *Hansard* parliamentary written answer on 22 May 2006, the numbers of commencements on drug or alcohol rehabilitation programmes in community sentences during 2005–6 were as follows: for DIDS, 4665; for ASRO, 2943; for OSAP, 928.

Delivery and management

Implementing the kinds of changes in practice such as the above and on the scale required by the CRP has represented a mammoth undertaking for the probation service. At national and area levels it has necessitated a massive investment in training, the pivotal importance of which is perennially obvious and has been underlined by a recent meta-analysis (Dowden and Andrews 2004). The role of probation officers in supervising offenders has altered considerably, and numerous additional tasks have arisen, associated with the programmes enterprise. Local areas have had to address internal organisational issues, such as communication between case managers and programme delivery teams, and extra responsibilities such as collecting and recording data for monitoring integrity of delivery have posed further challenges and in many instances led to rapid and sometimes uneasy re-adjustment of priorities. Process evaluation of the opening stages of delivering programmes revealed the complexity of the demands that were placed on probation staff (Hollin *et al.* 2002).

To compound the situation, the inauguration of Pathfinder programmes was accompanied by several types of administrative change occurring in parallel. Judging by numerous comments made throughout that period, this resulted in con-siderable confusion and uncertainty, and ultimately, it is alleged, in a decline in working morale among criminal justice professionals. The causes to which this has been attributed are numerous and include: the reduction in the number of probation local areas; centralisation of management in the National Probation Service; what was felt by many to be a concentration of resources into its headquarters; the implementation of numerous other components of the CRP, forging many changes in day-to-day practice; an almost continuous programme of legislative change, both leading up to and issuing from the Criminal Justice Act 2003; integration with the prison service and establishment of the National Offender Management Service; associated fears of being 'swallowed up' by a larger and more powerful agency.

The outstanding problem that has faced the implementation of offending behaviour programmes themselves has been the very large proportion of offenders who have failed to commence them despite being mandated to do so, together with a comparably high rate of attrition from programmes after commencement. The axiomatic outcome is completion rates for programmes that have been disappointingly low, particularly so in the period just after their initial inception. In 2001 the average completion rate across programmes stood at only 37 per cent. However, completions have risen in consecutive years to an average of 68 per cent in 2005 (National Offender Management Service 2005), and considerable efforts continue to be expended to maintain and amplify those improvements. A closely associated issue is that of geographical unevenness: as annual reports have shown, there has been significant variation in programme completions across the 42 probation areas.

Several studies have been conducted at local area level to investigate the factors influencing attrition, for example, in Northumbria (Westmarland *et al.* 2002), West Yorkshire (Turner 2006), in a study of Think First across three probation areas (Roberts 2004b), and another study of several programmes conducted across five areas (National Probation Service 2006). One initial hypothesis was that the materials contained in the programmes required a literacy level that was too high for many participants and, following research into this, a series of recommendations has been made and implemented (Davies *et al.* 2004). However, most studies suggest that non-commencement and non-completion of programmes is frequently due to factors that are not a function of the programmes themselves: arising instead, for example, from events in individuals' lives that detract from their ability to maintain attendance; organisational difficulties (programmes unavailable at appropriate times) or levels of case management support. Various 'barriers to attendance' accumulate for many offenders and to the extent that they do so early on in programme attendance the likelier it is that an individual will not complete. Inevitably a proportion of non-completion is also due to non-compliance, and the reasons for that also warrant further investigation (Turner 2006). The majority of the direct feedback obtained from participants in offending behaviour programmes is positive in tone and many endorse the use of the programmes and cite examples of personal benefits of participation.

Despite numerous drawbacks of these and other kinds, there has been a steady consolidation in the usage and delivery of programmes and massive efforts have been undertaken to sustain the process. Developments at national level are communicated through Probation Circulars and other bulletins such as *Interventions News* (a successor to *What Works* news from April 2005). Programme delivery at area level is also supported by an extensive network of telephone contacts in the Offending Behaviour Programmes Team, and a telephone helpdesk. With reference to the background research, it is indisputable that the process of implementation was badly marginalised in previous work (Gendreau, Goggin and Smith 1999). Much better guidance is now available on the pitfalls of transferring results from research into practice (Bernfeld, Farrington and Leschied 2001).

International context

The UK is by no means the only location where programmes of the type discussed here are in use in probation services. A questionnaire-based survey conducted by the Home Office for the National Probation Service (Home Office 2005b) has shown that in recent years such programmes have been applied in several other countries.

As this was an exploratory study, questionnaires were sent to countries 'that were English speaking or were likely to have a good command of English' (p.1); this included several countries in Europe, plus Australia, New Zealand, the US and South Africa. On the basis of initial expressions of interest, 24 jurisdictions were approached, and 14 returned questionnaires. Replies were received from Belgium, Denmark, Finland, the Netherlands, Norway, Portugal, Sweden, two US states (Arizona, North Carolina), three Australian states (Capital Territory, Tasmania, Western Australia), and New Zealand. Several other locations where it is known programmes are used unfortunately did not respond. Offending behaviour programmes were defined as employing a cognitive-behavioural approach, which may have excluded interventions grounded in other theoretical frameworks.

Arizona reported the widest range of programme types, with 18 focused on substance abuse alone, bringing its total portfolio of programmes to 24. England and Wales, however, remained the most prolific user of the programmes, judged in terms of numbers of offenders required to attend, presumably a function of the impact of the Crime Reduction Programme. During 2004–5, programme orders exceeded 35,000 as compared with the next highest, the US state of North Carolina with 4569 offenders mandated. However, the completion rate in England and Wales was lower than elsewhere; though these data were available for only a few countries. Many of the issues raised by respondents, concerning referral processes, delivery problems, attrition, staff training, resource provision and associated matters were common across all jurisdictions.

Recent evaluations

The evidence briefly outlined earlier shows that cognitive-behavioural approaches emerge from many reviews as most frequently producing the largest effect sizes. The effectiveness of the approach has also been specifically tested in five meta-analyses (Landenberger and Lipsey 2005; Lipsey, Chapman and Landenberger 2001; Lipton *et al.* 2002; Tong and Farrington 2006; Wilson, Bouffard, and MacKenzie 2005), yielding effect sizes that are larger than for educational, vocational and related interventions (Wilson, Gallagher, and Mackenzie 2000). Fuller information is given by McGuire (2006).

A series of four follow-up evaluations has been published from the large-scale use of programmes in prisons in England and Wales. However, the findings have been variable and the overall pattern somewhat discouraging with regard to their impact on recidivism. In an initial study, 667 participants in RandR and ETS between 1992 and 1996 were compared with 1801 non-participants matched on a number of relevant variables. Two years following release there was a 14 per cent reduction in reconviction among medium-low-risk offenders, an 11 per cent reduction among medium-high-risk offenders and a 5 per cent reduction among high-risk offenders across the two programmes. The overall effect was highly significant (Friendship *et al.* 2002). However, analysing two-year reconviction rates for a later cohort, Falshaw *et al.* (2003) found no significant differences between treatment and comparison samples. Subsequently Cann *et al.* (2003) reported programme outcomes for both adult and young offenders, finding only small (though significant) reductions in recidivism for those completing programmes at a one-year follow-up, but no difference at two years. In a later study with women prisoners Cann (2006) found no statistically significant differences in reconviction rates between programme and comparison groups, but added that given relatively low risk levels, and poor targeting of criminogenic needs, the participants might not have been suitable for the programmes. None of these studies gives information on the timing of delivery of the programmes, and if attendance occurred some time before release it is feasible that initial beneficial effects may have diminished or been undermined by other influences.

The most extensive outcome study of probation-based programmes to date is the Pathfinder Evaluation Project which has reported recidivism rates for samples of participants over variable follow-up periods up to 18 months (as a function of programme delivery schedules within the research study period). These studies have found significant effects on recidivism for those completing programmes across several of the interventions described above, including RandR, ETS, Think First, ART and DIDS. The study also encompassed evaluation of other offence-specific programmes, but the numbers completing were in some instances insufficient for the testing of intervention effects.

The evaluation of general programmes was conducted in two phases (retrospective and prospective), the first analysing data on 2141 probationers allocated to RandR, ETS or Think First across 16 probation areas during 2001; the second, 2409 from 15 probation areas similarly allocated during 2002. The comparison group consisted of a random sample of 3305 offenders given community sentences during 2001 and 2002 without a requirement to attend an offending behaviour programme. In both studies data for those who attended all programme sessions and those who did not do so were first of all analysed in combination, forming an 'intent-to-treat' experimental study. The groups were also disaggregated, and analysis conducted separately for those who completed programmes, those who commenced but failed to complete, and those who did not even commence, constituting a 'treatment received' study. As the groups were non-equivalent (and not randomly allotted to treatment conditions), statistical controls were employed to take account of prior differences, most importantly in risk levels for future offending as measured by the OGRS-2.

With respect to recidivism a similar pattern of findings was obtained across all three programmes in both studies. Direct comparisons between each experimental group as a whole and the control sample showed a higher rate of recidivism amongst the former. However, the predicted reconviction scores for those allocated to programming were significantly higher than for the controls in both cohorts.

When these prior differences between the samples were taken into account through the use of multivariate analysis, the results of both studies showed that participants who completed a general offending behaviour programme were significantly less likely to be reconvicted relative to non-completers and the comparison group (in the retrospective study, by 3.4 %; in the prospective study, by 38.7%). Those who did not complete were considerably more likely to be reconvicted relative to completers and the comparison group (Hollin *et al.* 2005; Hollin *et al.* 2004; Palmer *et al.* 2007). This type of evaluation cannot dismiss a possible explanation of the results in terms of prior inter-group differences: notably in motivational levels or readiness to change. However, these evaluations were conducted during the early phase of implementation when completion rates for programmes were very low. Alongside other research, the marked increase in completions since then suggests that programme commencement and sustained attendance was much more a factor of organisational than of intrinsic individual factors.

There are also positive findings for some of the specific programmes included in the Pathfinder evaluation. For the DIDS programme, completers were significantly less likely to be reconvicted than the comparison sample and non-completers, with respective reconviction rates of 13 per cent, 29 per cent and 44 per cent. Reductions were observed in drink-driving offences but were non-significant. Equivalent results have been obtained from a separate, internal evaluation by the Offending Behaviour Programmes team (National Probation Service 2006). For ART, an outcome evaluation using one-to-one matching between experimental and comparison groups showed that programme completers were 13 per cent less likely to be reconvicted (Hatcher *et al.* forthcoming). However, this was based on a fairly small sample size and follow-up was feasible over a ten-month period only.

Some researchers remain cautious and wary of overinterpreting the data from these studies, and unresolved issues remain about the findings from practice-based evaluation of the probation programmes. Disagreements revolve around the usage of different research designs – randomised controlled trials (RCTs) as opposed to quasi-experiments in which groups cannot be regarded as equivalent; and different types of analysis – 'intention-to-treat' in which all drop-outs are included, versus 'treatment received' in which completers, non-completers and comparison samples are analysed separately.

In consequence Home Office researchers (Debidin and Lovbakke 2005; Friendship and Debidin 2006) regard the majority of the results to date as merely promising at best, and some observers are only likely to be convinced to the contrary through evidence gained from RCTs. It would clearly be advantageous were some RCTs to be carried out, and the ethical and legal aspects of such work could be made manageable. But this research design also poses challenges with regard to translating results into messages for practice, as has been repeatedly found in research on psychotherapy (Aveline, Strauss and Stiles 2005). Lipsey (1999) has noted that while the results of 'practical programmes' may often appear less satisfactory than those obtained from 'demonstration programmes' (i.e. strictly controlled experimental evaluations), the latter lack external validity and still leave unanswered the question of how to decipher findings and implement services in the 'real world' of criminal justice. Similarly other researchers such as Sherman (2003) have argued that the findings of quasi-experiments can be sufficiently valid both to test theory and to furnish valuable guidance for service delivery.

Conclusion: Debates and controversies

The usage of offending behaviour programmes has been the subject of a high level of criticism and controversy. Among other things it has been argued, first, that the evidence base is much less substantial than enthusiasts claim, indeed it is highly suspect. Second, it has been contended that the overemphasis on offenders' thinking and other factors at the individual level *ipso facto* means excluding and thereby ignoring social, cultural, economic and political forces that are the main influences on crime. Third, it is claimed that 'cognitive-behaviouralism' neglects diversity: the use of structured programmes coerces individuals into a 'one-size-fits-all' approach; a drawback that is particularly nefarious with reference to gender and ethnicity.

Regrettably space does not permit detailed coverage of these points in the present chapter. For discussion of the disputes arising from the use of different research designs, interpretation of results and associated scientific questions, see Hollin (2006). Concerning the general impact of programmes, Raynor (2004b) compares various competing explanations for disappointing results, while elsewhere (Raynor 2004a) he rectifies some inaccurate impressions concerning the use of evidence in probation. With reference to other apparently widespread mis-conceptions regarding programmes, both in terms of the ideas behind them, how they have been received, and cultural resistance to them, see McGuire (2005c).

Whether any of the kinds of interventions described here can have a discernible impact on the national crime statistics is fairly doubtful. But to raise the prospect that any form of tertiary prevention can succeed in doing so is almost certainly unrealistic. Some years ago Tarling (1993) convincingly demonstrated the limits of incapacitation through imprisonment for reducing the overall rate of crime. His calculations showed that to achieve a reduction of just 1 per cent in the crime rate in England and Wales, the prison population would have to increase by 25 per cent. Temporal variations in crime rates on a societal level are probably a function of other large-scale factors such as demographic change, or fluctuations in the avail-ability of different kinds of goods. Recently Garside (2006) has argued that the capacity of governmental action to manage the rate of crime through the penal system is severely limited, and that it would be more valuable if ministers were to help the public to understand this, rather than offering futile promises that something meaningful can be done about it.

None of these circumstances, however, detracts from the importance of working with people who have been convicted of crimes, or of retaining the reduction of re-offending as an objective with them. It is surely one of the purposes of social work to address that issue – in contemporary jargon we might call it 'social inclusion' – for the sakes both of those individuals themselves, and of the communities of which they remain a part.

References

Andrews, D.A. (1989) 'Recidivism is Predictable and can be Influenced: Using Risk Assessments to Reduce Recidivism.' *Forum on Corrections Research 1*, 11–18.

Andrews, D.A. (2001) 'Principles of Effective Correctional Programs.' In L.L. Motiuk and R.C. Serin (eds) *Compendium 2000 on Effective Correctional Programming*. Ottawa: Correctional Service Canada.

Andrews, D.A., and Bonta, J. (2003) *The Psychology of Criminal Conduct* (3rd edn). Cincinnati, OH: Anderson Publishing.

Andrews, D.A., Bonta, J., and Hoge, R.D. (1990) 'Classification for effective rehabilitation: Rediscovering psychology.' *Criminal Justice and Behavior 17*, 19–52.

Andrews, D.A., Zinger, I., Hoge, R.D., Bonta, J., Gendreau, P. and Cullen, F.T. (1990) 'Does correctional treatment work? A clinically relevant and psychologically informed meta-analysis.' *Criminology 28*, 369–404.

Antonowicz, D.H. (2005) 'The Reasoning and Rehabilitation Programme: Outcome evaluations with offenders.' In M. McMurran and J. McGuire (eds) *Social Problem Solving and Offending: Evidence, Evaluation and Evolution*. Chichester: John Wiley and Sons.

Aveline, M., Strauss, B. and Stiles, W.B. (2005) 'Psychotherapy research.' In G.O. Babbard, J.S. Beck and J. Holmes (eds) *Oxford Textbook of Psychotherapy*. New York, NY: Oxford University Press.

Babcock, J.C., Green, C.E. and Robie, C. (2004) 'Does Batterers' Treatment Work? A Meta-analytic Review of Domestic Violence Treatment.' *Clinical Psychology Review 23*, 1023–1053.

Bandura, A. (2001) 'Social Cognitive Theory: An Agentic Perspective.' *Annual Review of Psychology 52*, 1–26.

Bernfeld, G.A., Farrington, D.P., and Leschied, A.W. (eds) (2001) *Offender Rehabilitation in Practice: Implementing and Evaluating Effective Programmes*. Chichester: John Wiley and Sons.

Bilby, C. and Hatcher, R. (2004) *Early Stages in theDdevelopment of the Integrated Domestic Abuse Programme (IDAP): Implementing the Duluth Domestic Violence Pathfinder*. Online Report 29/04. London: Home Office.

Blud, L. and Travers, R. (2001) 'Interpersonal Problem-solving Skills Training: A Comparison of RandR and ETS.' *Criminal Behaviour and Mental Health 11*, 251–261.

Bottoms, A., Rex, S. and Robinson, G. (2004) 'How did We get Here?.' In A. Bottoms, S. Rex and G. Robinson (eds) *Alternatives to Prison: Options for an Insecure Society*. Cullompton: Willan Publishing.

Bush, J. (1995) 'Teaching Self-risk-Management to Violent Offenders.' In J. McGuire (ed.) *What Works: Reducing Reoffending: Guidelines from Research and Practice*. Chichester: John Wiley and Sons.

Cann, J. (2006) *Cognitive Skills Programmes: Impact on Reducing Reconviction Among a Sample of Female Prisoners.* Findings 276. London: Home Office Research, Development and Statistics Directorate.

Cann, J., Falshaw, L., Nugent, F., and Friendship, C. (2003) *Understanding What Works: Accredited Cognitive Skills Programmes for Adult Men and Young Offenders.* Research Findings No. 226. London: Home Office Research, Development and Statistics Directorate.

Clark, D.A. (2000) *Theory Manual for Enhanced Thinking Skills.* Prepared for the Joint Prison-Probation Accreditation Panel. London: Home Office.

Cook, T.D. and Campbell, D.T. (1979) *Quasi-Experimentation: Design and Analysis Issues for Field Settings.* Chicago, IL: Rand McNally.

Cooper, H. and Rosenthal, R. (1980) 'Statistical Versus Traditional Procedures for Summarising Research Findings.' *Psychological Bulletin 87,* 442–449.

Copas, J., and Marshall, P. (1998) 'The Offender Group Reconviction Scale: A Statistical Reconviction Score for Use by Probation Officers.' *Applied Statistics 47,* 159–171.

Davies, K., Lewis, J., Byatt, J., Purvis, E. and Cole, B. (2004) *An Evaluation of the Literacy Demands of General Offending Behaviour Programmes.* Findings 233. London: Home Office Research, Development and Statistics Directorate.

Dawson, P., Walmsley, R.K. and Debidin, M. (2005) *A Process Evaluation of the Cognitive Skills Booster Programme Initial Roll-out in 14 Probation Areas and 12 Prisons.* Home Office Online Report 41/05. London: Home Office Research, Development and Statistics Directorate.

Debidin, M., and Lovbakke, J. (2005) 'Offending Behaviour Programmes in Prison and Probation.' In G. Harper and C. Chitty (eds) *The Impact of Corrections on Re-offending: A Review of 'What Works'.* Home Office Research Study 291, 2nd edn. London: Home Office.

Dobash, R.P., Dobash, R.E., Cavanagh, K. and Lewis, R. (1996) *Re-education Programmes for Violent Men – An Evaluation.* Research Findings No. 46. London: Home Office Research and Statistics Directorate.

Dowden, C., and Andrews, D.A. (2004) 'The Importance of Staff Practice in Delivering Effective Correctional Treatment: A Meta-analytic Review of Core Correctional Practice.' *International Journal of Offender Therapy and Comparative Criminology 48,* 203–214.

Duncan, E.A.S., Nicol, M.M. and Ager, A. (2004) 'Factors that Constitute a Good Cognitive Behavioural Treatment Manual: A Delphi study.' *Behavioural and Cognitive Psychotherapy 32,* 199–213.

Ellis, T. and Winstone, J. (2002) 'The Policy Impact of a Survey of Programme Evaluations in England and Wales.' In J. McGuire (ed.) *Offender Rehabilitation and Treatment: Effective Programmes and Policies to Reduce Re-offending.* Chichester: John Wiley and Sons.

Falshaw, L., Friendship, C., Travers, R., and Nugent, F. (2003) *Searching for 'What Works': An Evaluation of Cognitive Skills Programmes.* Research Findings No. 206. London: Home Office Research, Development and Statistics Directorate.

Friendship, C., Blud, L. Erikson, M., and Travers, R. (2002) *An Evaluation of Cognitive Behavioural Treatment for Prisoners.* Research Findings No. 161. London: Home Office Research, Development and Statistics Directorate.

Friendship, C. and Debidin, M. (2006) 'Probation and Prison Interventions.' In A.E. Perry, C. McDougall and D.P. Farrington (eds) *Reducing Crime: The Effectiveness of Criminal Justice Interventions.* Chichester: John Wiley and Sons.

Garrett, C.J. (1985) 'Effects of Residential Treatment on Adjudicated Delinquents: A Meta-analysis.' *Journal of Research in Crime and Delinquency 22,* 287–308.

Garside, R. (2006) *Right for the Wrong Reasons: Making Sense of Criminal Justice Failure.* Monograph Number 2. London: Crime and Society Foundation.

Gendreau, P., Goggin, C. and Smith, P. (1999) 'The Forgotten Issue in Effective Correctional Treatment: Program Implementation.' *International Journal of Offender Therapy and Comparative Criminology 43*, 180–187.

Gendreau, P. and Ross, R.R. (1980) 'Effective Correctional Treatment: Bibliotherapy for Cynics.' In R.R. Ross and P. Gendreau (eds) *Effective Correctional Treatment.* Toronto: Butterworths.

Goldstein, A.P., Glick, B. and Gibbs, J.C. (1998) *Aggression Replacement Training: A Comprehensive Intervention for Aggressive Youth.* Rev. edn. Champaign, IL: Research Press.

Goldstein, A.P., Nerwen, R., Daleflod, B. and Kalt, M. (eds) (2004) *New Perspectives on Aggression Replacement Training.* Chichester: John Wiley and Sons.

Gray, N.S., Snowden, R.J., MacCulloch, S., Phillips, H., Taylor, J. and MacCulloch, M. (2004) 'Relative Efficacy of Criminological, Clinical, and Personality Measures of Future Risk of Offending in Mentally Disordered Offenders: A Comparative Study of HCR-20, PCVL:SV and OGRS.' *Journal of Consulting and Clinical Psychology 72*, 523–530.

Hatcher, R.M., Palmer, E.J., McGuire, J., Hounsome, J.C., Bilby, C.A.L., and Hollin, C.R. (submitted, 2007) *Aggression Replacement Training with Adult Male Offenders in Community Settings: A Reconviction Analysis*

Henning, K.R. and Frueh, B.C. (1996) 'Cognitive-behavioral Treatment of Incarcerated Offenders: An Evaluation of the Vermont Department of Corrections' Cognitive Self-Change Program.' *Criminal Justice and Behavior 23*, 523–542.

HM Inspectorate of Probation (2006) *An Independent Review of a Serious Further Offence Case: Damien Hanson and Elliot White.* London: HM Inspectorate of Probation.

Hollin, C.R. (ed.) (2001) *Handbook of Offender Assessment and Treatment.* Chichester: John Wiley and Sons.

Hollin, C.R. (2006) 'Offending Behaviour Programmes and Contention: Evidence-based Practice, Manuals, and Programme Evaluation.' In C.R. Hollin and E.J. Palmer (eds) *Offending Behaviour Programmes: Development, Application, and Controversies.* Chichester: John Wiley and Sons.

Hollin, C.R. and Palmer, E.J. (eds) (2006) *Offending Behaviour Programmes: Development, Application, and Controversies.* Chichester: John Wiley and Sons.

Hollin, C.R., McGuire, J., Palmer, E.J., Bilby, C., Hatcher, R. and Holmes, A. (2002) *Introducing Pathfinder Programmes into the Probation Service: An Interim Report.* Home Office Research Study No. 247. London: Home Office.

Hollin, C.R., Palmer, E.J., McGuire, J., Hounsome, J., Hatcher, R., and Bilby, C. (2005) 'An Evaluation of Pathfinder Programmes in the Probation Service.' Unpublished research report to the Home Office Research, Development and Statistics Directorate.

Hollin, C.R., Palmer, E., McGuire, J., Hounsome, J., Hatcher, R., Bilby, C. and Clark, C. (2004) *Pathfinder Programmes in the Probation Service: A Retrospective Analysis.* Online Report 66/04. London: Home Office.

Home Office (2002) *Working with offenders: Offending Behaviour Programmes.* Accessed on 20/04/07 at http://www.crimereduction.gov.uk/workingoffenders3.htm.

Home Office (2005a) *Interventions News 20.* London: National Probation Service for England and Wales.

Home Office (2005b) *International Survey of Community-based Offending Behaviour Programmes.* London: National Probation Service.

Howard, P. (2006) *The Offender Assessment System: An Evaluation of the Second Pilot.* Findings 278. London: Home Office Research, Development and Statistics Directorate.

Howells, K. and Day, A. (2003) 'Readiness for Anger Management.' *Clinical Psychology Review* 23, 319–337.

Kendall, P.C., Chu, B., Gifford, A., Hayes, C. and Nauta, M. (1998) 'Breathing Life into a Manual: Flexibility and Creativity with Manual-based Treatments.' *Cognitive and Behavioral Practice 5*, 177–198.

Landenberger, N.A. and Lipsey, M.W. (2005) 'The Positive Effects of Cognitive-Behavioral Programs for Offenders: A Meta-analysis of Factors Associated with Effective Treatment.' *Journal of Experimental Criminology 1*, 451–476.

Laub, J.H. and Sampson, R.J. (2001) 'Understanding Desistance from Crime.' *Crime and Justice: A Review of Research 28*, 1–70.

Lewis, C. (2005) 'Working for Community Justice: A Home Office Perspective.' In J. Winstone and F. Pakes (eds) *Community Justice: Issues for Probation and Criminal Justice.* Cullompton: Willan Publishing.

Lipsey, M.W. (1999) 'Can Rehabilitative Programs Reduce the Recidivism of Juvenile Offenders? An Inquiry into the Effectiveness of Practical Programs.' *Virginia Journal of Social Policy and the Law 6*, 611–641.

Lipsey, M.W., Chapman, G.L., and Landenberger, N.A. (2001) 'Cognitive-behavioral programs for offenders.' *Annals of the American Academy of Political and Social Science 578*, 144–157.

Lipton, D.S., Pearson, F.S., Cleland, C.M., and Yee, D. (2002) 'The Effectiveness of Cognitive-behavioral Treatment Methods on Recidivism.' In J. McGuire (ed.) *Offender Rehabilitation and Treatment: Effective Programmes and Policies to Reduce Re-offending.* Chichester: John Wiley and Sons.

Lipton, D.S., Thornton, D., McGuire, J., Porporino, F.J. and Hollin, C.R. (2000) 'Program accreditation and correctional treatment.' *Substance Use and Misuse 35*, 1705–1734.

Lloyd, C., Mair, G. and Hough, M. (1994) *Explaining Reconviction Rates: A Critical Analysis.* Home Office Research Study No.136. London: HMSO.

Lösel, F. and Schmucker, M. (2005) 'The Effectiveness of Treatment for Sexual Offenders: A Comprehensive Meta-analysis.' *Journal of Experimental Criminology 1*, 117–146.

Marshall, W.L., Fernandez, Y.M., Marshall, L.E. and Serran, G. A. (2006) *Sexual Offender Treatment: Controversial Issues.* Chichester: John Wiley and Sons.

Martinson, R. (1974) 'What Works? – Questions and Answers about Prison Reform.' *The Public Interest 10*, 22–54.

Martinson, R. (1979) 'New Findings, New Views: A Note of Caution Regarding Sentencing Reform.' *Hofstra Law Review 7*, 243–258.

McGuire, J. (2000) *Think First: Programme Manual.* London: National Probation Service.

McGuire, J. (2001) 'Defining Correctional Programs.' In L.L. Motiuk and R.C. Serin (eds) *Compendium 2000 on Effective Correctional Programming.* Ottawa: Correctional Services of Canada.

McGuire, J. (ed.) (2002) *Offender Rehabilitation and Treatment: Effective Practice and Policy.* Chichester: John Wiley and Sons.

McGuire, J. (2004) *Understanding Psychology and Crime: Perspectives on Theory and Action.* Maidenhead: Open University Press/McGraw-Hill Education.

McGuire, J. (2005a) 'Social Problem Solving: Basic Concepts, Research, and Applications.' In M. McMurran and J. McGuire (eds) *Social Problem Solving and Offending: Evidence, Evaluation and Evolution.* Chichester: John Wiley and Sons.

McGuire, J. (2005b) 'The Think First Programme.' In M. McMurran and J. McGuire (eds) *Social Problem Solving and Offending: Evidence, Evaluation and Evolution.* Chichester: John Wiley and Sons.

McGuire, J. (2005c) 'Is research working? Revisiting the research and effective practice agenda.' In J. Winstone and F. Pakes (eds) *Community Justice: Issues for Probation and Criminal Justice.* Cullompton: Willan Publishing.

McGuire, J. (2006) 'General Offending Behaviour Programmes: Concept, Theory, and Practice.' In C.R. Hollin and E.J. Palmer (eds) *Offending Behaviour Programmes: Development, Application, and Controversies.* Chichester: John Wiley and Sons.

McGuire, J. and Clark, D. (2004) 'A national dissemination program.' In A.P. Goldstein, R. Nensén, B. Daleflod and M. Kalt (eds) *New Perspectives on Aggression Replacement Training.* Chichester: John Wiley and Sons.

McGuire, J., and Hatcher, R. (2001) 'Offense-focused Problem-Solving: Preliminary Evaluation of a Cognitive Skills Program.' *Criminal Justice and Behavior 28,* 564–587.

McGuire, J. and Priestley, P. (1985) *Offending Behaviour: Skills and Stratagems for Going Straight.* London: Batsford.

McIvor, G. (1995) 'Practitioner Evaluation in Probation.' In J. McGuire (ed.) *What Works: Reducing Reoffending: Guidelines from Research and Practice.* Chichester: John Wiley and Sons.

McMurran, M. and Duggan, C. (2005) 'The Manualisation of a Treatment Programme for Personality Disorder.' *Criminal Behaviour and Mental Health 15,* 17–27.

McMurran, M. and McGuire, J. (eds) (2005) *Social Problem Solving and Offending: Evidence, Evaluation and Evolution.* Chichester: John Wiley and Sons.

McMurran, M. and Priestley, P. (2004) 'Addressing Substance-related Offending (ASRO).' In B. Reading and M. Weegman (eds) *Group Psychotherapy and Addiction.* London: Whurr Publishers.

National Offender Management Service (2005) *Annual Report for Accredited Programmes 2004–2005.* London: National Probation Directorate Interventions Unit, National Offender Management Service.

National Offender Management Service (2006) *Interventions: A Guide to Interventions in the National Probation Service.* London: National Offender Management Service.

National Probation Service (2002) *Briefing: Introduction to OASys.* London: National Probation Service.

National Probation Service (2004) *General Offending Behaviour/Cognitive Skills Programmes: Evaluation Manual and Scoring Supplement.* London: Home Office, National Probation Directorate.

National Probation Service (2006a) *Annual Report 2005–2006.* London: National Offender Management Service.

National Probation Service (2006b) *Interventions News: Special Edition.* London: National Offender Management Service.

National Probation Service (2007) *Bulletin (1 June 2007).* London: National Offender Management Service.

O'Beirne, M., Denney, D. and Gabe, J. (2004) 'Fear of Violence as an Indicator of Risk in Probation Work.' *British Journal of Criminology 44,* 113–126.

Palmer, E.J., McGuire, J., Hounsome, J.C., Hatcher, R.M., Bilby, C.A. and Hollin, C.R. (2007) 'Offending behaviour programmes in the community: The effects on reconviction of three programmes with adult male offenders.' *Legal and Criminological Psychology 12,* in press.

Porporino, F.J., and Fabiano, E.A. (2000) *Theory Manual for Reasoning and Rehabilitation, revised.* Ottawa: T3 Associates.

Priestley, P. (2000) *Manual for One-to-One Programme.* Prepared for the Joint Prison-Probation Accreditation Panel. London: Home Office.

Raynor, P. (2004a) 'Seven Ways to Misunderstand Evidence-based Probation.' In D. Smith (ed.) *Social Work and Evidence-Based Practice.*. London and Philadelphia: Jessica Kingsley Publishers.

Raynor, P. (2004b) 'The Probation Service 'Pathfinders': Finding the Path and Losing the Way?' *Criminal Justice 4*, 309–325.

Raynor, P. and Vanstone, M. (1996) 'Reasoning and Rehabilitation in Britain: The Results of the Straight Thinking on Probation (STOP) programme.' *International Journal of Offender Therapy and Comparative Criminology 40*, 272–284.

Roberts, C. (2004a) 'An Early Evaluation of a Cognitive Offending Behaviour Programme ('Think First') in Probation Areas.' *Vista: Perspectives on Probation 8*, 130–136.

Roberts, C. (2004b) 'Offending Behaviour Programmes: Emerging Evidence and Implications for Practice.' In R. Burnett and C. Roberts (eds) *What Works in Probation and Youth Justice: Developing Evidence-Based Practice.* Cullompton: Willan.

Robinson, D., and Porporino, F.J. (2001) 'Programming in Cognitive Skills: The Reasoning and Rehabilitation Programme.' In C.R. Hollin (ed.) *Handbook of Offender Assessment and Treatment.* Chichester: John Wiley and Sons.

Ross, R.R., and Fabiano, E.A. (1985) *Time to Think: A Cognitive Model of Delinquency Prevention and Offender Rehabilitation.* Johnson City, TN: Institute of Social Sciences and Arts, Inc.

Ross, R.R., Fabiano, E.A., and Ewles, C.D. (1988) 'Reasoning and Rehabilitation.' *International Journal of Offender Therapy and Comparative Criminology 32*, 29–36.

Scourfield, J.B. and Dobash, R.P. (1999) 'Programmes for Violent Men: Recent Developments in the UK.' *Howard Journal of Criminal Justice 38*, 128–143.

Sherman, L.W. (2003) 'Misleading Evidence and Evidence-led Policy: Making Social Science More Experimental.' *Annals of the American Academy of Political and Social Science 589*, 6–19.

Sherman, L.W., Farrington, D.P., Welsh, B.C., and MacKenzie, D.L. (eds) (2002) *Evidence-Based Crime Prevention.* London: Routledge.

Steele, R. (2002) 'Reconviction of Offenders on Think First.' Unpublished report, Research and Information Section, National Probation Service, Merseyside.

Stephens, K., Coombs, J. and Debidin, M. (2004) *Black and Asian Offenders Pathfinder: Implementation Report.* Development and Practice Report 24. London: Home Office Research Development and Statistics Directorate.

Sugg, D. (2000) 'Wiltshire Aggression Replacement Therapy (ART): One-year Reconvictions and Targeting.' Unpublished report, Research Development and Statistics Directorate, Home Office.

Tarling, R. (1993) *Analysing Offending: Data, Models and Interpretations.* London: HMSO.

Tong, L.S.J. and Farrington, D.P. (2006) 'How Effective is the "Reasoning and Rehabilitation" Programme in Reducing Re-offending? A Meta-analysis of Evaluations in Three Countries.' *Psychology, Crime and Law 12*, 3–24.

Turner, R. (2006) *Developing Understanding of Accredited Programmes Completion: The Role of Case-management and Barriers to Completion.* Research Section, National Probation Service, West Yorkshire.

Underdown, A. (1998) *Strategies for Effective Offender Supervision: Report of the HMIP What Works Project.* London: Home Office.

Vanstone, M. (2000) 'Cognitive-behavioural Work with Offenders in the UK: A History of Influential Endeavour.' *Howard Journal of Criminal Justice 39*, 171–183.

Vennard, J., Sugg, D. and Hedderman, C. (1997) *Changing Offenders' Attitudes and Behaviour: What Works?* Home Office Research Study No. 171. London: HMSO.

Westmarland, N., Hester, M., Reid, P., Coulson, S. and Hughes, J. (2002) *An Investigation into the Factors Associated with Attrition in the Northumbria Probation Think First Programme.* Sunderland: International Centre for the Study of Violence and Abuse, University of Sunderland.

Wilson, D.B., Bouffard, L.A. and MacKenzie, D.L. (2005) 'A Quantitative Review of Structured, Group-oriented, Cognitive-behavioral Programs for Offenders.' *Criminal Justice and Behavior 32*, 172–204.

Wilson, D.B., Gallagher, C.A., and MacKenzie, D.L. (2000) 'A Meta-analysis of Corrections-based Education, Vocation and Work Programs for Adult Offenders.' *Journal of Research in Crime and Delinquency 37*, 568–581.

Winogron, W. (2006) 'Anger Management has the Power to Rehabilitate Offenders.' Letter. *Guardian*, 2 May.

CHAPTER 10

Case Managing Offenders within a Motivational Framework

Frank Porporino and Elizabeth Fabiano

Introduction

Our attempts to translate evidence into practice in corrections have evolved rather strangely. To the chagrin of watchful critics (Farrall 2002; Mair 2004; Rex 2001), undeserved prominence has been bestowed on the delivery of 'appropriate' programmes, defined most commonly as interventions that are structured, apply cognitive-behavioural methods and focus on dynamic risk factors. We can speculate as to whether this takeover of correctional practice, caricatured easily as 'programme fetishism' (Her Majesty's Inspectorate of Probation 2002, p.8), was spurred on more by froth or substance, but clearly the 'What Works' paradigm, in some variation or other, has been legitimised and systematised by one jurisdiction after another over the last decade or so. Some credit certainly has to be given to the meta-analytic reviews for quantifying the notion that some sorts of things may work better than others when we are trying to intervene purposefully with offenders (Harper and Chitty 2004; McGuire 1995, 2002; Pearson *et al.* 2002; Sherman *et al.* 1997). But the momentum that can flow when pragmatism and optimism combine to give new direction to the field also has to be credited. Programmes are a very tangible thing, with a beginning and end, incorporating a set of identifiable and predictable methods and procedures, that are relatively easily quality controlled, and that can be organisationally standardised into an approach for managing offenders that brings visibility, focus and accountability to the aim of public protection. If there are programmes that work and we organise to deliver those programmes to as many offenders as possible, then we are doing our job.

Unfortunately, of course, we know that appropriate programmes also require appropriate delivery in an appropriate context, something exceedingly difficult to get right in any broad-based, real-world implementation (Harris and Smith 1996; Lipsey 1999; Van Voorhis *et al.* 2004). It is when we slip into formulaic application of these programmatic solutions, as if interventions had some inherent transformative power to create good citizenship, that a 'fix the offender' misconceptualisation of 'what works' is being pursued (Porporino 2004). This is at the crux of many of the critic's concerns but, curiously, though not acknowledged by the critics, it is also at the crux of the concerns expressed by many of its proponents (Gendreau, Goggin and Smith 1999, 2001; Porporino 1995, 2004; Raynor 2002; Underdown 2001; Vanstone 2000).

Timed for when they can make a difference, and targeted for whether they can, good delivery of quality programmes is quite obviously one piece of the assistance we might be able to provide individuals in helping them transition towards desistance. But 'What Works' was supposed to be about more than this. Stripped of the methods that might be applied, the paradigm is about how correctional practice can become a more deliberate force towards pro-social change for offenders.[1] As an underlying principle, the paradigm accepts the social-cognitive notion that in their 'exercise of self-influence' (Bandura 1989), offenders react out of the multiple, cumulative and interactive impact of both personal and social factors. At least partially, then, they are constructing the limitations of their situation by the way they see it. Effective practice with offenders is about helping them clarify these influences in their lives and equipping them to exercise some greater choice and control.

'What Works' concludes optimistically that we can help activate, accelerate and solidify some relevant change for offenders rather than merely waiting for that interest in change to emerge. It is not the one thing that we can do *to* offenders that will change them, it is how offenders might end up responding differently to problems, the options and strategies they might attend to, the resources and capabilities they might acquire, after they experience *all* of the things we do with them that *might* help them change. The operative notion here, of course, is that we are exposing them to a *process* of service delivery, implying some kind of interaction

---

1   Some would find exception with this very aim, suggesting that it is merely another instance of the neo-liberal agenda to responsibilise the individual offender. In its own way, this criticism grants the methods and techniques of 'what works' exaggerated power to fix offenders. It also refuses to acknowledge how 'social agencies of control' can possibly have any genuine motives for social inclusion and betterment of individual lives.

with individuals over the course of time, with multiple components, that work together to influence.

Creating an effective practice framework that is responsive to change, encouraging it to start, alert to noticing it when it begins, sensitive to mutually reinforcing ways of supporting it when it does, is supposed to have an underlying integrative theme to it. It is complicated by an ever present need to balance conflicting imperatives to protect (the public) and to serve (the offender). It begs the question as to whether an essentially coercive system can accommodate, or claim to be supporting, a non-coercive practice framework. It is challenging in the way it strains resources, requires skilled, human-service oriented staff and so heavily depends on timely accessibility to a range of community services that are at best spotty in their availability. And there is no escaping that this process, especially in the community context, cannot be made to come to life simply with more flexible, more refined or better targeted programmes and services. What will always underpin or undermine effectiveness is how we 'relate' with offenders throughout the process, what we refer to as case management.

Arguably, the case management of offenders is the Achilles heel of a 'What Works' aspiration for corrections. Case management is seen as something that needs to be and should be done well, but it is typically left unspecified as to what this actually means in practice. It is the glue that should work but that we haven't figured out exactly how to apply. Though there are expectations about what good case managers should be able to achieve, the process seems to take direction more from the agency culture and/or structures that are superimposed, or from the interpersonal style, rapport-building skills, dedication, resourcefulness, biases and personal perspectives of case managers. As a force of influence, any articulated theory or model of how to case manage offenders seems to pale in comparison. Indeed, arguments continue to be made for why even the extremes of traditional approaches to case managing offenders are entirely compatible with a 'What Works' paradigm.

For example, a simple 'support and assistance' aim falling out of the traditional casework model remains as the principal orientation for many aftercare agencies (Raynor 2004). Yet we know that such offers of support may only influence those with some pre-existing readiness to accept them (Prochaska and Levesque 2002). When faced with the resistance that we can expect from the majority of offenders, much of the time, the orientation will also tend towards premature withdrawal (not wishing to impose) or resort to ineffective convincing and persuading. A consequence is that there may be limited uptake of the assistance offered, which in turn discourages workers who are offering it, and further leads to labelling of offenders as unmotivated, untreatable and ungrateful. A simple motivational analysis of this dynamic offers a different interpretation. It would suggest that support and assistance should not be expected to be well received when it is mistimed (i.e. offered too soon), misapplied (i.e. to the wrong issue or concern), or misinterpreted by the caseworker (i.e., presented as a solution to a problem not acknowledged by the offender). Even if the assistance is temporarily taken up, it is just as easily let go when it no longer serves a purpose. So offenders may take employment assistance, seemingly willingly, but the job is then rejected in short order as not worth the effort.

At the other extreme is a continued articulation of offender case management as being most effective when it takes seriously the enforcement of conditions and sets clear, non-negotiable expectations for offenders to follow (i.e. objectives, action steps). Compliance becomes the indicator and measured focus of progress. The trap here, of course, is that significant numbers of offenders will boldly defy the perceived impositions (challenging the workers to do something about it when they know little can be done). Others may pretend they are trying while all the while keeping the worker at bay with rationalisations for their limited efforts. Still others may seem to be doing all that is expected, but knowing all along that this is rote effort being expended for the time being, simply because it is preferable to the alternative (i.e. a violation or breach). Again, a motivational analysis would suggest that simple monitoring or threat of enforcement, especially with a correctional clientele, may ensure some degree of compliance, but only temporarily or superficially. When the approach is escalated into becoming more confrontational or intrusive, it can itself become an additional aggravating factor towards re-offending. This has become clear in the indisputable failure of various intensive supervision and surveillance schemes (Gendreau, Goggin and Fulton 2000), yet the enhancing constraints approach in corrections predictably re-emerges with renewed vigour (Reinventing Probation Council 2000).

Administratively, case managers will always have to reconcile formal accountabilities and policy or standards-driven procedures, even if at times overwhelming and seemingly inconsistent. Agencies experience significant degrees of consternation when, in the hindsight of investigations of community incidents, it becomes apparent that policy was not adhered to. But articulation of case management policy, in whatever level of detail it may be provided, does not give any compelling underlying rationale for why offenders should be 'managed' as individuals in a particular way. The action of case management will always occur in the nature and sequencing of interactions that case managers have with offenders, and the performance measurement of administrative 'actions' or the refinement of case management guidelines and frameworks that agencies are preoccupied with will never fully ensure that these interactions unfold as they should. For that to happen we need a sound and integrated theory of case management that becomes the professions' standard, its identity and basis for training.

Form or function

If offenders are to be exposed to a meaningful process of supervision, we know that case managers will need to assess, plan and co-ordinate, support and reinforce, refer and broker, review and record and, if and as necessary, monitor and enforce. These are functions of case management that certainly deserve to be defined more clearly. They generalise across other areas of human service (Hasenfeld 1983). Within corrections, though, it is the fact that we are working with offenders that should give some specific form to these functions. For practitioners, the essential challenge of case management is 'relational', how do we get offenders to do what they need to do. For managers, on the other hand, the essential challenge becomes 'administrative', what structures and mechanisms do we put in place to ensure that staff will do what they need to do. Practitioners inevitably find the structures inflexible and the mechanisms burdensome. Managers keep trying to readjust in an effort to simplify and better focus the work that practitioners need to do. This fundamental dilemma characterises the history of efforts to derive the right case management model for corrections; we attempt to simplify the task of executing the 'functions' of case management by giving precise direction regarding what 'form' these should take with which offenders.

In the early 1980s, for example, the Client Management Classification System (CMC) was very actively disseminated as model practice by the US National Institute of Corrections.[2] It built on pioneering work in Wisconsin in developing offender risk/needs assessment (Baird, Heinz and Bemus 1979; Harris 1994) and sought to provide a practical, easily understood alternative to the various personality and/or cognitive development-based typologies that had emerged in the decade predating 'nothing works' (Megargee and Bohn 1979; Quay 1983; Warren 1983; Van Voorhis 1997). The CMC differentiated five offender profiles (Selective Intervention: 1. Situational or 2. Treatment, 3. Environmental Structure, 4. Casework-Control, and 5. Limit-Setting), wherein for each profile or

2   For a time, its popularity also spilled over into Canada where Correctional Service of Canada senior managers considered it an easy and sensible case management strategy. Seeing it as too simplistic and inflexible, field staff rejected it quickly.

grouping of offenders there was a certain matching with specific goals for treatment, types of programmes that should be relied upon and particular methods and approaches for supervision. A simple face valid typology with no real empirical grounding took hold as the case management fad of the decade and it has been estimated that about one quarter of probation/parole agencies that practice case classification in the US still adhere to the approach (Jones *et al.* 1999). A recent quasi-experimental test of this differential supervision model, controlling for risk and eliminating the possibility of contamination by studying cases in two geographically distinct areas, found that the experimental group showed similar or higher rates of rule violations and arrests. The authors conclude that if CMC practice had any effect, it was only in giving officers the 'appearance of favourable outcomes' (Harris, Gingerich and Whittaker 2004).

Our contemporary effective practice paradigm has given us a more empirically robust way to classify offenders; according to their level of risk and range of 'criminogenic' needs (Andrews and Bonta 1998). It was intended, and is clearly useful, to generally direct level of effort in working with offenders (and to caution practitioners that they should avoid the trap of working *most* with those offenders *easiest* to work with). The highest risk and greatest need offenders are the most likely to re-offend and we should concentrate and attempt to intensify our work with these offenders relative to those lower in risk and need. For case management, of course, it is straightforward to derive the axiom that service delivery should be structured so that 'resources follow risk/need'[3] (Grapes 2004). Various permutations of case management models can flow from this so that offenders can be managed consistent with their categorisation, as reflected, for example, in case-load formulas, development of specialist or team models of case supervision, elaboration of case management assistant roles, prioritisation for programming, etc. For the higher risk/need offenders, case management *ipso facto* becomes more intensive (i.e. greater frequency of contact), and since more needs implies more complexity of intervention, it is something which should be done by the most skilled or seasoned practitioners in situations where they can access more services and/or programmes. Since needs have to be addressed as soon as we identify them, arrangements are made to load a range of services and programmes to counteract risk at the front-end of supervision. And since length of sentence constrains how much effort we can deliver, we triage out those offenders where we forecast limited prospect for success.

---

3   Risk of harm is commonly added as another dimension to further specify and adjust the resource allocation philosophy.

In the terminology of a recent review of case management models in the UK (Partridge 2004), the 'drivers' of the effort become how to achieve consistency and make the best use of scarce staff resources in the unfolding of risk-minimisation strategies. When carried to an extreme, there may be some merits in the argument that this has created a new politics of punishment, transmuting the notion of *intervenable needs* into a new conception of risk (Hannah-Moffat 2005). But there is an effective practice argument to be made as well, since in striving to structure how we can perform the *functions* of case management more sensibly and efficiently, we can easily lose sight of the imperative to preserve its *form* as an effective interpersonal process.

The risk/needs framework speaks to focus but not to timing of intervention. It gives no guidance on how we should sequence our efforts to address *intervenable* needs. It suggests a general approach for working with offenders but doesn't prescribe particular methods for dealing with particular *intervenable* needs in given individuals. It does not claim, nor is there any evidence that might lead us to conclude, that the greater the number of *intervenable* needs the more complex the intervention plan should be.

When we try to define, *a priori*, which and how much of various functions case managers should do, with whom and when, case management models become more about pragmatics than process. We justify limits to practitioner discretion rather than highlighting ways to enhance it. We work under the illusion that we are trying to achieve efficiency but have no idea how much inefficiency this is breeding in the end as offenders fail to be engaged by the early and frequent intrusion of case management contact, reject and antagonise the services we attempt to have them access, and fail to attend or fail to complete the programmes they are assigned to.

Style and skill

It has been more than a quarter century since Andrews and Kiessling (1980) outlined the key dimensions under which we can subsume effective correctional practice. Importantly for practitioners the framework calls for an alert and consistent blending of *style* and *skill* in:

1. attending to their use of authority to clarify and enforce rules and requirements

2. promoting pro-social and counteracting anti-social sentiments and behaviours

3. problem-solving to help remove obstacles and reduce dysfunctional levels of personal distress (i.e. in dealing with community/interpersonal and emotional issues)

4. steady steering of individuals towards use of appropriate and supportive community resources

5. communicating and relating meaningfully (i.e., in an open, warm and enthusiastic way).

A recent meta-analysis of 273 studies found that the presence of these 'core correctional practices' was indeed related positively with outcome (Dowden and Andrews 2004).

In ethnographic studies of probation practice that are at least not apparently influenced by social learning conceptualisations (Bailey and Ward 1992; Ditton and Ford 1994; Rex 1999), the blending of style and skills that seems to emerge as *core* in importance is strikingly consistent. It includes:

•   a demeanour that shows sensitivity and understanding of the offender's perspective (without collusion)

•   an ability to negotiate active participation

•   an attuned sense of how offenders may tend to *react to and/or reject* what is proposed to them

•   focusing on encouraging the offender to arrive at sensible and reasonable conclusions (through analysis of their own decisions/thinking)

•   providing 'critical' and 'problem-solving' advice when it seems welcomed, but grounded in a 'demonstrated understanding of the offender's situation'

•   talking convincingly about the consequences of and alternatives to offending

•   providing encouragement that is perceived as genuine, coming from a desire for 'wishing you make a success of your life'

•   attending to promoting self-determination and change in the offender's 'self-identity and sense of maturity and responsibility'.

None of these descriptive studies were at all theoretically biased by the extensions and refinement of pro-social modelling principles with offenders (Trotter 1996, 2000) or by contemporary notions of 'motivational' practice for working with resistant clients (MCMurran 2002; Miller and Rollnick 2002; Prochaska and Levesque 2002). But the conclusions are clearly in line with both those perspectives as well.

The style and skills that are called for in case managing offenders are generally well understood. They should be applied to influence subtly and progressively so that effort towards pro-social change is sustained. Fundamentally, perceived coercion has to be transformed into perceived choice. It serves little purpose to debate whether what probation officers do has any relationship with whether offenders can overcome their obstacles to desistance (Farrall 2004). The fact that offenders are not always able to easily identify a relationship is no proof that one does not exist. Success of efforts to overcome difficult personal and social circumstances hinges on both the kinds of approaches we take and the supports we receive. Crystallisation of a new pro-social identity for offenders occurs over time. The aim in the end should be to have offenders self-attribute its primary cause (Maruna 2000), not necessarily to recognise the external influences that brought it about.

It needs to be acknowledged that many offenders will respond genuinely and positively to very simple avenues of assistance they might receive with community supervision. In motivational terms, though, this would be seen as occurring because they are already 'in readiness' for change. Effective case management should be a much more powerful force. It should do more that simply pick up on pre-existing readiness to change; it should awaken it, strengthen it and support is as necessary. While the field debates what truly matters in working with offenders, and positions are counterposed to exaggerate the differences, the truth may be that the same thing is being said much of the time, only in a different way, with some different emphasis. Interestingly enough, despite a growing evidence base for effective practice, it is disconcerting to note that we have perhaps made case management even more unclear and confusing for practitioners. An illustration with a brief case example may be helpful.

> Jonathan Q. is a 24-year-old serving his second probation term of 18 months for common assault and driving while impaired. He has a record of driving offences for which he was given fines or received community punishment and he has a prior assault for which he served six months probation. On this occasion, he assaulted his work supervisor for 'getting on his case' and was arrested for drunk driving after an evening at the pub commiserating with his mates. In his first meeting with his probation officer, he has a relatively friendly demeanour but announces that he has found new employment that suits him much better, is planning to get married and that he neither wishes to nor has the time to attend the Anger Management Programme that he was ordered to by the court.

Imagine you are the probation officer/case manager, relatively new to the job, who is struggling with how to respond to Jonathan Q. Your responsibility to get offenders into targeted accredited programmes, and the offender's supervision plan, suggest that you have to inform Jonathan Q. quite unequivocally to attend the next scheduled start of the Anger Management Programme regardless of whether that means asking for time away from his current employment. A focusing on desistance or 'good life' model would argue that forcing the offender to risk losing his employment is folly, especially for such an unproven intervention as a cognitive-behavioural treatment he seems to be so uninterested in pursuing. Adopting a pro-social modelling orientation might suggest that one should fairly immediately take on Jonathan's views that 'rich chaps get away with drunk driving because they have the money to hire a good solicitor'. And the motivational skills training seminar you just completed suggests that this offender is likely in pre-contemplation and needs to first admit and become aware that he has a problem if he is to benefit from any intervention. In the background, the advice of an experienced colleague who is informally mentoring you rings in your ear; always remember that if you give an offender an inch, they will ask for a yard. So what is our case manager to do?

An organising framework for case management

The case manager in the example should not feel torn or pulled between different evidence-based models of work with offenders. There is the possibility for a thoughtful and integrative case management response that capitalises on *style* and *skill* in:

1. case conceptualising

2. orchestrating desistance planning

3. contextual intervening

4. influencing pro-social consolidation.

A timeline for case management is depicted in Figure 10.1.

How long we might have to move from beginning to end of this process is, of course, constrained by sentence length, but shortcutting or accelerating is not likely to be successful. Indeed, it is what typically unravels the whole process (e.g. moving the offender too quickly into channelling action). The phases of the timeline have to tolerate a degree of elasticity. There is only one iteration of this process that we can help the offender pass through, and the focus should be to make it significant for the offender; not necessarily so multi-faceted so that they are required to deal with all of their problems but meaningful in helping them see 'why they should' and 'how they can'.

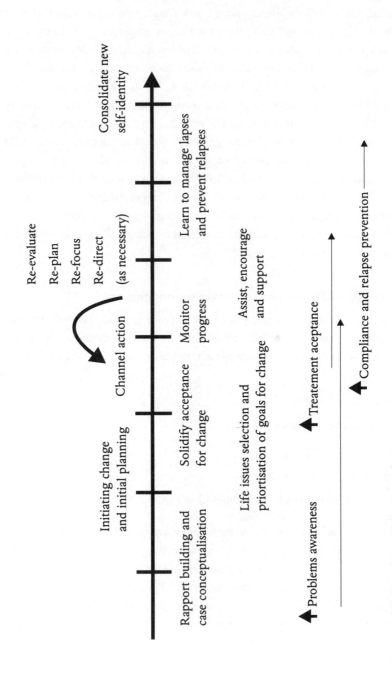

Figure 10.1 Timeline for orchestrating desistance planning

There are a few simple questions that underlie all human change (Egan 1998), and that the supervision process should help engender some answers to:

What are the problems I should be working on?	Issues, concerns, undeveloped opportunities
What do I need or want in place of what I have?	Aspirations, wishes, preferences
What do I have to do to get what I need or want?	Strategies for goal-accomplishing action
How can I make all this happen?	Moving from planning to action

At the heart of good case management is getting at the reasons for why offenders may not be *asking* or may not be *answering* these questions in the pro-social fashion we would like them to. It behoves us to look at the correlates of offending from every available perspective: dynamic risk (Andrews and Bonta 1998), social factors related to desistance (Farrall 2002; May 1999; Sampson and Laub 1993), a broader human agency and goal-seeking Good Lives Model (McMurran and Ward 2004; Ward and Stewart 2003), and our understanding of how the ebb and flow of motivational states to tackle problems might be influenced interpersonally (Fabiano and Porporino 1999; Lopez Viets, Walker and Miller 2002).

The following is an attempt to outline what it might mean to 'case manage' offenders within this sort of organising framework.

Case conceptualising

It should be easier to work with the individual offender if we understand why he or she offends. If we ask them we may get their theory, which may have some validity, but undoubtedly will be coloured by their view of the world, themselves and the person asking the question. If we derive our own theory too quickly or too narrowly, we can seriously bias the nature of our response. As competent case conceptualisers, case managers need to exercise their expertise, as a starting point for supervision, to develop an explicit parsimonious understanding of offenders and their problems that can effectively guide intervention. It should be evident that case managers need the time to do this (i.e. before a supervision plan is set) and that it requires seeing the offender as more than the sum of their criminogenic risk factors. It has to encompass, as well, an appreciation of the offender's goals, motives

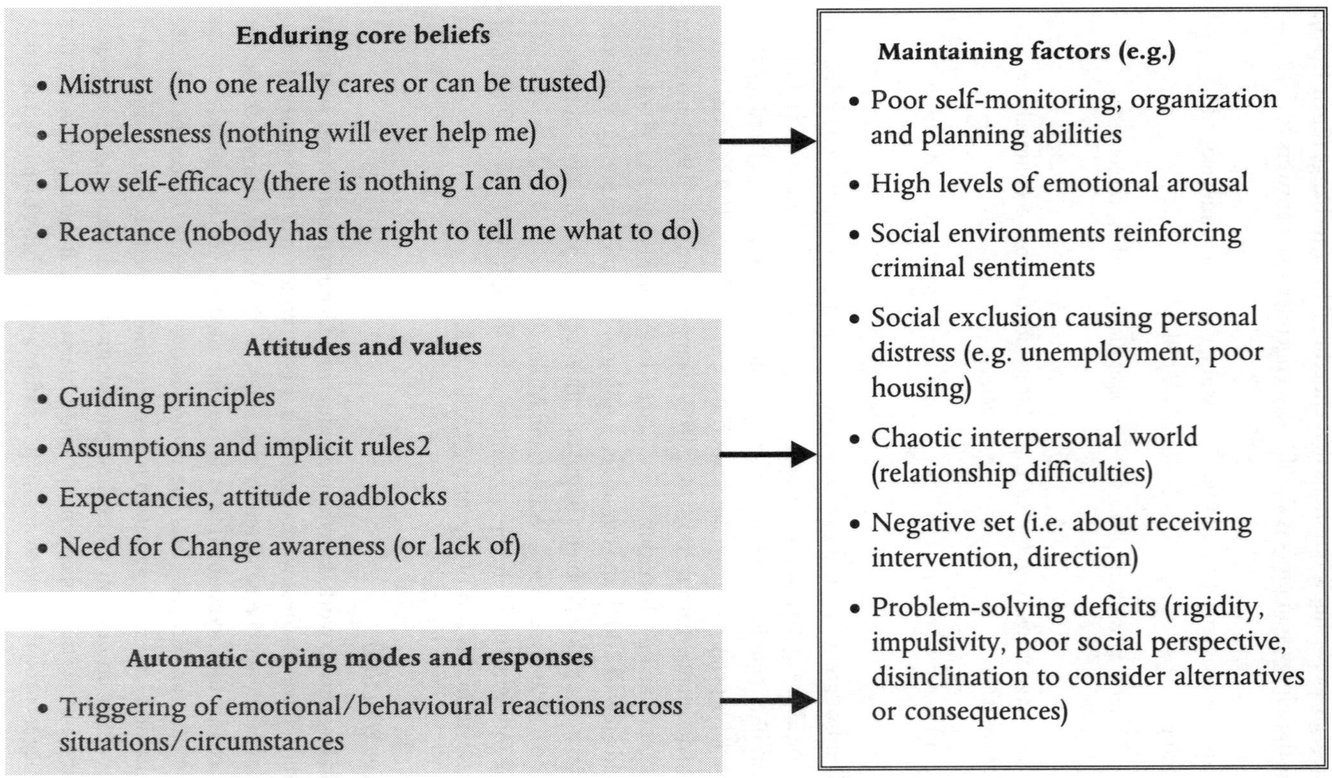

Maintaining factors (e.g.)

- Poor self-monitoring, organization and planning abilities
- High levels of emotional arousal
- Social environments reinforcing criminal sentiments
- Social exclusion causing personal distress (e.g. unemployment, poor housing)
- Chaotic interpersonal world (relationship difficulties)
- Negative set (i.e. about receiving intervention, direction)
- Problem-solving deficits (rigidity, impulsivity, poor social perspective, disinclination to consider alternatives or consequences)

Enduring core beliefs

- Mistrust (no one really cares or can be trusted)
- Hopelessness (nothing will ever help me)
- Low self-efficacy (there is nothing I can do)
- Reactance (nobody has the right to tell me what to do)

Attitudes and values

- Guiding principles
- Assumptions and implicit rules2
- Expectancies, attitude roadblocks
- Need for Change awareness (or lack of)

Automatic coping modes and responses

- Triggering of emotional/behavioural reactions across situations/circumstances

Figure 10.2 Case conceptualising offenders

and expectations, as it relates to the supervision experience and their life more generally (Needleman 1999; McMurran and Ward 2004).

Borrowing some social-cognitive terminology, just for purposes of illustration, Figure 10.2 describes how we might go about conceptualising the factors that may be operating as obstacles to change for the offender; the individual's core beliefs, their attitudes and values supportive of crime, coping modes and patterns of response to distress, and the range of both external and internal forces impinging on current behaviour.

Taken together, these are the influences that may be keeping the offender stuck, either unwilling to consider the need for change or unable to see themselves negotiating it with any success (Lopez Viets *et al.* 2002). Though there is certainly a considerable amount of personal data to elicit, process and integrate, it is in attempting to do so, patiently and without inquisition, that we can arrive at a tentative model for understanding:

1. how the offender experiences and reacts to the world

2. the inter-relatedness of problems linked to offending

3. the attitude roadblocks that may have to be overcome so they can accept putting effort into changing

4. the timing, sequencing and nature of services and interventions that might help.

The starting point for this is that we listen to their perspective and not try to impose our own from the onset. We listen for any expressed interest in change to assess where the offender may be positioned motivationally and how much acknowledgement of problems they may have developed. We listen, without judgement, for why they may see their behaviour as necessary, to achieve what primary goals, in giving them what sorts of satisfactions or rewards. We listen for rehearsed rationalisations and justifications, attempting to determine as best we can what the supporting core beliefs and attitudes might be. We listen as well, of course, for concerns and/or feelings of ambivalence (i.e. that not all may be fine). In short, we prepare to help the offender build a case for change by attempting to understand how well elaborated, how clear or how blocked their own personal case for change might be.

Though intuitively practitioners will accept the notion of crime as seductive (Katz 1988), routinely they also express some degree of frustration (or exasperation, puzzlement) at having to deal with so many offenders who 'don't want to do anything to help themselves'. It is as if there was an obvious reality that all offenders should be aware of, that change is necessary and in their best interest. Ward's Good Lives Model (Ward and Stewart 2003) is insightful in reminding us that offenders, like us all, are striving to satisfy some primary human needs. He summarises the difficulties they can encounter as falling out of the:

1. *means* used to secure these needs

2. lack of *scope* or coherence in their overall life plan

3. *conflict* among goals

4. lack of the *capacities* or skills to adjust to changing life circumstances.[4]

Another way to reformulate this is that offenders may be prone to confuse their 'wants' and 'needs', often behaving in ways that forego their basic and longer-term needs in satisfying their more immediate wants (which is clearly also a dispositional feature or dynamic risk factor).

Motivational theorists suggest that problem awareness will give momentum to change only when individuals see problems as:

- *necessary to deal with* (i.e. the costs of not dealing with the issue or problem are seen as outweighing the costs of change)

- *important to deal with* (i.e. triggered by a discrepancy in values or desires between how things are and how they would like them to be; the benefits or rewards of change are seen as outweighing the comforts of the status quo)

---

4   Though it is sensible to assume that with offenders there is goal-directed pursuit of the same array of human needs as us all, the Good Lives Model does not account for what may be propelling offenders, in particular, into anti-social trajectories. The dynamic risk model gives us a predictive level of explanation for criminal behaviour and tries to clarify how some individuals, with a particular mix of dispositional traits, exposed to a complex interplay of circumstances and experiences, can be propelled towards rejecting conventional norms and developing anti-social sentiments that underpin anti-social lifestyles (Andrews and Bonta 1998; Farrington 1997; Sampson and Laub 1993; Porporino and Fabiano 1999; Zamble and Quinsey 1997). The GLM is a complimentary descriptive level of explanation that tells us what kind of distortions in goal-directed behaving may be characterising anti-social conduct. The dynamic risk model tells us how this originates and what may be maintaining it. Both models can assist in helping us redirect offenders towards pro-social living.

- *where resolution is within their reach* (i.e. triggered by self-efficacy expectations or confidence about personal and other resources for handling the issue).

The motivational enhancement techniques of seeding doubt or creating dissonance, raising concerns and/or removing obstacles in tipping the balance towards change, and working to increase self-efficacy all hinge on our ability to get a full sense of what the offender 'thinks and feels'. They are techniques that rely on our insights about what may be most relevant for the individual offender.

The essential aim for case conceptualising is to decipher offending behaviour patterns, from the offender's subjective though still rational optic, but informed also by our analysis of dynamic risk factors, impinging and exerting their toll often without awareness (e.g. impulsivity, emotional reactivity, poor problem-solving, criminal thinking distortions and neutralisations, etc.). As the grounding for case management, we need to conceptualise critical information for the individual offender regarding:

1. problem 'un-awareness', how much of it there may be and with relevance to what issues

2. what exploration of conflict in needs or values, or what compelling rationale of self-interest, might help create more urgency about change

3. what enhancement of personal 'capacities' and what changes in immediate circumstances might be key to reducing risk of re-offending (both in the immediate and medium to longer-term)

4. what supervision-resistant and supervision-interfering factors will have to be dealt with (i.e. thoughts, feelings and behaviours)

5. what tolerable level and type of initial expectations and contingencies should be put in place as external controls.

This is the material that should inform and support the next phases of the process.

Orchestrating desistance planning

This is essentially about creating collaboration with the offender where they begin to gain greater clarity about *their* plan for change, the steps required and the level of effort *they* accept as necessary, the outcomes *they* realistically wish for, and the refocusing of new actions that *they* come to see as important.

Most probation practitioners appreciate the notion of 'therapeutic alliance' as it applies to working with offenders. The difficulty, of course, is that when we *know* so clearly what offenders should be doing, it is terribly difficult to resist telling them. So for, example, we tell offenders they *should* be looking for employment, *should* be getting assistance from a local employment agency, *should* stop giving excuses about lack of transportation (they can work on this later), and *should* settle for whatever job they can get, at least in the beginning. If an offender has participated in some cognitive-behavioural intervention then they might be told as well that they *should be* 'problem-solving' rather than rationalising or justifying. Offenders who seem to be unwilling to take concrete action in dealing with risk factors and resettlement issues, despite the fact that they may have participated in some intervention, are seen as needing *more* intervention. Case management with offenders is clearly vulnerable to the 'righting' reflex (Miller and Rollnick 1991, 2002), perhaps in part because there are so many apparent issues to right. But desistance planning may lose momentum in direct proportion to how much imposition offenders might experience.

Orchestrating a sustainable desistance plan with offenders requires a steady and focused emphasis. It involves applying the right skills and techniques to garner movement, issue by issue, from 1. problem awareness, to 2. treatment acceptance to 3. compliance and relapse prevention (Fabiano and Porporino 2003, 2004). Importantly, however, the process is not sequential. Depending on the key risk issue or social factor being dealt with, the work of case management may have to help bolster:

- movement from 1 to 2, e.g. in dealing with an outstanding anger problem

- movement from 2 to 3, e.g. in controlling an ongoing alcohol problem

- staying in 3, e.g. in keeping the offender on track in retaining employment.

Key areas of need should be seen by offenders as personal goals and projects. Working on resolving too many things all at the same time is difficult and overwhelming. Some prioritising is essential. Again, though, a motivational approach means we take steps to actively involve the offender in this process so they can accept any sorting, classifying or redefining and reframing of goals as their own. We have had some success in this regard by encouraging offenders to visualise or 'plot' the relationships between resettlement goals rather than simply listing or ranking them (Fabiano and Porporino 2003). Figure 10.3 illustrates such a plotting. Goals are related in one of three ways:

1. Importance: the space or distance between the goals with the most important laid in the centre (the bulls-eye) and the least in the outer most ring of a target.

2. Clustering: describing which goals might be able to be addressed at the same time with the same means (e.g. learning to control one's temper should help us to 'get along better with partner' and 'not have so many fights with friends').

3. Enabling: when achieving one goal will lead, and may be a prerequisite, to achieving another.

Plotting by both relationship and importance

The offender would work on goal 1, then 3 [by doing so would also accomplish 5 and 6] and then 4 which would enable him/her to achieve 7, and then when possible 2.

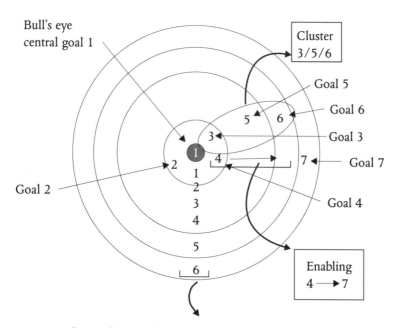

Traditional way of indicating 'Importance' of goals

The offender would work on all goals one after another and it might appear as though it will never end. If there is more personal or emotional valence attached to goals that are ranked lower in priority, the individual might conclude they are not doing what they 'want' or 'think' they should'…which increases resistance talk and possible 'failure'. They give up because…'it is too much…it is not working…nothing every works anyway'!

Figure 10.3: Goals sorting and plotting (Source: Porporino and Fabiano 2005).

Working in a reflective listening mode, the aim in the process is to alternate fluidly between helping offenders refine their vague wishes into SMART goals Specific, Meaningful, Achievable, Realistic and Timely, and helping them notice relationships they may not have been sensitive to. Discussion of goals is turned into a motivational way of communicating priority. Ambivalence about tackling some issues can be dealt with by clarifying how dealing with one thing before another can be more beneficial and in some instances easier than at first envisioned. Including positive approach goals the offender aspires to can add to conviction. Asking them to consider and take account of those strategies that may not have worked for them in the past adds to self-efficacy. And arriving at a coherent picture of how their goals might fit within a broader life plan should help reduce distress, anxiety or fear about implementation (Emmons 1999; McMurran and Ward 2004).

It is certainly true that compliance with the basic conditions of a probation order (e.g. attending appointments with the case manager) may come about in response to constraint or coercion, habit, calculation of self-interest or moral obligation (Bottoms 2001). There needs to be a constant organisational tuning into the balance and force of incentives and disincentives that operate on offenders. Orchestrating a desistance plan, however, is about the interpersonal influence we can have on offenders in 'choosing' to do the right things. A level of comfortable compliance has to be engendered in order to allow case managers to pursue the ongoing work of reinforcing/supporting action. At times even simple gestures may make a considerable difference. It has been noted, for example, that reminder calls or a structured calendar can double the number of aftercare sessions that problem drinkers might attend (Intagliata 1976). At other times, offenders may need to get themselves over and past some critical tough spots, periods of emotional turmoil that clearly relate to risk of re-offending (Zamble and Quinsey 1997). Alertness and flexibility are needed to case manage the ups and downs that normally accompany change, and skill in responding appropriately when the issue might require:

1.   a resolution of some hesitation or ambivalence (where it could be a matter of simply reminding the offender of the reasons they started all of this and showing them the gains made so far)

2.   the removal of an emerging obstacle for the offender (where there may be need for an adjustment or modification in the 'plan for change')

3.   contending with a slip or relapse (where there may be a need to revisit concerns and highlight benefits for change, build greater self-efficacy, learn

to anticipate and avoid high-risk situations, monitor and challenge negative self-talk, and build a strong network of supports and positive influences).

Contextual intervention

In a Correctional Service of Canada consultation report on ways to improve the community reintegration of offenders, a refreshingly honest reference was made to the fact that 'individual PO/client contacts are not being acknowledged as structured clinical contacts ... parole officers have become dispatchers' (Correctional Service of Canada 1999, p.34). In every jurisdiction, as availability of intervention options rises, community case management can easily deteriorate into a simple dispatching or brokering function.

Contextual intervention implies that we are trying to get a good sense of what type of programme, service, support or counselling approach may be needed (and will make most sense to the offender) at what point in that 'desistance planning' timeline we have been referring to. The aim should be to achieve a steady improvement in the offender's life context and our 'case conceptualising' of the individual should lead us to ask what is it that he/she needs most to stabilise, settle down a bit, become more optimistic about their future? In view of this offender's present life context, and what seems to have blocked them in the past, what little success or victory might they need at this juncture to move forward?

Case managing as contextual intervention should not restrict itself to simply 'boosting' or reinforcing treatment gains from other interventions, be it by reminding offenders of what they should have learned, rehearsing it over again or asking them how they are applying it in real life. Remaining aware of the offender's current 'motivational state', appropriate strategies should be applied to help give formal interventions (i.e. programmes) some greater power of influence. In the beginning, if there is 'ambivalence' in accepting the treatment pathway being offered, there may be need to explore whether lack of motivation or lack of self-efficacy may be underpinning it (Fabiano and Porporino 1999). Offenders may have had a history of unsuccessful treatment experiences or believe that other less intrusive and bothersome ways to deal with their problems may be just as effective. They may harbour doubts about their own ability to learn or master any new 'thinking or behaving' skills. Brief but focused exploration of the right concerns may move them forward.

As the formal treatment pathway proceeds or is completed, different strategies for reinforcing effort and action need to be put in place. The case manager who is contextually intervening not only looks for opportunities to reinforce but also has to create conditions and suggest approaches wherein offenders learn to *self-reinforce*. Prochaska and Levesque (2002) have outlined some of the motivational matching strategies that can be used with offenders under ten broad categories. They range from consciousness-raising techniques to help offenders become more aware of the 'causes, consequences and cures for a particular problem', approaches that might move offenders emotionally, self-reevaluation techniques (e.g. self-narratives), and a range of behavioural and social-learning techniques such as contingency management and stimulus control to increase the likelihood that healthier, positive behaviours are given more opportunity to emerge.

The effect of sequencing in services and interventions is relatively unexplored and needs to be taken much more seriously. Stacking of programmes, for example, originates in the notion that dynamic risk factors can be segmented into broad areas or 'domains', and some sort of formal intervention may be required to tackle or eliminate each, one by one, sometimes with repetitions of dose. In a substance abuse programme evaluation we conducted a few years ago (Porporino *et al.* 2002), it was found that when a prison-based cognitive-behavioural intervention was followed through with a community 'booster' type intervention, there was a statistically significant additive effect. But the additive effect occurred as well, and was actually even more pronounced, when offenders followed through on their prison-based cognitive-behavioural intervention with self-help AA/NA type support. This type of pro-social peer support, though not an accredited intervention, may be the counter-influence that matters, especially within the chaotic life contexts of some offenders who may be moving in some ways towards change, but who may still be gravitating towards their anti-social networks for more underlying, self-validating feedback. Interestingly, in a recent survey of substance-abuse clinicians and counsellors working within the cognitive-behavioural tradition (Laudet 2003), it was noted that these professionals were much less enthusiastic about encouraging their clients to attend AA/NA support groups, even though they acknowledged that this sort of support might be beneficial!

Case management practice has to progress to understanding how we can 'lever' change for offenders where with some effective case work together with other supportive influences, an unravelling of risk factors can begin to occur, and a whole range of dynamic risk factors are impinged upon meaningfully. We have to begin to pay more than lip service and seriously explore how other settings and contexts, the work or educational setting, the pro-social support group, the mentor relationship, our own probation offices…etc. can become places for generalising, intertwining and solidifying the change experience for offenders into their real lives.

Influencing pro-social consolidation

An offender says 'I've taken anger management twice and I know about self-talk and all that…it just doesn't help when I get angry'. This encapsulates the central failing of cognitive-behavioural methods, especially in working with offenders who are particularly emotionally volatile. We teach them self-management and other skills, but we do not manage to tap into their underlying schemas and self-protective motives that keep spiralling them to react maladaptively. Angry offenders, for example, are not typically looking to learn skills but rather are:

1. seeking advice on how to change others

2. wanting to vent about being the targets of unfairness at the hands of others

3. looking for verification that others are indeed deserving of the anger they elicit.

In group-work, these anger-related beliefs turn easily into resistance and/or withdrawing and, when challenged, can be perceived by the offender as invalidating their personal experience. So any learning that occurs is not personalised or deeply absorbed. To breakthrough more powerfully and credibly, the message giver may have to display certain characteristics, and be able to deliver the message in a more trusting interpersonal relationship, where the offender decides it may be worth self-disclosing meaningful and sensitive information. Case managers may be the only persons in the offender's life who might be able to do this. There is an untapped knowledge base in social psychology on the characteristics of credible 'message givers' (Moskowitz 2005), and it is perhaps the reason why ex-addicts have such success in treating addicts even when their methods may not be especially consistent with love in the cognitive-behavioural tradition.

When we ask offenders to change anti-social lifestyles, we have to remember that we are asking them to accept quite fundamental 'change'. Letting go of the entrenched attitudes and beliefs that have marked their experience may be a persistent and long-term challenge. As a counter-force, powerful and credible messages need to be delivered in the interpersonal context of supervision, directed to them personally and connected to other meaningful experiences they have related to us.

Sue Rex concluded from her study of experiences of probation that probation officers 'may be hampered by their own tentativeness about engaging probationers fully in the making of plans to tackle the issues underlying their offending' (1999 p.380). In Dowden and Andrews' (2004) meta-analysis of core correctional practices, evidence of some reliance on these practices could be detected only 3 per cent to 16 per cent of the times. A recent Canadian study by James Bonta and his colleagues (2004) methodically examined audio taped interviews of probationer officers with their offenders for evidence of how 'criminogenic' needs were actually being addressed in supervision. Though anti-social attitudes was one of the most frequently noted areas of need in Primary Risk Assessments (noted in 55.8 per cent of adult offenders), it was one of the areas least attended to in supervision discussions with offenders. Moreover, though pro-social reinforcement (i.e. expressions of approval for pro-social activities reported by probationers) was one of the methods probation officers used most frequently in attempting to shape change, discouragement of anti-social sentiments was one of the methods used least.

Case management with offenders is a task that has to be approached with some degree of tenacity and patience to tackle the relevant and substantial issues connected to offending. As offenders struggle to consolidate some of their emerging pro-social sentiments with their remaining anti-social views, we have to be ready to provide compelling arguments of incompatibility and inconsistency. This would be easier to do if we have truly understood the offender's perspective and succeeded in identifying some personally valued goals that we could orient them towards (creative, educational, vocational, physical or health related, volunteerism for giving back, relationship enhancing, etc.). The Good Lives Model (Ward and Stewart 2003) points us in the right direction in this respect. The last challenge of case management may have to be to leave offenders with more scope and coherence in their pro-social life plan. We need to ask ourselves what else offenders might need to stay on track and see the possibility of growing satisfaction in their lives, where anti-social sentiments become more easily appraised for what they are, illogical and unhelpful.

Conclusion

In the end, we have no choice but to acknowledge that everything we do in corrections will influence offenders regardless, our systems, procedures, methods and all of our interactions with them. We can choose to do it to make a difference with every bit of evidence we can find about what truly works and why, or we can go about doing it as efficiently as we can and risk losing the original intent.

Direction for improving the case management of offenders cannot come only, or even primarily, from the structures and mechanisms we might put in place to organise it. To a degree this might even be counterproductive. Staff will not be genuinely exuberant about working with us if they feel boxed-in, if they believe they have little choice in defining their roles, if they become frustrated at their inability to connect with other components of the system, and if they see their work as having too little rhythm and not enough accommodation with what they desire and feel able to do.

Direction for improving case management has to come more from continued articulation of an overarching model of practice that is comprehensively evidence driven and theoretically inclusive. Debate regarding discipline-based differences in perspective should turn into efforts to merge them. This chapter has argued for the meshing of motivational principles into the fabric of offender case management, while keeping an eye on what else we know about offending and its desistance. It has been suggested that there is risk of punitive drift in promoting rehabilitative work with offenders under a broader public protection "meta-narrative' for probation (Robinson and McNeill 2004). That risk could be lessened substantially if the uniqueness and complexity of probation case work in motivating offenders to redirect their lives was acknowledged. It is time we concentrated our research, resourced our correctional systems, reorganised and realigned our procedures, and trained and developed our staff to help achieve the full benefits of good probation work.

References

Andrews, D.A. and Bonta, J. (1998) *The Psychology of Criminal Conduct.* 2nd edn. Cincinnati, OH: Anderson Publishing Co.

Andrews, D.A. and Kiessling, J.J. (1980) 'Program Structure and Effective Correctional Practices: A Summary of the CaVic Research.' In R.R. Ross and P. Gendreau (eds) *Effective Correctional Treatment.* Toronto: Butterworth.

Bailey, R. and Ward, D. (1992) *Probation Supervision: Attitudes to Formalised Helping.* Belfast: Probation Board for Northern Ireland.

Baird, C., Heinz, R. and Bemus, B. (1979) *The Wisconsin Case Classification/Staff Deployment Project. Project Report No 14.* Madison, Wisconsin: Department of Health and Social Services.

Bandura, A. (1989) 'Human Agency in Social Cognitive Theory.' *American Psychologist 44,* 1175–84.

Bonta, J., Rugge, T. Sedo, B, and Cole, M. (2004) *Case Management in Manitoba Probation.* Corrections Research Report No. 2004-01. Ottawa: Public Safety and Emergency Preparedness Canada.

Bottoms, A. (2001) 'Compliance and Community Penalties.' In A. Bottoms, L. Gelsthorpe and S. Rex (eds) *Community Penalties: Change and Challenges.* Cullompton: Willan.

Correctional Service of Canada (1999) *Consultation Report Prepared in Development of an Integrated Community Corrections Strategy.* Ottawa: Correctional Service of Canada

Ditton, J. and Ford, R. (1994) *The Reality of Probation: A Formal Ethnography of Process and Practice.* Aldershot: Avebury.

Dowden, C. and Andrews D. (2004) 'The Importance of Staff Practice in Delivering Effective Correctional Treatment: A Meta-analysis.' *International Journal of Offender Therapy and Comparative Criminology 48,* 203–214.

Egan, G. (1998) *The Skilled Helper: A Problem-Management Approach to Helping.* Pacific Grove: Brooks/Cole Publishing Company.

Emmons, R.A. (1999) *The Psychology of Ultimate Concerns.* New York: Guilford Press.

Fabiano, E. and Porporino, F.J. (1999) *Manual for Cognitive-Motivational Tools for Negotiating Behaviour Change.* Ottawa: T3 Associates Inc.

Fabiano, E. and Porporino, F.J. (2003) *Focussing on Resettlement Part 2: Community Case Management Guidelines.* Ottawa: T3 Associates Inc.

Fabiano, E. and Porporino, F.J. (2004) *Cognitive Motivational Case Management Unravelled: Three Phases.* Ottawa: T3 Associates Inc.

Farrall, S. (2002) *Rethinking What Works With Offenders: Probation, Social Context and Desistance from Crime.* Cullompton: Willan.

Farrall, S. (2004) 'Supervision, Motivation and Social Context: What Matters Most When Probationers Desist.' In G. Mair (ed.) *What Matters in Probation.* Cullompton: Willan.

Farrington, D.P. (1997) 'Human Development and Criminal Careers.' In M. Maguire, R. Morgan and R. Reiner (eds) *Oxford Handbook of Criminology,* 2nd edn. Oxford: Clarendon Press.

Gendreau, P., Goggin, C. and Fulton, B. P. (2000). 'Intensive Probation in Probation and Parole Settings.' In C.R. Hollin (ed.) *Handbook of Offender Assessment and Treatment.* Chichester: John Wiley and Sons.

Gendreau, P., Goggin, C. and Smith, P. (1999) 'The Forgotten Issue in Effective Correctional Treatment: Program Implementation.' *International Journal of Offender Therapy and Comparative Criminology 43,* 180–187.

Gendreau, P., Goggin, C. and Smith, P. (2001) 'Implementation Guidelines for Correctional Programs in the Real World.' In G.A. Bernfeld, D.P. Farrington and A.W. Leschied (eds) *Offender Rehabilitation in Practice: Implementing and Evaluating Effective Programs.* Chichester: John Wiley and Sons.

Grapes, T. (2004) *The NOMS Offender Management Model.* London: Home Office.

Hannah-Moffat, K. (2005) 'Criminogenic Needs and the Transformative Risk Subject.' *Punishment and Society 7,* 1, 29–51.

Harper, G. and Chitty, C. (eds) (2004) *The Impact of Corrections on Offending: A Review of 'What Works.* Home Office Research Study No 291. London: Home Office.

Harris, P.M. (1994) 'Client Management Classification and Prediction of Probation Outcome.' *Crime and Delinquency 40,* 154–174.

Harris, P.M., Gingerich, R. and Whittaker, T.A. (2004) 'The "effectiveness" of differential supervision.' *Crime and Delinquency 50,* 2, 235–271.

Harris, P. and Smith, S. (1996) 'Developing Community Corrections: An Implementation Perspective.' In A.T. Harland (ed.) *Choosing Correctional Options That Work: Defining the Demand and Evaluating the Supply.* Thousand Oaks, CA: Sage Publications.

Hasenfeld, Y. (1983) *Human Service Organisations.* Englewood-Cliffs, NJ: Prentice Hall.

Her Majesty's Inspectorate of Probation (2002) *Annual Report 2001–2002.* London: HMIP.

Intagliata, J. (1976) 'A Telephone Follow-up Procedure for Increasing the Effectiveness of a Treatment Program for Alcoholics.' *Journal of Studies on Alcohol 37,* 1330–1335.

Jones, D.A., Johnson, S. Latessa, E. and Travis, L.F. (1999) 'Case Classification in Community Corrections: Preliminary Findings from a National Survey.' In. *Topics in Community Corrections: Annual Issue on Classification and Risk Assessment.* Washington, DC: National Institute of Corrections.

Katz, J. (1988) *Seductions of Crime: Moral and Sensual Attractions in Doing Evil.* New York: Basic Books.

Laudet, A.B. (2003) 'Attitudes and Beliefs about 12-step Groups among Addiction Treatment Clients and Clinicians: Toward Identifying Obstacles to Participation.' *Substance Use and Misuse: An International Interdisciplinary Forum 38,* 2017–2047.

Lipsey, M. (1999) 'Can Rehabilitative Programs Reduce the Recidivism of Juvenile Offenders? An Inquiry into the Effectiveness of Practical Programs.' *Virginia Journal of Social Policy and the Law 6,* 611–641.

Lopez Viets, V., Walker, D. and Miller, W.R. (2002) 'What is Motivation to Change? A Scientific Analysis.' In M. McMurran (ed.) *Motivating Offenders to Change: A Guide to Enhancing Engagement in Therapy.* Chichester: John Wiley and Sons.

Mair, G. (2004) 'The Origins of what Works in England and Wales: A House Built on Sand?' In G. Mair (ed.) *What Matters in Probation.* Cullompton: Willan.

Maruna, S. (2000) *Making Good: How Ex-Convicts Reform and Rebuild Their Lives.* Washington: American Psychological Association.

May, C. (1999) *Explaining Reconviction Rates Following a Community Sentence: The Role of Social Factors.* Home Office Research Study No 192. London: Home Office

McGuire, J. (ed.) (1995) *What Works: Reducing Re-Offending: Guidelines for Research and Practice.* Chichester: John Wiley and Sons.

McGuire, J. (2002) 'Criminal Sanctions versus Psychologically-based Interventions with Offenders: A Comparative Empirical Analysis.' *Psychology, Crime and Law 8,* 183–208.

McMurran, M. (ed.) (2002) *Motivating Offenders to Change: A Guide to Enhancing Engagement in Therapy.* Chichester: John Wiley and Sons.

McMurran, M. and Ward, T. (2004) 'Motivating Offenders to Change: An Organizing Framework.' *Legal and Criminal Psychology 9,* 295–311.

Megargee E. and Bohn, M. (1979) *Classifying Criminal Offenders: A New System Based on the MMPI.* Beverly Hills, CA: Sage Publications.

Miller, W.R., and Rollnick, S. (1991) *Motivational Interviewing: Preparing People to Change Addictive Behaviours.* New York: Guilford Press.

Miller, W.R. and Rollnick, S. (2002) *Motivational Interviewing: Preparing People to Change Addictive Behaviours,* 2dn edn. New York: Guilford Press.

Moskowitz, G.B. (2005) *Social Cognition: Understanding Self and Others.* New York: Guilford Press.

Needleman, L.D. (1999) *Cognitive Case Conceptualisation: A Guidebook for Practitioners.* Mawmah, NJ: Erlbaum.

Partridge, S. (2004) *Examining Case Management Models for Community Sentences.* Home Office Online Report 17/04. London: Home Office.

Pearson, F.S., Lipton, D.S., Cleland, C.M. and Yee, D.S. (2002) 'The effects of behavioural/cognitive-behavioural programs on recidivism.' *Crime and Delinquency 48*, 3, 476–496.

Porporino, F.J. (1995) 'Intervention in Corrections: Is "Cognitive" Programming an Answer or just a Passing Fashion.' In *The State of Corrections: Proceedings of the American Correctional Association Annual Conference.* Lanham, MD: American Correctional Association

Porporino, F.J. (2004) 'Revisiting Responsivity: Why What Works Isn't Working.' In *What Works and Why: Effective Approaches to Reentry.* Lanham, MD: American Correctional Association.

Porporino, F.J. and Fabiano, E. (1999) *Program Overview of Reasoning and Rehabilitation Revised: Theory and Application Manual.* Ottawa: T3 Associates Inc.

Porporino, F.J. and Fabiano, E. (2005) *The Focusing on Resettlement Programme (F.O.R.): Theory and Conceptual Overview.* Ottawa: T3 Associates Inc.

Porporino, F.J., Robinson, D., Millson, B. and Weekes, J. (2002) 'An Outcome Evaluation of Prison-based Treatment Programming for Substance Abusers.' *Substance Use and Misuse: An International Interdisciplinary Forum 37*, 1047–1077.

Prochaska, J.O. and Levesque, D.A. (2002) 'Enhancing Motivation of Offenders at Each Stage of Change and Phase of Therapy.' In M. McMurran (ed.) *Motivating Offenders to Change: A Guide to Enhancing Engagement in Therapy.* Chichester: John Wiley and Sons.

Quay, H. (1983) *Technical Manual for the Behavioral Classification System for Adult Offenders.* Washington: Department of Justice.

Raynor, P. (2002) 'What Works: Have we Moved On?' In D. Ward *et al.* (eds) *Probation: Working for Justice* 2nd edn.. Oxford: Oxford University Press.

Raynor, P. (2004) 'Opportunity, Motivation and Change: Some Findings from Research on Resettlement.' In R. Burnett and C. Roberts (eds) *Evidence-Based Practice in Probation and Youth Justice.* London: Willan.

Reinventing Probation Council (2000) *Transforming Probation Through Leadership: The 'Broken Windows' Model.* New York: Centre for Civic Innovation, The Manhattan Institute.

Rex, S. (1999) 'Desistance from offending: Experiences of Probation.' *The Howard Journal 38*, 4, 366–383.

Rex, S. (2001) 'Beyond Cognitive-behaviouralism? Reflections on the Effectiveness Literature.' In A. Bottoms, L. Gelsthorpe and S. Rex (eds) *Community Penalties: Change and Challenges.* Cullompton: Willan.

Robinson, G. and McNeill, F. (2004) 'Purposes Matter: Examining the "Ends" of Probation.' In G. Mair (ed.) *What Matters in Probation.* Cullompton: Willan.

Sampson, R.J. and Laub, J.H. (1993) *Crime in the Making: Pathways and Turning Points Through Life.* Cambridge, MA: Harvard University Press.

Sherman. L., Gottfredson, D., McKenzie, D., Eck, J., Reuter, P. and Bushway, S. (1997) *Preventing Crime: What Works, What Doesn't, What's Promising.* Washington, DC: Office of Justice Programs.

Trotter, C. (1996) 'The Impact of Different Supervision Practices in Community Corrections: Cause for Optimism.' *Australian and New Zealand Journal of Criminology 29*, 29–46.

Trotter, C. (2000) 'Social Work Education, Pro-social Orientation and Effective Probation Practice.' *Probation Journal 47*, 256–261.

Underdown, A. (2001) 'Making "What Works" Work: Challenges in the Delivery of Community Penalties.' A. Bottoms, L. Gelsthorpe and S. Rex (eds) *Community Penalties: Change and Challenges.* Cullompton: Willan.

Vanstone, M. (2000) 'Cognitive-behavioural Work with Offenders in the UK: A History of Influential Endeavour'. *Howard Journal 39*, 171–183.

Van Voorhis, P. (1997) 'Correctional Classification and the 'Responsivity' Principle.' *Forum on Corrections Research 9*, 1, 46–50.

Van Voorhis, P., Spruance, L.M., Ritchey, P.N., Listwan, S.W. and Seabrook, R. (2004) 'The Georgia Cognitive Skills Experiment: A Replication of Reasoning and Rehabilitation.' *Criminal Justice and Behaviour 31*, 3, 282–305.

Ward, T., and Stewart, C. (2003) 'Criminogenic Needs and Human Needs: A Theoretical Model'. *Psychology, Crime and Law 9*, 125–143.

Warren, M. (1983) 'Application of Interpersonal Maturity Theory to Offender Populations.' In W. Laufer and J. Day (eds) *Personality Theory, Moral Development and Criminal Behavior.* Lexington, NC: Lexington Books.

Zamble, E. and Quinsey, V.L. (1997) *The Criminal Recidivism Process.* Cambridge: Cambridge University Press.

CHAPTER 11

Pro-Social Modelling

Chris Trotter

Introduction

What is pro-social modelling? The term 'pro-social modelling' in its most limited sense refers to the way in which probation officers, or others who work with involuntary clients, model pro-social values and behaviours in their interactions with clients. The term is, however, often interpreted more broadly to include a group of skills which include supervisors modelling pro-social values, reinforcing clients' pro-social expressions and actions and negatively reinforcing or confronting pro-criminal actions and expressions of those clients. The term 'pro-social practice' or 'pro-social model' is also often used by practitioners to describe a still broader approach to the supervision of offenders which includes collaborative problem-solving and role clarification (see Trotter 1999, 2004). The definition of pro-social modelling that is used in this chapter includes modelling, positive and negative reinforcement and confrontation.

Research on the pro-social model

The importance of pro-social modelling in the supervision of offenders has been shown in studies as early as 1964. Martinson, Lipton and Wilks (1975) in their now famous (or infamous) study on what works in corrections refer to a study by Schwitygebel published in 1964 which found reduced numbers of arrests and incarcerations, compared to a matched control, among young offenders who were given positive reinforcement for successful accomplishments. For example, they were rewarded with cash for attending sessions and talking in detail about their experiences. Subsequent studies using pro-social modelling and reinforcement found similar outcomes (e.g. Fo and O'Donnell 1974, 1975; Sarason and Ganzer 1973).

Don Andrews and his colleagues (1979) examined tape recordings of interviews between Canadian probation officers and their clients and found that probation officers who modelled and reinforced pro-social values and who also made use of reflective listening practices had clients with lower recidivism rates in comparison to other probation officers. Probation officers who scored above the mean on a socialisation scale (a measure of pro-social orientation) and an empathy scale (a measure of workers' understanding of others' points of view) also had clients with lower recidivism. The value of pro-social modelling in the supervision of offenders has been further demonstrated in meta-analyses undertaken by Don Andrews and James Bonta (Andrews 2000; Andrews and Bonta 2003; Andrews *et al.* 1990; Bonta 2004).

I found in a study undertaken in Australia (Trotter 1990) that volunteer probation officers had clients with lower recidivism if they scored above the median on the socialisation scale regardless of the levels of empathy of the clients. In other words pro-social officers did better. A later study (Trotter 1996) which again replicated aspects of the Andrews *et al.* 1979 study found that professional probation officers also did better when they had high levels of socialisation and when their file notes indicated that they reinforced pro-social expressions and actions of their clients. This again was regardless of empathy levels.

A similar study (Trotter 2004) found that child protection workers, who in many cases work with young people and families who are involved in the criminal justice system, did better on a range of outcome measures, including client and worker satisfaction with outcome and earlier case closure, if they used the skills of pro-social modelling and reinforcement and appropriate confrontation.

How do workers model pro-social values?

The Gough socialisation scale which was used in the Andrews *et al.* study (1979) and my studies (Trotter 1990, 1996) places individuals on a continuum from pro-social to pro-criminal behaviours and forecasts the likelihood that they will transgress mores accepted by their particular culture (Megargee 1972). The scale was originally developed as a delinquency scale. It reflects a person's 'social maturity, integrity and rectitude'. It reflects family cohesiveness, social sensitivity, empathy, optimism and self-confidence (Megargee 1972).

How do people who score high on the scale behave in comparison to those who score low on the scale? In both the Canadian and Australian studies those who scored high on the scale were more likely to model and to express views which support the value of a law-abiding lifestyle. Some examples of the practice of pro-social modelling are set out below. These are based on my studies in corrections and child protection (Trotter 1996, 2004) and on comments from participants in many seminars I have undertaken with professional workers examining the process of pro-social modelling.

Pro-social modelling involves the worker keeping appointments, being punctual, honest and reliable, following up on tasks, respecting other people's feelings, expressing views about the negative effects of criminal behaviour, expressing views about the value of social pursuits such a non-criminal friends, good family relations and the value of work. It involves interpreting peoples motives positively, e.g. 'most police are people trying to do a job and they have similar needs to most of us' rather than 'all police are pigs'. It involves being open about problems the worker may have had which are similar to the offender's, e.g. 'I spent a period of time unemployed at one time and I found it depressing.' It also involves being optimistic about the rewards which can be obtained by living within the law.

One finding from the child protection study referred to earlier (Trotter 2004) which clearly illustrates the importance of simple modelling processes, was that when the clients reported that their workers were in the habit of responding to phone calls and keeping appointments, both the clients and the workers were almost twice as likely to be satisfied with the outcome of the intervention. The cases were also likely to be closed earlier. This was independent of client risk levels.

The following comments illustrate the differences between the kind of things more pro-social probation officers say in comparison to the things which less pro-social officers say. I have constructed these examples however they are consistent with the comments which have been made in the research studies and with the views expressed by practitioners in workshops. More detail is provided about the kind of conversations conducted by pro-social workers in Trotter (2004) albeit in a child protection setting.

The following comments are not pro-social:

- I know you are doing well and complying with the conditions but I need to see you more often anyway because you have still got problems.

- The police seem to be having a go at a lot of my clients lately. They never leave you alone do they?

- It is good that you went for the interview – but with the unemployment situation the way it is you can't expect too much, can you.

The first comment effectively punishes a pro-social action, the second is not supportive of a law-abiding perspective and the third is pessimistic. The following comments are more pro-social.

- Because you have been keeping your appointments and doing your community work you will have to report monthly from now on.

- It must be frustrating if you feel that the police are really out to get you. I think most police are really just doing their job. Is there some way that you can change what you are doing so that they are less interested in you?

- That is great that you went for the employment interview and that you have kept the appointment with me today. I can see that you are really making an effort.

The first comment rewards pro-social behaviour, the second responds to the issue of police harassment with a more pro-social perspective and the third is more optimistic and acknowledges the pro-social actions of the client.

Pro-social reinforcement

It was evident in both the Canadian study (Andrews *et al.* 1979) and the Australian studies (Trotter 1996, 2004) that more pro-social workers were inclined to reinforce pro-social comments and actions by their clients. Some examples of pro-social actions and comments include those related to compliance with the order such as keeping appointments, being punctual, completing community work, not offending and complying with special conditions such as attending for drug treatment. Other client pro-social actions include working through problem-solving processes with the worker, accepting responsibility for offences, comments about the harm that crime can do to others and yourself, empathy for the victim and comments that crime is wrong. Pro-social workers are also inclined to reinforce comments and actions which value non-criminal activities and associations including family, sport, non-criminal friends, hobbies and attending school or work. Pro-social workers are likely to reinforce expressions which are fair, non-sexist and non-racist. They also reinforce optimistic attitudes, for example expressing a belief that life without crime is achievable, that goals can be achieved, that workers can help, and that clients can change.

How do the workers reinforce these things? The first and most obvious method of providing reinforcement is through body language (e.g. smiling, attentive listening, leaning forward) and the use of praise. Rewards can also be provided by the worker giving time to the client, attending court with the client and providing positive evidence, reducing the frequency of contact, helping the client find a job or accommodation, doing home visits or meeting a client outside the office, compiling a positive report for a court or parole board, speaking to other agencies/professionals such as social security or the police about the client's needs and making positive comments in file notes.

The idea of pro-social reinforcement is that the rewards should be contingent on the behaviour. The reinforcement should be offered clearly in response to the pro-social behaviour. The clients need to clearly see the link. The clients should understand that the reduction in visits, the praise used by the supervisor or a visit to court is directly linked to their pro-social behaviour, for example the fact they have kept appointments, been punctual, been attending job interviews, and not re-offended.

One of the most powerful rewards available to the probation officer in his/her day-to-day work is the capacity to reduce the frequency of contact. It is important in using this model to make the link between reduced frequency of contact and the pro-social activities of the client. It should not be seen simply as usual procedure; rather, it should be seen as reward for good progress. In this way the client gains a sense that his or her goals can be achieved through pro-social behaviour.

The other aspect of pro-social modelling as I have defined it in this chapter is negative reinforcement. How do more effective workers use negative reinforcement? Let's look first at confrontation, the most common form of negative reinforcement? The issue of confrontation in work with involuntary clients is a complex one. There is little support in the research for aggressive or critical confrontation. A small qualitative study (Burns 1994) undertaken with probation officers in Australia found that the more effective probation officers (those with clients who had low recidivism rates) focused almost exclusively on the positive things that their clients said and did and made little if any use of confrontation.

My child protection study (Trotter 2004) found that the confrontation most likely to be related to positive outcomes was confrontation which:

1. suggests more positive ways of dealing with the situation

2. acknowledges that negative feelings may be justified

3. explores the reasons why clients feel and act the way they do.

On the other hand, confrontation which gives the client a sense of being criticised or confrontation which points out the likely ill effects of the clients' views was related to poorer outcomes in the view of both the clients and the workers. Ignoring pro-criminal or anti-social comments and actions was also related to poorer outcomes in this study.

Care needs to be taken therefore in the use of confrontation. The Canadian study referred to earlier suggests a 'four to one' rule (Andrews 1982). For every negative comment give four positive ones. Evidence from my studies (Trotter 1996, 2004) certainly confirms that people are more likely to learn from positive reinforcement rather than negative reinforcement. Similarly, care needs to be exercised in relation to more active forms of negative reinforcement such as increasing frequency of appointments or writing negative reports.

Empathy, pro-social modelling and legitimacy

The concept of pro-social modelling and legitimacy has been raised by Sue Rex (Rex and Matravers1998) referring to the moral authority of the worker. It seems clear that the pro-social orientation of supervisors relates to the ongoing recidivism of those under supervision. Is this influence greater, however, if the client identifies with the worker, if the worker is young or old or if the worker understands the client's point of view? Are supervisors effective if they have a pro-social orientation but at the same time have little understanding or empathy for the client's perspective?

Some of the work which has been done on this issue is contradictory. I referred earlier to the Canadian study (Andrews *et al.* 1979) which found that probation officers who had high levels of empathy and high levels of socialisation had clients with lower recidivism. On the other hand, probation officers with high levels of socialisation and low levels of empathy had clients with higher recidivism rates than other clients. It seems that a pro-social disposition accompanied by a lack of understanding of the clients' perspective was counterproductive. While both of my Australian studies in corrections found that high scores on the socialisation scale were related to lower recidivism, regardless of levels of empathy, it was also apparent that judgemental comments in file notes (e.g. no hoper, lazy) were related to higher recidivism even after taking risk levels into account.

It does seem, therefore, that a pro-social disposition needs to be accompanied at least by a willingness to be reasonably non-judgemental. Further research on the notion of pro-social modelling and legitimacy might shed further light on the situations in which pro-social modelling is most effective.

Peer group association

Modelling pro-social values by workers appears to influence the re-offence rates of their clients. There is also some evidence that modelling by other offenders also influences re-offence rates. I found in an Australian study (Trotter 1995) that clients placed on community work sites with other offenders had higher re-offence rates than clients placed on community worksites with community volunteers or by themselves. This was particularly so with young offenders (aged 17 to 21) and was evident after risk levels had been taken into account. This is certainly consistent with theories of differential association and a range of research studies pointing to the influence of peer group association (see Trotter 1995 for more detail on this issue).

Strengths of pro-social modelling

The greatest strength of pro-social modelling is that the research evidence suggests that it works. It does seem to be related to client outcomes with offenders and with a range of involuntary clients. The evidence from my studies (Trotter 1996, 2004) shared that the use of the approach was also significantly correlated with a number of client satisfaction measures. The success of this approach can also be explained theoretically by reference to learning theory.

The pro-social approach seems to work because it provides a method for discouraging and challenging anti-social comments and behaviours within a positive framework. It puts into practice the idea that people learn best by encouragement rather than discouragement. The approach also helps workers to take control of a reinforcement process which occurs anyway. Whether they are aware of it or not workers with involuntary clients do make judgements about the things they wish to encourage in their clients and they do in turn influence their clients' behaviour. By understanding the process and using this approach, workers are able to take some control over this process.

Criticisms of pro-social modelling

The concept of pro-social modelling has nevertheless received some criticism. Outlined below are some of these criticisms and my responses to them. The issues are addressed in more detail in *Working with Involuntary Clients* (Trotter 2006).

One of the most common comments made in my workshops is 'I do it anyway'. Some workers feel that the pro-social approach merely describes a process which they use unconsciously. However, there is evidence that those who work with involuntary clients do not routinely use these skills. Two Canadian studies (Andrews *et al.* 1979; Bonta and Rugge 2004) and the Australian studies (Burns 1994; Trotter 1990, 1996, 2004) found that workers used the pro-social approach very erratically. Some workers use it and some don't. Some use it sometimes. The qualitative study referred to earlier found that many probation officers inadvertently reinforced the very behaviour they were hoping to change, often through use of smiling and body language as much as direct comment or actions (Burns 1994).

There seems little doubt that while pro-social skills might come naturally to some workers they do not come naturally to everyone. One of the strongest arguments in favour of this approach relates to the notion that the modelling process occurs anyway. It seems that whether they are conscious of it or not, to one degree or another, workers reinforce different behaviours in their clients. As I mentioned earlier, it is preferable that they are explicit about this process both with themselves and their clients and that they take some control over it.

It might be argued that the approach is superficial and symptom-focused and it is therefore unlikely to address the complex long-term issues which have led offenders into the criminal justice system, for example, peer group influence, unemployment, family breakdown, drug use, homelessness and school failure. It is certainly true that pro-social modelling will not address all the problems faced by clients of the criminal justice system. It is, however, one skill which will address some issues, it relates to client outcomes and it can be used along with a range of other skills.

It can be argued that the pro-social approach is manipulative – it attempts to change the behaviour of the client often without the client's knowledge, in directions set by the worker. On the other hand, the reinforcement and modelling process inevitably occurs in worker/client relationships and the process is less likely to be manipulative if it is explicit and if the worker understands and attempts to take some control of the process.

Pro-social modelling may also be criticised as being judgemental. It is based on value judgements. The term pro-social has connotations of social control, of there being a right way of doing things. It suggests that what is socially acceptable is best. Again probation officers and others who work with offenders inevitably make judgements about what are acceptable and unacceptable standards in relation to such issues as drug use, reporting patterns or minor offending. A number of studies (Andrews *et al.* 1979; Trotter 1990, 1996, 2004) suggest that workers reinforce different expressions and behaviours regardless of whether they have any awareness of doing so. Again it is better that they take some control over this process.

It is important nevertheless that pro-social behaviour is defined in explicit and limited terms. It should not be interpreted as meaning having values consistent with the worker. As discussed earlier, the Canadian study in corrections (Andrews *et al.* 1979) found that supervisors who practised the pro-social approach were only effective if they also practised reflective listening and had high levels of empathy. It does seem that if this approach is in any way used as an excuse for moralising on the part of the worker it is not going to work. Perhaps one of the strongest arguments for focusing on clients' pro-social actions and comments rather than their pro-criminal or anti-social actions and comments is that it is likely to avoid the possibility that the pro-social approach will come across as moralistic and disapproving.

Confrontation should be limited to factors which relate to the presenting problem (or the mandate for the worker's involvement with the client). For the most part this relates to illegal behaviour, for example, offending, domestic violence, truancy or failure to comply with the court order. Other 'desirable' behaviours which the worker may wish to encourage such as seeking employment, mixing with pro-social peers or returning to study, should be encouraged if the worker believes they are pro-social. The clients' failure to do these things should not, however, result in confrontation by the worker.

It could be argued that pro-social modelling may by inappropriate with clients with particular cultural backgrounds. Definitions of pro-social are inevitably entrenched in social and cultural mores. Punctuality, work ethic, domestic violence, child neglect may mean different things in different cultures. Workers and clients are influenced by their racial, social, religious and economic milieu. It is important therefore that workers attempt to understand the views and actions of their clients in terms of their cultural context. In forming views about what is pro-social in any given situation the worker should take the client's cultural background into account. This involves talking to the client about cultural differences. Pro-social modelling aims to help make explicit the cultural issues in the supervision of offenders and in turn to contribute to culturally sensitive practice.

Pro-social modelling may also be criticised because of the difficulties involved in judging the genuineness of clients. Clients may make pro-social comments, however, their behaviour may not be consistent with those comments. This is certainly part of the challenge in using this approach. The aim of pro-social modelling is to reward pro-social behaviour and comments, that is comments and behaviour which are honest and genuine. A dishonest or frivolous array of comments about how a client may have changed, for example, should not be defined as pro-social and should not be rewarded.

At the same time it can be difficult to determine whether someone is genuine or not. The worker clearly needs to avoid being 'conned' and should avoid reinforcing behaviour which attempts to do this. Nonetheless, if in doubt, it seems that the most appropriate approach is to accept the client's word – at least until the worker has information that what the client is saying is incorrect.

One final criticism which is sometimes made about pro-social modelling is that it is very difficult to carry out because many clients do not say or do anything pro-social. How do you identify pro-social comments and actions when a client has a severe drug addiction, no work, no personal or family supports and is resistant to supervision? However, the challenge in these situations is for the worker to search for the pro-social actions and comments. There is no evidence that the client will be helped by a focus on things that he or she has done wrong. The worker should instead search for pro-social comments and actions as they occur (for example, keeping an appointment and talking to the worker).

Training

Can pro-social modelling be taught? Personality traits and beliefs such as optimism, fairness, punctuality, reliability and honesty are hard to develop or change. Is effective use of the skills of pro-social modelling limited to workers with these personality traits?

Some light on the extent to which training can influence the use of pro-social modelling and in turn client outcomes is provided in my Australian study (Trotter 1994). Workers with high levels of socialisation (more pro-social workers) had clients who offended less often than other clients in the one- and four-year follow-up periods. Workers who completed training in pro-social modelling also had clients with low re-offence rates at one and four years. Workers with high socialisation were however more inclined to participate in pro-social modelling training and to complete the training. Which factor was influential – training or socialisation? A regression analysis of the data found that socialisation levels and training were independently related to client re-offence rates after taking risk factors into account. In other words some workers by virtue of their socialisation levels did better with their clients, however, they did better still if they had undertaken training in pro-social modelling. Workers with low socialisation, although they tended to drop out of training and to have clients with high recidivism, did better with their clients if they completed the training.

The particular training involved in this study included an initial five-day seminar followed by monthly two-hour seminars plus the availability of consultation with a coach if requested. The workers were however, supervised by senior workers who had little knowledge of pro-social modelling. In most cases their colleagues also had limited knowledge. The impact of the training might have been greater if it had been more supported through supervision and collegiate support at the local office level. It seems likely that attempts to increase the use of pro-social modelling among direct practice staff will be most successful if they are part of a concerted effort involving training, supervision, collegiate support and modelling by senior staff.

Conclusion

In this chapter I have acknowledged the difficulties of defining pro-social modelling. I have, nevertheless, defined it in this chapter as an approach to the supervision of offenders which involves workers modelling pro-social values, comments and actions, re-inforcing pro-social values, comments and actions of offenders and appropriately confronting pro-criminal values, actions and expressions. The research consistently points to the value of pro-social modelling in work with offenders and other involuntary clients. In fact research in Australia and elsewhere suggests that it can make considerable difference to the re-offence rates of those under supervision.

The chapter has outlined the specific ways in which pro-social modelling is undertaken and discusses and responds to some criticisms of pro-social modelling. It goes on to discuss the extent to which training can impact on the skills and practices of probation officers and others who work with offenders. Certainly, in my research and in more recent research by James Bonta and Tanya Rugge (2004) it was apparent that for every probation officer who used the skills of pro-social modelling another probation officer would not be using the skills. This may be changing with widespread training in the UK and elsewhere in pro-social modelling. Nevertheless, the challenge today is how to help probation services implement these practices and how to encourage individual workers to participate in training and to make use of the principles with their clients.

References

Andrews, D. (1982) *The Anti-criminal Dimension of Correctional Counselling.* Ottawa: Carlton University.

Andrews, D., Zinger, I., Hoge, R., Bonta, J., Gendreau, P. and Cullen, F. (1990) Does Correctional Treatment Work – A Clinically Relevant and Psychologically Informed Meta-analysis', *Criminology 28*, 3, 369–401.

Andrews, D. (2000) 'Effective Practice: Future Directions.' In D. Andrews, C. Hollin, P. Raynor,C. Trotter and B. Armstrong (eds) *Sustaining Effectiveness in Working with Offenders.* Cardiff: Cognitive Centre Foundation.

Andrews, D. and Bonta, J. (2003) *The Psychology of Criminal Conduct.* Cincinnati: Anderson Publishing Co.

Andrews, D.A., Keissling, J.J., Russell, R.J. and Grant, B.A. (1979) *Volunteers and the One to One Supervision of Adult Probationers.* Toronto: Ontario Ministry of Correctional Services.

Bonta, J. (2004) 'Effective Practice: The State of the Art (or Science?).' In *Conference Proceedings Cognitive Centre Foundation: Personal Effectiveness in Working with Offenders.* Cardiff: Cognitive Centre Foundation.

Bonta, J. and Rugge, T. (2004) *Case Management in Manitoba Probation.* Ottawa: Solicitor General, Canada.

Burns, P. (1994) 'Pro-social Practices in Community Corrections.' Honours thesis, Monash University, Dept of Social Work, Melbourne.

Fo, W.S. and O'Donnell, C. (1974) 'The Buddy System: Relationship and Contingency Conditions in a Community Prevention Program for Youth with Non-professionals as Behaviour Change Agents.' *Journal of Counselling and Clinical Psychology 42,* 163–169.

Fo, W.S. and O'Donnell, C. (1975) 'The Buddy System: Effect of Community Intervention on Delinquent Offences.' *Behaviour Therapy 6,* 522–524.

Martinson, R., Lipton, D. and Wilks, J. (1975) *The Effectiveness of Correctional Treatment: A Survey of Treatment Evaluation Studies.* New York: Praeger Publishers.

Megargee, E.I. (1972) *The California Psychological Inventory Handbook.* London: Jossey Bass Inc.

Rex, S. and Matravers, A. (eds) (1998) *Pro-Social Modelling and Legitimacy.* Cambridge: University of Cambridge Institute of Criminology.

Sarason, I.G. and Ganzer, V.J. (1973) 'Modelling and Group Discussion in the Rehabilitation of Juvenile Delinquents.' *Journal of Consulting Psychology 20,* 5, 442–449.

Trotter, C. (1990) 'Probation Can Work: A Research Study Using Volunteers.' *Australian Journal of Social Work 43,* 2, 13–18.

Trotter, C. (1995) 'Contamination Theory and Unpaid Community Work.' *Australian and New Zealand Journal of Criminology 28,* 2, 163–177.

Trotter, C. (1996) 'The Impact of Different Supervision Practices in Community Corrections.' *Australian and New Zealand Journal of Criminology 29,* 1, 29–46.

Trotter, C. (2006) *Working with Involuntary Clients: A Guide to Practice.* Sydney: Allen and Unwin.

Trotter, C. (2004) *Helping Abused Children and their Families.* Sydney: Allen and Unwin.

Trotter, C. (1994) 'The Effective Supervision of Offenders.' Unpublished PhD thesis, LaTrobe University, Melbourne.

CHAPTER 12

Giving Up and Giving Back: Desistance, Generativity and Social Work with Offenders

Fergus McNeill and Shadd Maruna

Introduction

Criminality can appear – maybe especially to the overworked social work practitioner – to be a frustratingly intractable pattern of behaviour in the lives of many individuals. Young people living in disadvantaged areas can appear to be caught up in a never-ending cycle of drugs, debt, crime and incarceration that is near impossible to escape. Yet, research on crime in the life course suggests that a very large percentage (over three-quarters) of young people involved in crime do indeed manage to desist from crime and 'go straight' (see Farrington 1997, p.373).

In recent years, a number of academic writers have begun to explore the implications of 'desistance' research for probation and social work practice (Farrall 2002; Maruna, Immarigeon and LeBel 2004; McNeill 2003, 2004, 2006). By seeking to explore and understand the processes through which people come to cease offending – with or without intervention by criminal justice agencies – desistance research provides a rich seam of knowledge for social work practice with offenders. Indeed, the findings of desistance studies have begun to direct those involved in 'offender management' towards a series of issues that have been, until recently, somewhat neglected in the pursuit of effective practice. For example, desistance research has played a significant part in the revival of interest in the significance of officer–offender relationships in the process of rehabilitation (Burnett and McNeill 2005). It has also directed attention towards the importance in practice of social support and advocacy in order to build the social capital required to support desistance in the long term (Farrall 2002; McCulloch 2005).

224

Though we discuss such issues briefly below, our aim in this chapter is to build upon this previous work by focusing on another important message from desistance research concerning the concept of 'generativity' (see Maruna 2001). The predictability of 'self-reform' with increasing age has led more than a few commentators to suggest that the best strategy for criminal justice agencies would be to allow young people to 'grow out' of criminality 'on their own'. Others have argued in favour of interventions that 'work in partnership with self-restorative forces where these exist' (Toch 1997, p.97). One such self-restorative force, we argue, is the developmental challenge that Erikson (1963) refers to as 'generativity'. McAdams and de St Aubin (1998) define generativity as:

> The concern for and commitment to promoting the next generation, manifested through parenting, teaching, mentoring, and generating products and outcomes that aim to benefit youth and foster the development and well-being of individuals and social systems that will outlive the self (p.xx).

In this chapter, we explore in greater depth Maruna's (2001) argument that the normative developmental process of 'generativity' plays a significant role in the desistance process (or, as in the title of this chapter, 'giving back' to others plays a part in 'giving up' crime). Moreover, we discuss the implications of this argument for social work practice. That is, can generativity be sponsored and supported in social work practice? The chapter proceeds by first defining desistance, then providing a brief and selective overview of some relevant findings from desistance studies and their implications for social work practice. Next we introduce the concept of generativity and explore its relationships with desistance from crime. The concluding discussion addresses the implications for practice of these relationships.

What is desistance?

Although 'desistance from crime' is a relatively unambiguous concept, it has been very difficult to operationalise in criminological research. To 'cease and desist' any activity is to stop doing something (to cease) and refrain from repeating it again (to desist). Hence, individuals who are at one point engaged in a pattern of criminal pursuits could be said to 'desist from crime' when they cease this involvement and, importantly, abstain from additional behaviours deemed to be illegal. Like the colloquial term 'going straight' or 'going legit', desistance should not be seen so much as an event or state, but rather a process or an ongoing work in progress. One goes straight. One does not talk about having *turned* legit or having *become* legit – the 'going' is the thing.

Maruna *et al.* (2004) argue that desistance might be better understood by borrowing from the literature on criminal aetiology. A half century ago, Edwin Lemert introduced considerable clarity into the debate on the origins of 'deviance' by differentiating between two categorical phases in this developmental process: primary deviation and secondary deviation. Primary deviation involved the initial flirtation and experimentation with deviant behaviours. Secondary deviation, on the other hand, is deviance that becomes 'incorporated as part of the "me" of the individual' (Lemert 1951, p.76), that is, criminality becomes a core aspect of the person's identity. Primary and secondary deviation had distinctly different causes according to Lemert, and his real interest was less on why some people initially experimented with primary deviance (as this was highly common) but rather why some of those individuals graduated into secondary deviation.

Maruna and colleagues argue that the same framework might clarify some issues in the study of desistance. Perhaps there are (at least) two, distinguishable phases in the desistance process: primary and secondary desistance. Primary desistance would take the term desistance at its most basic and literal level to refer to any lull or crime-free gap in the course of a criminal career. However, the real interest of practitioners and academics would be secondary desistance: the movement from the behaviour of non-offending to the assumption of the role or identity of a 'changed person.' In secondary desistance, crime not only stops, but 'existing roles become disrupted' and a 'reorganization based upon a new role or roles will occur' (Lemert 1951, p.76). Indeed, recent research (e.g. Burnett 2004; Farrall 2002; Maruna 2001) provides compelling evidence that long-term desistance does involve identifiable and measurable changes at the level of personal identity or the 'me' of the individual.

What causes desistance?

Easily the best predictor of whether a person will desist from crime or not is his or her age. Basically, crime (or at least street crimes such as housebreaking, assault and vandalism) is a young person's game as is obvious from the well-known 'age–crime curve' (or the relationship between age and criminal behaviour). For example, Figure 12.1 shows that in the year 2000, 19-year-old males in England and Wales had a rate of offending 50 or more times higher than the rate for men over the age of 50. Something happens to those 19-year-olds as they age. Some die or spend their lives in prison, but we know from a variety of research sources that the majority desist from criminal lifestyles. Longitudinal, self-report studies following young people who have offended into later adulthood, for instance, indicate that

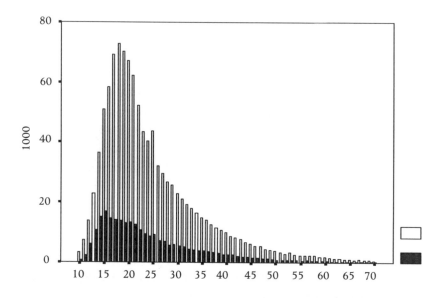

Source: Bottoms *et al.* 2004

Figure 12.1 Recorded offender rates per 1000 relevant population by age-year and sex. England and Wales, 2000

most young offenders stop committing crimes after turning 23 years old (Farrington 1997, p.373).

This clear relationship between ageing and 'going straight' has led numerous observers to argue that desistance from crime is a 'natural' or even biological process (e.g. Glueck and Glueck 1937; Goring 1915). Gottfredson and Hirschi suggest, 'Crime declines with age. Spontaneous desistance is just that, change in behavior that cannot be explained and change that occurs regardless of what else happens' (1990, p.136). According to proponents of this view, the effect of age on criminal behavior is 'direct', natural and invariant across social, temporal and economic conditions.

More recently, criminologists have sought to 'unpack' the 'meaning' of age (Sampson and Laub 1992). Age indexes a range of different variables, including biological changes, social transitions and life experiences. For age to be a meaningful explanation of social behaviour, according to this argument, one must ask which features indexed by age 'constitute the mediating mechanisms' at work in this process (Rutter 1996). Farrall, for instance, stresses the significance of the relationships between 'objective' changes in the offender's life and his or her 'subjective' assessment of the value or significance of these changes: 'Most of these factors are related to acquiring 'something' (most commonly employment, a life partner or a family) which the desister values in some way and which initiates a re-evaluation of his or her own life' (2002, p.11). Thus, Farrall argues, desistance resides somewhere in the interfaces between developing personal maturity, changing social bonds associated with certain life transitions, and the individual subjective narrative constructions which offenders build around these key events and changes. It is not just the events and changes that matter; it is what these events and changes *mean* to the people involved.

Burnett's (1992, 2004; Burnett and Maruna 2004) study of the post-prison experiences of 130 adult property offenders is particularly illustrative of this combination of subjective and objective factors in the desistance process. Burnett found that while 8 out of 10 of her sample, when interviewed pre-release, wanted to 'go straight', only 4 out of 10 were able to avoid criminality for even a year after release. For many, the intention to be law-abiding was provisional in the sense that it did not represent a confident prediction; only one in four reported that they would definitely be able to desist. Importantly, Burnett discovered that those who were most confident and optimistic about desisting – whom she labelled 'converts' – had the greatest success in doing so.

> The most resolute and certain among the desisters...had found new interests that were all-preoccupying and overturned their value system: a partner, a child, a good job, a new vocation. These were attainments that they were not prepared to jeopardize or which over-rode any interest in or need for property crime. (2000, p.14)

Although Burnett notes that, for most of the men involved in her study, processes of desistance were characterised by ambivalence and vacillation, the overturning of value systems and all-preoccupying new interests that characterised the 'converts' seem to imply the kind of identity changes invoked in the notion of secondary desistance. Moreover, in similar vein but in relation to women's experience of desistance, Rumgay (2004) has suggested that desistance is best understood as a process initiated by the perception of an opportunity to claim a pro-social identity during a period of readiness to reform, which is subsequently sustained by the deployment of strategies of resilience and survival in conditions of adversity.

Supporting desistance in social work practice

Researchers have long wondered whether the study of how people reform 'on their own' could aid in the improvement of professional activities conducted in the name of offender reform (see e.g. Farrall 2002; McCulloch 2005; Rex 1999). In the words of Glueck and Glueck in their classic desistance study: 'Can educators, psychologists, correctional workers, and others devise means of 'forcing the plant," as it were, so that benign maturation will occur earlier than it seems to at present?' (1937, p.205).

In one such study of 'assisted desistance', Rex (1999) explored the experiences of 60 probationers. She found that those who attributed changes in their behaviour to probation supervision described it as active and participatory. Probationers' commitments to desist appeared to be generated by the personal and professional commitment shown by their probation officers, whose reasonableness, fairness and encouragement seemed to engender a sense of personal loyalty and accountability. Probationers interpreted advice about their behaviours and underlying problems as evidence of concern for them as people, and 'were motivated by what they saw as a display of interest in their well-being' (Rex 1999, p.375). Such evidence resonates with other arguments about the pivotal role that relationships play in effective interventions (Barry 2000; Burnett 2004; Burnett and McNeill 2005; McIvor 2004; McNeill *et al.* 2005; Raynor 2004). If, as we have suggested above, secondary desistance requires a narrative reconstruction of identity, then it seems obvious why the relational aspects of practice are so significant. Who would risk engaging in such a precarious and threatening venture without the reassurance of sustained and compassionate support from a trusted source?

However, workers and working relationships are neither the only nor the most important resources in promoting desistance. Related studies of young people in trouble suggest that their own resources and social networks are often more significant factors in resolving their difficulties than professional staff (Hill 1999). The potential of social networks is highlighted by 'resilience perspectives' which, in contrast with approaches that dwell on risks and/or needs, consider the 'protective factors and processes' involved in positive adaptation in spite of adversity. In terms of practice with young people, such perspectives entail an emphasis on the recognition, exploitation and development of their competences, resources, skills and assets (Schoon and Bynner 2003).

In the most substantial study of probation and desistance to date, Farrall (2002) explored the progress or lack of progress towards desistance achieved by a group of 199 probationers. Though over half of the sample evidenced progress towards desistance, Farrall found that desistance could be attributed to specific interventions by the probation officer in only a few cases, although help with finding work and mending damaged family relationships appeared particularly important. Desistance seemed to relate more clearly to the probationers' motivations and to the social and personal contexts in which various obstacles to desistance were addressed.

Farrall (2002) goes on to argue that interventions must pay greater heed to the community, social and personal contexts in which they are situated (see also McCulloch 2005). After all, 'social circumstances and relationships with others are *both* the object of the intervention and the medium through which...change can be achieved' (Farrall 2002, p.212). Necessarily, this requires that interventions be focused not solely on the individual person and his or her perceived 'deficits.' As Farrall (2002) notes, the problem with such interventions is that while they can build human capital, for example, in terms of enhanced cognitive skills or improved employability, they cannot generate the social capital which resides in the relationships through which we achieve participation and inclusion in society. Vitally, it is social capital that is necessary to encourage desistance. It is not enough to build *capacities* for change where change depends on *opportunities* to exercise capacities: '...the process of desistance is one that is produced through an interplay between individual choices, and a range of wider social forces, institutional and societal practices which are beyond the control of the individual' (Farrall and Bowling 1999, p.261).

Barry's (2004) recent study provides another key reference point for exploring how themes of capital, agency, identity and transition play out specifically for younger people desisting from offending. Through in-depth interviews with 20 young women and 20 young men, Barry explored why they started offending and what influenced or inhibited them in that behaviour as they grew older. The young people revealed that their decisions about offending and about desisting were related to their need to feel included in their social world, through friendships in childhood and through wider commitments in adulthood. The resolve displayed by the young people in desisting from offending seemed remarkable to Barry, particularly given that they were from disadvantaged backgrounds and were limited in their access to mainstream opportunities (employment, housing and social status) both because of their age and because of their social class. Barry recognises crucially that:

> Because of their transitional situation, many young people lack the status and opportunities of full citizens and thus have limited capacity for social recognition in terms of durable and legitimate means of both accumulating and expending capital through taking on responsibility and generativity... Accumulation of capital requires, to a certain extent, both responsibilities and access to opportunities; however, children and young people rarely have such opportunities because of their status as 'liminal entities' (Turner 1969), not least those from a working class background. (Barry 2004 p.328–329)

Summarising the findings from the growing literature on desistance from crime, we can conclude the following: that desistance is a process associated with maturation but often characterised by ambivalence and vacillation; that it may be provoked by life events, depending on the meaning of these events for the offenders; that it may be 'sponsored' by someone involved in a significant relationship with the offender who 'believes in' the offender; that it probably involves more than the development of cognitive skills – it involves the re-storying of narrative identities; and that it requires the development of social as well as human capital. A further important message of one recent study (Maruna 2001) is that secondary desistance often involves earning 'redemption' (or 'giving back') through generative activities. It is to this message that we now turn in more detail.

Generativity and desistance

According to Erikson, generativity emerges as a key developmental theme for most individuals at approximately the same time that delinquent and criminal behaviours typically dissipate – around mid-adulthood. Maruna (2001) has argued that this correlation is not coincidental. Generative commitments seem to fill a particular void in the lives of former offenders, providing a sense of purpose and meaning, allowing them to redeem themselves from their past mistakes, and legitimising the person's claim to having changed (see Maruna 2001, Chapter 6). For the individual engaged in generative commitments and concerns, criminal behaviour either seems pointless (for example, its role in establishing one's masculinity no longer needed) or else too risky (in the sense that it could jeopardise the person's generative self-identity). Similarly, Goodstein speculates that women's traditional gender roles in caring for children, younger siblings and community members (that is, their socially expected involvement in *certain* gendered generative pursuits) may be one reason why they are so dramatically under-represented in criminal statistics (cited in Cullen 1994).

Further evidence of a link between generativity and rates of offending can be drawn from one of the best known studies of desistance. Sampson and Laub empirically demonstrated the role of steady employment, marriage and family creation in providing young people with a route out of criminal behaviour. They found that former offenders who assume the responsibility of providing for their spouses and children are significantly more likely to successfully desist from crime than those who make no such social commitments. Interestingly, they also found that desistance from crime is also correlated with assuming social and financial responsibility for one's ageing parents or one's siblings in need (1993, pp.219–220).

More recently, Uggen and Janikula investigated the question of whether involvement in volunteer work can induce a change in a person's likelihood of anti-social conduct. Focusing on young offenders (under 21 years old) involved in a variety of civic volunteer activities 'exemplified by persons stocking food shelves or visiting elderly persons at a hospital' (Uggen 1999, p.350), they found a robust, negative relationship between such volunteer work and arrest (after statistically controlling for the effects of 'anti-social propensities', pro-social attitudes, and commitments to conventional behaviour). Citing de Tocqueville's (1835/1956) argument that, 'By dint of working for one's fellow-citizens, the habit and the taste for serving them is at length acquired' (Uggen and Jankula 1999, p.334), they conclude that volunteerism may reduce criminality through a gradual process of pro-social socialisation (see also Van Voorhis 1985).

Maruna's (2001) own research on the phenomenology of the desistance process provides additional hints at the possible relationship between generativity and desistance. Maruna found that the self-narratives of ex-offenders who were able to 'go straight' (and stay that way) were often care-oriented, other-centred and focused on promoting the next generation. In contrast with active offenders in the sample, the desisters in his study expressed a desire for lasting accomplishments or 'something to show' for one's life. They described newfound pleasures in creative and productive pursuits, and often expressed a special attachment or duty to some particular community, group or cause. Frequently, the desisters in the study based their self-conceptions on identities as 'wounded healers' (White 2000). That is, they tried to find some meaning in their life histories by turning their negative experiences into cautionary tales or hopeful stories of redemption, which they share with younger offenders in similar situations. One participant in Maruna's (2001) research describes this as a desire to '*give people my life* – you know, experiences – what I been through' (male, 31). Another says:

> Hopefully, I'll be something to other people. To a few people down by ours, I already am. I led through example. I get a lot of people now, everyone else's ma's whose (kid is) on drugs, have got me harassed all the time, saying 'Can you help our boy, Joe, or whatever?' 'What if you just come round for a couple of nights and spend time?' (male, 36.)

The stories that these desisters develop out of their life histories are frequently intended, in particular, to be gifts for the next generation. One interviewee states:

> I was saying to [my brother's] kids the other day. I'd sat both of them down the other day, and I said, 'Listen, me and your dad have wasted our lives. I don't want yous to do what we've done. For 15 or 16 years, me and your dad (who also served a prison sentence) wasted our lives, and now we want you to take a leaf out of our book' (male, 33.)

Ironically, even though the speaker says that his life has been wasted, by living to tell the tale, he has in fact found a social purpose or meaning for this part of his life. It has produced a 'book' that he can pass on to the next generation. Indeed, the moral heroism of the 'wounded healer' role 'serves to make acceptable, explicable and even meritorious the guilt-laden, "wasted" portions of an Actor's life' (Lofland 1969, p.287). Narratives like these can help facilitate the difficult process of identity change involved in desisting from crime, by helping ex-convicts 'make sense' of their past lives in crime.

Despite this evidence, the transition from the supposed self-centredness and self-destructiveness of much criminal behaviour to a new identity as a generative role model may sound suspicious to some. A change at the margins, perhaps from egocentrism to some small degree of empathy or consideration for others, might seem the more likely transition. Yet, Maruna (2001) argues that the sense of higher moral purpose that accompanies generative commitments might be necessary for sustaining desistance. For all of its problems, being an offender provides individuals with at least momentary escapes into excitement, power and, sometimes, notoriety, not to mention other material and social benefits. If going straight means little more than accepting docility, self-hatred and stigma, there is little reason to desist from such diversions. The intrinsic rewards and social respectability of generative roles provides a more appealing alternative. Finally, it may be that a degree of 'hypermoralism' on the part of desisters may be required in order for community members, who are necessarily hesitant about re-welcoming former 'deviants', to accept that an ex-offender has really changed his or her ways.

Conclusions: Supporting generativity in practice

The argument developed above suggests that the development, encouragement and facilitation of generativity should be at the heart of effective practice with offenders (see especially Cullen, Sundt and Wozniak 2001; Toch 2000). Although originally conceived by Erikson as a distinct, age-graded stage in the life course, contemporary generativity theory suggests that adults of all ages engage in some level of generative behaviour (see especially McAdams, Hart and Maruna 1998). This literature suggests that such *generativity* is a product not only of inner desire, but also of social and cultural demands; therefore, social institutions can both foster and impede its development. Ironically, no institution does a better job of hindering generativity than prison with its unique ability to separate individuals from their social responsibilities and civic duties. We would argue that this obstruction of normative development undermines the justice system's ability to reduce crime. If instead, the justice system were to become an environment in which generative commitments were modelled and nurtured, and opportunities for generative activities were promoted and rewarded, it would be more effective at reducing re-offending. Put another way, if we want to encourage offenders to 'give up' crime, we would do well to create opportunities for them to engage in 'giving back.'

This claim is built on the assumption that, on some level, generativity is an acquired taste. In the same way that one learns to enjoy drug use and find this a pleasurable experience through an interactive, sub-cultural process, one conceivably learns generativity by *doing* generative things in a setting or niche in which such behaviour is defined as rewarding and good. The latter part of this equation, the enabling niche (Taylor 1997), is critical because there may not be anything inherent about parenting, productivity or mentoring the next generation that makes these behaviours appealing. Frankly, generativity can be very hard work. When it is modelled and appreciated by significant others, however, one learns to intrinsically enjoy and even to 'need' or crave the feelings one gets when doing this work. When these generative motivations become internalised through such social interactions, rehabilitation (or more aptly, moral reintegration) is beginning to happen. Once again therefore, generativity drives us back to the recognition of the pivotal role that relationships play in desistance processes (Burnett and McNeill 2005).

In other areas of social work practice the importance of seeking out every opportunity to support and hasten the development of generativity seems better developed and established than in work with offenders (for example, Saleebey 1997); we refer to this trend as a 'strengths-based' paradigm, though it has many features in common with developing desistance-focused approaches to probation work (McNeill 2003, 2006). The term 'strengths-based' should be seen as an umbrella term that encompasses numerous approaches. Indeed, strengths-based themes have been a staple of progressive criminal justice reforms for much of the last century (Erickson *et al.* 1973; Grant 1968). The term 'strengths-based' highlights the primary difference between this vision for practice and models that we label 'risk-based' (or control) narratives and 'need-based' (or treatment) narratives in probation and social work with offenders (Maruna and LeBel 2003). Arguments in favour of tighter controls or additional 'treatment' programmes both concentrate on offenders' deficits. By contrast, the strengths-based approach is less concerned with a person's 'deficits' and more concerned with the positive contribution that the person can make. How can their lives become useful and purposeful? This shift represents a move 'away from the principle of entitlement to the principle of social exchange' (Levrant *et al.* 1999, p.22) or to what Bazemore (1999) calls 'earned redemption'. The strengths-based paradigm calls for opportunities for offenders and ex-offenders to make amends, demonstrate their value and potential, and experience success in support and leadership roles.

At the heart of the strengths approach is the so-called 'helper principle' of the 1960s New Careers Movement (Caddick 1994): it is better (that is, more reintegrative) to give help than to receive it. The central premise of the New Careers Movement was that disadvantaged people (including ex-offenders) could be trained and placed in entry-level social service jobs that would take advantage of their life experiences as well as their geographic, cultural, and functional similarities to other persons in need. The goal of strengths-based practice, like the New Careers Movement before it, would be to devise ways of creating more helpers. More specifically, the question would be how to transform receivers of help (cast as welfare recipients) into dispensers of help; how to structure the situation so that 'receivers of help will be placed in roles requiring the giving of assistance' (Pearl and Riessman 1965, pp.88–89).

Even though contemporary community penalties lack a coherent or systematic vision for the promotion of generative ideals and behaviours, potentially generative projects and activities can be found (with a little effort) scattered throughout the system; community service is the most obvious example. Quasi-experimental evaluations of community service for offenders consistently show that such penalties outperform both standard probation and custodial sentences in reducing reconviction (Schneider 1986). Participants in community service work almost always rate the experience as a positive one, particularly where there is contact with the beneficiaries of the service (McIvor 1992, p.177). Moreover, there is some evidence that this sort of constrained public service often promotes and preserves things of value for future generations and can aid in moral development and personal growth (Van Voorhis 1985). Yet despite its origins as a rehabilitative panacea, dating back to the Wootton Committee (Advisory Council on the Penal System 1970), community service is no longer primarily justified using a strengths-based narrative. According to Bazemore and Maloney, 'Punishment now appears to have become the dominant objective of service sanctions in many jurisdictions' (1994 p.25). This shift was made explicit in England and Wales (see Halliday 2001, p.40) by the much criticised (and, as it turn out, temporary) re-branding of community service as community *punishment.* Some critics have gone so far as to suggest that community service orders in England and Wales tend to be 'almost exclusively manual, menial and arduous' (Caddick 1994, p.450; see also Blagg and Smith 1989) although this trend seems to be changing. Rex and Gelsthorpe (2002) argue convincingly that regardless of its name, community service work in England and Wales is 'rediscovering reintegration' and undergoing a return to its origins as a rehabilitative and educational intervention (see e.g. Advisory Council on the Penal System 1970).

The potential of generativity and of strengths-based perspectives should not and need not be limited to a consideration of community service/punishment however. With regard to other community-based sentences, at least where these have genuine rehabilitative intentions (as opposed to a more limited focus on control and/or punishment), the evidence from desistance research clearly suggests a necessary emphasis on relationships, networks, social capital and generativity. This is not to say that such interventions should not seek to directly address risk and need factors, but it does require that such interventions must look beyond an unhelpful and disabling preoccupation with risks and needs. The problem with these preoccupations and with the practices that they produce is that that 'they tend to accentuate precisely those aspects of an offender's history, behaviour and attitudes which intervention aims to diminish' (McNeill 2003, pp.155–156). By contrast, the 'strengths-based' or 'desistance-focused' approach requires a more positive focus on what kinds of 'giving back' or 'making good' can and should be facilitated on the basis of an individual's potential, rather than a negative focus on what kinds of controls, sanctions and treatments need to be imposed in order to address an individual's riskiness or neediness (see also Maguire and Raynor 2006). Whereas the former approach recognises and requires the possibility of the reconstruction of a new generative identity, the latter approach, by identifying the offender with his or her needs/risks/offending, runs the risk of unwittingly reinforcing the passivity and fatalism of the old identity.

Of course, in order to fully apply a strengths-based or desistance-focused approach, not only would the practice of 'offender management' need to be reconceived (see McNeill 2006), but society would also need to change. After all, providing opportunities for ex-offenders to 'make good' is only the first step. Generativity – like reintegration or reciprocity – is a two-way process. The ex-offender must be willing to contribute, and society (or at least generative sub-cultures within society) must be willing to accept and recognise those contributions and consequently re-accept the ex-offender. 'Giving up' and 'giving back' will only make sense to offenders in social contexts within which they are offered the realistic prospect of 'getting back' (or perhaps enacting for the first time) their status as fully included citizens. Thus the challenges posed by taking the issue of generativity seriously direct interventions not only towards supporting the development of the individual but also towards developing the communities from which offenders come, to which they belong and for whom *ex*-offenders represent critical but neglected resources. Ironically, perhaps, just as the reconstruction of probation as offender management (in England and Wales, at least) may be finally signalling the demise of its role in community crime prevention initiatives aiming to prevent the *development* of criminal careers, desistance research perhaps re-opens the door to a serious, complex and challenging re-engagement with communities as partners in the processes of sponsoring, supporting and sustaining rehabilitation.

References

Advisory Council on the Penal System (1970) *Non-Custodial and Semi-Custodial Penalties.* London: HMSO.

Barry, M. (2000) 'The Mentor/Monitor Debate in Criminal Justice: What Works for Offenders.' *British Journal of Social Work 30*, 575–595.

Barry, M.A. (2004) *Understanding Youth Offending: In Search of 'Social Recognition'.* PhD dissertation, University of Stirling, Stirling.

Bazemore, G. (1999) 'After Shaming, Whither Reintegration: Restorative Justice and Relational Rehabilitation.' In G. Bazemore and L. Walgrave (eds) *Restorative Juvenile Justice: Repairing the Harm of Youth Crime.* Monsey, NY: Criminal Justice Press.

Bazemore, G. and Maloney, D. (1994) 'Rehabilitating Community Service: Toward Restorative Service Sanctions in a Balanced Justice System.' *Federal Probation 58*, 1, 24–35.

Blagg, H. and Smith, D. (1989) *Crime, Penal Policy and Social Work.* Harlow: Longman.

Bottoms, A., Costello, A. Holmes, D. Muir, G. and Shapland, J. (2004) 'Towards Desistance: Theoretical Underpinnings for an Empirical Study'. *Howard Journal of Criminal Justice 43*, 4, 368–389.

Burnett, R. (1992) *The Dynamics of Recidivism: Summary Report.* Oxford: University of Oxford, Centre for Criminological Research.

Burnett, R. (2000) 'Understanding Criminal Careers Through a Series of In-Depth Interviews.' *Offender Programs Report 4*, 1, 1–16.

Burnett, R. (2004) 'To Re-offend or Not to Re-offend? The Ambivalence of Convicted Property Offenders.' In S. Maruna and R. Immarigeon (eds) *After Crime and Punishment: Pathways to Offender Reintegration.* Cullompton: Willan Publishing.

Burnett, R. and Maruna, S. (2004) 'So 'Prison Works', Does It? The Criminal Careers of 130 Men Released from Prison under Home Secretary Michael Howard.' *Howard Journal of Criminal Justice 43*, 390–404.

Burnett, R. and McNeill, F. (2005) 'The Place of the Officer-offender Relationship in Assisting Offenders to Desist from Crime.' *Probation Journal 52*, 3, 247–268.

Caddick, B. (1994) 'The 'New Careers' Experiment in Rehabilitating Offenders: Last Messages from a Fading Star.' *British Journal of Social Work 24*, 449–460.

Cullen, F.T. (1994) 'Social Support as an Organizing Concept in Criminology: Presidential Address to the Academy of Criminal Justice Sciences.' *Justice Quarterly 11*, 527–559.

Cullen, F.T., Sundt, J.L., and Wozniak, J.F. (2001) 'The Virtuous Prison: Toward a Restorative Rehabilitation.' In H.N. Pontell and D. Shichor (eds) *Contemporary Issues in Crime and Criminal Justice: Essays in Honor of Gilbert Geis.* Upper Saddle River, NJ: Prentice-Hall.

Erikson, E.H. (1963) *Childhood and Society,* 2nd edn. New York: Norton.

Erickson, R.J., Crow, W.J., Zurcher, L.A. and Connet, A.V. (1973) *Paroled But Not Free.* New York: Behavioral.

Farrall, S. (2002) *Rethinking What Works With Offenders: Probation, Social Context and Desistance From Crime.* Cullompton: Willan Publishing.

Farrall, S., and Bowling, B. (1999) 'Structuration, human development and desistance from crime.' *British Journal of Criminology 39*, 253–268.

Farrington, D.P. (1997) 'Human development and criminal careers.' In M. Maguire, R. Morgan and R. Reiner (eds) *The Oxford Handbook of Criminology*, 2nd edn. Oxford: Clarendon.

Glueck, S. and Glueck, E.T. (1937) *Later Criminal Careers.* New York: Commonwealth Fund.

Goring, C. (1919) *The English Convict.* London: His Majesty's Stationery Office.

Gottfredson, M., and Hirschi, T. (1990) *A General Theory of Crime.* Stanford: Stanford University Press.

Grant, J.D. (1968) 'The Offender as a Correctional Manpower Resource.' In F. Riessman and H.L. Popper (eds) *Up From Poverty: New Career Ladders for Nonprofessionals.* New York: Harper and Row.

Halliday, J. (2001) *Making Punishments Work: Report of a Review of the Sentencing Framework for England and Wales.* London: Home Office.

Hill, M. (1999) 'What's the problem? Who can help? The perspectives of children and young people on their well-being and on helping professionals.' *Journal of Social Work Practice 13*, 2, 135–45.

Lemert, E.M. (1951) *Social Pathology.* New York: McGraw-Hill.

Levrant, S., Cullen, F.T., Fulton, B. and Wozniak, J.F. (1999) 'Reconsidering Restorative Justice: The Corruption of Benevolence Revisited?' *Crime and Delinquency 45*, 3–27.

Lofland, J. (1969) *Deviance and Identity.* Englewood Cliffs, NJ: Prentice-Hall.

Maguire, M. and Raynor, P. (2006) 'How the Resettlement of Prisoners Promotes Desistance from Crime: Or Does it?' *Criminology and Criminal Justice 6*, 1, 19–38.

Maruna. S. (2001) *Making Good: How Ex-convicts Reform and Rebuild their Lives.* Washington, DC: American Psychological Association.

Maruna, S. and LeBel, T. (2003) 'Welcome Home? Examining the Re-entry Court Concept from a Strengths-based Perspective.' *Western Criminology Review 4*, 2, 91–107.

Maruna, S., Immarigeon, R. and LeBel, T. (2004) 'Ex-Offender Reintegration: Theory and Practice.' In S. Maruna and R. Immarigeon (eds) *After Crime and Punishment: Pathways to Ex-Offender Reintegration.* Cullompton: Willan.

McAdams, D.P. and de St Aubin, E. (1998) 'Introduction.' In D.P. McAdams and E. de St Aubin (eds) *Generativity and Adult Development: How and Why We Care for the Next Generation.* Washington, DC: American Psychological Association.

McAdams, D.P., Hart, H. and Maruna, S. (1998) 'The anatomy of generativity.' In D.P. McAdams and E. de St Aubin (eds) *Generativity and Adult Development: How and Why We Care for the Next Generation.* Washington, DC: American Psychological Association.

McCulloch, P. (2005) 'Probation, Social Context and Desistance: Retracing the Relationship.' *Probation Journal 52*, 1, 8–22.

McIvor, G. (1992) *Sentenced to Serve: The Operation and Impact of Community Service by Offenders.* Aldershot: Avebury.

McIvor, G. (2004) 'Getting Personal: Developments in Policy and Practice in Scotland.' In G. Mair (ed.) *What Matters in Probation.* Cullompton: Willan.

McNeill, F. (2003) 'Desistance-Focused Probation Practice.' In W.-H. Chui and M. Nellis (eds) *Moving Probation Forward: Evidence, Arguments and Practice.* Harlow: Pearson Longman.

McNeill, F. (2004) 'Desistance, Rehabilitation and Correctionalism: Developments and Prospects in Scotland', *Howard Journal of Criminal Justice 43*, 4, 420–436.

McNeill, F. (2006) 'A Desistance Paradigm for Offender Management.' *Criminology and Criminal Justice 6*, 1, 39–62.

McNeill, F., Batchelor, S., Burnett, R. and Knox, J. (2005) *21st Century Social Work. Reducing Re-offending: Key Practice Skills*. Edinburgh: Scottish Executive.

Pearl, A. and Riessman, F. (1965) *New Careers for the Poor: The Nonprofessional in Human Service*. New York: The Free Press.

Raynor, P. (2004) 'Rehabilitative and Reintegrative Approaches.' In A. Bottoms, S. Rex and G. Robinson (eds) *Alternatives to Prison: Options for an Insecure Society*. Cullompton: Willan.

Rex, S. (1999) 'Desistance from Offending: Experiences of Probation.' *Howard Journal of Criminal Justice 38*, 366–383.

Rex, S. and Gelsthorpe, L. (2002) 'The Role of Community Service in Reducing Offending: Evaluating Pathfinder Projects in the UK.' *Howard Journal of Criminal Justice 41*, 311–325.

Rumgay, J. (2004) 'Scripts for Safer Survival: Pathways out of Female Crime.' *Howard Journal of Criminal Justice 43*, 405–419.

Rutter, M. (1996) 'Transitions and Turning Points in Developmental Psychopathology: As Applied to the Age Span Between Childhood and Mid-adulthood.' *Journal of Behavioral Development 19*, 3, 603–626.

Saleebey, D. (ed.) (1997) *The Strengths Perspective in Social Work Practice*, 2nd edn. New York: Longman.

Sampson, R.J. and Laub, J. (1992) 'Crime and deviance in the life course.' *Annual Review of Sociology 18*, 63–84.

Sampson, R.J. and Laub, J. (1993) *Crime in the Making: Pathways and Turning Points through Life*. Cambridge, MA: Harvard University Press.

Schneider, A. (1986) 'Restitution and Recidivism Rates of Juvenile Offenders: Results from Four Experimental Studies.' *Criminology 24*, 533–552.

Schoon, I.J. and Bynner, H. (2003) 'Risk and Resilience in the Life Course: Implications for Interventions and Social Policies.' *Journal of Youth Studies 6*, 1, 21–31.

Taylor, J.B. (1997) 'Niches and Practice: Extending the Ecological Perspective.' In D. Saleebey (ed.) *The Strengths Perspective in Social Work Practice*, 2nd edn. New York: Longman.

Toch, H. (1997) *Corrections: A Humanistic Approach*. Guilderland, NY: Harrow and Heston.

Toch, H. (2000) 'Altruistic Activity as Correctional Treatment.' *International Journal of Offender Therapy and Comparative Criminology 44*, 3, 270–278.

Tocqueville, A. de (1835/1956) *Democracy in America*. New York: Knopf. (First published 1835.)

Turner, V. (1969) *The Ritual Process: Structure and Anti-Structure*. Chicago, IL: Aldine.

Uggen, C. and Janikula, J. (1999) 'Volunteerism and Arrest in the Transition to Adulthood.' *Social Forces 78*, 331–362.

Van Voorhis, P. (1985) 'Restitution outcome and probationers' assessments of restitution: The effects of moral development.' *Criminal Justice and Behavior 12*, 259–287.

White, W.L. (2000) *Toward a New Recovery Movement: Historical Reflections on Recovery, Treatment and Advocacy*. Retrieved 2 December 2001, from http://www.unhooked.com/sep/wmwhite_advocacy21.pdf.

CHAPTER 13

Restorative Justice

Gwen Robinson

Introduction

As many of its proponents have pointed out, responses to offending which we now understand under the umbrella of 'restorative justice' have a long history, and have been found in a variety of social and cultural contexts. Restorative justice, then, is not a recent invention; but few commentators would doubt that it is currently enjoying unprecedented attention and investment. As Dignan (2005, p.1) observes, a distinctive restorative justice agenda has taken just a quarter of a century to 'leap from a position of virtual obscurity to one of increasing international influence'. This is evident both in the growing prominence of restorative justice in government policy, but also in a burgeoning academic literature: according to Daly (2004), the period 1993–2004 has seen the publication of over 60 books on restorative justice written in English, a crescendo of scholarly attention which no other justice practice has previously commanded.

In this chapter the focus is the practice(s) of restorative justice, with a particular emphasis on questions about how those practices have been evaluated. Whilst there is some reference to theory, where restorative justice practice is closely associated with a particular theoretical stance, the chapter does not consider in any depth the rich theoretical and philosophical heritage of what is often referred to as the restorative justice 'movement'. Readers interested in this aspect of restorative justice are referred to Dignan (2005), which is an excellent starting point.

Defining restorative justice

'Restorative justice' is a term which has been used to denote a wide variety of practices, carried out in a number of different social, cultural and historical contexts. Indeed, restorative justice is perhaps best described as a 'conceptual umbrella' under which a number of different practices have found common ground. Perhaps not surprisingly, then, there is no single agreed definition. At its broadest, restorative justice denotes a strategy or set of strategies oriented toward the resolution of conflicts or disputes, not necessarily acts defined as criminal offences. Thus, it has been deployed to deal with anything from school bullying to the resolution of political conflicts (e.g. Dignan and Lowey 2000). In the more specific context of offending, restorative justice is perhaps best described as an approach which seeks to deal with or respond to offending by involving both offender and victim, and sometimes members of the wider community. This 'essence' of restorative justice is neatly captured in Marshall's popular definition: 'Restorative Justice is a process whereby parties with a stake in a specific offence collectively resolve how to deal with the aftermath of the offence and its implications for the future' (1999, p.5). Restorative justice can, thus, be characterised as a way of working with offenders, but its scope is much broader than 'traditional' social work or probation practice, in that it potentially involves a range of stakeholders[1], and is not focused solely on the offender. As Schiff has argued: 'As a justice strategy, restorative justice is concerned with much more than simply what is done to or with offenders, and as such it is a much more ambitious justice response [than] either retribution, deterrence, rehabilitation or incapacitation, all of which have far more modest, offender-centred goals' (2003, p.330).

Indeed, the current restorative justice 'boom' is commonly understood in the context of a 'victim's movement' which has sought over a number of years to raise the profile of crime victims, forefront their needs and promote their involvement in justice processes in a number of ways (e.g. Miers 2004; see also Dignan 2005).[2] As Marshall (1999) explains, the objectives of restorative justice include offender-focused ones such as encouraging offenders to assume responsibility for their actions and reintegrating offenders into their communities; however, victim-focused objectives, such as attending to the material, financial and emotional needs of victims, are also central to the majority of restorative justice initiatives. Other potential objectives are not specific to individual stakeholders: for example,

1   Unlike most areas of social work, restorative justice does not usually involve a 'primary client': in fact many restorative justice theorists and practitioners would probably say that there is no client as such, and that their focus is a crime or conflict and its resolution.

2   For a sociologically oriented analysis of the rise of restorative justice, see Bottoms (2003).

the prevention of re-offending is generally recognised as a key aim of restorative justice which is likely to benefit the whole community (see generally Johnstone 2002). It should be noted, though, that reflecting the contested nature of restorative justice and the difficulties of reaching a definitional consensus, producing an agreed set of aims or objectives has proved equally problematic. This is an issue which will resurface later in the chapter.

Restorative justice and criminal justice

For some of its advocates, restorative justice constitutes a way of responding to offending which is radically different from criminal justice. Advocates of restorative justice commonly trace the roots of this movement to the 'traditional' dispute resolution practices of pre-modern and non-western cultures which, it is argued, represent a radical (and favourable) alternative to western criminal justice, with its tendency to sideline the victim and to favour retributive punishment, rather than the more 'positive' outcomes of reconciliation, reparation and restoration (e.g. Barnett 1977; Wright 1991; Zehr 1985; see also von Hirsch *et al.* 2003). There are indeed a small number of contemporary communities in which restorative justice operates outside the formal criminal justice system (e.g. see Roberts and Roach (2003) on restorative justice in Canada, and Miles (2004) on the Parish Hall Enquiry system in Jersey). It is also the case that, in some jurisdictions, the recent development of restorative justice has reflected a concern with involving or empowering communities for whom criminal justice is perceived as discriminatory or illegitimate. For example, the reform of the youth justice system in Northern Ireland has been understood as an attempt to establish a system that is seen as legitimate by Republican/Catholic and Unionist/Protestant groups alike (Dignan 2005). Similarly, in New Zealand the establishment of restorative justice has been associated with attempts to develop a system of justice which is culturally sensitive, taking into account the cultural values of its indigenous populations (Daly 2002; Maxwell and Morris 1993).

However, despite the opposition, or juxtaposition, of restorative and criminal justice in some theoretical work, the contemporary development of restorative justice practice has tended to take place in the context of, rather than outside, 'mainstream' criminal justice – albeit not always at active 'decision points' in the criminal justice process[3]. Restorative justice has, thus, been deployed in the context of diversionary measures (e.g. a police caution or warning); between conviction and sentence; as part of a sentence; and following the imposition and completion of a sentence. It should be noted, however, that the extent to which restorative justice has become a 'mainstream' response to offending differs between jurisdictions. For example, in New Zealand conferencing has become an integral part of the criminal justice process for juveniles, whilst in Australia some states have introduced restorative justice on a legislated basis whilst others have not (see McIvor 2004).

Further, restorative justice projects have tended to be managed and run by criminal justice personnel, most notably police and probation officers, albeit often seconded from their agencies to undertake this specialist area of practice[4]. Indeed, one of the most interesting, but least discussed, aspects of restorative justice, certainly in the UK, has been its role in confronting and breaking down the 'traditional' practices of criminal justice professionals. For example, as we shall see below, restorative justice has developed quite rapidly in the police service. Whilst in the past police officers have largely allied themselves with the interests and protection of victims, involvement in restorative justice schemes has entailed the adoption of a more balanced approach, requiring respect for the needs and situations of both victims and offenders (Dignan and Lowey 2000; Young and Hoyle 2003). Similarly, for professionals like probation officers who have traditionally identified with the needs and problems of offenders, restorative justice is one of a number of developments which has encouraged an awareness of and sensitivity to the needs of victims. For both professional groups, restorative justice has necessitated specialist training and the acquisition of new skills.

3   Wright (1991) helpfully distinguishes between restorative justice schemes which are *relatively independent* from and those which are *dependent* on criminal justice processes. The former deal with cases which have already entered the criminal justice process, but are referred unconditionally, such as where a police caution has been issued and referral is recommended; or a case has gone through the system and is referred at the end, such as during a prison sentence. 'Dependent' schemes offer restorative justice at a point where the criminal justice process has not yet run its course: for example, between conviction and sentence.

4   Not all restorative justice schemes have been run by criminal justice personnel, however. For example, one of the schemes currently being evaluated under the Crime Reduction Programme (see further below) employs experienced community mediators as well as probation and prison officers.

Restorative justice in practice

Reflecting the ongoing debate about how restorative justice should be defined, there is no 'definitive' typology of restorative justice practices (cf. McIvor 2004; Dignan 2005). However, the most common operational examples of restorative justice fall under two main headings.

Victim-offender mediation: in which contact between offender and victim is facilitated by a specially trained, neutral third party (mediator or facilitator). Contact between the two parties may be direct (i.e. face-to-face) or indirect, involving the relaying of questions and/or information by a mediator/facilitator. The Victim/Offender Reconciliation Program (VORP), which began life in the mid-1970s in Kitchener, Ontario, is generally recognised as the first victim/offender mediation scheme bringing convicted offenders and their victims face to face; whilst the first 'diversion' scheme utilising mediation dates back to 1971 in Columbus, Ohio (Wright 1991). Recent research indicates that victim–offender mediation is currently the most common form of restorative justice practice in both the USA and Europe.

Restorative conferencing: differs from victim-offender mediation principally in that it tends to involve members of the wider community as well as the victim and offender. Dignan (2005) distinguishes between two main variants: family group conferencing, and police-led community conferencing. *Family group conferencing* originated in New Zealand as a means of dealing with offending by young people, and as an antidote to criminal justice processes which tended to offer little opportunity for victim involvement, and which were perceived as potentially discriminatory in respect of the Maori population (Maxwell and Morris 1993). *Police-led community conferencing,* in contrast, originated in the early 1990s in the small town of Wagga Wagga in New South Wales, Australia. Subsequently, this particular conferencing model spread not just to other parts of Australia (most notably Canberra, where the well-known 'reintegrative shaming experiment' – RISE – was instituted in 1995)[5], but also to the USA, and the UK (see further below). These two models differ on a number of important dimensions, but one of the key differences is that police-led conferencing, unlike family group conferencing, has been heavily influenced by Braithwaite's (1989) theory of

5   Daly (2001) notes that since 1993, whilst the Wagga Wagga model has spread to and proved popular in other parts of the world, it has in Australia largely been replaced by New Zealand-style family group conferencing.

'reintegrative shaming'. This means that conferences tend to be 'scripted' in order first to encourage feelings of shame on the part of the offender; and second to facilitate the offender's reintegration into his or her community.

A further model of restorative justice centres on the deployment of *community panels*, which are common in the USA but have been established in a number of other jurisdictions, including UK youth justice systems. These involve panels of specially trained lay people, usually in the sanctioning of young people, and often with an emphasis on negotiating reparation for victims. In England and Wales the Referral Order, introduced by the Youth Justice and Criminal Evidence Act 1999, involves the referral of a young offender[6] to a youth offender panel which allows victims, if they choose, to play a role in deciding how the offender can make amends (Crawford and Newburn 2003). For a description of other, less common, operational examples of restorative justice, see McIvor (2004) and Dignan (2005).

Restorative justice in the UK context

Restorative justice practice has developed in the UK context over a number of years, only recently reaching a crescendo of activity. During the 1980s a number of police- and probation-led mediation schemes developed on an ad hoc basis. The majority deployed mediation in conjunction with a police caution and targeted juvenile offenders having committed relatively minor offences, but a small number focused on adult offenders and sometimes quite serious offences (Marshall 1984). In the mid-1980s, in the context of a growing interest in victims and reparation, the Home Office funded a small number of experimental schemes for a short period, but 'official' interest in mediation was not sustained (Davis 1992).

However, restorative justice was to receive a significant boost in the late 1990s, when the incoming Labour government announced plans to put restorative justice principles at the heart of a reformed youth justice system (Home Office 1997). The 'new youth justice' sought to implement restorative justice principles in three main ways: through the introduction of two new penalties (the Reparation Order and the Action Plan Order) and the reform of the system of cautioning (Holdaway *et al.* 2001). All three initiatives were conceived with a strong emphasis on reparation to victims (including an apology) (Bottoms and Dignan 2005; see also Chapter 2 in this volume). Subsequently the Referral Order was introduced for 10–17-year-olds

6   Available to 10–17-year olds pleading guilty and convicted by the courts
     for the first time.

(see above). Meanwhile, the Thames Valley police service, which had been developing restorative justice initiatives for a number of years, decided to move wholesale toward a model of 'restorative cautioning', along the lines of the police-led conferencing model described above (Hoyle, Young and Hill 2002).

In 2001 the Home Office decided to provide funding to three restorative justice schemes under the auspices of its Crime Reduction Programme. These schemes were to test the potential of victim-offender mediation and conferencing in a variety of contexts, targeting both juvenile and adult offenders, and a range of offences from the relatively minor to very serious assault and property offences (Shapland *et al.* 2004). The Home Office has subsequently published a 'restorative justice strategy' (Home Office 2003)[7] and, building on experience in Thames Valley, the Criminal Justice Act 2003 has introduced a statutory basis for restorative justice as part of a police caution. The Home Office has also announced a new pilot restorative justice project involving the diversion of adult offenders from court.

Evaluating restorative justice

As Miers (2004, p.29) has recently noted, there is 'no shortage of evaluations of the many forms assumed by restorative justice programmes'. Whilst much of the research comes from overseas (most notably Australia, New Zealand and North America), where restorative justice is more firmly established, there is also a growing body of UK research. This includes the programme of evaluation of mediation schemes coordinated by the Home Office in the 1980s (Marshall and Merry 1990) and a more recent Home Office evaluation of seven restorative justice schemes (Miers *et al.* 2001); as well as an evaluation of the SACRO mediation project in Scotland (Warner 1992). There are also the recent evaluations of the Referral Order pilots (Crawford and Newburn 2003; Newburn *et al.* 2002) and restorative cautioning in Thames Valley (Hoyle *et al.* 2002; Wilcox, Young and Hoyle 2004), as well as a national evaluation of the Youth Justice Board's restorative justice projects (Wilcox and Hoyle 2004). A substantial ongoing study, from which only interim findings are available at the time of writing, is the Crime Reduction Programme (CRP) evaluation on behalf of the Home Office (Shapland *et*

---

7   The Home Office strategy document makes it clear that the government
      sees restorative justice as an effective way of putting victims' needs at the
      heart of the criminal justice system, as well as encouraging offenders to
      take responsibility and make amends for their behaviour, and for involving
      the community in responses to crime and anti-social behaviour.

al. 2004)[8]. Most of these studies have been referred to above. Additionally, there are a growing number of authoritative reviews of the evaluative literature, including those by Dignan (2005; Dignan and Lowey 2000), Kurki (2000, 2003) and Miers (2001, 2004). It will be clear that, in the face of this recent proliferation of evaluative literature, this chapter is able to do no more than skim the surface of what we know about the effectiveness of restorative justice. With this in mind, this section will describe the typical ways in which restorative justice has been evaluated, with some reference to the main findings, before moving on to raise some issues about the evaluation of restorative justice.

Participation and participant satisfaction

As Miers (2004) points out, evaluative research commonly focuses on two aspects of restorative justice: the process itself; and the products or outcomes which may or may not follow.

As far as the process of restorative justice is concerned, one focus of existing evaluative research has been assessing levels of participation, particularly among 'eligible' victims. As Dignan and Lowey (2000) have observed, the available research consistently shows that the majority of victims are willing in principle to participate in restorative justice, given adequate notice and preparation, and arrangements that are convenient. However, such positive findings are not universal. For example, in their study of the Referral Order pilot schemes, Newburn *et al.* (2002) found very low rates of victim attendance in the context of youth offender panels – just 13 per cent. Hoyle *et al.* (2002), similarly, found a victim participation rate in restorative cautioning conferences of just 14 per cent.

For those who do take part in restorative justice, measures of short-term satisfaction have produced generally positive results. As Kurki (2003, p.294) has explained, the measurement of participant satisfaction is almost universal in evaluative studies, typically ascertained not only by asking participants directly about levels of satisfaction, but also whether they would recommend the process to others; whether they would choose to do it again, and so on. In a small number of studies, these 'satisfaction' measures have been compared for those participating in 'ordinary' criminal justice proceedings, who form a control group. For example, the

---

8   The latter is at a very preliminary stage in terms of published results, whilst the former evaluation is complete with the exception of a reconviction analysis.

Canberra RISE experiment has compared the effects of a diversionary conference with those of 'standard' court processing for four categories of case/offender (Sherman *et al.* 1998). Most reviews of research on this dimension of effectiveness point to high levels of satisfaction with restorative justice processes amongst both victims and offenders taking part in mediation and conferencing (Dignan and Lowey 2000). However, there have been some exceptions. For example, in an early study of conferencing in New Zealand only half of victims reported being satisfied, and just over a quarter (27%) said they felt worse as a result of participating in a conference (Maxwell and Morris 1993). It has been suggested that some victims may have felt coerced into participating (Marshall 1999), thus rendering the experience a less than positive one for them. A degree of perceived coercion was also found among young offenders in the restorative cautioning study: two-thirds of the young offenders involved in restorative cautioning reported feeling that they had no meaningful choice about taking part (Hoyle *et al.* 2002). In the recent Home Office evaluation, Miers *et al.* (2001) found that a few offenders felt worse for having taken part, although they were in a minority. In this context it is also worth noting that whilst offenders generally report high levels of satisfaction, they do not perceive restorative justice as an 'easy option': in the RISE experiment offenders participating in conferences found the experience more stressful than their counterparts who took the court route (Sherman *et al.* 1998).

Another common set of 'satisfaction' measures relates to the notion of procedural justice, which essentially refers to perceptions of fairness. Again, restorative justice programmes appear to perform well in respect of this dimension. For example, in the recent Youth Justice Board evaluation, the majority of both victims and offenders perceived the process as fair (Wilcox and Hoyle 2004), whilst the RISE experiment reports higher levels of perceived procedural fairness amongst both victims and offenders taking part in conferences, than amongst those attending court (Sherman *et al.* 1998).

Outcomes for victims

The potential outcomes of restorative justice for victims may be both 'tangible' and 'symbolic' (Dignan and Lowey 2000). In respect of the former, evaluations consistently report not only that a high proportion of restorative justice cases result in an agreement being reached (typically involving the payment of compensation or the performance of other kinds of reparation), but also that rates of completion are high. 'Symbolic' outcomes usually refer to the receipt of apologies, which many victims value more than material forms of reparation (e.g. Marshall and Merry

1990). Again, restorative justice has been shown to perform well in respect of securing symbolic forms of reparation. For example, in the RISE study, whilst victims received apologies in none of the court proceedings observed, in the context of conferencing 67 per cent of victims in property cases received apologies, as did an even higher proportion (82%) of victims of violence (Sherman *et al.* 1998).

Kurki (2003) further reports that several studies have indicated that restorative justice can significantly reduce victims' feelings of anger, anxiety and fear of revictimisation. For example, in a combined evaluation of four Canadian mediation programmes, Umbreit (1995, cited in Kurki 2003, p.297) found that whilst 11 per cent of victims still feared revictimisation by the same offender after mediation, this figure was significantly higher (31%) for victims who had been referred to the scheme but had not ultimately participated.

Offender recidivism

As a number of commentators have observed, interest in the capacity of restorative justice to impact on recidivism has increased in recent years. For example, the impact of restorative justice on recidivism rates was one of the key variables considered by Miers *et al.* (2001), and the Thames Valley restorative cautioning evaluation has also included a reconviction study (Wilcox *et al.* 2004). The current CRP evaluation will also be investigating the impact of restorative justice on reconviction rates. Reviews of research on the impact of restorative justice on recidivism rates invariably conclude that, to date, findings have been mixed. Whilst some studies – and some programmes – appear to demonstrate an impact on reconviction rates, others do not. For example, only one of the seven schemes investigated by Miers *et al.* (2001) yielded a reduction in reconviction amongst participants two years after taking part. In this (West Yorkshire) scheme (which dealt with more serious, adult offenders – over half of whom had received custodial sentences), participating offenders were less likely to be reconvicted within two years (44%) than a control group (56%). More recently, Wilcox *et al.* (2004) reported no significant differences in terms of the frequency or seriousness of subsequent offending between offenders subject to restorative cautions and control groups receiving 'ordinary' cautions.

Findings to date also suggest that there may be differential impacts in terms of reconviction for different types of offender. In the RISE study, which compared the impact of restorative justice on four groups of offenders, Sherman, Strang and Woods (2000) reported that conferencing reduced recidivism rates for juveniles who committed violent crimes, but there were no differences for shoplifters or property offenders, and drunk drivers were actually slightly *more* likely to be reconvicted after conferencing. Meanwhile, Miers (2004) speculates that the positive findings for the West Yorkshire scheme suggest that mediation works more effectively with 'higher tariff' cases than with the more minor cases which are the bread-and-butter of most restorative justice programmes.

Issues in evaluation

This brief overview of research findings has highlighted the emergence of a small number of 'standard' measures of effectiveness, which have tended to be common to restorative justice evaluations. This apparent consensus may well give the impression that the evaluation of restorative justice is an unproblematic enterprise. However, this is not the case. Dignan and Lowey (2000, p.34) are amongst a number of commentators who have noted that, despite a proliferation of research studies, the evaluation of restorative justice is very much in its infancy and, for a number of reasons, the findings of evaluative studies should not necessarily be taken at face value. In this final section, a number of issues relevant to the evaluation of restorative justice are identified.

Establishing evaluation criteria

One problem in the evaluation of restorative justice has been establishing suitable criteria against which to assess effectiveness. Schiff (2003) argues that before we can assess whether restorative justice is effective, we first need to ask some fundamental questions about how the 'success' and 'failure' of programmes should be measured. Of course this is not just true for restorative justice, but for all programmes subject to evaluation. Nonetheless, restorative justice poses particular problems in this respect.

First, as noted at the beginning of the chapter, the aims of restorative justice programmes have not always been explicitly stated, and in some cases have been particularly vague, abstract and/or ambiguous. Aims such as 'restoration of victims, offenders and communities' may be laudable, but they are not easily operationalised and therefore are extremely difficult to measure. It is probably for this reason that evaluations so far have tended to focus on individual-level outcomes and have used measures that are typical of research on conventional criminal justice programmes: for example, with short-term satisfaction issues and, more recently, recidivism rates, dominating evaluative efforts (Kurki 2003). Von Hirsch, Ashworth and Shearing (2003, pp.23, 29) have argued that the abstract nature of restorative justice objectives creates a problem of 'dangling standards for evaluation'. What they mean by this is that it is not always clear just how evaluation criteria are related to the purposes of a restorative justice programme; reasons are rarely provided as to why a given evaluation norm, rather than another, has been chosen. However, as Kurki (2003, p.293) has rightly observed, it has proved difficult to develop 'more innovative measures that would better capture the goals and values of restorative justice'.

A second issue is that restorative justice programmes have commonly been associated with multiple aims or objectives, which have not always been prioritised – or indeed shared – by all of the programme's stakeholders. For example, when the Home Office commissioned research to evaluate a number of schemes it was funding in the mid-1980s, it was noted by the project manager of one of the schemes that different stakeholders did not always share the same objectives or priorities. Thus, whilst the government was at that time primarily interested in finding new ways to secure reparation for victims, the probation service was principally interested in providing alternatives to custody, whilst advocates of mediation were mostly concerned with the potential of restorative justice as an alternative to the formal criminal justice system (Ruddick 1989). In their ongoing CRP evaluation, Shapland *et al.* (2004) have similarly found that stakeholders claim to be pursuing a variety of aims – not always clearly prioritised – in relation to the programmes with which they are working.

In the absence of clearly stated, agreed aims which can be ranked in some kind of order of priority, the researcher faces a dilemma. Whilst it is clearly possible to assess separately the achievement of a variety of different objectives, when it comes to answering the question 'does restorative justice work?' the researcher is in some difficulty. For example, if a scheme has been shown to meet victims' emotional needs, but does not reduce re-offending, is it a success?

Getting inside the 'black box': What exactly happens in restorative justice?

As a number of reviews of evaluative research have made clear, much of what has been done in the name of restorative justice appears to have produced positive outcomes in terms of participant satisfaction and procedural justice, and in a small number of cases reductions in reconviction have been reported. However, researchers know relatively little about how and why these positive outcomes occur. This is because, as Kurki (2003) has observed, few studies have captured the *quality* of the restorative justice encounter and are therefore unable to relate processes to outcomes. Indeed, much of the evaluative research has been conducted retrospectively, such that researchers have tended not to have access to direct observations of restorative justice proceedings. There are, however, some exceptions to this. For example, in their evaluation of restorative cautioning, Hoyle *et al.* (2002) observed 79 restorative justice encounters, the majority of which were also tape-recorded. On the basis of their initial observation of 23 encounters, the researchers concluded that 'implementation failure' was such that only 2 of the 23 cases actually merited the label 'restorative justice'. Each of the other 21 cases involved significant variation from the prescribed (and scripted) model: for example, with facilitators dominating the exchanges which took place and/or sidelining one or more participants.

Kurki (2003, p.307) has argued that it seems 'more and more important to focus resources and research on the restorative quality of initiatives'. In other words, we need to be asking not just whether restorative justice practices are capable of producing positive outcomes, but also *why* they do: what conditions need to be present, in which particular contexts? On the basis of existing research, Kurki argues, victim presence, the expression of genuine apology and remorse by the offender, equal participation in decision-making and consensus on decisions have been reported as factors that are related to lower rates of recidivism; however, much more research is needed in order to refine the 'ingredients' of effective restorative justice practice.

Reconviction as an outcome measure

This brings us rather neatly to another potentially problematic issue in restorative justice evaluation: namely, the growing interest in reconviction as an outcome measure. As Hoyle *et al.* (2002, p.46) have observed, achieving reductions in reoffending 'for most policy-makers is the litmus test'. But whilst this is almost certainly true, it does pose various problems.

First, there is the problem of 'dangling standards for evaluation' which has already been referred to (von Hirsch *et al.* 2003). That is, it is not actually at all clear just *how* reducing recidivism is linked with the stated purposes of restorative justice, or *why* we should expect restorative justice to contribute to the reduction of offending. Indeed, it has been argued that reducing recidivism is perhaps the goal least likely to be achieved because of the limited ability of most approaches to impact upon the wider 'criminogenic' factors that contribute to and sustain offending behaviour (Dignan 2001; Dignan and Lowey 2000; McIvor 2004).

But even if we accept recidivism as a relevant outcome measure, there are other issues to consider. How are we to make sense of a reduction in recidivism following restorative justice? It is surely possible that any observed reductions in reoffending on the part of offenders taking part in restorative justice may not be a direct result of their participation in restorative justice, but rather a reflection of 'selection effects' (Hudson 2003). For example, participation in restorative justice may be for an offender a means of reinforcing a prior decision to desist from further offending. In this case, taking part in restorative justice would be a *correlate* rather than a *cause* of desistance. A related issue concerns offenders for whom restorative justice is only one element in a sanction which may have other 'rehabilitative' elements – such as a probation order or a prison sentence which offers access to offending behaviour programmes or other services. Here it may be extremely difficult to isolate the specific impact of the restorative justice intervention. This is an interesting issue, particularly when considering the growing interest in utilising restorative justice with more serious offences and offenders. The use of experimental designs involving random allocation to restorative justice or a control group, as in the RISE and CRP evaluations, arguably goes some way toward resolving this particular issue, but it will not necessarily enable researchers to unravel all of these issues effectively.

Assuming recidivism reduction to be the 'ultimate' goal of restorative justice is also problematic in that it arguably diminishes the importance or salience of other goals, particularly victim-centred ones. Whilst it may be argued that the prevention of further offending may be viewed by victims as a favourable outcome – and even possibly as part of the process of 'making amends' (von Hirsch *et al.* 2003) – there is also a danger that a set of practices which for many of its advocates derives legitimacy from its claim to balance the interests of both victims and offenders may wind up as just another means toward the end of crime reduction. And if restorative justice should come to be primarily conceived in such terms, the costs of 'failure' are high: poor performance in respect of reducing reconviction could in theory result in the abandonment of restorative justice in favour of (allegedly) more effective means of crime reduction, such as incapacitation. Thus, as Hudson (2003, p.190) points out, the crime reduction claims of restorative justice are 'risky': '[crime] reduction is not the ground on which restorative justice should be selling itself, because it is a "competition" which restorative justice is bound to lose'.

Dignan provides a fitting conclusion to this section, with his observation that:

> policy makers need to retain a sense of realism about the crime reduction potential of restorative justice initiatives…and to accept that there may be other sound reasons for supporting such developments even if the hoped-for reduction in re-cidivism rates does not materialise or turns out to be more modest than might have been anticipated. (2001, p.344)

Conclusion

This chapter has been able to do little more than skim the surface of restorative justice, presenting an overview of its practical forms, its development and the ways in which it has been (and is currently being) evaluated. There is little doubt that, in the UK context, restorative justice is increasing in popularity, and enjoying unparalleled political support. However, its future is not guaranteed:

> Looking back in 2024, will we see the current fascination with [restorative justice] as a short-term fad that stayed at the margins or as a turning point in the history of justice? Will we see it as a failed experiment or as a start of a great transformation? (Daly 2004, p.500)

These are interesting and pertinent questions. Part of the answer will depend upon the findings of current and future research into the outcomes and potential benefits of restorative justice. Whilst it should be borne in mind that developments in criminal justice (and social work) have not always depended upon clear evidence of their effectiveness, it is nonetheless crucial that research informs future policy and practice. Despite its current popularity, restorative justice is unlikely to prove a suitable approach to dealing with crime across the board, and the role of researchers is to help inform practitioners and policy makers about the kinds of circumstances, cases, victims and offenders most likely to benefit from this type of process. Research can also, hopefully, expand the knowledge base about the forms that process should take. At present we know remarkably little about how different forms or styles of restorative justice impact on offenders, victims and other participants.

Acknowledgement

The author is a member of the research team currently evaluating a number of restorative justice schemes for the Home Office. Although I have benefited from discussions with other team members, the views expressed in this chapter are my own and do not necessarily reflect those of other members of the team.

References

Barnett, R.E. (1977) 'Restitution: A New Paradigm of Criminal Justice.' *Ethics 87*, 4, 279–301.
Bottoms, A.E. (2003) 'Some Sociological Reflections on Restorative Justice.' In A. von Hirsch, J. Roberts, A.E. Bottoms, K. Roach and M. Schiff (eds) *Restorative Justice and Criminal Justice: Competing or Reconcilable Paradigms?* Oxford: Hart Publishing.
Bottoms, A. and Dignan, J. (2004) 'Youth Crime and Youth Justice: Comparative and Cross-national Perspectives.' *Crime and Justice: A Review of Research 31*, 21–183.

Braithwaite, J. (1989) *Crime, Shame and Reintegration.* Cambridge: Cambridge University Press.

Crawford, A. and Newburn, T. (2003) *Youth Offending and Restorative Justice: Implementing Reform in Youth Justice.* Cullompton: Willan.

Daly, K. (2001) 'Conferencing in Australia and New Zealand.' In A. Morris and G. Maxwell (eds) *Restorative Justice for Juveniles: Conferencing, Mediation and Circles.* Oxford: Hart Publishing.

Daly, K. (2002) 'Restorative Justice: The Real Story.' *Punishment and Society 4,* 1, 55–79.

Daly, K. (2004) 'Pile it on: More Texts on RJ.' *Theoretical Criminology 8,* 4, 499–507.

Davis, G. (1992) *Making Amends: Mediation and Reparation in Criminal Justice.* London: Routledge.

Dignan, J. (2001) 'Restorative Justice and Crime Reduction: Are Policy Makers Barking up the Wrong Tree?' In E. Fattah and S. Parmentier (eds) *Victim Policies and Criminal Justice on the Road to Restorative Justice.* Belgium: Leuven University Press.

Dignan, J. (2005) *Understanding Victims and Restorative Justice.* Maidenhead: Open University Press.

Dignan, J. and Lowey, K. (2000) *Restorative Justice Options for Northern Ireland: A Comparative Review.* Belfast: Northern Ireland Office.

Holdaway, S., Davidson, N., Dignan, J., Hammersley, R., Hine, J. and Marsh, P. (2001) *New Strategies to Address Youth Offending: The National Evaluation of the Pilot Youth Offending Teams.* RDS Occasional Paper 69. London: Home Office.

Home Office (1997) *No More Excuses – A New Approach to Tackling Youth Crime in England and Wales.* Cm 3809. London: Stationery Office.

Home Office (2003) *Restorative Justice: The Government's Strategy.* London: Home Office.

Hoyle, C., Young, R. and Hill, R. (2002) *Proceed With Caution: An Evaluation of the Thames Valley Police Initiative in Restorative Cautioning.* York: Joseph Rowntree Foundation.

Hudson, B. (2003) 'Victims and Offenders.' In A. von Hirsch, J. Roberts, A.E. Bottoms, K. Roach and M. Schiff (eds) *Restorative Justice and Criminal Justice: Competing or Reconcilable Paradigms?* Oxford: Hart Publishing.

Johnstone, G. (2002) *Restorative Justice: Ideas, Values, Debates.* Cullompton: Willan.

Kurki, L. (2000) 'Restorative and Community Justice in the United States.' In M. Tonry (ed.) *Crime and Justice: A Review of Research 26.* Chicago: University of Chicago Press.

Kurki, L. (2003) 'Evaluating Restorative Justice Practices.' In A. von Hirsch, J. Roberts, A.E. Bottoms, K. Roach and M. Schiff (eds) *Restorative Justice and Criminal Justice: Competing or Reconcilable Paradigms?* Oxford: Hart Publishing.

Marshall, T.F. (1984) *Reparation, Conciliation and Mediation.* Home Office Research and Planning Unit Paper 27, London: Home Office.

Marshall, T.F. (1999) *Restorative Justice: An Overview.* London: Home Office.

Marshall, T.F. and Merry, S. (1990) *Crime and Accountability: Mediation and Reparation Projects in Great Britain.* Home Office Research and Planning Unit Paper 33. London: Home Office.

Maxwell, G. and Morris, A. (1993) *Family, Victims and Culture: Youth Justice in New Zealand.* Wellington: Social Policy and Administration and Victoria University of Wellington.

McIvor, G. (2004) 'Reparative and Restorative Approaches.' In A. Bottoms, S. Rex and G. Robinson (eds) *Alternatives to Prison: Options for an Insecure Society.* Cullompton: Willan.

Miers, D. (2001) *An International Review of Restorative Justice.* Crime Reduction Series Paper 10. London: Home Office.

Miers, D. (2004) 'Situating and Researching Restorative Justice in Great Britain.' *Punishment and Society 6,* 1, 23–46.

Miers, D., Maguire, M., Goldie, S., Sharpe, K. *et al.* (2001) *An Exploratory Evaluation of Restorative Schemes.* Crime Reduction Research Series Paper 9. London: Home Office.

Miles, H. (2004) 'The Parish Hall Enquiry: A Community-based Alternative to Formal Court Processing in the Channel Island of Jersey.' *Probation Journal 51,* 2, 133–143.

Newburn, T., Crawford, A., Earle, R., Goldie, S. *et al.* (2002) *The Introduction of Referral Orders into the Youth Justice System.* RDS Occasional Paper 70. London: Home Office.

Roberts, J. and Roach, K. (2003) 'Restorative Justice in Canada: From Sentencing Circles to Sentencing Principles'. In A. von Hirsch, J. Robert, A.E. Bottoms, K. Roach, and M. Schiff, (eds) *Restorative Justice and Criminal Justice: Competing or Reconcilable Paradigms?* Oxford: Hart Publishing.

Ruddick, R. (1989) 'A Court-referred Scheme'. In M. Wright and B. Galaway (eds) *Mediation and Criminal Justice: Victims, Offenders and Community.* London: Sage.

Schiff, M. (2003) 'Models, Challenges and the Promise of Restorative Conferencing Strategies'. In A. von Hirsch, J. Roberts, A.E. Bottoms, K. Roach and M. Schiff (eds) *Restorative Justice and Criminal Justice: Competing or Reconcilable Paradigms?* Oxford: Hart Publishing.

Shapland, J., Atkinson, A., Colledge, E., Dignan, J. *et al.* (2004) *Implementing Restorative Justice Schemes (Crime Reduction Programme): A Report on the First Year.* Home Office Online Report 32/04. London: Home Office.

Sherman, L.W., Strang, H., Barnes, G.C., Braithwaite, J., Inkpen, N. and Teh, M.-M. (1998) *Experiments in Restorative Policing: A Progress Report on the Canberra Reintegrative Shaming Experiments (RISE).* Australian Institute of Criminology. Accessed on 23/04/07 at: www.aic.gov.au/rjustice/rise/progress/1998.html

Sherman, L.W., Strang, H. and Woods, D.J. (2000) *Recidivism Patterns in the Canberra Reintegrative Shaming Experiments (RISE).* Australian Institute of Criminology. Accessed on 23/04/07: www.aic.gov.au/rjustice/rise/recidivism/.

von Hirsch, A., Ashworth, A. and Shearing, C. (2003) 'Specifying Aims and Limits for Restorative Justice: A 'Making Amends' Model?' In A. von Hirsch, J. Roberts, A.E. Bottoms, K. Roach and M. Schiff (eds) *Restorative Justice and Criminal Justice: Competing or Reconcilable Paradigms?* Oxford: Hart Publishing.

von Hirsch, A., Roberts, J., Bottoms, A.E., Roach, K. and Schiff, M. (eds) (2003) *Restorative Justice and Criminal Justice: Competing or Reconcilable Paradigms?* Oxford: Hart Publishing.

Wilcox, A. and Hoyle, C. (2004) *Restorative Justice Projects: The National Evaluation of the Youth Justice Board's Restorative Justice Projects.* Youth Justice Board.

Wilcox, A., Young, R. and Hoyle, C. (2004) *Two-Year Resanctioning Study: A Comparison of Restorative and Traditional Cautions.* Home Office Online Report 57/04. London: Home Office.

Wright, M. (1991) *Justice for Victims and Offenders: A Restorative Response to Crime.* Milton Keynes: Open University Press.

Young, R. and Hoyle, C. (2003) 'New, Improved Police-led Restorative Justice?'. In A von Hirsch, J. Roberts, A.E. Bottoms, K. Roach and M. Shiff (eds) *Restorative Justice and Criminal Justice: Competing or Reconcilable Paradigms?* Oxford: Hart Publishing.

Zehr, H. (1985) *Retributive Justice, Restorative Justice.* Elkhart, IN: Mennonite Central Committee, US Office of Criminal Justice.

CHAPTER 14

Paying Back – Unpaid Work by Offenders

Gill McIvor

Introduction

The option of requiring convicted offenders to undertake unpaid work for the benefit of the community has been available in the UK for around three decades. However the focus, nature and purpose of unpaid work by offenders in England and Wales have undergone significant changes in recent years, reflecting varying emphasis on its punitive, rehabilitative, reintegrative and reparative potential. This chapter begins with a brief historical overview of the development and use of community service[1] in the UK. However, its primary focus is upon those changes which have occurred in more recent years such as the redefinition of community service as community punishment in England and Wales, the development of evidence-informed community punishment Pathfinders and Enhanced Community Punishment and, most recently, its reincarnation as Community Payback, comprising unpaid work with an emphasis upon community involvement and enhanced visibility. The chapter will conclude by considering the possible consequences of these changes for the potential for community service to fulfil different sentencing aims.

1   Although the term 'community service' was replaced in England and Wales
     by 'community punishment' and is currently referred to as 'unpaid work',
     'community service' is widely recognised in different jurisdictions and
     continues to have currency in Scotland. It is therefore used throughout this
     chapter unless referring to specific legislative and policy initiatives.

Community Service: An overview of issues

In England and Wales, the option of requiring offenders to undertake unpaid work of benefit to the community has been available to the courts for more than three decades (and for just under a similar period of time in Scotland). When the option of requiring offenders to undertake unpaid work for the benefit of the community was first introduced in the UK its strength was thought to lie in its ability to appeal to a number of different sentencing aims (Advisory Council on the Penal System 1970). While representing a fine on the offender's free time, community service also offered the potential for offenders to make reparation to their communities and, it was believed, could in some cases have a 'reforming' influence on offenders by bringing them into contact with other, non-offending, volunteers.

In most jurisdictions community service is available as a sanction of the court at first sentence. This is so throughout the UK and in many other western jurisdictions, though in some jurisdictions – such as Germany – community service operates as an alternative to imprisonment for fine default. Interestingly, Immarigeon (1998) has observed that despite community service by offenders having its origins in the US, very little is known about its operation there, though its use is reported to be widespread. Usually, community service is imposed in the US and in other jurisdictions in conjunction with other sanctions and often as part of an intensive supervision package.

In England and Wales, community service was initially introduced as a 'stand-alone' option, whereas in Scotland unpaid work could also be imposed as a condition of a probation order. Subsequently, provisions were made for community service orders to be imposed in England and Wales in conjunction with probation orders (as combination orders) or, as they were subsequently referred to, community rehabilitation orders (as community punishment and rehabilitation orders). More recently, existing community sentences in England and Wales – community rehabilitation orders, community punishment orders and drug treatment and testing orders – were replaced under provisions in the Criminal Justice Act 2003 with a single generic community order with a range of possible requirements including between 40 and 300 hours of unpaid work.

Whatever the change in terminology, community service has proved to be a relatively popular and enduring sentencing option, not least because of its relatively tangible nature in comparison to other disposals such as probation (Carnie 1990). In England and Wales the use of community service orders rose steadily throughout the 1980s before stabilising in the mid-1990s at around 45,000 orders per annum. The use of combination orders – introduced in 1992 – increased until 1998 before decreasing to around 15,500 orders annually (Home Office 2004). In Scotland the number of community service orders made by the courts has continued to rise steadily over the last decade, with 8330 community service orders (including 2757 Probation Orders with a Requirement of Unpaid Work) made in 2004–5 (Scottish Executive 2006).

Despite its apparent popularity with the courts, concern has been expressed that community service is permeated by the ideology that it is a 'young man's punishment' and is, as such, a highly gendered disposal (Worrall 1996). In recent years the proportion of female offenders required to undertake unpaid work has increased in England and Wales, though probation (community rehabilitation order) remains a more widely used disposal with women (Home Office 2004). In Scotland, women represented 12 per cent of those given community service and probation orders with a requirement of unpaid work in 2004–5 (Scottish Executive 2006), which is identical to the percentage of women given similar orders in England and Wales in 2002 (the latest year for which relevant data are available) (Home Office 2004).

Although the gender difference in the proportionate use of community service with men and women has now largely disappeared in the UK, there are still clear differences in the characteristics of men and women sentenced to community service. For example, in Scotland women given community service in 2004–5 tended to be older than men who were similarly sentenced: 64 per cent of orders made on women related to over 25-year-olds while this was true of only 49 per cent of orders made on men (Scottish Executive 2006). Similarly, Rex *et al.* (2003a) found that 43 per cent of women given community punishment orders were 30 years of age or older compared with 31 per cent of men. Women who are given community service are more likely than men who receive the disposal to be first offenders (Hine 1993; McIvor 1998a). There also appears to be less consistency in the use of community service with women, suggesting that factors other than offence and previous criminal history may play a greater part in the sentencing to community service of women than of men (Hine and Thomas 1996). That said, it appears that women given community service – in Scotland at least – are more likely than men to successfully complete their orders: in 2004–5 74 per cent of women completed their orders successfully (including early discharge following review) compared with 70 per cent of men, while revocation following breach was more common among men (18%) than among women (13%) (Scottish Executive 2006).

In August 2006 the Lord Chief Justice of England and Wales, Lord Phillips of Worth Matravers, undertook a day of community service near Milton Keynes (subsequently reported in The *Observer* newspaper on 8 October 2006). To make the experience as authentic as possible, his real identity was not disclosed to the supervisor or co-workers and his 'cover story' was that he was a solicitor who had been sentenced to 150 hours of unpaid work for drunk driving. He was required to clear weeds from a path and paint an underpass. His conclusion about what had clearly been a demanding but rewarding experience was as follows:

> I was left in no doubt that, at its best, community work is a punishment that is positive. Both the self-discipline and the work make greater demand than a spell in prison, and the experience can rehabilitate those who have lost, or never had, self-respect... Community work is much less expensive to provide than prison places, and it must make sense to provide the resources needed to fund the provision of this alternative to custody. (Lord Phillips of Worth Matravers 2006)

The apparent popularity of community service with sentencers has not, however, been reflected in a lowered use of imprisonment. Indeed, just as the numbers of community service orders has risen over the last two decades, so too has the use of imprisonment across the UK. At the time of writing, the prison populations in England and Wales and in Scotland stood at their highest recorded levels. Despite plans for a further 900 prison places to be available by autumn 2007 and 8000 additional places to subsequently be made available in England and Wales (Home Secretary's statement to the House of Commons, 20 July 2006), penal establishments were, by autumn 2006, approaching capacity, with the result that some convicted prisoners were being detained in police cells and the Home Office was proposing to commission ships to provide further prison places (*Observer*, 22 October 2006).

Community service outcomes

Even though it has not traditionally been regarded as an explicitly rehabilitative disposal, community service may, it appears, have a positive impact upon recidivism (McIvor 2002). Comparisons of recidivism between different sanctions suggest that while prison sentences and community-based disposals have similar reconviction rates (e.g. Barclay and Tavares 1999), offenders on community service often have lower reconviction rates than would be predicted by their criminal history, age and other relevant characteristics (Lloyd *et al.* 1995). For example, May (1999) found that reconviction rates among offenders given community service were better than predicted even when social factors such as unemployment and drug use were taken into account. In a Swiss study, Killias, Aebi and Ribeaud (2000) found lower reconviction rates among offenders sentenced to community service than among those given short prison sentences.

There is some evidence that the quality of the community service experience for offenders may be associated with reductions in recidivism. For example, McIvor (1992) found that reconviction rates were lower among offenders who believed community service to have been worthwhile. More positive experiences of community service were found among those whose work placements were characterised by high levels of contact with the beneficiaries, opportunities to acquire new skills and work that was readily recognisable as having some intrinsic value for the recipients. Killias *et al.* (2000) reported a relationship between the perceived fairness of the sentences offenders received and reconviction, leading Rex and Gelsthorpe (2002) to suggest that perceiving a community service sentence as 'fair' makes offenders more receptive to re-integrative opportunities that arise when they undertake court-ordered unpaid work. In a similar vein, McIvor has observed that:

> community service placements which were viewed by offenders as most rewarding – and which were associated with reductions in recidivism – might best be characterised as re-integrative and as entailing a degree of reciprocity or exchange. In many instances, it seems, contact with the beneficiaries had given offenders an insight into other people and an increased insight into themselves; the acquisition of skills had instilled in them greater confidence and self-esteem; and the experience of completing their community service orders had placed them in a position where they could enjoy reciprocal relationships – gaining the trust, confidence and appreciation of other people and having the opportunity to give something back to them in return. (1998b, pp.55–56)

The reintegrative potential of community service was illustrated by a survey of placement providing agencies in Scotland (McIvor 1992). Around half of the agencies surveyed indicated that on at least one occasion a community service worker had stayed on in a voluntary (and sometimes paid) capacity after they had completed the work that had been ordered by the court. This was more likely to occur in agencies in which community service workers were better integrated with agency staff and other volunteers and in which they enjoyed direct contact with the service users who would benefit from the work they carried out. A recent inspection by Her Majesty's Inspectorate of Probation (HMIP 2006) also reported instances of offenders being employed by a beneficiary or continuing to work on a voluntary basis after completing their court-ordered unpaid work.

An emphasis upon the re-integrative potential of community service or, as McNeill and Maruna suggest (Chapter 12 in this volume), its potential for generativity, is congruent with Bazemore and Maloney's observation that 'offenders are capable of making positive contributions and, having paid their debt, should be allowed to be accepted back into community life. (1994, p.26)' These authors advocated the development of community service in such a way that it might provide added value both to the offender and to the community and might help to strengthen the bond between them. Examples they offer of 'service on its highest plane' (p.30) include mentoring; economic development; citisenship and civic participation; helping the disadvantaged; and crime prevention projects. This, importantly, would require a redefinition of offenders as resources rather than as 'the problem' and would be consistent with more recent strengths-based approaches that emphasise resilience rather than risk. As Bazemore and Maloney have noted:

> A competency development strategy would require that offenders be placed in positive, productive roles in the community which allow them to experience, practice and demonstrate ability to do something well that others value... Opportunities of learning and personal development are 'wrapped around' engagement in productive activity rather than being presented as ends in themselves... Meeting competency development objectives would require that the work be clearly useful for the community, that the offender and his or her labor be viewed as a resource, and that the offender be engaged in such a way that cognitive, social and occupational skill development can occur. (1994, pp.29–30)

However, Immarigeon (1998) has argued that community service has been employed in the US primarily as a punishment, with little attempt to maximise its potential to effect offender change. Bazemore and Maloney (1994) have similarly contended that the increasingly punitive emphasis on community service in the US appeared to 'remove incentives for creativity in developing either competency building or otherwise meaningful service options for offenders' (p.25). As they pessimistically conclude, 'If the goal is meaningful restoration to the community or offender rehabilitation...community service as now practiced in most jurisdictions would be viewed as a failure' (p.25).

Punishment in the community

In Scotland, community service has remained relatively unchanged since its introduction in the late 1970s. This is despite a heightened sensitivity to the risks posed by offenders given community-based social work disposals (reflected, for instance, in more recent versions of the National Objectives and Standards for Community Service produced by the Scottish Executive (e.g. Scottish Executive 2004)) and occasional attempts by politicians to enhance its punitiveness (through, for example, proposing that offenders' visibility is enhanced by requiring them to wear distinctive uniforms). In England and Wales, by contrast, community service has undergone important transformations linked to broader penal objectives and related to wider policy concerns.

In England and Wales, interest grew during the 1990s in the reintegrative potential of community service, or what was referred to in some probation areas as 'value-added' community service. This resulted, in some probation areas, in the accreditation of skills acquired by offenders on community service. Offenders worked towards a variety of awards with the assistance of specialist Education, Training and Employment staff (Rex and Gelsthorpe 2002). The aim was to increase the employability of offenders and, consequently, their likelihood of finding work or undertaking further education or training after they had completed their orders.

In April 2001 the Criminal Justice and Court Services Act 2000 came into force, resulting in the community service order in England and Wales being renamed the 'community punishment order'. Ironically, perhaps, legislation enacted to emphasise the punitive nature of community service (and therefore 'sell' it to courts and to the public) coincided with a government initiative – the Community Punishment Pathfinders – aimed, in essence, at enhancing the rehabilitative and reintegrative potential of unpaid work by offenders.

Community Punishment Pathfinders had previously been established in 2000 under the Home Office's Crime Reduction Programme. A total of seven pathfinders were set up across ten probation areas and, like the other Home Office Pathfinders, they were subject to evaluation (Rex and Gelsthorpe 2002; Rex *et al.* 2003a). The projects focused upon the use of pro-social modelling (Trotter 1999), skills accreditation and addressing the problems underlying offending behaviour in various combinations. In some projects attempts were also made to improve the quality of work placements and, hence, their perceived value to offenders. One project focused specifically upon enhancing the integration of the community service and probation elements of combination orders through improved induction and supervision planning.

The evaluation found that short-term outcomes were encouraging, with offenders showing reductions in perceived problems and pro-criminal attitudes (as measured by Crime-Pics II, a standardised tool for assessing offenders' problems and their attitudes towards offending). Two-thirds of offenders on orders were viewed by staff as having undergone positive change and as having good prospects of future change while (no doubt because they were relatively low risk in the first place) three-quarters were thought by staff to be unlikely to re-offend. A similar proportion of offenders considered that their experience of community service had made them less likely to re-offend. Importantly, the features of community service that were most strongly linked with changes in offenders' attitudes were whether they perceived the work to have been of value to themselves and to the beneficiaries.

Following the community punishment Pathfinders, the 'Enhanced Community Punishment' initiative was launched in October 2003, building upon the experiences of the Pathfinders and upon a model of practice that had been granted Recognised Status by the Joint Accreditation Panel in September 2004 (Rex *et al.* 2003b). Enhanced Community Punishment built upon the experiences of the Pathfinders by focusing upon skill acquisition and attitude change through teaching offenders pro-social attitudes and behaviour, and employment-related and problem-solving skills. The aim was to combine elements of reparation and retribution while maximising the rehabilitative potential of community punishment through addressing some offenders' needs to help them avoid offending in the future. The key elements of enhanced community punishment were integrated case management, pro-social modelling, cognitive skills modelling, guided skills learning and placement quality standards. The latter were intended to ensure that placements had characteristics – such as contact with the beneficiaries and meaningful work – that would encourage compliance and support the other elements of the disposal ((National Probation Service 2002). However a thematic inspection of Enhanced Community Punishment suggested that not all projects were providing the intended benefits to offenders and there were wide variations in the quality of case management across the areas inspected (Her Majesty's Inspectorate of Probation 2006).

Community payback and visible unpaid work

The community punishment order was relatively short-lived, being replaced through provisions in the Criminal Justice Act 2003 by unpaid work as a condition of a generic community order, with a renewed emphasis upon 'paying back' to the community. Emphasising the visibility of community punishment had been highlighted in the Carter Report (Carter 2003) and was reflected in the establishment of 'visibility pilots' in six probation areas in July 2005 followed by a national roll-out to other probation areas across England and Wales. Visible Unpaid Work is one of three elements of a national strategy for unpaid work aimed at ensuring that the work undertaken by offenders should be recognisable by the local community, and it has been taken forward alongside the Home Office three-year Community Sentences Communication campaign, the purpose of which is to 'raise the profile of Community Sentences and promote public confidence that offenders receive demanding punishments which reflect the seriousness of the crime' (National Probation Service 2005, para. 2).

The Visible Unpaid Work campaign is linked to Civil Renewal and Community Safety Strategies though promoting unpaid work as a resource to communities that can enhance community safety and well-being and through encouraging community involvement in the identification of community service projects at the local level. The latter has been taken forward through the Community Payback Scheme, which was launched November 2005 as part of a wider government initiative to increase the involvement of local communities in criminal justice systems. It is intended that Visible Unpaid Work will overlap with the Enhanced Community Punishment, with the latter being used for offenders who are assessed as presenting a medium or high likelihood of reconviction. While Enhanced Community punishment is aimed primarily at capitalising upon the rehabilitative potential of community service, with reparation to the community serving as a subsidiary aim, the Visible Unpaid Work campaign is more explicitly reparative. As the National Probation Service has indicated, the primary focus of Visible Unpaid Work 'is on the value of unpaid work to society, both economically and in terms of promoting strong communities' (2005, para. 27).

Arguably, offering local communities the opportunity to identify suitable projects for offenders or the contracting out of community service to other providers (in the context of contestability and requirements that Probation Boards contract out an increasing proportions of their services to other organisations (Home Office 2006; National Probation Service 2006)) *may* provide greater opportunities for the reparative potential of unpaid work to be realised, though this is by no means a foregone conclusion. Indeed there is a risk that with a huge increase in the proposed volume of unpaid work undertaken by offenders in England and Wales (from 5 million hours of unpaid work per annum in 2005/6 to almost 10 million hours in five years' time (Home Office 2006b) the quality of placement provision (however quality might be defined) may suffer and unpaid work may become even more distanced from other elements of community orders.

It is clear that policy thinking on the purpose and ethos of community service in England and Wales has shifted dramatically in a very short space of time such that the 'balance' has moved from the offender to the community as the primary intended beneficiary of unpaid work. This has become even more apparent in recent months as Home Office rhetoric about criminal justice has reflected an increasing punitive slant. For instance, as originally conceived, the Visible Unpaid Work campaign explicitly ruled out the use of uniforms for offenders 'the intention of which is to humiliate or stigmatise', stressing instead that the emphasis would be on 'badging the work, not the offender' (National Probation Service 2005, para. 6.i). However, the possible introduction of uniforms was subsequently raised through the publication of leaked Home Office correspondence in July 2006 that indicated that the new Home Secretary regarded such a move as appropriate to ensure that unpaid work is portrayed and perceived as 'penance and contrition', prompting the General Secretary of NAPO to respond that 'the notion of "penance and contrition" as the cornerstone of unpaid work is extraordinary. Orders need to be seen as purposeful by offenders and raise self-esteem, not severely diminish it' (*Guardian*, 22 July 2006).

Conclusions

Community service has become a well established addition to the repertoire of community sentences available to courts in the UK. Although the core elements of community service have remained largely unchanged since its introduction – undertaking unpaid work for the benefit of the community – how that work should be conceptualised has evolved in recent years. In the 25 years following the establishment of the first pilot schemes in England and Wales, debates centred largely around the relative advantages and disadvantages of team and agency placements or practical versus more personalised work. Gradually, however, increasing interest was shown in how the reintegrative potential of community service might be maximised by providing offenders with knowledge and skills that might facilitate their path into education, training and employment. The community punishment Pathfinders trialled the use of pro-social modelling by supervisors and an emphasis upon placement provision aimed at enhancing the satisfaction offenders gained from carrying out unpaid work with a view to promoting the rehabilitative potential of the disposal. The most recent developments, with an emphasis on heightened visibility and a concern to accentuate the benefits to be accrued through the carrying out by offenders of unpaid work, signal a return to more explicitly reparative aims which engage with the wider community justice agenda. They offer scope for the value to communities of unpaid work by offenders to be maximised while retaining those elements of Enhanced Community Punishment that, research would suggest, may encourage offender integration and change. The challenge will lie in treading a line between ensuring that the contribution made by offenders performing unpaid work is duly recognised and acknowledged and avoiding projects or experiences of carrying them out that are perceived by offenders as demeaning. As Ahmed *et al.* (2001) have argued, the process of shaming and its outcomes are complex and effective 'shame management' is required for its restorative or reintegrative potential to be invoked.

References

Advisory Council on the Penal System (1970) *Non-custodial and Semi-custodial Penalties.* London: HMSO.

Ahmed, E., Harris, N., Braithwaite, J., and Braithwaite, V. (2001) *Shame Management Through Reintegration.* Cambridge: Cambridge University Press.

Barclay, G.C. and Tavares, C. (eds) (1999) *Information on the Criminal Justice System in England and Wales: Digest 4.* London: Home Office Research and Statistics Directorate.

Bazemore, G. and Maloney, D. (1994) 'Rehabilitating Community Service: Toward Restorative Service Sanctions in a Balanced Justice System.' *Federal probation 61,*1, 24–35.

Carnie, J. (1990) *Sentencers' Perceptions of Community Service by Offenders.* Edinburgh: Scottish Office.

Carter, P. (2003) *Managing Offenders, Reducing Crime. A New Aproach.* London: The Strategy Unit, Home Office.

Her Majesty's Inspectorate of Probation (2006) *Working to Make Amends: Inspection Findings 1/06.* London: HMIP.

Hine, J. (1993) 'Access for Women: Flexible and Friendly?' In D. Whitfield and D. Scott (eds) *Paying Back: Twenty Years of Community Service.* Winchester: Waterside Press.

Hine, J. and Thomas, N. (1996) 'Evaluating Work with Offenders: Community Service Orders'. In G. McIvor (ed.) *Working With Offenders.* London: Jessica Kingsley Publishers.

Home Office (2004) *Probation Statistics 2002.* London: Home Office.

Home Office (2006) *A Five Year Strategy for Protecting the Public and Reducing Re-offending.* Cm 6717. London: Stationery Office

Immarigeon, R. (1998) 'Sentencing Offenders to Community Service: 30 Years of Practice, Promise and Pessimism.' *Community Corrections Report 5,* 2, 19–20, 28.

Killias, M., Aebi, M. and Ribeaud, D. (2000) 'Does Community Service Rehabilitate Better than Short-term Imprisonment? Results of a Controlled Experiment'. *The Howard Journal 39,* 1, 40–57.

Lloyd, C., Mair, G. and Hough, M. (1994) *Explaining Reconviction Rates: A Critical Analysis.* Home Office Research Study No. 136. London: Home Office.

Lord Phillips of Worth Matravers (2006) 'Community Payback Day – A Lord Chief Justice's experience.' Judiciary of England and Wales. Accessed on 25/04/07 at http://www.judiciary.gov.uk/about_judiciary/judges_in_the_community/lcj_170806.htm.

May, C. (1999) *Explaining Reconviction Following Community Sentences: The Role of Social Factors.* Home Office Research Study 192. London: Home Office.

McIvor, G. (1992) *Sentenced to Serve: The Operation and Impact of Community Service by Offenders.* Aldershot: Avebury.

McIvor, G. (1998a) 'Jobs for the boys?: Gender Differences in Referral to Community Service.' *The Howard Journal 37,* 3, 280–91.

McIvor, G. (1998b) 'Prosocial Modeling and Legitimacy: Lessons from a Study of Community Service.' In S. Rex and A. Matravers (eds) *Prosocial Modeling and Legitimacy: The Clarke Hall Day Conference.* Cambridge: University of Cambridge Institute of Criminology.

McIvor, G. (2002) 'What Works in Community Service?' Criminal Justice Social Work Briefieng Paper No. 6. Edinburgh: Criminal Justice Social Work Development Centre for Scotland. Accessed on 25/04/07 at http://lomond.mis.ed.uk/pls/portal 30/docs/8396.pdf.

National Probation Service (2002) *NPS Briefing: Enhanced Community Punishment.* London: Home Office.

National Probation Service (2005) *Visible Unpaid Work: Probation Circular 66/2005.* London: Home Office.

National Probation Service (2006) *The Development of Sub-Contracting Plans: Probation Circular 33/2006.* London: Home Office.

Rex, S. and Gelsthorpe, L. (2002) 'The Role of Community Service in Reducing Offending: Evaluating Pathfinder Projects in the UK.' *The Howard Journal 41,* 4, 311–325.

Rex, S., Gelsthorpe, L., Roberts, C. and Jordan, P. (2003) *An Evaluation of Community Service Pathfinder Projects: Final Report 2002.* London: Home Office.

Rex, S., Lieb, R., Bottoms, A. and Wilson, L. (2003) *A Process-based Evaluation of the Joint Prison/Probation Services Accreditation Panel.* London: Home Office.

Scottish Executive (2004) *National Objectives for Social Work Services in the Criminal Justice System: Standards – Community Service.* Edinburgh: Scottish Executive. Acessed on 25/04/07 at: http://www.scotland.gov.uk/Publications/2004/12/20475/49355.

Scottish Executive (2006) *Criminal Justice Social Work Statistics, 2004–05.* Edinburgh: Scottish Executive.

Trotter, C. (1999) *Working with Involuntary Clients.* London: Sage.

Worrall, A. (1996) 'Gender, criminal justice and probation'. In G. McIvor (ed.) *Working with Offenders: Research Highlights in Social Work 26.* London: Jessica Kingsley.

PART THREE

Issues and Needs

CHAPTER 15

Developments in Work with Drug Using Offenders

Iain Crow

Introduction

It is useful to start by defining some parameters. What drugs are we talking about? What is the nature of this 'work', and where should a discussion of developments in work with drug using offenders start? Taking the last question first, it could be some 40 years ago when the Brain Committee was reconvened as a result of a sudden rise in the number of known addicts. This was mainly a result of prescribed drugs being sold on, rather than used by those for whom they were intended. It led to responsibility for treatment being vested in licensed drug clinics, where withdrawal took precedence over maintenance, and eventually to the Misuse of Drugs Act 1971. There have been many developments since then, but the main legal framework remains in place. What has been more gradual, but in many ways more significant, has been the inexorable shift from drug misuse being seen as a medical concern, to one where it is primarily considered to be a matter of crime control. This has been particularly marked during and since the 1990s, and this is the period that I shall be mainly concerned with. I shall argue that while some of the developments over this period have been welcome, evidence is still lacking about what works best, with whom and in what circumstances. It is therefore important in working with drug using offenders to look not just at the treatment of individuals, but at how to address the factors that lead to drug-related offending in the first place.

As far as the second question – types of drug – is concerned, it is dangerous to categorise drugs because such categorisations (for example, between 'hard' and 'soft' drugs) often lead to false assumptions, because drug taking patterns change, and because many drug users use more than one kind. Even so, if this chapter is to have any meaningful focus it is useful to concentrate on the Class A drugs of addiction, heroin and cocaine, which are of most concern with regard to offending. Turning to the third of the opening questions, the nature of the work, this is most likely to be thought of in terms of working with individual drug users. But there is also work that may be one or more steps removed from the users. It can mean work with the families of users, and the communities of which they are part. It means agencies and government departments working together to develop co-ordinated strategies. There has always been a mixture of direct work with using offenders and more indirect work, but indirect work, involving more broadly-based initiatives and strategies, has grown in prominence over the years. Furthermore, work with drug misusing offenders, important as it is, is only one aspect of tackling drug misuse. Prevention and reducing supply also need to be addressed.

When talking about two problems in juxtaposition, such as drug use and offending, there is a danger of assuming that one implies, or is caused by, the other, when there may be a more complex relationship involved. Nevertheless, what work is done with drug misusing offenders depends on what the problem is perceived to be, so it is useful to start with a brief consideration of the problem of drug misusing offenders before going on to look at the responses to it.

Drug misuse and offending

Use of certain drugs is illegal, so there is an inherent relationship between drug misuse and offending. However, what is usually thought of as the relationship between drug misuse and crime also has a more specific character, involving not only the criminal activities that occur as part of the transaction of drugs, but the commission of crimes in furtherance of drug misuse. While generalisations are dangerous, the drug culture of the 1960s and 1970s was not markedly criminogenic in this sense; it was largely associated with lifestyles and culture. It was the transformation of the drugs market in the 1980s that marked a significant transition in the relationship between drug misuse and offending. This transformation was one of both scale and nature. The transformation of scale occurred because of the increasing numbers involved. For much of the twentieth century drug addiction in the UK was limited to a fairly small number (around 500) of what were termed 'therapeutic' addicts – people who had become dependent on opiates during the course of medical treatment – or to members of the medical profession. During the 1960s this increased to around 3,000 registered opiate addicts, mainly attributed to irresponsible prescribing by a small number of doctors, which resulted in the introduction of stricter controls, and led to the Misuse of Drugs Act 1971.

Known use gradually increased during the 1970s, but it was the early 1980s which saw a significant increase, to around 12,000 registered addicts by the middle of the decade. Estimates of regular users far exceeded this figure, ranging up to some 50,000 (Pearson 1987). But it was not just the size of the problem that attracted attention. The 1980s 'boom' was also identified as having a particular character. The new users were increasingly likely to be working-class young people in certain run down areas of towns and inner cities, and in some areas particular housing estates were identified as being at the centre of the problem. These areas were often characterised by their high levels of poverty and deprivation, poor social provision and high levels of alienation among the young. In particular drug misuse came to be associated with high unemployment and the development of an informal economy (e.g. Fazey 1988; Parker *et al.* 1988) and, later in the decade, with other social problems such as the growth in homelessness. It was around this time that drug misuse began to be characterised as criminogenic in terms of organised crime related to drug supply, and crime by users to support a habit, which had not been so marked in the past (Mott 1989). Thus, what developed during the 1980s was a triangular relationship between drug misuse, social deprivation and criminal activity in a way which meant that drug misuse, hitherto largely perceived as a medical problem, had come into the mainstream of social and criminal justice concern. A review in the mid-1990s summarised the position then by concluding that: 'our current knowledge about the volume and cost of drug-related crime is so patchy that all we can say with any certainty is that problem drug misuse is responsible for a significant minority of crime in England and Wales' (Hough 1996, p.18).

Since then the relationship between drug misuse and offending has become more fully documented. A study of crack cocaine users (Parker and Bottomley 1996) reported that the annual drugs bill per person was £20,000, and that acquisitive crime was the single most important source of funding for a drugs habit. Of particular relevance have been studies of the testing of arrestees. Using this method, drug use and crime have been found to be strongly correlated (Bennett 1998). In this study almost two-thirds of arrestees who provided a urine specimen tested positive for a drug apart from alcohol. Arrestees held for property offences were more likely to test positive than arrestees held for other offences, and almost half of arrestees who said they had used drugs in the last 12 months said there was a connection between their drug use and crime. In particular there was evidence for the idea that crime is committed to support drug use. Arrestees who said that their crime and drug use were connected reported illegal incomes which were two to three times higher than those who said that their crime and drug use were not connected. The use of heroin and crack cocaine were especially likely to result in increased illegal activity. Despite this it is worth considering that although many people with a drug problem may commit crimes (other than use of illegal substances), and some of those who commit offences take illegal drugs, the relationship between drug misuse and crime may be a complex one, involving other personal and social factors. It may also be relevant to ask whether some people would nonetheless be offenders even if they had not started using drugs. Furthermore, it is important to note that drug misusing offenders are not a homogeneous group and work with them will depend on their age, gender, ethnic group and social background. To review this work in detail would involve more than one chapter, but it is necessary to bear in mind the diversity of drug misusing offenders.

Responding to drug misuse: Policy development

Not surprisingly the changing nature of drug use has been accompanied by a series of changing responses, ranging from government strategies and initiatives, to the treatment of drug misusing offenders. Government policies for dealing with drug misuse have covered various aspects of the problem, and work with individual drug misusing offenders has only been one part of these policies. In addition they have included prevention programmes, reducing supply and promoting inter-agency working. In 1990, for example, the then Conservative Government established the Drugs Prevention Initiative to further a community-based approach to drugs prevention. In 1995 this became part of a broader strategy, *Tackling Drugs Together* (Central Drugs Co-ordination Unit 1995). The Drug Prevention Initiative was subsequently replaced in 1999 by the Drug Prevention Advisory Service, to work with Drug Action Teams to help young people resist drug misuse and protect communities from the adverse criminal and social consequences of drug misuse.

Tackling Drugs Together, intended to be a strategy for the period 1995–8, had three main elements. The first was concerned with reducing the availability and acceptability of drugs to young people, by expanding the Drugs Prevention Initiative, training teachers and supporting innovative projects in drug education and prevention. The second focused on reducing the health risks and other damage related to drug misuse by ensuring access to advice, counselling, treatment and rehabilitation. The third was aimed at reducing drug related crime, and included the reduction of drug misuse in prisons, involving mandatory drug testing, and the introduction of effective treatment services. Locally the strategy was to be carried forward by Drug Action Teams (DATs) composed of senior representatives from the police, prisons, local authorities, probation service and health authorities. Drug Reference Groups (DRGs) would provide local expertise to the DATs and harness local communities to tackle drug misuse. The approach was an improvement on previous policy. Rather than just being 'tough on drugs' it highlighted the importance of education, advice and improving treatment services, and it emphasised partnership in dealing with drug misuse.

Following the General Election in May 1997, the new Labour Government issued *Tackling Drugs to Build a Better Britain* in 1998 (Central Drugs Co-ordination Unit 1998), described as a ten-year strategy for tackling drugs misuse. This strategy had four main objectives:

• To help young people resist drug misuse, with the aim of reducing the proportion of under 25s reporting use of illegal drugs.

• To protect communities from the adverse consequences of drug related behaviour. The key objective of this part of the strategy was to reduce levels of repeat offending amongst drug misusing offenders, and one of the main means of achieving this would be to increase the number of offenders entering treatment programmes as a result of arrests and the court process.

• To enable people with drug problems to overcome them. The main aim here was to increase the participation of drug misusers, including prisoners, in drug treatment programmes.

• To stifle the availability of illegal drugs. While this fourth element of the strategy included attempts to reduce the drug supply, the key objective was to reduce access to drugs among 5–16-year-olds, thus placing the emphasis on education as much as on enforcement.

A significant feature was the increased emphasis on the use of treatment as a way of achieving its objectives. This was based on the evidence that had become available from a National Treatment Outcome Research Study (NTORS: Gossop, Marsden and Stewart 1998) that effective and targeted treatment for drug misusing offenders could reduce subsequent offending.

Tackling Drugs to Build a Better Britain was amended in 2002 by the publication of an *Updated Drug Strategy*. This included a greater focus on reducing the availability of Class A drugs, the expansion of treatment services, especially residential treatment, and better throughcare for ex-prisoners. It was also concerned to do more work in communities affected by drugs, and to use a sports and arts activities programme called Positive Futures to engage young people at risk of drug misuse. The Updated Strategy said, 'Treatment works. It is the key to reducing the harm drugs cause to users, family and communities. Investing in treatment is cost effective

– for each £1 spent, an estimated £3 is saved in criminal justice costs alone' (Home Office 2002, p.10). In November 2004 the Government produced a progress report on its drugs strategy. Among other things, this highlighted the expansion of the drug treatment workforce to 9000 (an increase of 50% since 2002), an increase in the number of drug users in treatment (up 54% on 1998), and the fact that waiting times for treatment had decreased from 6–12 weeks in 2001 to 2–4 weeks. It also said that planned expenditure on the strategy would be increased from £1.3 billion in the current year to nearly £1.5 billion in 2005–6 (Home Office 2004a).

Despite the change in government in 1997 there has been some continuity in the strategies adopted during and since the 1990s, with greater commitment to the provision of treatment and to work with drug affected communities alongside enforcement measures. In addition to, or as part of such strategies, there have also been more specific initiatives. The Drugs Intervention Programme (DIP) is part of, the Updated Drugs Strategy. It was launched in April 2003, and was originally called the Criminal Justice Intervention Programme (CJIP). It aims to get drug users who come into contact with the criminal justice system into treatment at various points in the system from arrest onwards. The interventions include testing for cocaine and opiates for offenders charged with offences likely to be connected with drug use; referral of arrested drug users to treatment, restrictions on bail for those who test positive for certain Class A drugs to encourage defendants to enter treatment; greater use of community sentences with treatment conditions, such as Drug Treatment and Testing Orders (DTTOs); and use of the Counselling, Assessment, Referral, Advice and Throughcare (CARAT) service in prisons. Several of these interventions are not new in themselves, but DIP interventions are intended to produce what is referred to as 'beginning-to-end' support for drug using offenders as they pass through the criminal justice system. This is an important development, since it was all too often possible for people to be picked up more than once at various points in the system, but in an unco-ordinated manner.

However, one of the issues that arises from the growing number of initiatives is that they also have to meet the expectations of joined up working. Hence DIP needs to link up with the Government's Resettlement Strategy, with Local Criminal Justice Boards (LCJBs), Crime and Disorder Reduction Partnerships (CDRPs, now incor-porating DATs), and the Prolific and Other Priority Offender Strategy (POPOS), to name but a few. At a local level the people and agencies involved are likely to know each other and work together in a variety of contexts, with workers and managers donning their various 'hats' as appropriate to the occasion, and it is clearly important to ensure that the various initiatives are well co-ordinated overall. Having looked briefly at policy developments, I will now turn to look more at work with drug using offenders themselves.

Working with drug using offenders

Work with drug using offenders can be described in terms of what happens in custodial establishments and what happens in the community. However, it is important not to see this entirely as a segregation of effort. Community-based programmes may have the avoidance of imprisonment as a more or less explicit incentive, and a Government strategy launched in 2004, laying emphasis on the successful resettlement of prisoners as a way of reducing offending, means that it is important for any prison-based treatment to be followed through on release.

Since 1998 work with drug using offenders, like work with offenders of all kinds has revolved around identifying 'What Works'. The 'What Works?' movement developed in North America, especially Canada, in the 1980s as a response to the doctrine that arose in the 1970s that nothing worked in terms of rehabilitating offenders. It challenged the assumption that all the findings relating to work with offenders had been negative, and began to look at what kinds of interventions could be shown to be effective in terms of reducing re-offending. In the late 1980s and 1990s the 'What Works?' movement also developed in the UK with a series of conferences, and was adopted by the Probation Service under Graham Smith (Mair 2004a). The Research Development and Statistics Division of the Home Office followed up the possibilities by reviewing the effectiveness of various programmes (Vennard, Hedderman and Sugg 1997) as part of a coherent strategy to reduce crime (Goldblatt and Lewis 1998), and the Labour Government adopted a 'What Works?' approach as part of its Crime Reduction Programme announced in 1998. At one level the 'What Works?' approach is simply a commitment to trying to find out what interventions are most effective in working with offenders. However, as a result of various research studies and reviews (e.g. McGuire 1995) 'What Works?' has become very much associated with the application of cognitive behavioural therapy (CBT), and almost the only criterion of success has become preventing re-offending (or more correctly, reducing the likelihood of reconviction). It is also worth noting that in its early manifestations the phrase was followed by a question mark, but significantly it has since become common to drop the interrogative.

An important part of the 'What Works?' programme was the introduction of a Correctional Services Accreditation Panel (see Chapter 7 in this volume). This adjudicates on what programmes should be approved for treatment purposes. More programmes have received recognition or accreditation from the Panel for treating drug misuse than for any other type of treatment (including general offending, sex offending, and violence). Two programmes have been provisionally accredited for use in the community,[1] while a further eight programmes have been accredited for use in prison.[2] The prison programmes in particular tend to feature cognitive behavioural therapy as the main tool of treatment (Correctional Services Accreditation Panel 2003–4).

There are those who have reservations about a wholehearted commitment to the 'What Works?' programme generally (Mair 2004b), but putting these aside for the time being, there are particular considerations regarding its application to work with drug using offenders. Responding to drug misuse usually means addressing a range of problems with a range of outcomes. There is the drug use itself. There are also questions regarding harm minimisation and safer drug use, such as using clean needles, and avoiding HIV/AIDS and overdoses. There is the need to protect the families of addicts, especially their children. Drug use may also be related to mental health problems and to a range of social problems that need to be tackled (referred to as dual diagnosis). Finally, there is work to reduce drug-related crime. Consequently it is more difficult to look at the effectiveness of work with drug using offenders by reference to a single criterion. As Bean and Nemitz engagingly put it, 'There is little point in treating an addicted unemployed thief to see him become a non-addicted unemployed thief' (2004, p.10). It is also worth noting that the treatment of drug misuse had its own 'What Works?' review in the mid-1990s, the Department of Health's National Treatment Outcome Research Study (NTORS), which preceded the Home Office's 'What Works?' programme. Consequently it may be argued that considering work with drug misusing offenders solely in terms of the 'What Works?' programme is too narrow a focus.

Work in the community

Two main criminal justice based responses to drug misuse have been of particular importance in recent years: arrest referral and Drug Treatment and Testing Orders. Following the large increase in drug misuse in the early 1980s some areas set up

1   ASRO (Addressing Substance Related Offending) and PRISM (Programme for Reducing Individual Substance Misuse).

2   A prison version of ASRO, RAPT Substance Abuse Treatment Programme, Prisons Partnership 12-Step Programme, North-West Area Therapeutic Community, Ley prison programme, FOCUS, Action on Drugs, STOP.

experimental schemes to provide information and referral opportunities for people with drug problems at the point at which they were arrested. As mentioned earlier, studies have shown a high incidence of positive testing amongst people arrested by the police. However, only one-fifth of arrestees in one study said that they had received some form of treatment for drug dependence, while a similar proportion (22%) said that they would like to receive treatment. The author concluded that 'these findings suggest that there might be an opportunity to provide treatment advice or to make available some kind of treatment programme to arrestees at the point of contact with the criminal justice system' (Bennett 1998, p.60).

Another study found that almost half of a sample of 128 arrestees said that the arrest referral scheme was their first contact with any drug agency, even though most had long criminal histories, with an average of 21 previous convictions (Edmunds *et al.* 1998). The research also indicated that following contact there was a significant decline in both self-reported drug use and a corresponding reduction in expenditure on drugs and the number of crimes committed. A more extensive study examined a range of interventions for drug misusing offenders in London, Brighton, Derby and Salford, including arrest referral schemes, probation referral schemes and work in prisons, and concluded that such treatment services could have a significant impact both on drug taking and drug related crime (Edmunds *et al.* 1999). The study found that there was a fall in the reported use of illicit opiates from 83 per cent of the cases before contact with a drug worker to 55 per cent after contact, and that the average amount spent on drugs each week by offenders fell from £400 to less than £100 within nine months, with corresponding falls in the levels of offending to finance drug use. Such studies have provided the basis for policies directed at intervening with drug using offenders to refer them to treatment. Because referral by itself was insufficient to ensure involvement with treatment this subsequently became Enhanced Arrest Referral, with arrest referral workers taking on clients until they entered treatment.

For many years offenders with a drug problem could be given probation orders requiring them to attend drug treatment as a condition of probation. However, when in opposition the Labour Party put forward proposals for a specific drug treatment order. This proposal was enacted in the Crime and Disorder Act 1998, sections 61 to 63 of which provide for a drug treatment and testing order (DTTO). This consists of 'the treatment requirement' (s.62(1)) that an offender undergo treatment 'with a view to the reduction or elimination of the offender's dependency on or propensity to misuse drugs', and 'the testing requirement' (s.62 (4)) that the offender should provide samples 'for the purpose of ascertaining whether he has any drug in his body during the treatment and testing period'.

Section 63 of the Act provides for the periodic review of the order 'at intervals of not less than one month'.

In October 1998 DTTOs were introduced in three pilot areas for offenders who had committed an offence. An evaluation was carried out and produced a series of reports on how the pilots were doing. These showed, first, that less than four in ten of those assessed for a DTTO were selected for one, so clearly DTTOs are not suitable for all drug using offenders. However, those who were selected reported reductions in drug use and in offending, and a substantial reduction in spending on drugs from an average of £400 per week prior to commencing DTTOs, to less than £30 per week in the first weeks of the order (Turnbull 1999). While one may be sceptical about the reliability of self-reported reductions in a programme where offenders clearly have an incentive to appear to be doing well, the researchers report that urine testing did bear out the reported reductions in drug use. So the results thus far were encouraging. DTTOs were implemented nationally from October 2000. This was shortly after the second evaluation report, when the researchers suggested that the longer-term impact of the pilots needed to be established through a reconviction study, and prior to their third report giving the results of such a study. This is significant because even in the second report there were several notes of caution. The first was that it was *those who reached the end of their order* who managed to contain their drug use and to stop drug related offending. However, the number doing so was small (31 of the 210 offenders selected in the pilot areas at that stage). The authors also commented that it takes at least three months to engage successfully with DTTO offenders, and it was unrealistic to expect offenders to be drug-free in a few weeks (Turnbull, McSweeney and Hough 2000).

The third report underlined such qualifications. This presented the results of a two-year reconviction study comparing 161 offenders given DTTOs with 202 people not selected for the orders, and 81 people who had received Section 1A(6) orders (the forerunner of DTTOs) requiring them to attend drug treatment as a condition of probation. The two-year reconviction rate for DTTO offenders was high at 80 per cent. However, only 30 per cent completed their orders, and reconviction rates were significantly lower among completers than non-completers. Those who completed their orders reduced their annual conviction rate to levels well below those of previous years, but it was not possible to draw any conclusions about the relative effectiveness of the DTTO as against the Section 1A(6) approach. The researchers suggest that such disappointing outcomes are probably more to do with 'implementation failure' rather than 'theory failure'; in other words DTTOs may work well, but only if they are operated properly. The researchers conclude,

'There is no reason in principle why DTTO teams should not be able to surmount these hurdles (encountered by the pilot studies) and thus be more effective in retaining offenders on DTTO programmes', but 'If teams struggle to establish their programmes, and lack the resources to deliver rapid and appropriate responses, then DTTOs could become expensive precursors to imprisonment'. They further suggested that 'the point at which drug-dependent offenders decide – or can be persuaded – to address their drug problems is a product of more idiosyncratic characteristics. There is an obvious need for further research on desistance from problematic drug use' (Hough *et al.* 2003, p.6). So DTTOs seem to have benefits for those who take part in a well-implemented scheme and complete it. However, the evidence was that too often the orders were not operating as they should, and that they are not the answer to drug-related offending for all. Almost 26,000 DTTOs had been started up to September 2004, but the high level of non-completion was noted by the Government, and in its November 2004 progress report on its drugs strategy it was said that completion targets had been introduced as one of a range of measures to improve DTTO retention (Home Office 2004a). DTTOs have now been replaced by DRRs (drug rehabilitations requirements).

Some mention needs to be made of a development that has *not* occurred (at least not on a wide scale), and this is the adoption of drug courts. Like so many initiatives this originated in the US, in Miami. Offenders are not handed over to probation, but remain under the control of the court itself. The judge in a drug court decides on treatment and monitors offenders' progress. Individual judges handle cases and can occupy a mixture of roles. It therefore becomes reasonable to ask how meaningful the term 'defendant' is if, as the main proponent of the system in the UK has said, 'the judge operates somewhere between a judge, social worker, prosecutor and defender' (Bean, 1995). In such a situation who safeguards due process? Nonetheless, proposals were put forward that there should be similar developments in the UK (Bean 1997). Courts specialising in dealing with drug users started in Wakefield and Pontefract in 1998, but in Bean's view these were not proper drug courts in accordance with the Florida model, but 'traditional courts using probation orders with bells and whistles attached' (Bean 2002, p.91). The nearest the UK has come to adopting a true drug court approach is in Scotland, where a pilot project started in Glasgow in 2001, which has been described by one of the Sheriffs involved as having the purpose of reducing 'the level of drug related offending behaviour by reducing or eliminating the offender's propensity to misuse drugs by the use of court sanctioned treatment rather than traditional sentencing' (O'Grady

2003, p.56).[3] An early study of the operation of the court indicated that 'Its main strengths were perceived to be the "fast-tracking" of offenders, the existence of a trained and dedicated team in regular contact with each other, and the system of pre-court review meetings' (Barnsdale *et al.* 2004, p.77). A second Scottish drug court was established in Fife in 2002, operating under slightly different procedures (McIvor *et al.* 2006) and in England pilot drug courts have now also been implemented in London and Leeds.

Work in prison

Despite an earlier caution about making too clear a division between custodial and community-based work, it is nonetheless important to refer to the work that goes on in Prison Service establishments. Until the mid-1990s treatment in prison for people with drug dependency problems was limited, something that has been attributed to the impact of the 'nothing works' doctrine that took hold in the 1970s (Lipton 1996, p.14). The Annual Report of the Chief Inspector of Prisons for 1993–4 said, 'The treatment of those prisoners addicted to hard drugs…leaves much to be desired' (HM Chief Inspector of Prisons 1994, p.18, para. 2.27). Inspectors did not find any local prison with a regime for drug withdrawal that met the standards applied in NHS drug dependency clinics. During the 1990s, however, the Prison Service developed a policy towards dealing with drug misuse which was in line with the Government strategies outlined earlier. This included drug testing, reducing availability and increasing treatment, including cognitive behavioural programmes, and methadone provision. One of the most notable developments was the introduction of a programme run by the Rehabilitation for Addicted Prisoners Trust (RAPT) at Downview prison. It was based on a 12-step approach to abstinence similar to that of Alcoholics Anonymous. Following a study by Player and Martin (1996), the programme was extended to more prisons by the Home Office. Twenty-two establishments were involved in the initial wave of treatment programmes, which included therapeutic community approaches, detoxification units, intensive drug education and counselling services and community linked throughcare. In 1996 funding was increased to £5.1m and 59 establishments were involved (Tilt 1997). Despite this, concerns about the Prison Service's ability to deal with drug dependent prisoners was voiced by the All Party Parliamentary Drugs Misuse Group (All Party Parliamentary Drugs Misuse Group 1998).

---

3   For a fuller discussion of drug courts see Bean 2002, Chapter 5.

Although the Group was impressed by the Prison Service's efforts at tackling drug misuse, it was in no doubt that, in 1998 at least, provision was far from adequate.

The Prison Service's drug strategy was reviewed the same year, and in 1999 the Prison Service launched CARAT (Counselling, Assessment, Referral, Advice and Throughcare) aiming to provide a range of interventions, starting with an initial assessment on a prisoner's entry into custody, and linking prisons with community agencies in order to ensure continuity of care. More recently work relating to drug use among prisoners was reviewed in a report summarising the results of seven studies (Ramsay 2003). This reported that although good quality treatment can be effective in reducing drug use and re-offending, treatment needed to be tailored to individual need, to be of adequate duration, and to be followed up with high quality after care.

Effectiveness

Perhaps the most crucial question is how effective developments in work with drug using offenders are. As noted earlier, several criteria can be adopted to judge effectiveness. The emphasis is usually on the benefits for the public and society, rather than for drug users themselves, and consequently the main criteria tend to be reduced drug use, less being spent on drugs, and less drug related offending. There is a corresponding contrast here between the results from programmes whose main concern is with the treatment of drug dependency, and those which are more concerned with reducing offending. As noted earlier, there was an extensive evaluation of drug treatment programmes during the 1990s as part of the NTORS, and this produced favourable results. However, the NTORS stands out as a somewhat isolated example. Its findings contrasted with earlier suggestions that research had failed to demonstrate that medical treatment is successful in terms of long-term abstinence, resort to the illegal market, or reducing criminal activity (Jarvis and Parker 1990; South 1994, pp.416–418). Admirable as the NTORS was, it is now a decade since the work on which it was based was carried out and, as other commentators have noted, the dearth of research on drug treatment means there is little evidence on which to base the assertion that treatment works (Bean and Nemitz 2004).

Since the NTORS the emphasis has shifted to programmes directed at reducing offending as part of the 'What Works?' programme, and here the indications have been more qualified, and in many instances final results are not available (Merrington and Stanley 2004). An evaluation of 32 drug and alcohol programmes for young offenders undertaken for the Youth Justice Board reported considerable difficulty in obtaining worthwhile outcome data, reinforcing Bean and Nemitz's criticism of programmes which fail to provide a sound basis for evaluation. It noted that, 'Projects had often been designed quickly and without sufficient information about local needs.' Only 6 of the 32 projects reported outcome data, which was uniformly weak. The reconviction part of the research found that most young offenders referred to or treated by alcohol and drug services re-offended. Despite the design, start-up and operational difficulties that impeded outcome evaluation, the researchers found a substantial demand for substance services, and suggest that, properly run, such services can affect offending and substance use by some young offenders, but that more rigorous evaluations than were possible in this study were needed (Hammersley *et al.* 2004).

However, the most recent analysis of effectiveness comes from a systematic review of the effectiveness of criminal justice and treatment programmes in reducing drug-related crime (Holloway, Bennett and Farrington 2005). The review involved both a meta-analysis and a quantitative survey of evaluations, and the researchers describe the results as positive. Out of 52 studies reviewed, 44 found the programme evaluated to be effective in reducing crime, and the odds of a reduction in criminal behaviour were 41 per cent higher among treatment groups than in comparison groups. The most effective interventions were found to be therapeutic communities and drug courts. However, the researchers noted that most of the evaluations included in their review were from the US (and drug courts are a purely US phenomenon), and that there was a paucity of evaluations in the UK.

Getting a user into treatment as soon as possible when the opportunity to do so presents itself is critical to effective intervention (Hough 1996). In 2002 the National Treatment Agency analysed information provided by Drug Action Teams to provide a picture of the current state of drug treatment provision. The report showed that the average waiting times for various drug services, from when a user presented, to when the service started, were:

1. Inpatient detoxification   12 weeks

2. Specialist prescribing   14 weeks

3. GP prescribing   5.7 weeks

4. Counselling   7.6 weeks

5. Day programmes   6 weeks

6. Residential rehabilitation   9 weeks

The report also showed that there was wide variation in the levels of investment across the DATs, from less than £2 per head of the population in the DAT's area in 2002/3, to over £25 per head (National Treatment Agency 2002). Quite often the opportunity to get a drug using offender into treatment occurs when a court case is pending. If the offender has to wait for several weeks before getting treatment the opportunity may be lost. This is something that has been recognised by the government, and in its review of progress on its drugs strategy it reported that waiting times had been cut by 72 per cent compared with 2001.

Throughcare and resettlement

Some reference has already been made to what is variously termed throughcare, aftercare and resettlement, but it is worth making special mention of this aspect of work with drug using offenders, since the indications have been that all too often this is an aspect that has been neglected (All Party Parliamentary Drugs Misuse Group 1998), and a recent review of the effectiveness of treatment and criminal justice interventions noted that 'very little evaluation research has been undertaken looking at the effectiveness of supervision and aftercare' (Holloway *et al.*, 2005, p.v). Throughcare gained in importance following the introduction of early release provisions in the Criminal Justice Act 1991, which led to the drawing up of a national framework for throughcare (HM Prison Service 1993). However, implementation of the Correctional Services Review (Carter 2003), leading to the establishment of a National Offender Management Service (NOMS), bringing the Prison and Probation Service together, should lead to greater joint working and integrated case management. This, at least, is the intention. The problem is translating intentions into the delivery of more, swifter and more effective provision on the ground.

Improving aftercare provision was part of the Government's Updated Drug Strategy, with the intention that by April 2005 all Drug Action Teams would have a co-ordinated system of aftercare in place. In 2004 the Government launched a new initiative directed at addressing the resettlement of offenders, and this includes giving some priority to drug using offenders (Home Office 2004b). However the deficiencies in aftercare provision for drug dependent prisoners are still commented on (Turnbull 2004). The Correctional Services Accreditation Panel's Annual Report for 2003-4 noted that 'drug treatment programmes had performed particularly badly on throughcare' (Correctional Services Accreditation Panel 2004, para. 39). The intention of improving throughcare for drug dependent prisoners is therefore a welcome one, and the hope is that the developments intended to improve throughcare and resettlement will be addressed as a matter of urgency.

Where are we now? A summary and assessment

Research has shown that many drug using offenders had no contact with treatment services prior to arrest. Efforts are being made to change this, to get more people into treatment, and to reduce the time between referral and treatment. Much has happened over the last decade or so in terms of adopting a positive approach to the treatment and rehabilitation of drug using offenders, but there is clearly much more to do. Whether this is best served by the 'treatment or else...' approach of some politicians is open to question. In looking at recent developments in work with drug using offenders the three elements that stand out are the Government's Drug Strategy, Drug Treatment and Training Orders and the Drugs Intervention Programme, each of which holds out considerable promise of improvements in services. However, when rolling out large-scale programmes it is important to ensure that they address individual needs.

A dominant feature of work with drug using offenders over the last decade has been its absorption within a criminal justice agenda rather than a health service agenda. This has had its benefits in ensuring that drug treatment services are accorded a high priority and a supply of money, but it can also be a handicap. If an offender uses drugs then the tendency is to see the drug use as the root of the problem: stop the drug use and the offending will stop is the obvious inference. The difficulty with this is that it may mean that insufficient consideration is given to what is at the root of the drug use. To coin a phrase, the present policy may be tough on drug use, but is it tough on the causes of drug use?

It is important to recognise that recovering from a serious drug problem may be an arduous and lengthy journey. The use of drugs may be rooted in a violent and unhappy background, in areas where circumstances are less than ideal, and drug use and associated offending are part of a life response to those circumstances. In such a context moving towards drug and offending free behaviour may well not happen because of a single event, but as part of a sustained period of change in one's life. Moving away from drug use and offending needs to be seen as a process rather than an event. It is here that the work on how people cease to offend becomes significant. Writers such as Shadd Maruna (2000) have charted the changes that sometimes make this possible and, welcome though more rigorous evaluations of treatment programmes are, studies of desistance may be more significant.

Suggested further reading

More information can be obtained from Bean and from Bean and Nemitz (2004). There is a good article by Judith Rumgay (2003) in *Probation Journal*. For general background, the chapter 'The Treatment of Drug Misuse' in my book *The Treatment and Rehabilitation of Offenders* may also be useful (Crow 2001).

References

All Party Parliamentary Drugs Misuse Group (1998) *Prisons and Drug Misuse.* London: Houses of Parliament.

Barnsdale, L., Brown, A., Eley, S., Malloch, M., McIvor, G. and Yates, R. (2004) 'Evaluation of the Pilot Drug Court in Glasgow.' *Scottish Journal of Criminal Justice Studies 9*, 77.

Bean, P. (1995) 'Drug Courts USA.' *Druglink 10*, 3, 13–14.

Bean, P. (1997) 'New Ideas in the Field'. *Druglink 12*, 2, 12–13.

Bean, P. (2002) *Drugs and Crime.* Cullompton: Willan.

Bean, P. and Nemitz, T. (2004) *Drug Treatment: What Works.* London and New York: Routledge.

Bennett, T. (1998) *Drugs and Crime: The Results of Research on Drug Testing and Interviewing Arrestees.* Home Office Research Study No. 183. London: Home Office.

Carter, P. (2003) *Managing Offenders, Reducing Crime.* London: Home Office.

Central Drugs Co-ordination Unit (1995) *Tackling Drugs Together.* Cm 2846. London: HMSO.

Central Drugs Co-ordination Unit (1998) *Tackling Drugs to Build a Better Britain: The Government's 10-Year Strategy for Tackling Drug Misuse.* Cm 3945. London: Stationery Office.

Correctional Services Accreditation Panel (2004), *Annual Report, 2003–04.* London: HM Prison Service. Accessed on 25/04/07 at http://www.probation.homeoffice.gov.uk/files/pdf/CSAP_report03to04.pdf.

Crow, I. (2001) *The Treatment and Rehabilitation of Offenders.* London: Sage.

Edmunds, M., Hough, M., Turnbull, P.J. and May, T. (1999) *Doing Justice to Treatment: Referring Offenders to Drug Services.* Drugs Prevention Advisory Service, Paper 2. London: Home Office.

Edmunds, M., May, T., Hearnden, I. and Hough, M. (1998) *Arrest Referral: Emerging Lessons From Research.* Drugs Prevention Initiative, Paper 23. London: Home Office.

Fazey, C. (1988) *Heroin Addiction, Crime and the Effect of Medical Treatment.* Report to the Home Office. London: Home Office.

Goldblatt, P. and Lewis, C. (eds) *Reducing Offending: An Assessment of Research Evidence on Ways of Dealing with Offending Behaviour.* Home Office Research Study 187. London: Home Office.

Gossop, M., Marsden, J. and Stewart, D. (1998) *NTORS at One Year: The National Treatment Outcome Research Study – Changes in Substance Use, Health and Criminal Behaviours One Year after Intake.* London: Department of Health.

Hammersley, R., Reid, M., Oliver, A., Genova, A. Raynor, P. Minkes, J. and Morgan, M. (2004) *The National Evaluation of the Youth Justice Board's Drug and Alcohol Projects.* London: Youth Justice Board.

Holloway, K., Bennett, T. and Farrington, D. (2005) *The Effectiveness of Criminal Justice and Treatment Programmes in Reducing Drug-Related Crime: A Systematic Review.* Home Office Online Report 26/05. London: Home Office.

HM Chief Inspector of Prisons (1994) *Report of Her Majesty's Chief Inspector of Prisons, 1993–94.* House of Commons Paper 688. London: HMSO.

Home Office (2002) *Updated Drugs Strategy.* London: Home Office.

Home Office (2004a) *Tackling Drugs, Changing Lives: Keeping Communities Safe from Drugs.* London: Home Office.

HM Prison Service (1993) *National Framework for the Throughcare of Offenders in Custody to the Completion of Supervision in the Community.* London: HM Prison Service.

Home Office (2004b) *Reducing Re-offending National Action Plan.* London: Home Office. Accessed on 25/04/07 at http://www.homeoffice.gov.uk/docs3/5505reoffending.pdf.

Hough, M. (1996) *Drug Misuse and the Criminal Justice System: A Review of the Literature.* Drug Prevention Initiative, Paper 15. London: Home Office.

Hough, M., Clancy, A., McSweeney, T. and Turnbull, P.J. (2003) *The Impact of Drug Treatment and Testing Orders on Offending: Two-year Reconviction Results.* Research Development and Statistics Directorate Findings 184. London: Home Office.

Jarvis, G. and Parker, H. (1990) 'Can Medical Treatment Reduce Crime Amongst Young Heroin Users?' *Home Office Research Bulletin 28*, 29–32.

Lipton, D.S. (1996) 'Prison-Based Therapeutic Communities: Their Success with Drug Abusing Offenders.' *National Institute of Justice Journal*, 12–20 February. Washington DC: US Department of Justice.

Mair, G. (2004a) 'The Origins of What Works in England and Wales: A House Built on Sand?' In G. Mair (ed.) *What Matters in Probation.* Cullompton: Willan.

Mair, G. (2004b) *What Matters in Probation.* Cullompton: Willan.

Maruna, S. (2000) *Making Good: How Ex-Convicts Reform and Rebuild their Lives.* Washington DC: American Psychological Association.

McGuire, J. (ed.) (1995) *What Works: Reducing Reoffending – Guidelines from Research and Practice.* Chichester: John Wiley and Sons.

McIvor, G., Barnsdale, L. Malloch, M., Eley, S. and Yates, R. (2006) *The Operation and Effectiveness of the Scottish Drug Court Pilots.* Edinburgh: Scottish Executive Social Research.

Merrington, S. and Stanley, S. (2004) 'What Works?: Revisiting the Evidence in England and Wales.' *Probation Journal 51*, 1, 7–20.

Mott, J. (1989) 'Reducing Heroin Related Crime'. *Home Office Research and Planning Unit Research Bulletin 26*, 30–33.

National Treatment Agency (2002) *Key Findings on Drug Treatment.* National Treatment Agency. Accessed on 25/04/07 at www.nta.nhs.uk/factsand figures/dat_analysis.htm

O'Grady, M. (2003) 'Drug Courts – The Scottish Experience.' *Scottish Journal of Criminal Justice Studies 9*, 55–67.

Parker, H. and Bottomley, T. (1996) *Crack Cocaine and Drugs: Crime Careers.* Research Findings No. 34. London: Home Office.

Parker, J., Pool, Y., Rawle, R. and Gay, M. (1988) 'Monitoring Problem Drug-Use in Bristol.' *British Journal of Psychiatry 152*, 214–221.

Pearson, G. (1987) *The New Heroin Users.* Oxford: Blackwell.

Player, E. and Martin, C.A. (1996) *ADT Drug Treatment Programme at HMP Downview. Preliminary Evaluation.* Research Findings No.31, Home Office Research and Statistics Department. London: Home Office.

Ramsay, M. (2003) *Prisoners' Drug Use and Treatment: Seven Studies.* Research Development and Statistics Directorate Findings 186. London: Home Office

Rumgay, J. (2003) 'Drug Treatment and Offender Rehabilitation: Reflections on Evidence, Effectiveness and Exclusion.' *Probation Journal 50*, 1, 41–51.

South, N. (1994) 'Drugs: Control, Crime and Criminological Studies'. In M. Maguire, R. Morgan and R. Reiner (eds) *The Oxford Handbook of Criminology*. Oxford: Clarendon Press.

Tilt, R. (1997) 'Prison Service Drugs Strategy'. *CJCC Newsletter, Issue 7*. London: Criminal Justice Consultative Council.

Turnbull, P.J. (1999) *Drug Treatment and Testing Orders – Interim Evaluation*. Research Development and Statistics Directorate Findings 106. London: Home Office.

Turnbull, P., McSweeney, T. and Hough, M. (2000) *Drug Treatment and Testing Orders – The 18 Month Evaluation*, RSD Research Findings 128. London: Home Office.

Turnbull, P. (2004) 'Drug Treatment: The Importance of Aftercare'. *Criminal Justice Matters 56*, 28–29.

Vennard, J., Hedderman, C. and Sugg, D. (1997) *Changing Offenders' Attitudes and Behaviour: What Works?* Home Office Research Study No. 171. London: Home Office

CHAPTER 16

Dealing with Diversity

Loraine Gelsthorpe

Introduction

The issue of diversity is never far from media reports at present whether one is talking about race, gender, mental health or sexual orientation, for example, and a host of issues spring to the fore: is there evidence to suggest discrimination? How can we best interpret the evidence on the basis that no facts speak for themselves? Other questions revolve around the various attempts to avoid negative discrimination and to ensure that anti-discriminatory policy is translated into practice. Moreover, there are substantive issues as to whether or not any one group of offenders deserves to be dealt with differently on grounds of their differential needs and risks.

These questions are not easily answered because there might be different issues depending on whether or not one was talking about racial discrimination, gender, sexual orientation, mental health or, indeed, age. Moreover, the very notion of 'dealing with diversity' demands attention from other directions too, for it cannot be assumed that equality of penal outcome is, in fact, the most desirable goal, although we might agree that a broadly equitable approach is necessary to ensure that sentencing and the criminal justice system as a whole achieve legitimacy for the public, offenders, sentencers and other criminal justice system professionals themselves. Thus one question is how diversity can be addressed without completely dislodging the principles of justice, fairness, and equity in approach. This chapter focuses on race and gender issues, although the broader precepts and principles find resonance when dealing with other forms of diversity too.

The concept of discrimination

First, it is important to consider ways in which diversity amongst offenders is already dealt with and here we turn to notions of negative discrimination. Discrimination is a notoriously difficult concept to define. In the criminal justice context the term is commonly taken to mean unfavourable treatment based on a person's sex, gender, social class, 'race', ethnicity, age or disability, for instance. It is a concept that is frequently tied to the concept of prejudice against particular people on the grounds that they are, for example, 'inferior' or 'difficult'. Under the Race Relations Act 1976 (revised by the Race Relations (Amendment) Act 2000)[1], *direct* racial discrimination arises when a person treats another less favourably on racial grounds than that person would treat someone else. 'Racial grounds' under the Act meant on grounds of colour, race, nationality (including citizenship) or ethnic or national origins. *Indirect* discrimination on the other hand, consists of treatment which may be described as equal in a formal sense (say between black and white offenders) but discriminatory in its actual effect. Arguably, indirect discrimination is far more significant and pervasive than direct discrimination, and this is as likely to be the case in the field of criminal justice as it is in other areas of social policy.

Complaints relating to the treatment of BME (black and minority ethnic) offenders in the criminal justice system often lead to claims that there should be *less disparity* in the delivery of justice; complaints about the treatment of women in the system often lead to the opposite conclusion. Here it is suggested that women and men should be treated *rather more* differently than they are. Thus 'dealing with diversity' is challenging and especially so in attempts to avoid dislodging notions of fairness, equality and justice in the process.

Concerns about discrimination

The key complaints about negative *racial* discrimination are that whilst black and ethnic minority groups represent just 7.9 per cent of the population in Britain, they represent around 24 per cent of the prison population (Home Office 2005a). Whilst this is an area of research which is beset with difficulties (because of the limits to conclusions that can be drawn from 'snap-shot' studies which focus on single

---

1 Whereas the Race Relations Act 1976 exempted key agencies within the criminal justice system, the Race Relations (Amendment) Act 2000 makes it possible for an individual who has been directly discriminated against within those agencies to bring a challenge to the courts.

decision-making stages in the system, limits to comparisons between evidence from different geographical areas and types of courts, and other methodological deficiencies such as weak data on ethnicity) and whilst data concerning ethnicity and crime always need to be treated with caution (Bowling and Phillips 2002) the evidence shows that people from BME groups continue to be disproportionately represented in the criminal justice system. For instance, black people are over six times more likely to be stopped and searched by the police, three times more likely to be arrested, and seven times more likely to be in prison than white people (Home Office 2005a). There is no evidence to suggest that this imbalance is a result of people from BME groups committing more crime than others (Flood-Page *et al.* 2000; Graham and Bowling 1995; Home Office 2005b).

A number of studies have pointed to notable differences in the trajectory of white offenders and black offenders (particularly African-Caribbean offenders) through the criminal justice system. It shouldn't be assumed that these differences are always evidence of clear discrimination however, indeed, taken together, the available research findings suggest that some differences may be explained by a combination of legal factors and social factors. Nonetheless, in many studies, residual, unexplained ethnic differences remain after these differences have been taken into account.

Overviews of the evidence can be sought in other texts (for example, Bowling and Phillips 2002) or in statistical compilations (Home Office 2005a). Beyond studies of entry points to the criminal justice system (Phillips and Brown (1998) who looked at police arrests and outcomes, and Mhlanga (1999) who looked at Crown Prosecution Service and court decision-making), both of which are worthy of mention because of their methodological robustness, attention should be drawn to Hood and Cardovil's (1992) study of sentencing in the Crown Court which showed a greater risk of custody for black males than for whites with the same characteristics (in terms of offence seriousness, previous convictions and so on). The study showed both the cumulative effect of discriminatory decisions and the discriminatory effects of social factors such as unemployment – which can affect decisions to remand people in custody and thereby create a 'custodial momentum'. Further, a recent study by Hood, Shute and Seemungal (2003) found that one in ten black defendants in the Crown Court and one in five in magistrates' courts believed that they had experienced unfair treatment by being given a more severe sentence than their white counterparts.

There have also been concerns about race equality issues within court reports (formerly social inquiry reports, now pre-sentence reports; HM Inspectorate of Probation 2000). And there is concern about differential access to community penalties for BME adults and young offenders (Bowling and Phillips 2002; Feilzer and Hood 2004), as well as the suggestion that BME offenders' needs have been neglected. Indeed, there are now a number of forceful accounts that BME offenders have experienced considerable social exclusion (Social Exclusion Unit 2002) and that the particularities of the disadvantages that they have experienced are not captured either by risk assessment instruments or by the caring gaze of probation officers (Cole and Wardak 2006; Raynor and Lewis 2006).

Concerns about negative or neglectful treatment of BME offenders have been so great as to suggest that there is 'institutional bias' whereby organisations fail to provide a professional service to people on the basis of their 'colour, culture and ethnic origin'. Whilst the claim originally concerned the police in response to a catalogue of police failures following the murder of black teenager Stephen Lawrence (Macpherson 1999), it is a term which has been taken up by other criminal justice system agencies too in their attempts to deal with diversity (Bowling and Phillips 2002; Lewis *et al.* 2006).

Turning to *gender*, there is a popular view that women receive lenient treatment in criminal justice compared to men, but little to support this claim beyond superficial analysis of criminal statistics which show that more women than men receive cautions (or reprimands and warnings in the case of young offenders in the English and Welsh system) and conditional discharges and probation, and that fewer women than men receive custodial penalties. But what such claims ignore is the fact that these differences reflect the seriousness of crimes committed and the number of previous convictions and so on. As a result of these varying views, debates about whether women receive lenient or harsh treatment have abounded (Gelsthorpe 2001a).

Hedderman and Gelsthorpe (1997) attempted to address the question of differential treatment once and for all in research involving some 13,000 offenders. But even here the finding was that there was no consistently different pattern in the sentencing of women and men. Women were less likely to be fined than men, but *some* of the women got a more severe penalty, for instance, not all of them got a lower penalty. Interviews with the magistrates, however, suggested that they drew clear distinctions between 'troubled' and 'troublesome' women, those who conformed to gender role expectations and those who did not. Family circumstances, appearance and demeanour, for instance, all played their part in determining how a women offender would be viewed and sentenced (Gelsthorpe 2001a; Heidensohn 2002).

More recently, there have been huge concerns about the increase in the number of women sentenced to custody (the number has almost tripled within a decade and is way out of proportion to the level of increases in crime or seriousness of crimes committed by women (Fawcett Society 2004; Gelsthorpe and Morris 2002; Home Office 2003). Women generally commit less serious offences than men and are far less likely to commit violent or sexual offences or to persist in crime. Moreover, it is thought that women's routes into crime are often quite distinct from men's and there are strong links between women's offending and financial and other kinds of hardship (see chapters in McIvor 2004 for an overview). Women prisoners are thought to be a particularly disadvantaged group with high levels of poverty, low levels of educational attainment and poor employment histories (Fawcett Commission 2004). For example, a disproportionately high number of women prisoners have a history of abuse or victimisation (Loucks 2004; Rumgay 2004, 2005).

One of the key issues, however, is that imprisoning women is not only damaging and often counterproductive for the individual, but that it has a disproportionate impact on their families as they are far more likely than men to be primary carers. More than 17,000 children are thought to be separated from their mothers each year through imprisonment and only 5 per cent of children remain in the family home after their mother is sentenced (Fawcett Society 2004).

Another concern is that prisons are often designed for men in terms of security and regimes (Carlen 2002). Similarly, community provision is primarily designed for men, meaning that women's needs are neglected (Mair and May 1997). At times, probation has been considered the default sentence for women and as befitting their perceived condition as 'troubled' more than 'troublesome'. Yet modern developments within the Probation Service have not necessarily accommodated women or women's needs. Not only has there been little recognition of the need to take into account gender lifestyle differences with regard to community service orders (under the Criminal Justice Act 2003 now called the 'unpaid work' requirement of a Community Order), but standard community penalties involving 'rehabilitative' interventions (cognitive- behavioural programmes, for instance) have largely been based on white men and pay little heed to the distinctive needs of women (Kendall 2002; Roberts 2002; Shaw and Hannah-Moffat 2004; Worrall 2003; see also Hannah-Moffat and Shaw 1999 who argue that risk and classification schemes disadvantage women). Further, a woman with a history of domestic violence or sexual exploitation may be placed on a probation programme where she is the only woman in a group of men, some of whom themselves may have a history of abusing women (Worrall 2002).

Needless to say, it is important to consider how ethnicity and gender (and indeed social class) might inter-relate, but few studies so far have got anywhere near the methodological sophistication and robustness required for this (see Gelsthorpe

2006 who writes about the other 'other' – the experiences of female minority ethnic offenders).

To summarise, the evidence is that BME offenders have been treated in a discriminatory way that undermines equality and fairness and the possibility of distinctive needs and disadvantages have not been properly explored. Women have been treated differently from men, but not always on the basis of *relevant* factors, instead reflecting gender-role stereotyping. Whilst some women benefit from gender-role stereotyping, some are disadvantaged by it. The criminal justice system appears to neglect women's needs, and subjects women to sentencing provision and prison regimes which to a large extent have been designed for men (and white men at that). What does it mean to 'deal with diversity' then?

Dealing with diversity: The law

The law can be utilised to guard against negative discrimination in a number of ways. First, there is the Race Relations legislation which we has already been mentioned. Second, Section 95 of the Criminal Justice Act 1991 requires the Secretary of State to publish information 'to avoid discriminating against any persons on the ground of race or sex or any other improper grounds'. Sentencing data alone, of course, serves no practical purpose unless the findings are reflected in policy but, symbolically, s.95 is taken to signify that discrimination is of concern. Equally, the Crime and Disorder Act 1998 (s.28) places a new emphasis on racial harassment which signifies that racial discrimination must be viewed as serious aggravation in offending behaviour. The Human Rights Act 1998 also carries particular import in attempts to frame the rights and freedoms of individuals, including the right, without discrimination, to life, liberty and security of the person, and the right not to be subject to inhuman or degrading treatment or punishment (see Cheney *et al.* 1999). However, it has yet to be tested in terms of negative discrimination and it would be a long route to justice (via the European Court of Human Rights).

But the most important legislation to mention here is the Equality Act 2006 which creates the Commission for Equality and Human Rights (taking on the work of existing Commissions)[2] and extending the equality purview to include religion/belief, age and sexual orientation. In particular, the Act contains a duty on

2   The Commission for Racial Equality, the Equal Opportunities Commission and the Disability Rights Commission.

public bodies to promote equality of opportunity between women and men ('the gender duty') and specifies duties and good practice in relation to equality and diversity. This means that all bodies carrying out 'public functions' will be required to take account of the differences between women and men, and ethnic majority and minority offenders. All criminal justice system agencies, the Sentencing Guidelines Council and the Sentencing Advisory Panel, for example, will be subject to the duty when it comes into force – in early 2007. One question to put to Regional Offender Managers (serving the National Offender Management System), for example, is whether there is sufficient and appropriate provision for women and BME offenders in the community. It would be a mistake to think that dealing with diversity effectively is a matter of making new legislation, however. Law is often only as good as its enforcement; arguably policy and practice are equally important.

Dealing with diversity: Policy and practice

Over the years there have been a number of policy initiatives which have attempted to deal with ethnic diversity and discrimination within the criminal justice system agencies. Such initiatives include equal opportunities policies in recruitment (including target-setting). Positive action measures (pre-entry training and experience) under the terms of the Race Relations Act 1976 have also been introduced both to encourage new entrants to agencies and to ensure equality of opportunity for promotion and career development (although recruitment strategies may be rendered useless without strong retention strategies: Holdaway and Barron 1997).

There have been other policy initiatives in training, but training is unlikely to be effective unless it is supported and legitimated by clear policy and commitment emanating from the top. Also, much depends on how racism, say, is conceived in training – a few rotten apples in a profession who have to be got at? personal racism? or appreciation that the system itself may be racist in effect if not in intention? Single training events may not be enough – there may need to be 'topping-up' or consolidation sessions and imaginative approaches since experiential learning is deemed to have greater impact than traditional didactic styles of teaching). But, arguably, training needs to be part of a broader strategy of political commitment and policy change, and personal commitment to improve practice (Luthra and Oakley 1991).

Action research approaches (linking local policy decision-making with research evidence by providing rapid feedback to managers) may also be useful. For example, the Prison Service has revised its race relations policy several times during the past 18 years, but until recently the focus has been on the diversity agenda for staff, rather than prisoners' experiences. In 1999, research was commissioned to measure the extent to which discrimination against BMEs could be reduced and to identify the process by which this is best achieved (Ellis, Tedstone and Curry 2004). The conclusion was that much can be achieved through a rapid response to problems.

Some of these policy initiatives are quite recent, however. For example, according to Denney (1992) probation policy ignored ethnic minority offenders until the late 1970s. It wasn't until the mid-1970s that the Home Office encouraged the appointment of specialist officers in each area to develop services for ethnic minorities. The thinking at the time was that specialists could mediate any 'cultural misunderstandings'. Following the urban disturbances in the 1980s (the Brixton riots) there was emerging acknowledgment of the need to recognise institutional forms of racism and to promote anti-racist probation practice – mainly through local initiatives and projects. But since the 1990s there has been rapid development of policy initiatives to recruit and retain BME staff for example (HM Inspectorate of Probation 2000) and to promote positive leadership in relation to race equality (HM Inspectorate of Probation 2004). (There have been similar concerns about women within the Service and their role in managerial positions.) The National Probation Service's (NPS) report (2001) *A New Choreography* established 'diversity' as a key business objective for the NPS. The subsequent publication of *The Heart of the Dance* by the NPS (2003) translates the objectives into priority actions to guide probation practice on the ground and to ensure that the culture of probation is one which recognises appropriate service delivery.

A key question is how far anti-racist practice has become embedded within the Service, and how far it has succeeded in addressing perceptions of inequality of treatment. There are differing perspectives on this (see Dominelli *et al.* 1995; Lavalette, Penketh and Jones 1998) and certainly major concerns that not enough has been done to establish an anti-discriminatory culture (Chouhan 2002; HM Inspectorate of Probation 2000; 2004).

There was relatively little research on BME offenders' needs and on what might 'work' for them until the early 1990s, but since then there have been a number of significant developments in efforts to address perceptions of inequality in provision (Williams 2006) and to establish more clearly what BME offenders' needs and experiences might be. One such development involved a survey of Probation Service provision (group work programmes and so on) specifically targeting black and Asian offenders (Powis and Walmsley 2002), but whilst some staff showed a preference for running separate programmes for BME offenders, others advocated mixed group-work provision and there was little empirical evidence (in terms of effectiveness) to substantiate either position. Unfortunately the research did not include a focus on offenders' views. But another study did involve interviews with nearly 500 black and Asian offenders under supervision by the Probation Service in order to produce some evidence on their 'criminogenic needs' (Calverley *et al.* 2004). The research found that black, Asian and mixed heritage offenders showed less evidence of crime-prone attitudes and beliefs, and lower levels of self-reported problems than white counterparts. Interestingly, only a third of the offenders wanted to be supervised by someone from the same ethnic group, while most thought that it would make no difference. Moreover, there was very limited support from those attending programmes for groups of offenders containing only members from ethnic minority groups. Given this, it will be important to ensure that the Equality Act 2006 does not lead to ready assumptions that ethnic diversity *has* to mean difference in delivery. But it is another story when we turn to gender.

There has been no shortage of alternative proposals to deal with female offenders in a way which would reduce the use of imprisonment and reflect more closely what we know about women's pathways into crime. The proposals have ranged from the fanciful notion of a 'sex neutral sentencing system' (discrimination is rarely conscious and direct, but is rather unconscious and indirect) to the case for a feminist conception of justice (Heidensohn 1986).

Since the mid-1990s, in particular, there have been numerous attempts by researchers (and some politicians and policy-makers) to make criminal justice policy less discriminatory against some women (attempting to reduce gender-role stereo-typing), but generally more gender sensitive (responding to women's particular needs; see, for example, Carlen 2002; Fawcett Society 2004; Hedderman 2004; HM Inspectorate of Prisons 1997; Morris *et al.* 1995; Prison Reform Trust 2000). Policy recommendations include the need for increased diversion from court on the grounds that women generally commit offences of relatively low seriousness. Indeed, Wedderburn suggested a co-ordinated network of Women's Supervision, Rehabilitation and Support Centres (Prison Reform Trust 2000, Recommendation 4.ii) which would facilitate a reduction in the use of imprisonment and which, at the same time, would serve to address women's needs for support and social integration. Two such centres have been identified in Yorkshire and Humberside and in the North West of England and they are now being implemented – following the Scottish Executive initiative in setting up a community support centre for women in Glasgow (Loucks *et al.* 2006). Other recommendations include the reintroduction of unit fines[3] (so as to reflect the fact that women, as a group, are relatively poor and that fines should be imposed according to means) and a requirement that sentencers take into account the distinctive position of female offenders (for instance, their economic position, their mental health, their childhood or recent experiences of physical or sexual abuse, or their responsibilities towards children, partners, parents or other family or household members). Combined, these recommendations (and others) stem from an understanding of the lower seriousness of women's offending, their comparatively lower likelihood of re-offending and the strong evidence that the lives of female offenders are characterised by individual and social problems.

Welcome as such proposals are, there is also the need to question whether or not such moves are enough, and whether or not initiatives which promulgate new policies for women but not for men run the risk of creating as many discrepancies as they resolve. Whilst claims that women commit less serious crimes and pose fewer risks than men are grounded in incontrovertible evidence which legitimates calls for the differential treatment of men and women, there is some difficulty in applying this same logic of differentiation on the basis of women's *social* backgrounds. Few would dismiss indications of social hardship amongst men in prison, although there might be variation in degree (Howden-Windell and Clark 1999; Prison Reform Trust 1991).

Importantly, there has been a general push to ensure that provision is 'gender-sensitive' in Home Office sponsored initiatives such as the Government's Women's Offending Reduction Programme (WORP) which attempts to co-ordinate work across departments and agencies in working more effectively with women offenders in the community and reducing imprisonment. The Fawcett Society's Gender and Justice Policy network – working with both Home Office departments and voluntary organisations – similarly serves to bring women's distinctive needs to the foreground in policy and practice.

Given what is known about women's distinctive needs, the implications for practice in work with offenders are unmistakable but not easy to address. The relatively low number of women given community orders or prison sentences point to generic offender intervention programmes (on grounds of logistics and cost). The Home Office continues to focus on similarities rather more than on differences (e.g.

3   Unit fines were proposed in the Criminal Justice Act 1991 (s.13). Based
     on the notion of a 'day fine' as used in part of the USA and Scandinavia,
     the idea was to fine people according to their means as well as in relation
     to the seriousness of offence (Easton and Piper 2005).

in relation to Enhanced Thinking Skills: Cann 2006) but 'What Works' principles (McGuire 2002) suggest that targeting and responsivity are important. As Anne Worrall amongst others has pointed out, 'women who commit offences are often driven to do so not by 'cognitive behavioural deficits' but by the complexity of the demands placed upon them' (2002, p.144). She goes on to suggest that:

> They not only believe that they have few positive legitimate options, but in reality, they have few positive legitimate options. Important as enhanced thinking skills are, they can only be, at best, a prerequisite to empowering women to make better choices, if the choices genuinely exist. (p.144)

If there is need for further evidence of what is likely and what is less likely to work for women, in the context of strong suggestions that provision should be multi-modal (Roberts 2002), there is scope to draw on the research literature in relation to learning styles. Most educational researchers and cognitive psychologists acknowledge the significant effect that learning styles have on the learning process (Vincent and Ross, 2001). Amongst the foundational work on gender and learning is Belenky *et al*.'s (1986) *Women's Ways of Knowing*, which argues that women's learning differs from men's learning both in terms of its developmental sequence and in terms of its underlying theory (see also Covington 1998). Belenky *et al*. (1986) argue that women view knowledge more as a set of connections than a set of distinctions, and that most women prefer to learn in collaborative, rather than competitive, settings. If we put this alongside evidence which suggests that women-only environments facilitate growth and development (Zaplin 1998) we can see that the evidence adds up to a need for work with women in non-authoritarian co-operative settings, where women are empowered to engage in social and personal change. (Although as Roberts (2002) has indicated, women-only provision remains controversial for economic, political and other reasons.)

Conclusion

The concluding argument is that more attention needs to be given to diversity in the conception and delivery of interventions for offenders – not only to meet 'equality criteria' now enshrined in law, but to maximise any potential for effectiveness (the discussion of women's needs and learning styles highlights the importance of recognising gender differences). This general point has resonance for other groups too – including BME offenders where proper research on distinctive needs is perhaps only just beginning.

Moreover, it could be argued that any moves towards compliance or desistance on the part of offenders will perhaps come via interventions (though not exclusively criminal justice interventions) which are thought to be *legitimate* (Bottoms 2001). In this regard, there is evidence that where authorities act fairly (where there is procedural justice) it has a significant impact on notions of legitimacy (Paternoster *et al.* 1997; Tyler 1990). The ingredients of justice here include ethicality or what might be termed as 'respect' for offenders. In this regard, to be treated not as a composite offender but as a fully human, socially and culturally differentiated offender is perhaps to engender reciprocal 'respect' and to indirectly promote compliance (Gelsthorpe 2001b).

In this chapter consideration has been given to ways in which the criminal justice system *does* give consideration to ethnic and gender differences and the possibility has been raised that there are ways in which the system *should* perhaps make differentiated provision. Whilst the focus has been on race and gender issues, it is possible to extrapolate from this points which are relevant to sexual orientation, religion, disabilities, and mental health factors. The conclusion is to suggest that the system needs both to avoid negative discrimination and to accommodate diversity in order to work out 'What Works' (or at least what might work) and in order to promote legitimacy.

References

Belenky, M., Clinchy, B., Goldberger, N. and Tarule, J. (1986) *Women's Ways of Knowing.* New York: Basic Books.

Bottoms, A.E. (2001) 'Compliance and Community Penalties.' In A.E. Bottoms, L. Gelsthorpe and S. Rex (eds) *Community Penalties: Changes and Challenges.* Cullompton: Willan.

Bowling, B. and Phillips, C. (2002) *Racism, Crime and Justice.* Harlow: Longman.

Calverley, A., Cole, B., Kaur, G., Lewis, S. *et al.* (2004) *Black and Asian offenders on probation.* Home Office Research Study 277. London: Home Office.

Cann, J. (2006) *Cognitive Skills Programmes: Impact on Reducing Reconviction Among a Sample of Female Prisoners.* Home Office Findings 276. London: Home Office.

Carlen, P. (ed.) (2002) *Women and Punishment: The Struggle for Justice.* Cullompton: Willan.

Cheney, D., Dickson, L., Fitzpatrick, J. and Uglow, S. (1999) *Criminal Justice and the Human Rights Act 1998.* Bristol: Jordans.

Chouhan, K. (2002) 'Race Issues in Probation.' In D. Ward, J. Scott and M. Lacey (eds) *Probation: Working for Justice.* Oxford: Oxford University Press.

Cole, B. and Wardak, A. (2006) 'Black and Asian Men on Probation: Social Exclusion, Discrimination and Experiences of Criminal Justice.' In S. Lewis, P. Raynor, D. Smith and A. Wardak (eds) *Race and Probation.* Cullompton: Willan.

Covington, S. (1998) 'The Relational Theory of Women's Psychological Development: Implications for the Criminal Justice System.' In R. Zaplin (ed.) *Female Offenders: Critical Perspectives and Effective Interventions.* Gaithersburg, MD: Aspen Publishers.

Denney, D. (1992) *Racism and Anti-racism in Probation.* London: Routledge.

Dominelli, L., Jeffers, L., Jones, G., Sibanda, S. and Williams, B. (1995) *Anti-racist Probation Practice.* Aldershot: Arena.

Easton, S. and Piper, C. (2005) *Sentencing and Punishment: The Quest for Justice.* Oxford: Oxford University Press.

Ellis, T., Tedstone, C. and Curry, D. (2004) *Improving Race Relations in Prisons: What Works?* Home Office Online Report 12/04. London: Home Office.

Fawcett Society (2004) *Women and the Criminal Justice System: A Report of the Fawcett Society's Commission on Women and the Criminal Justice System.* London: Fawcett Society.

Feilzer, M. and Hood, R. (2004) *Differences or Discrimination? Minority Ethnic Young People in the Youth Justice System.* London: Youth Justice Board.

Flood-Page, C., Campbell, S., Harrington, V. and Miller, J. (2000) *Youth Crime: Findings from the 1989/90 Youth Lifestyles Survey.* Home Office Research Study 209. London: Home Office.

Gelsthorpe, L. (2001a) 'Critical Decisions and Processes in the Criminal Courts.' In E. McLaughlin and J. Muncie (eds) *Controlling Crime.* London: Sage/Open University.

Gelsthorpe, L. (2001b) 'Accountability, Difference and Diversity in the Delivery of Community Penalties.' In A.E. Bottoms, L. Gelsthorpe, and S. Rex (eds) *Community Penalties: Change and Challenges.* Cullompton: Willan.

Gelsthorpe, L. (2006) 'The Experiences of Female Minority Ethnic Offenders: the Other "Other".' In S. Lewis, P. Raynor, D. Smith and A. Wardak (eds) *Race and Probation.* Cullompton: Willan.

Gelsthorpe, L. and Morris, A. (2002) 'Women's Imprisonment in England and Wales: A Penal Paradox.' *Criminal Justice 2,* 3, 277–301.

Graham, J. and Bowling, B. (1995) *Young People and Crime.* London: Home Office Research Study 145.

Hannah-Moffat, K. and Shaw, M. (1999) 'Women and Risk: A Genealogy of Classification.' Paper presented to the British Society of Criminology Conference, Liverpool, July.

Hedderman, C. (2004) 'The Criminogenic Needs of Women Offenders.' In G. McIvor (ed.) *Women Who Offend.* Research Highlights in Social Work 44. London: Jessica Kingsley Publishers.

Hedderman, C. and Gelsthorpe, L. (1997) *Understanding the Sentencing of Women.* Home Office Research Study 170. London: Home Office.

Heidensohn, F. (1986) 'Models of Justice: Portia or Persephone? Some Thoughts on Equality, Fairness and Gender in the Field of Criminal Justice.' *International Journal of Sociology of Law 14:* 287–298.

Heidensohn, F. (2002) 'Gender and Crime.' In M. Maguire, R. Morgan and R. Reiner (eds) *The Oxford Handbook of Criminology.* Oxford: Oxford University Press.

HM Inspectorate of Prisons (1997) *Women in Prison. A Thematic Review by HM Chief Inspector of Prisons.* London: Home Office.

HM Inspectorate of Probation (2000) *Towards Race Equality: A Thematic Inspection.* London: HM Inspectorate of Probation.

HM Inspectorate of Probation (2004) *Towards Race Equality Follow-up Inspection Report.* London: HM Inspectorate of Probation.

Holdaway, S. and Barron, A.-M. (1997) *Resignation: The Experience of Black and Asian Police Officers.* Basingstoke: Macmillan.

Home Office (2003) *Statistics on Women and the Criminal Justice System.* London: Home Office Section 95 Report.

Home Office (2005a) Race and the Criminal Justice System: An Overview to the Complete Statistics 2003–2004. A Section 95 report. London: Home Office.

Home Office (2005b) *Ethnicity and Crime: Findings from the (Crime and Justice) Survey.* London: Home Office Crime and Justice Survey.

Hood, R. and Cordovil, G. (1992) *Race and Sentencing – A Study in the Crown Court.* Oxford: Clarendon Press.

Hood, R., Shute, S. and Seemungal, F. (2005) *A Fair Hearing? Ethnic Minorities in the Criminal Courts.* Cullompton: Willan.

Howden-Windell, J. and Clarke, D. (1999) *The Criminogenic Needs of Female Offenders: A Literature Review.* London: Home Office Prison Service.

Kendall, K. (2002) 'Time to Think Again about Cognitive Behavioural Programmes.' In P. Carlen (ed) *Women and Punishment: The Struggle for Justice.* Cullompton: Willan.

Lavalette, M., Penketh, L., and Jones, C. (eds) (1998) *Anti-Racism and Social Welfare.* Aldershot: Ashgate.

Lewis, S. (2006) 'Minority Ethnic Experiences of Probation Supervision and Programmes.' In S. Lewis, P. Raynor, D. Smith and A. Wardak (eds) *Race and Probation.* Cullompton: Willan.

Lewis, S. Raynor, P., Smith, D. and Wardak, A. (eds) (2006) *Race and Probation.* London: Jessica Kingsley.

Loucks, N. (2004) 'Women in Prison.' In G. McIvor (ed.) *Women who Offend.* London: Jessica Kingsley Publishers.

Loucks, N., Malloch, M., McIvor, G. and Gelsthorpe, L. (2006) *Evaluation of the 218 Centre.* Edinburgh: Scottish Executive Justice Department.

Luthra, M. and Oakley, R. (1991) *Combating Racism Through Training: A Review of Approaches to Race Training in Organisations.* Policy Paper 22. Warwick: Centre for Research in Ethnic Relations, University of Warwick.

Macpherson, Sir William (1999) *The Stephen Lawrence Inquiry,* Cm. 4262-1. London: Stationery Office.

Mair, G. and May, C. (1997) *Offenders on Probation.* Home Office Research Study 167. London: Home Office.

McGuire, J. (ed.) (2002) *Offender Rehabilitation and Treatment.* Chichester: John Wiley and Sons.

McIvor, G. (ed.) (2004) *Women Who Offend.* London: Jessica Kingsley Publishers.

Mhlanga, B. (1999) *Race and Crown Prosecution Service Decisions.* London: Stationery Office.

Morris, A., Wilkinson, C., Tisi, A., Woodrow J. and Rockley, A. (1995) *Managing the Needs of Female Prisoners.* London: Home Office.

National Probation Service (2001) *A New Choreography.* London: Home Office.

National Probation Service (2003) *The Heart of the Dance: a Diversity Strategy for the National Probation Service for England and Wales 2002–2006.* London: Home Office.

Paternoster, R., Bachman, R., Brame, R. and Sherman, L. (1997) 'Do Fair Procedures Matter? The Effect of Procedural Justice on Spouse Assault.' *Law and Society Review 31,* 163–204.

Phillips, C. and Brown, D. (1998) *Entry into the Criminal Justice System: A Survey of Police Arrests and their Outcomes.* Home Office Research Study 185. London: Home Office.

Powis, B. and Walmsley, R. (2002) *Programmes for Black and Asian Offenders on Probation: Lessons for Developing Practice.* Home Office Research Study 250. London: Home Office.

Prison Reform Trust (1991) *The Identikit Prisoner.* London: Prison Reform Trust.

Prison Reform Trust (2000) *Justice for Women, the Need for Reform: Report of the Committee on Women's Imprisonment.* London: Prison Reform Trust.

Raynor, P. and Lewis, S. (2006) 'Black and Asian men on Probation: Who are They, and What are their Needs?.' In S. Lewis, P. Raynor, D. Smith and A. Wardak (eds) *Race and Probation*. Cullompton: Willan.

Roberts, J. (2002) 'Women-centred: The West Mercia Community-based Programme for Women Offenders.' In P. Carlen (ed.) *Women and Punishment: the Struggle for Justice*. Cullompton: Willan.

Rumgay, J. (2004) 'Scripts for Safer Survival: Pathways out of Female Crime.' *Howard Journal of Criminal Justice 43*, 405–19.

Rumgay, J. (2005) *When Victims Become Offenders: In Search of Coherence in Policy and Practice*. Occasional Paper. London: Fawcett Society.

Shaw, M. and Hannah-Moffat, K. (2004) 'How Cognitive Skills Forgot about Gender and Diversity.' In G. Mair (ed.) *What Matters in Probation*. Cullompton: Willan.

Social Exclusion Unit (2002) *Reducing Re-offending by Ex-prisoners*. London: Office of the Deputy Prime Minister.

Tyler, T. (1990) *Why People Obey the Law*. New Haven, CT: Yale University Press.

Vincent, A. and Ross, D. (2001) 'Learning Style Awareness: A Basis for Developing Teaching and Learning Strategies.' *Journal of Research on Technology in Education 33*, 5.

Williams, P. (2006) 'Designing and Delivering Programmes for Minority Ethnic Offenders.' In S. Lewis, P. Raynor, D. Smith and A. Wardak (eds) *Race and Probation*. Cullompton: Willan.

Worrall, A. (2002) 'Rendering them Punishable.' In P. Carlen (ed.) *Women and Punishment: The Struggle for Justice*. Cullompton: Willan.

Worrall, A. (2003) '"What Works" and Community Sentences for Women Offenders.' *Criminal Justice Matters 53*, 40–41.

Zaplin, R. (ed.) (1998) *Female Offenders: Critical Perspectives and Effective Interventions*. Gaithersbers, MD: Aspen Publishers.

CHAPTER 17

The Resettlement of Prisoners in England and Wales: Learning from History and Research

Maurice Vanstone

Throughout the history of the probation service work with prisoners and ex-prisoners has been aligned closely to its rehabilitative tradition. Initially, such work was based on voluntary contact, but in recent years such contact has been superseded by systems of automatic and discretionary conditional release and an accompanying concentration of resources. This chapter explores ways of undertaking work with people who have been imprisoned that are likely to be effective in providing appropriate help and reducing the likelihood of further offending after release. In so doing, it draws on the findings of research undertaken into the resettlement Pathfinder projects (Lewis *et al.* 2003; Vanstone, Lewis and Raynor 2004),[1] and examines what can be learned from other research and the history of work with those people who have been imprisoned.

---

1   The 'Resettlement Pathfinder' projects were set up by the Probation Service in 1999 as one of several evaluated pilots of new services and programmes which were an important part of the Service's *Effective Practice Initiative*. Initially, this involved six Pathfinder projects which tested a variety of resettlement strategies with adult prisoners sentenced to less than 12 months, who are released under the system of Automatic Unconditional Release (AUR) which offers only voluntary supervision. Three of the projects were based on the efforts of voluntary organisations and three on local probation services. The second phase involved the implementation of the FOR a Change programme (see below) in three prisons.

Early history

A reasonably full history of voluntary effort in the provision of welfare to prisoners can be found in Maguire *et al.* (1997), so a briefer summary will suffice here. From the beginning of the nineteenth century to 1862 independent discharged prisoners' aid societies (DPAS) provided a service at local county gaols. Then, following their first conference in 1871 (NADPAS 1956) the numbers increased, paradoxically as Davies (1974) suggests, leading to demands for central control. However, despite the fact that the Gladstone Report (Departmental Committee on Prisons 1895) concluded that the rehabilitation of prisoners was the responsibility of the penal system, discharged prisoners' aid societies exercised voluntary responsibility for most ordinary prisoners both inside and outside the prisons for the next 70 years.

Probation involvement began in the second half of the nineteenth century with the police court mission helping prisoners when they were discharged (Jarvis 1972; Vanstone 2004) operating on the same evangelical principles as their court work. Following the creation of the Probation Service, probation officers continued the role in parallel with the DPAS (Bochel 1976), and in 1928 the Advisory Committee on Probation was changed to that of Probation and AfterCare. After care work by officers primarily involved the supervision of boys released from Approved School and Borstal, but it did include some work with discharged prisoners. As King (1964) has argued, the voluntary supervision of discharged prisoners remained on the fringes of probation activity. In contrast, responsibility for the statutory aftercare of prisoners released from preventive detention and corrective training was ensconced in the 1948 Criminal Justice Act, the Maxwell Report 1953, Morison Report 1962 and most significantly the Advisory Council's Report of 1963 (Home Office 1963) which laid the basis on which the Probation Service would become the prime agency responsible for aftercare. By the time of the Home Office Circular 144/1965 (*The Organisation of Aftercare*), the purpose of which was to regulate this change, 50 probation areas had already assumed responsibility (Maguire *et al.* 1997).

The shift to compulsion

The subsequent history of the Probation Service's involvement in aftercare has been dominated by the expansion of its compulsory component. This has occurred during a period when the focus of the Service and, some would argue, its values have undergone significant change not only in terms of the managerialist agenda of increased control and surveillance but also in increased work with people whose offending is more serious and persistent (Nellis 1995; Vanstone 1995). The Day Training Centre experiment marked the beginnings of a shift to greater use of additional conditions in orders (Vanstone 1993), and the Carlisle Report (Home Office 1988c) prefigured an extension in parole and conditional release. At the same time, the offence was rediscovered as a focus of probation work (McGuire and Priestley 1985), public protection was promulgated by government as a key function of probation, and optimism in the capacity of offence-focused work was generated by emerging research into effectiveness (Ross, Fabiano and Ross 1986; Trotter 1993; Raynor and Vanstone 1994). The term aftercare which defined probation officers' work as post-release (although in reality that work had always involved contact with prisoners while they were serving their sentence) was replaced by *throughcare* which gave more weight to the process of continuous reha-bilitative work and later would lead to the concept of the seamless sentence.

Like the more general change in the focus of probation work, the inexorable shift in emphasis from voluntary to statutory supervision can be discerned in a number of government interventions, the first, and most significant of which, was the Statement of National Objectives and Priorities (Home Office, 1984). It lowered the priority of 'social work for offenders released from custody', and can be seen as sounding the first knell of the decline of voluntary aftercare. This was followed by a series of consultative papers (Home Office 1988a, 1988b, 1990, 1990a), sets of National Standards (Home Office 1992a, 1995, 2000) and Three Year Plans (Home Office 1992b, 1993) which introduced the concept of punishment in the community and continued the redefining of probation activity so that it involved intensive probation programmes; public protection and crime prevention and the supervision of people released on licence. One in particular expounded the notion that work such as voluntary aftercare could at least in part be provided by other bodies in partnership with probation who could provide information and help for released prisoners (Home Office 1990a). By 1995 National Standards focused exclusively on supervision of licences with no reference to voluntary throughcare and, perhaps inevitably, emphasised control rather than welfare as a more dominant concern.

Coupled with the Criminal Justice Act 1991, these unprecedented government interventions heralded the most significant changes in policy and practice in probation history. Automatic Conditional Release (ACR) and Discre-tionary Conditional Release (DCR) expanded statutory supervision (Maguire *et al.* 1996) and the National Framework for the Throughcare of Offenders (Home Office Probation Services Division and Prison Service 1993) established new guiding principles and core procedures for throughcare. The concept of sentence planning (inaugurated in 1992 with DCR prisoners) and its plan of action for each individual prisoner, drawn up by prison officers in conjunction with Probation, set a trail which was to lead to the seamless sentence ideal, the Carter Review recommendations and the National Offender Management System.

It is no surprise, therefore, that at the end of the twentieth century a survey of voluntary aftercare provision by the probation service found 'that the extent of voluntary aftercare being undertaken is considerably less than one might deduce from official returns and, moreover, that its use is declining rapidly' (Maguire *et al.* 1997, p.13). In addition, the survey found that some high-risk AUR (Automatic Unconditional Release) prisoners who might be termed high priority were unlikely to receive any aftercare service because officers were preoccupied with statutory ACR and DCR cases. In fact, the issue raised by this survey was taken up by Halliday (2001) who argued that the idea of short sentence prisoners making a voluntary commitment to working on their offending behaviour cut across the grain of current criminal justice policies. Such thinking, as Lewis *et al.* (2003) have pointed out, has a long history: at the beginning of the 1970s probation with a condition of attendance at a Community Training Centre was proposed by Priestley (1970) albeit for reasons of need rather than risk. During the same period, Davies (1974, p.51) threw doubt on the relevance of the voluntary principle to the problems of ex-prisoners:

> The voluntary nature of the relationship is bound to restrict the probation officer's potential for involvement, and where the client actually appears to want help, the problems are often of such complexity and depth that we are taken out of the realm of aftercare and into the question of how society as a whole should or could care for its inadequate adults – single or married.

In the past, some commentators have argued that the key to successful voluntary engagement with prisoners is the degree to which officers are client-centred (Corden and Clifton 1985). (In their evaluation of the Socially Isolated Prisoners Project set up by West Yorkshire Probation Service they discovered a take-up rate of 63 per cent.) In the context of current policy demands even success of this magnitude might not be enough. The final development in this short history is the introduction of the term resettlement in place of throughcare (Home Office 1998, 2001). Emerging for the first time from the prisons and Probation Review, it purports to more accurately describe the purpose of work with prisoners who have temporarily been taken out of their communities. Some have argued persuasively that it encompasses contradictory concepts (Raynor 2004), but it does perhaps give more credence to the idea of the imprisoned person as citizen. Admittedly, this runs against the grain of aspects of what happens to the individual's citizenship when they enter prison: the imposition of uniform and the removal of possessions are examples of the symbolic removal of citizenship, and the denial of the right to vote is an example of an actual removal of citizenship. However, the official recognition of one of the goals of work with prisoners as 'successful resettlement in the community' is an acceptance of the prisoner as at least a potential citizen (Home Office 1998, p.9). An individual cannot return to his or her community and *settle* or *integrate* or become *re-included* unless he or she is a citizen, so in this sense (for once) a change in official language may have positive results.

The case for helping prisoners

It may well be that exigencies of public protection from offending justify a compulsory component to all throughcare of prisoners whether short- or long-term. The avoidance of future offending following release from prison is surely in the interests of both public and prisoner, and it is the focus on offending that adds a moral dimension to the question of what kind of response the state should make to the problems of prisoners during and after their sentence. We know that reduction of offending is associated with a problem-solving approach to criminogenic factors such as unemployment, lack of accommodation and drug misuse (Berntsen and Christiansen 1965; May 1999; Raynor *et al.* 2000; Ross and Fabiano 1985); that state-imposed imprisonment often exacerbates (or even creates) such problems – as Haines (1990, p.9) asserts, 'the experience of prison exacerbates the social isolation of many prisoners, and that social isolation militates against successful integration into society' – and that most prisoners (but particularly short-term prisoners) have various combinations of them. Indeed, the latter point has been made consistently by research over the past 40 years.

One of the earliest research studies (National Council of Social Services 1961) concluded from interviews with 170 prisoners at 10 prisons and analysis of 280 cases dealt with by the Royal London Discharged Prisoners' Aid Society that the problems of ex-prisoners were loss of integrity, severe material losses, loss of employment, loss of family supports, wife and children's pain, and psychological difficulties. Four years later, Morris's (1965) study focused on prisoners and their families. Based on interviews with 824 men (837,330 of whom were first-time prisoners, 330 recidivists and 177 civil prisoners), 588 wives, and the families of 100 prisoners from London, the study found that 'many of these families are living in conditions of considerable poverty, and that there can be little left over for food, let alone household goods and cleaning materials' (p.84), and that they had multiple problems. Moreover, the men had problems such as unemployment, marital and psychiatric problems. The study created a profile particularly of short-term prisoners that has remained constant since (Corden 1983; Corden, Kuipers and Wilson 1978, 1979, 1980; Fairhead 1981; Hagell, Newburn and Rowlington 1995; Holborn 1975; McWilliams 1975; Haines 1990; Nacro 1993, 2000). Paylor (1992, p.30) highlighted the fact that imprisonment has a detrimental effect on people's housing status, advocated reform of the benefit system, and concluded 'that the situation for prisoners upon release in 1991 appears not to be a great deal different from that faced by ex-offenders in Corden, Kuipers and Wilson's study conducted over fourteen years ago'.

Some research has clarified differences in terms of the degree of problems between short-, medium- and long-term prisoners: Banks and Fairhead (1976) using a sample of 300 prisoners compared the problems of short-term prisoners (up to and including 18-month sentences) and medium- and long-term, and revealed that the former had a greater degree of personal and social problems, particularly those associated with recidivism; for example 38 per cent of the short-term men were homeless compared to 14.5 per cent of the medium- and long term, and 34 per cent were deemed to be unable to settle or inadequate as opposed to 5 per cent of the medium-term prisoners and 16 per cent of the long-term.

Other researchers have exposed the additional problems of minority groups in the prison system. The needs of women prisoners overlap those general needs outlined above but research has also exposed particular needs. Carlen (1983) carried out two in-depth interviews with 20 women over 21 years old in a Scottish prison who were either serving or had previously served a short term of imprisonment, or had been on remand, or had previous convictions, and found that as well as the usual catalogue of problems they had experienced separation from parents at an early age, physical violence from husbands, social isolation, and felt ensnared in dependence on men by their economic and social situation. Carlen argues also that the 'structural characteristics of women's lawbreaking and imprisonment' have 'been ignored in favour of the ever-elusive psychological ones' (2002, p.83); moreover, the official response to these problems was seen to be irrelevant with aftercare low on the social work departments' list of priorities. Other research has confirmed Carlen's findings and revealed the core problems faced by men plus additional problems such as childcare and substance abuse (Maguire *et al.* 2000). A recent report by Nacro (2001) underlines the different impact of imprisonment on women, manifesting itself as it does in higher incidence of self-harm and attempted suicide, higher use of medication, fewer accredited programmes, and greater dislocation from their communities (an even greater problem for Black and Asian women situated far from support and help with religious and cultural requirements).

It accepts that their needs are broadly similar to men, but exacerbated by problems of childcare, family responsibilities and discrimination in the labour market (Caddle and Crisp 1997; Hamlyn and Lewis 2000; Home Office 1999a). For those from minority ethnic groups there are the needs for recognition of difference, help with the effects of institutional racism, information in the relevant language, and appropriate skin care and food. All of which prescribes the need for what Nacro describes as an 'integrated model of resettlement practice which involves assessment, motivational and planning work before release, and cognitive work and practical guidance after release' (Nacro 2004, p.16).

While latterly the problems faced by women who have been imprisoned have been well documented, those of ethnic minority prisoners have been given less attention, although Lewis and her colleagues included a focus on the involvement of minority ethnic prisoners in the Pathfinder programmes (Lewis *et al.* 2003) and Nacro (2002) exposed their under-representation in such programmes. Research shows that men and women from ethnic minority groups are disproportionately represented in the prison population (Home Office 1994), and that they face different experiences in their contact with criminal justice agencies (Agozino 1997; Chigwada-Bailey 1997; Fitzgerald 1993; Home Office 1999a, 2002; Hood 1992); but we know too that the resettlement needs of these prisoners are often more acute. As Nacro put it:

> In this climate of neglect, the difficulties surrounding resettlement for black and minority ethnic (BME) prisoners are compounded for two reasons. Firstly, BME groups are less likely to access general resettlement services in prison, and facilities to address their particular cultural needs are often inadequate. Secondly, it is well known that BME groups experience social and economic disadvantage in housing, employment, education, health and social services, meaning that on release they are more likely to encounter social exclusion, which could have contributed to their incarceration in the first place (2002, p.3).

Interestingly, the Pathfinder resettlement research reveals that after entry into the project Black and Asian prisoners are as likely to experience a high continuity service while in prison or be involved in post-release contact as white prisoners. However, it provides confirmation of the Nacro assertion in as much as that in the majority of the projects (the exception being those prisons where there was a higher proportion of either Black or Asian prisoners) there were indications of under-representation of minority ethnic groups. The reasons for this are not transparent, but it is interesting that the project in which the highest number of Asian prisoners was involved had an Asian worker.

The unintended consequences of imprisonment have been given attention only relatively lately. Pope (1987) used the experiences of two children, Ben aged 6 and Karen aged 12, to illustrate child response to loss of father to prison. (Ben, for example, was withdrawn at school, making no academic progress, and having difficulty in dealing with the family secret that dad was in prison and a social outcast.) In the same year, Shaw (1987, p.79) had called for 'extensive research into the long-term effects of fathers' imprisonment on children'. Five years later, commenting on research findings that show that most prisoners are not adequately prepared for release, that families experience multiple problems and that spouses, partners and other relatives receive sparse help from responsible agencies, he asserted that 'these undesirable consequences of imprisonment are the inevitable effects of a sentencing culture which cannot afford to consider the consequences to innocent parties' (Shaw 1992, p.193). White (1989) added a focus on children in prison. In an examination of three mother and baby units in Holloway, Styal and Askham Grange, she attacked complacency about the punitive impact on the children. The paper illuminates the artificiality of the babies' lives, and the particular difficulties of women from minority groups. Among the problems emphasised are institutionalisation and the lack of *loco parentis* powers which means that the mother and father can decide a baby can be removed even into a risk situation. The author does not pose any easy solutions because the alternatives of, for instance, separation or removal into care are also identified as problematic, and children left behind suffer isolation, rejection and behavioural problems.

Paylor and Smith (1994) argue that the family ties of prisoners are often 'diverse and complex' (p.131), and that the traditional focus on partners excludes relatives of prisoners who have no partners or children: thereby excluding the majority of prisoners. They point out that the usual focus is on marital families. They go on to suggest that while the received wisdom is that a stable home to return to is an important factor in staying out of trouble, 'it is, however, not clear what the social and psychological processes might be through which kin support could work to reduce the re-offending risk' (p.133). They point to research that shows that kin relationships are important – that parents and other relatives are key sources of support – and elucidate the concept of imprisonment as a crisis involving the obligation to support. The experience of ex-care people demonstrates that those with 'highly disruptive family relationships' (p.135) have no access to any kinship support network. Moreover, they endorse the argument of Peelo *et al.* (1992) that the split between core work (tackling offending) and non-core work (which includes that with families) is simplistic because the latter could equally impact on offending behaviour. Probation officers should, therefore, identify support networks. In arguing this they repeat Haines' support for control theory, and explore two questions which relate first to the relevance of help in reducing offending and second to the problem of caring for the carers.

The research findings referred to above provide ample evidence of the multiple problems experienced by those offenders who end up in prison. Of course, the reasons for those problems are diverse and complex: inevitably, they will be a mixture of individual failings and limitations alongside those of society. However, the findings lend considerable weight to the argument that imprisonment if not creating some of those problems certainly exacerbates them. Prison, therefore, involves the deliberate and sometimes non-deliberate infliction of pain. With echoes of Sykes' (1958) elucidation of the pains of imprisonment, Williams (1991) highlights the significance of separation from family and friends; loss of touch with reality; fear and lack of trust of other prisoners; sexual deprivation; loss of privacy; loss of independence and loss of structure. It is the pain imposed by this form of state punishment, perhaps, that provides the strongest argument for the state having a responsibility to help prisoners during the time they are in prison and after they are released, but it is not the only one. Others include humanity in the face of suffering, reduction of offending to reduce future harm to the public and the prisoner, basic justice which involves the need to limit adverse consequences of imprisonment which prolong the punitive effects of the sentence beyond what justice or proportionality required, and obligations to the relatives innocently embroiled in the application of punishment. Combined, they more than justify the work of resettlement, but they do not resolve the central dilemmas of how to reconcile the demands of public protection from crime and the needs of people imprisoned (including their relatives), and justice for victims and offender. Both dilemmas are encompassed in rehabilitation, which itself lies at the heart of resettlement. As Raynor (1997, p.259) points out, rehabilitation needs to be 'limited by desert', but when effective it 'serves the end of justice by offering one route to the reintegration of some of our fellow citizens who are in trouble with the law', and it follows, therefore, that the same applies to resettlement. Prisoners, however, have a responsibility to take that route, and it could be argued that the moral obligation of the state to provide help is justifiably rescinded in its absence. Rightly, therefore, the process of helping prisoners has moved from its beginnings as a gift conditional upon Christian conformity to collaborative work on the reduction of harm caused by offending. So, how can the lessons learned from that process and the research findings that have accompanied it be applied, or put another way, how can the response to the problems of those imprisoned be best carried out?

Best practice

If we accept that the broad aims of resettlement are to reduce re-offending; to encourage and sustain personal change; to reduce criminogenic need and thereby improve social reintegration and ex-prisoners' prospects of improving their quality of life; to ensure public protection and to maintain and improve community ties and involve the families of prisoners where appropriate, then to achieve them we need to take account not only of research evidence about the needs of ex-prisoners and how they are best met but also evidence of what might be effective in helping them to attain a non-offending way of life. Both managers and practitioners need to understand, therefore, not only the historical context of work with short-sentence prisoners but also the research evidence that might inform best practice.

The detail of what has become known as 'What Works' and the principles of effective practice can be found in a number of publications (see, for example, Chapman and Hough 1998; McGuire 1995; Underdown 1998), and does not need repeating. What is important here is to understand that the lessons of that story and the principles of effective practice apply equally to prisoners. Two recent studies suggest that desistance is likely to be related to the way offenders think as well as their social situation (Maruna 2000; Zamble and Quinsey 1997). The first, a study of ex-prisoners in Canada, show that whether they re-offended or not depended to some extent on their state of mind and level of optimism about their ability to deal effectively with the problems they encountered. In effect, their low levels of optimism and emotions such as anger and depression in the face of difficulties led them to give up and re-offend. The second, a study of offenders in Liverpool, suggests that whether people see themselves as in control of their lives, and therefore responsible for what happens to them, or the victims of circumstance influences the likelihood or otherwise of re-offending. In other words, repeat offenders tend to see themselves as not being responsible or to blame for the circum-stances in which they find themselves; whereas those who desist have strategies to resolve problems without offending.

Combined, these studies confirm the view that the successful resettlement of prisoners depends on help being focused both on opportunities and thinking: put another way, the response to welfare needs should be ensconced in a frame of reference that challenges offence-prone attitudes and thinking. This accords both with the conclusion of Haines (1990), that if a prisoner returns to an environment in which offending is acceptable or where there are few normative controls or too low rewards plus high needs, there is a greater likelihood that he or she will re-offend (Hirschi's (1969) Control Theory), and with the evidence presented by May (1999) of the link between drug use (highly related), unemployment (significantly related), accommodation, money and peer group pressure (statistically significant) and re-offending. May also demonstrates that those with multiple problems are at highest risk of reconviction. Earlier research has shown a connection between levels of supervision and contact and re-offending. Shaw (1974) showed that an experimental group of prisoners who went through an 18-month treatment programme of one-hour weekly sessions during the last six months of sentence reconvicted less than a control group who did not undergo the programme. Soothill and Holmes (1981) in a ten-year follow-up of 63 men helped by APEX to find employment, while demonstrating that there was no insulation from reconviction from starting work straight after release did show a relationship between length of time in the APEX job and subsequent reconviction. Berntsen and Christiansen (1965) found that short-sentence prisoners who participated in an intensive programme involving help with family problems, addictions, emotional difficulties, accommodation, work and contacts with relevant agencies plus a two-year period of post-release supervision after six years had a reconviction rate 17 per cent less than a control group. Moreover, just as in the Reasoning and Rehabilitation and STOP experiments (Raynor and Vanstone 1997; Ross, Fabiano and Ewles 1988) those who did offend did so less seriously; they also offended later than the control group. The researchers also concluded that treatment had most effect with medium-risk prisoners.

Underlying all the evidence about effective work with prisoners is the notion that the process of help should be planned, coordinated within a clear strategy, and aimed at the amelioration of problems and the reduction of risk of further offending.[2] This means challenging crime-prone attitudes and if necessary using the concept of dissonance to increase levels of motivation. The use of dissonance is drawn directly from motivational interviewing where the worker's role is to tip the balance towards change (Miller and Rollnick 1991, 2002) and client-centred challenging where the worker's role is to highlight discrepancies, contradictions and inconsistencies in the personal matrix of behaviour, thinking and emotions of the individual (Egan 1994). Such an approach is best combined with Prochaska and DiClemente's (1984) Cycle of Change model and a focus on building motivation to

2   Shared work between prison staff and probation officers is not new. Shared Work in Prison Schemes were established in 1977, and Jepson and Elliott (1986) in their survey found 19 prisons operating in this way with another six running informal shared working schemes. In addition, they identified pre-release schemes involving prison staff in 20 prisons.

change. An interesting example can be found in the FOR a Change programme recently tested in the Pathfinder project referred to above (Fabiano and Porporino 2002).[3]

In addition, resettlement work should begin upon entry to prison, or as soon as possible thereafter. However, prison with its complex set of priorities, functions, objectives and demands, is a difficult environment within which to do such work. It is likely to require imaginative and resourceful ways of both exploiting the positive dimensions to that environment and responding to the constraints and obstacles to progress. Certain factors are crucial, however, to the success of any prison-based scheme.

Creating the right environment

> It is essential that probation officers should be prepared in their training for the special problems of aftercare and these problems underline the need for probation officers, as aftercare agents, to have the full support of their probation and case committees, as well as their supervisory grades.
>
> (Home Office 1962, p.45)

A strong message from the Pathfinder projects is that the support of senior prison staff is vital. Each of the project teams highlighted effective and committed leadership from all managers as one of the most important elements in resettlement work in as much as it predetermines good management (Lewis *et al.* 2003, p.17). Such management depends primarily on a designated resettlement manager within the prison with enthusiasm for and commitment to the project. This makes it much more likely that there will be clear communication to project staff about what the

3   This is a 13-session programme based on the concept of motivational interviewing developed by Miller and Rollnick which applies the principle that 'key "transitions" can interrupt life "trajectories" that have been consistently criminal and anti-social in character' (Fabiano and Porporino 2002, p.1), and aims to increase motivation and establish an agenda for change. The emphasis is on the individual's agenda; the individual is encouraged to think of life as a journey (trajectory), and then guided through five stages of acceptance of the need for change; problem recognition; problem definition; setting a plan for change and controlling for risks of relapse. The process involves work on factors relating to perception, interpretation, attitudes, values that might inhibit or enhance change; the setting of goals relevant to offending histories; relapse prevention and access to community resources.

project is trying to achieve and how this will be done. Management practice of this kind must be complemented by a shared, strategic approach that includes written plans, structures, lines of responsibility and accountability, policy agreements, objectives and strategy outlines within a framework of sentence management. Other features should include a shared protocol for risk assessment; mechanisms for clear communication and liaison between all staff involved in the resettlement process; resettlement managers and prison governors acting as advocates for re-settlement and ensuring that there is designated time for resettlement work, that the agreed level of priority to the task is maintained and that unnecessary transfers of prisoners do not take place; and finally a pro-social approach to leadership.

The latter requires managers to model appropriate levels of commitment and motivation, honesty and openness to self-challenge and challenge from within the team. (This would contribute to general levels of motivation and morale of the team involved in the resettlement programme.) In addition, they should promote the notion that diversity should inform practice and a commitment to equality of access. For the prison service this should involve ensuring commitment to the RESPOND and RESPECT programmes[4] and a strategy, policy and budget for the training and supervision of staff. That strategy should encompass regular training specific to need, and with a particular focus on the skills of engagement; the implementation and maintenance of risk management policies; systems for monitoring the process, ensuring quality assurance and evaluating the impact of the resettlement work; acknowledgement of staff skills and genuine empowerment through delegation; provision of appropriate budget levels and resources; ensuring the availability of 'a dedicated part of the prison estate' for resettlement work (Halliday 2001, p.24); and campaigning work with outside agencies.

Assessment and engagement

The resettlement process starts with an assessment of the risks and needs presented by the offender. While formal assessment procedures are important, and increasingly

---

4   The RESPOND programme is described in the Social Exclusion Report as intended to eliminate all forms of discrimination in the service and has five key elements – confrontation of harassment and discrimination; fair recruitment and promotion procedures; support of ethnic minority staff; equal opportunities for ethnic minority prisoners and recruitment of ethnic minority staff. The RESPECT programme is a part of that strategy and includes the Support Network for ethnic minority staff.

standardised as the Offender Assessment System (OASys) is being implemented in the Probation and Prison Services, it should be recognised that assessment begins in the first interaction, and continues throughout the resettlement process as the offender's circumstances change. Although assessment and engagement are discussed separately here, they are in fact intertwined. The assessment process can be used to motivate the offender, which, as will be shown below, is a key aspect of resettlement. For the assessment process to increase motivation it needs to be collaborative, with the prisoner engaged as a co-expert, because without the prisoner's perspective being accorded appropriate legitimacy there is unlikely to be real ownership of problems (Ginsburg *et al.* 2002; Miller and Rollnick 1991).

The process of assessment should include the gathering of background information (for example, from PSRs and pre-cons) and current relevant information; a portfolio of information that includes all the facts required to produce a supervision/action plan; and an individual supervision agreement. In turn, that agreement should specify the problems to be addressed and their priority; the degree and extent of response to risk (monitoring); the targets of change and the proposed actions to implement change. Crucial to these is the capacity and motivation of the prisoner to assist the process of change, and attention must therefore be given to inhibitors or enhancers of the prospects of success. These might include such characteristics as pro-criminal attitudes and values, lack of motivation, high motivation but no confidence, poor problem-solving skills, unrealistic or undefined goals, inability to achieve goals, impulsivity, addictive behaviour, and peer or family pressure. However, the focus on personal characteristics should not preclude the specification in the agreement of the social factors to address such as local availability of accommodation, unemployment, drug culture, health care provision and local criminal culture. The following comments from project staff in the resettlement projects provide pointers to good practice in relation to engaging and motivating offenders:

> Keeping [the offender] updated on issues, and funding bids, and housing requests. Writing them notes to say what is going on so that they are always engaged. They know that if I leave them and say that I am going to ring X up, they will get a note to say what the outcome of that was. Trying [to get] them to be pro-active in writing letters and engaging services from the cell. So [it is about] trying to empower people.

> It has become increasingly apparent that motivation of the women is best achieved when the same worker commences the work in the prison and continues to deliver in the community. The relationship which is developed between the [resettlement worker] and the woman is valued by the woman and offers a good pro-social

model. A second factor, which can affect the motivation of the women, is the speed at which the work commences, either in the prison or in the community. [Resettlement workers] meet with women within the first couple of days of their sentence and within a couple of days after release...[5]

As those quotes confirm, Pathfinder staff described the relationship between the practitioner and the prisoner and an early response to urgent resettlement problems as central to effective engagement and motivation. Both are dependent on the kind of empathy, concern, genuineness and concreteness that previous research tells us are the cornerstones of effective helping relationships (Miller and Rollnick 1991; Truax and Carkhuff 1967); and they are best conveyed by early attention to the most pressing problems identified in the Pathfinders and in previous research, namely, homelessness (or the risk of losing existing accommodation), unemployment, dependency on benefits, drug dependence and the maintenance of family ties.

Important though this kind of activity is, however, members of the Pathfinder teams also recognised the limited nature of such help without a concomitant effort to challenge the individual's anti-social attitudes, values and behaviour. Therefore, motivating the individual to recognise and address such cognitive factors is an integral part of the resettlement process. The application of motivational interviewing principles and techniques (Miller and Rollnick 1991) within Prochaska and DiClemente's (1984) Cycle of Change model is a vital part of encouraging individuals to think about change and decide what steps should be taken. Moreover, that change should encompass a determination to reducing re-offending, improve the prospects of reintegration into the community and ensure public protection through risk management.

Resettlement workers should also be familiar with the concept of dissonance, and be able to create dissonance in a prisoner to increase levels of motivation. In this context, creating dissonance means encouraging an awareness of the discordance between the individual's current circumstances and future aims and objectives. For example, a heroin addict with anger management problems needs to recognise that these factors prevent him from maintaining a good job and a stable relationship, and that he must address the former in order to achieve the latter.

In addition to the essential elements of effective engagement outlined above adherence to the principles and techniques of motivational interviewing and

5   M. Vanstone, S. Lewis and P. Raynor, Draft Good Practice Guide for the Resettlement of Short-term Prisoners (unpublished). (All project staff quotes are from this guide.)

sensitivity to, and action upon, the specific needs of women, and men and women from minority ethnic communities are pivotal. In organisational terms, practitioners should be responsible for such things as making judgements about criminogenic needs; assessing the level and the type of risk; verifying information as far as possible; identifying and engaging with appropriate resources for the process of assessment; managing the process of assessment; using approved or prescribed assessment tools; understanding motivational interviewing theory and techniques and responding to the special needs of prisoners. Managers should provide committed, imaginative and goal-oriented leadership; ensure adherence to the service's risk assessment and management policy and ensure that an appropriate level of resources is available. Leadership of this quality would also be concerned about the maintenance of a strategy for staff training, supervision and support; the development of a framework for effective relationships with key personnel both within and outside the prison and the proper implementation of an appropriate motivational programme. Other responsibilities would include the process of monitoring the work undertaken and its quality; assurance that assessment procedures are sensitive to the diverse needs of prisoners and, in particular, of women, men and women from minority ethnic groups, and prisoners with disabilities; and management of the application of effectiveness principles.

The use of motivational assessment practices and interviewing techniques should take place alongside structured cognitive motivational work on either an accredited group-work or one-to-one programme. Programmes such as FOR a Change are designed specifically to increase levels of motivation, while also addressing cognitive needs, and are, therefore, potentially helpful in the resettlement process. However, Pathfinder staff stressed the importance not of only being properly trained to deliver the pre and (where relevant) post-release phase of a programme but also of the need for adequate numbers of trained and dedicated programme deliverers.

Action planning

The reinforcement and maintenance of motivation generated through assessment and engagement is dependent on a realistic, tangible action plan. Although to all intents and purposes lost to mainstream help-related work (especially in the criminal justice field), two particular theoretical models still lend themselves to the production of effective action plans. The first, by Reid and Shyne (1969) showed that planned, short-term work increased the chances of success, that the improvements lasted, and that it was applicable to most situations. This model, with its principle of building on achievement, has particular relevance for the sustaining of motivation.

Building on this, Reid and Epstein (1972) developed and evaluated a model that targeted problems such as interpersonal conflict, role performance, social transition, insufficient resources and emotional stress. It involved several inter-related components. These included a tangible process of review of possible problem areas; agreement on the problem to be addressed; agreement on action within a specified time period and achievable intervention, and clarity about the role of the worker. In particular, the worker's role involved facilitating problem exploration, structuring the 'treatment relationship' and encouraging achievement. The application of the model was subjected to evaluation in three studies (Goldberg, Gibbons and Sinclair 1985; Reid and Epstein 1972). Although they were small (the biggest involving 20 cases) and the results somewhat unspecific and merely encouraging (in the biggest study 85 per cent of the clients showed some improvement), the research remains a significant early contribution to evidence-based practice.

The second, systems theory (Pincus and Minahan 1979) remains relevant in as far as it promotes the idea of collaborative effort within a framework of action systems and target systems – the former being the group of people involved in the change effort and the latter being those systems that are the focus of the change effort. Moreover, it formulates a number of important practice skill areas into a schema for work. These are assessing problems; collecting data; making initial contacts; negotiating contracts; forming action systems; maintaining and coordinating action systems; exercising influence and terminating the change effort.

This model remains potentially useful in action planning because it highlights the complexity and diversity of the context of change and demands clear and concrete priorities and objectives. Obviously, both approaches suffer from their age in as far as they were developed in an era when the 'client-centred' Non-Treatment Paradigm (Bottoms and McWilliams 1979), had legitimacy in the criminal justice field that is rather dubious now. However, a relatively recent attempt to update the paradigm might overcome this problem. Raynor and Vanstone (1994) provide a revision that fits current policy and preserves the paradigm's central contribution to improving probation practice. In Raynor and Vanstone's revision, Bottoms and McWilliams' three components, 'help', 'shared assessment' and 'collaboratively defined task', become respectively 'help consistent with a commitment to the reduction of harm', '[e]xplicit dialogue and negotiation offering opportunities for informed consent to involvement in a process of change' and '[c]ollaboratively defined task relevant to criminogenic needs, and potentially effective in meeting them' (p.402). Incorporating each of these models into the theoretical framework underpinning effective practice might create a solid platform for effective engagement, and the following may be considered central tenets of an effective action plan: a clearly written, collaboratively formulated plan that is informed by the prisoner's perspective, the assessment outcomes, and professional judgement; realistic and realisable short-term objectives put in order of priority; a planned timetable with a list of designated responsibilities – who does what, how and by when; the signatures of all parties to the plan to ensure understanding and agreement; a built-in monitoring mechanism and a date for review. A commitment to collaborative planning was demonstrated by one project worker who said:

> I am not going in there and telling them what they need. What I am doing is opening up the dialogue, so they are part of it...and letting [them] know that yes, we are about reducing offending, but that can only happen with their agreement. We work with them, and they are the most important part of the work we do.

In this part of the process the responsibilities of practitioners are to guarantee that the action plan relates to the key objective of reducing risk of re-offending; to make sure that the proposed programme matches the learning style of the prisoner; to monitor the action plan to check that it reflects the different needs of prisoners; to monitor the action plan; to formulate the action system; to facilitate the link between the people and agencies involved in the action system; to self-monitor to and implement the delivery of the action plan programme. Managers should provide supervision and support for key practitioners involved in the action plan; and monitor the implementation of risk management.

Developing support

The success of any action plan will hinge on the degree to which an effective network of support can be arranged. It is at this stage of the resettlement process that links with those resources relevant to resolving criminogenic need have to be established. There is a sense in which describing the development of support as a stage is inappropriate and misleading, because the early response to problems urged above inevitably involves that very activity, but the concept of a 'stage' will be retained for the sake of clarity.

As the Pathfinder evaluation revealed, there may well be problems in developing a strategy of support. For instance, short-term prisoners can be low down the list of priorities in an overstretched service like CARAT (see Chapter 15, this volume), the responsibility for the provision of post-release drug services might not fall to any single agency or there may be a shortage of funds. Furthermore, there may be a lack of local accommodation; housing associations and private landlords may refuse to consider ex-prisoners and local authorities may accord them low priority.

The development of support might be enhanced by a 'network map' or list of agencies to which offenders can be referred. One project worker described his team's experience of developing a 'network map' thus:

> When we did the [first] quarterly report [to the Home Office] we identified...maybe 40 different agencies around the area... We have a volunteer coming in, about once every couple of weeks, who will just sit at the 'phone and 'phone anything she can find – through the Yellow Pages – and build up resources.

> And we've got a file for each town [within the geographical area covered by the project] of resources we can access.

During such a process, it is important to check whether support projects for ethnic minority offenders exist locally (for instance, the Black Prisoners' Support Project in Manchester and the Black Prisoners' Support Scheme in Nottingham both provide a wide range of services for offenders both pre- and post-release). Moreover, the creation of links between offenders and post-release support workers at the pre-release stage, through one-to-one meetings, or attendance at a 'market place session' in which representatives of agencies are brought into the prison to meet with groups of prisoners (affording prisoners the opportunity to obtain information and make appointments with a range of agencies) or regular meetings of members of the action system including the prisoner, might be mechanisms to keep intact vital components of the prisoner's life outside.

Those components might include protecting accommodation and belongings, preventing rent arrears and childcare, particularly for women (Nacro 2001); training and education (including vocational skills) to enhance employment opportunity with particular attention paid to the particular needs of women and minority ethnic prisoners; mental health support systems; strategies for dealing with drug and alcohol problems; liaison with families and other key social contacts; involvement of relevant community organisations (including religious groups) for prisoners from minority ethnic groups; ongoing information on employment, education and housing opportunities and benefits.

Work in the Pathfinder projects provides some interesting illustrations of innovative responses to addressing problems. For example, faced with difficulties in finding housing for ex-prisoners, staff in one project used a variety of methods to secure accommodation. If an offender in one scheme had health problems, the project worker wrote to their GP requesting more information. If the medical condition was sufficiently serious, he then sent details to their housing department, in the hope that their poor health would enable them to jump the queue for council accommodation. Some project workers recognised the benefits of working not only with the offender but also with their family. A prisoner and former heroin addict from one project explained how his resettlement worker had agreed to work with him and his girlfriend, who was also in custody and had a history of substance misuse, on their release, to help them both to remain drug free. Many of the projects noted that clients wanting help with drug abuse issues post-release had to join the end of a long waiting list, often relapsing before receiving help. So, one project team got around a three-month waiting list for services by making arrangements with the local drug agency for their clients to jump to the front of the queue.

Attempts by project workers to sort out offenders' benefit entitlements prior to release were often hampered by bureaucracy and 'red tape'. The project manager and two resettlement workers from one scheme gave a presentation to representatives from all of the local job centres, to inform them of the project's aims and objectives. They eventually succeeded in getting a named contact at each local job centre who agreed to accept benefits claim forms that had been completed pre-release. It was also agreed that project participants could be given an appointment and interviewed on the day of release rather than, as was usually the case, having to go to the job centre to make an appointment to be interviewed at a later date, which delayed the first benefit payment. Two of the Pathfinder projects gave prisoners the opportunity to work with a volunteer mentor pre- and post-release. The mentors provided a wide range of practical help and support, including gathering information about local education and employment opportunities; helping to complete application forms and accompanying offenders to their accommodation or to meetings with service providers on release.

In providing support, practitioners should manage the programmes involved in developing support, and liaise with all relevant agencies and groups both inside and outside the prison. In order to make sure that support is effective they will need to provide the link to appropriate resources; ensure the integration of the cognitive-behavioural component and the attempt to resolve other criminogenic problems; offer a pro-social model to the prisoner (including the use of the problem-solving/thinking strategies being taught to the prisoner); provide specific group-work programmes where appropriate; maintain programme integrity in the delivery of those programmes where appropriate; keep the offender up to date on progress made in addressing practical resettlement needs and contribute to the maintenance of the motivation of the prisoner. Managers, on the other hand, should promote the programmes; identify the role and responsibilities of the members of the action system; ensure that strategies are in place to meet criminogenic needs;

monitor the responsiveness of the developing support strategy to the different needs of women, minority ethnic prisoners and disabled prisoners and monitor the delivery of agreed intervention.

Release and post-release

Relapse prevention work is a key aspect of resettlement work. Zamble and Quinsey (1997) show that if offenders doubt their ability to stay out of trouble they are more likely to re-offend. This highlights the importance of the maintenance and relapse stage in Prochaska and Di Clemente's Cycle of Change model. The maintenance stage (in which people are helped to develop ways of foreseeing the potential circumstance of failure and preventing it) and the relapse stage (in which people are helped to respond to failure as recoverable) are both pivotal to successful community integration. Such work should be a component of both individual and group work pre-release, and should continue on a one-to-one basis in the community.

Encouraging prisoners to maintain contact with resettlement staff and access services in the community post-release is also vital, particularly when they are not on licence, and is more likely to be successful if levels of motivation has been built up and sustained throughout the sentence. Possible impediments to take-up of services are a high level of social isolation; lack of coordination in resettlement work; poor quality contact during sentence; limited prisoner awareness of what is on offer; low priority given to resettlement work by key agencies; remoteness of relevant personnel and prisoners having a negative view of what is on offer. In order to increase the chances of overcoming such impediments, release and post-release work should involve consistent contact arrangements (where and when); pick up at gate by worker, volunteer or mentor; if an appointment is not kept, follow up by a telephone call, a letter, or a personal visit, or by checking with other agencies whether contact has been made; a reception environment that confirms the commitment to meeting the needs of ex-prisoners; an active advocacy role (for example, about benefits); help to set up a sustainable support network in the community and a focus on maintaining motivation through reference to agreed plans and achievements, and on reinforcing relapse prevention strategies.

At this stage practitioners should set up community appointments for the prisoner with resettlement workers and staff from other agencies; make arrangements for the prisoner to be met at the gate; monitor release date changes and prisoner response to appointments; provide practical help and support; guarantee access to specific resources for women, and prisoners from minority ethnic groups

(Howden-Windell and Clark 1999). The following quotes from project workers illustrate the practicalities of such work:

> [The post-release resettlement worker] is introduced to them when they are inside [prison], so they do not have the shock of 'hello, this is somebody new, are they going to help me at all?' Introducing them to staff at housing providers, going to see them at the initial stages to make sure that they are all right... Even helping them to buy toiletries – we have some money to do that so we will get them tea bags and things like that.

> If I am referring someone to CARAT [in the prison], and we are talking about [them] going on then to another agency [post release]...we will be talking to the other agency defining the person's needs, wants, and possible resistance... So it is about sharing information with the agency that they are going to...

> Where we have involved other agencies then we have informed them of what the action plan has been, where we are up to with it, and what the ongoing issues that need to be addressed are. So for example, ...X...had counselling while he was here, and then when he [went to supported housing on release] they provided counselling for him...to continue what had been started here... So it has been [about] liaising with outside agencies. Or liaising with GPs in the cases where...they haven't seen a GP for a few years, it is a case of putting them in touch with a GP to get a health assessment done. Arranging appointments with agencies outside...making appointments for them so that work can [be] continue[d] by another agency [on release].

Managers should be prepared to draw up service contracts with service providers, thus consolidating agencies' commitment to providing resettlement provisions, and increasing managers' capacity to troubleshoot if agencies do not meet their responsibilities; ensure necessary facilities are available for post-release meetings; troubleshoot for post-release problems, for example, by providing bus tokens to encourage offenders to attend meetings with their resettlement worker, volunteer mentor, or other service provider; make sure that safety procedures are in place and maintain existing and foster new community contacts.

The review stage

The way in which post-release contact with ex-prisoners is ended is of crucial importance. Every effort must be made to ensure that they are equipped to deal with subsequent problems. Moreover, some evaluation of the success of intervention needs to be undertaken at this point, and the mechanisms for evaluation should already be in place. Accordingly, a number of elements need to be in place. There should be an agreed point at which the service is terminated; a support network (with, when necessary, a particular focus on women, and women and men from minority ethnic groups) in place prior to termination; a process of evaluation championed by managers and supported by research expertise; an adherence to prescribed recording and monitoring tools (including repetitions); monitoring and evaluating and constructive feedback to both staff and prisoner.

The role of practitioners should involve management of the process of termination; checking of the existence of support network; the completion of necessary forms and instruments; a contribution to evaluation and the provision of feedback to the ex-prisoner. Managers should facilitate evaluation; monitor completion of forms and instruments and provide feedback to practitioners.

Conclusion

The continuing political commitment to imprisonment as a prime response to crime makes the effective resettlement of those people even more important. As has been argued in this chapter, the response to the needs of prisoners and ex-prisoners is directly related to the need of the community to be protected from offending. The fact that imprisonment involves pain for the guilty which may exceed what has been demanded by justice and proportionality and that offending inflicts pain on the innocent, adds a moral imperative to ensuring as far as possible that resettlement work is successful in its aims and objectives. This chapter, drawing on past and current research findings, has attempted to sketch out the features of successful resettlement practice. It is argued that if resettlement services were provided in a manner characterised by best practice of this kind some of the revolving-door problems identified for so long by research might be alleviated to some significant degree. As the Prison and Probation Inspectors assert in the foreword of their thematic review:

> The point is this. Unless something is done to tackle the causes of offending be-haviour, and the social and economic exclusion from which it commonly springs, and to which it contributes, prisons will continue to have revolving doors, and the public will not in the long term be protected. (Home Office 2001)

Inevitably, however, as long as people are imprisoned some of those problems of exclusion will remain. It is important then that good resettlement practice and policy is underpinned by policies which try to ensure that nobody goes unnecessarily to prison in the first place. Moreover, those policies are themselves dependent on imaginative, innovative and evidence-based ways of resolving and addressing those personal and social problems that place people at risk of imprisonment.

References

Agozino, B. (1997) *Black Women and the Criminal Justice System.* Aldershot: Ashgate.

Banks, C. and Fairhead, S. (1976) *The Petty Short Term Prisoner.* London: Howard League for Penal Reform.

Berntsen, K. and Christiansen, K. (1965) 'A Resocialization Experiment with Short-term Offenders'. *Scandinavian Studies in Criminology 1*, 35–54.

Bochel, D. (1976) *Probation and Aftercare. Its Development in England and Wales.* Edinburgh: Scottish Academic Press.

Bottoms, A.E. and McWilliams, W. (1979) 'A Non-treatment Paradigm for Probation Practice'. *British Journal of Social Work 9*, 159–202.

Caddle, D. and Crisp, D. (1996) Imprisoned Women and Mothers. Home Office Research Study 162. London: Home Office.

Carlen, P. (1983) *Women's Imprisonment. A Study in Social Control.* London: Routledge and Kegan Paul.

Carlen, P. (2002) 'Women's Imprisonment: Models of Reform and Change'. *Probation Journal 49*, 2, 76–87.

Chapman, T. and Hough, M. (1998) *Evidence Based Practice.* London: Home Office.

Chigwada-Bailey, R. (1997) *Black Women's Experiences of the Criminal Justice System.* Winchester: Waterside Press.

Corden, J. (1983) 'Persistent Petty Offenders: Problems and Patterns of Multiple Disadvantage'. *Howard Journal 22*, 68–90.

Corden, J. and Clifton, M. (1985) 'Helping Socially Isolated Prisoners'. *British Journal of Social Work 15*, 331–350.

Corden, J., Kuipers, J. and Wilson, K. (1978) *After Prison: A Study of Post-release Experiences of Discharged Prisoners.* York: Department of Social Administration and Social Work, University of York.

Corden, J., Kuipers, J. and Wilson, K. (1980) 'Prison Welfare and Voluntary Aftercare'. *British Journal of Social Work 10*, 71–86.

Davies, M. (1974) *Prisoners of Society. Attitudes and Aftercare.* London: Routledge and Kegan Paul.

Departmental Committee on Prisons (1895) *Report of the Departmental Committee on Prisons.* (The Gladstone Report) London: Home Office.

Egan, G. (1994) *The Skilled Helper: A Problem-management Approach to Helping.* Pacific Grove, CA: Brooks/Cole.

Fabiano, E. and Porporino, F. (2002) *Focus on Resettlement – A Change.* Canada: T3 Associates.

Fairhead, S. (1981) *Persistent Petty Offenders.* Home Office Research Study No. 66, London: Home Office.

Fitzgerald, M. (1993) *Ethnic Minorities in the Criminal Justice System.* Research Study No. 20, Royal Commission on Criminal Justice. London: Home Office.

Ginsburg, J.I.D., Mann, R.E., Rotgers, F. and Weekes, J.R. (2002) 'Motivational Interviewing with Criminal Justice Populations.' In W.R. Miller and S. Rollnick (eds) *Motivational Interviewing: Preparing People for Change,* 2nd edn. New York: Guildford Press.

Goldberg, E.M., Gibbons, J. and Sinclair, I. (1985) *Problems, Tasks and Outcomes.* London: Allen and Unwin.

Hagell, A., Newburn, T. and Rowlingson, K. (1995) *Financial Difficulties on Release from Prison.* London: Policy Studies Unit.

Haines, K. (1990) *Aftercare Services for Released Prisoners: A Review of the Literature.* Cambridge: Institute of Criminology.

Halliday, J. (2001) *Making Punishments Work. Report of a Review of the Sentencing Framework for England and Wales.* London: Home Office.

Hamlyn, B. and Lewis, D. (2000) *Women Prisoners: A Survey of their Work and Training experiences in Custody and on Release.* Home Office Research Study 208 London: HMSO.

Hirschi, T. (1969) *Causes of Delinquency.* Berkeley, CA: University of California Press.

Holborn, J. (1975) *Casework with Short-term Prisoners. Some Male Offenders Problems. Part 2.* Home Office Research Study 28, London: HMSO.

Home Office (1962) *Report of the Departmental Committee on the Probation Service.* London: HMSO.

Home Office (1963) The Organisation of Aftercare. The Report of the Advisory Council on the Treatment of Offenders. London: HMSO.

Home Office (1965) *The Organisation of Aftercare.* Circular 144/1965 London: Home Office.

Home Office (1984) *Probation Service in England and Wales. Statement of National Objectives and Priorities.* London: Home Office.

Home Office (1988a) *Punishment, Custody and the Community.* London: HMSO.

Home Office (1988b) *Tackling Offending: An Action Plan.* London: Home Office.

Home Office (1988c) *The Parole System in England and Wales: Report of the Review Committee,* Cm.532. London: HMSO.

Home Office (1990a) *Partnership in Dealing with Offenders in the Community. A Discussion Paper.* London: Home Office.

Home Office (1990b) *Supervision and Punishment in the Community. A Framework for Action.* London: HMSO.

Home Office (1992a) *National Standards for the Supervision of Offenders in the Community.* London: Home Office.

Home Office (1992b) *Three Year Plan 1993–1996.* London: Home Office.

Home Office (1993) *Three Year Plan 1994–1997.* London: Home Office.

Home Office (1994) *Race and the Criminal Justice System.* Home Office.

Home Office (1995) *National Standards for the Supervision of Offenders in the Community.* London: Home Office.

Home Office (1998) *Joining Forces to Protect the Public. Prisons-Probation. A Consultation Document.* London: Home Office.

Home Office (1999a) *Statistics on Women and the Criminal Justice System.* Section 95. A Home Office Publication under Section 95 of the Criminal Justice Act 1991. London: Home Office.

Home Office (1999b) *Statistics on Race and the Criminal Justice System.* Section 95. Home Office. A Home Office Publication under Section 95 of the Criminal Justice Act 1991. London: Home Office.

Home Office (2000) *National Standards for the Supervision of Offenders in the Community.* London: Home Office.

Home Office (2001) *Through the Prison Gate. A Joint Thematic Review by HM Inspectorates of Prison and Probation.* London: Home Office.

Home Office (2002) *Race and the Criminal Justice System 2001.* A Home Office Publication under Section 95 of the Criminal Justice Act 1991. London: Home Office.

Home Office Probation Services Division and Prison Service (1993) *National Framework for the Throughcare of Offenders.* London: Home Office.

Hood, R. (1992) *Race and Sentencing: A Study in the Crown Court.* Oxford: Clarendon Press.

Howden-Windell, J. and Clark, D.A. (1999) *Criminogenic Needs of Female Offenders: A Literature Review.* London: HM Prison Service.

Jarvis, F.V. (1972) *Advise, Assist and Befriend: The History of the Probation Service.* London: National Association of Probation Officers.

Jepson, N. and Elliot, K. (1986) *Shared Working between Prison and Probation Officers.* London: Home Office.

King, J.F.S. (ed.) (1964) *The Probation Service,* 2nd edn. London: Butterworths.

Lewis, S., Vennard, J., Maguire, M., Raynor, P. *et al.* (2003) *The Resettlement of Short-Term Prisoners: An Evaluation of Seven Pathfinders.* London: Home Office.

Maguire, M., Perroud, B. and Raynor, P. (1996) *Automatic Conditional Release – The First Two Years.* Home Office Research Study No.156. London: Home Office.

Maguire, M., Raynor, P., Vanstone, M. and Kynch, J. (1997) *Voluntary Aftercare.* Report to the Home Office. Cardiff: Michael and Associates.

Maguire, M., Raynor, P., Vanstone, M. and Kynch, J. (2000) 'Voluntary Aftercare and the Probation Service: A Case of Diminishing Responsibility'. *Howard Journal 39,* 234–248.

Maruna, S. (2000) *Making Good.* Washington: American Psychological Association.

May, C. (1999) *Explaining Reconviction Following a Community Sentence: The Role of Social Factors.* Home Office Research Study 192. London: Home Office.

McGuire, J. (ed.) (1995) *What Works: Reducing Re-offending.* Chichester: Wiley.

McGuire, J and Priestley, P. (1985) *Offending Behaviour: Skills and Strategems for Going Straight.* London: Batsford.

McWilliams, W. (1975) *Homeless Offenders in Liverpool. Some Male Offenders' Problems Part 1.* Home Office Research Study 28. London: HMSO.

Miller, W.R. and Rollnick, S. (1991) *Motivational Interviewing.* New York: Guilford Press.

Miller, W.R. and Rollnick, S. (2002) *Motivational Interviewing. Preparing people for Change,* 2nd edn. New York: Guilford Press.

Morris, P. (1965) *Prisoners and their Families.* London: George Allen and Unwin.

Nacro (1993) *Opening The Doors. The Resettlement of Prisoners in the Community.* London: Nacro.

Nacro (2000) *The Forgotten Majority: The Resettlement of Short Term Prisoners.* Nacro.

Nacro (2001) *Women Beyond Bars: A Positive Agenda for Women Prisoners' Resettlement.* London: Nacro.

Nacro (2002) *Resettling Prisoners from Black and Minority Ethnic Groups.* London: Nacro.

NADPAS (1956) *Handbook of the National Association of Discharged Prisoners' Aid Societies.* London: NADPAS.

National Council of Social Services (1961) *Problems of the Ex-Prisoner.* Report of the Pakenham/Thompson Committee. London: National Council of Social Services.

Nellis, M. (1995) 'Probation Values for the 1990s.' *Howard Journal 34,* 19–44.

Paylor, I. (1992) *Homelessness and Ex-Offenders: A Case for Reform.* Norwich: University of East Anglia.

Paylor, I. and Smith, D. (1994) 'Who are Prisoners' Families?' *Journal of Social Welfare and Family Law 2,* 131–144.

Peelo, M., Stewart, J., Stewart, G. and Prior, A. (1992) *A Sense of Justice: Offenders as Victims of Crime.* London: Association of Chief Officers of Probation.

Pincus, A. and Minahan, A. (1973) *Social Work Practice: Model and Method.* Itasca, IL: F.E. Peacock.

Pope, V. (1987) 'We All Went to Prison: The Distress of prisoners' Children. *Probation Journal 34,* 92–6.

Priestley, P. (1970) *The Problem of the Short Term Prisoner.* London: Nacro.

Prochaska, J. and DiClemente, C. (1984) *The Transtheoretical Approach: Crossing Traditional Boundaries of Therapy.* Homewood, IL:, Dow Jones-Irwin.

Raynor, P. (1997) 'Some Observations on Rehabilitation and Justice'. *Howard Journal 36*, 248–62.

Raynor, P. (2004) 'Opportunity, Motivation and Change: Some Findings from Research on Resettlement.' In R. Burnett and C. Roberts (eds) *What Works in Probation and Youth Justice.* Cullompton: Willan.

Raynor, P., Kynch, J., Roberts, C. and Merrington, M. (2000) *Risk and Need Assessment in Probation Services: An Evaluation*, Research Study 211. London: Home Office.

Raynor, P. and Vanstone, M. (1994) 'Probation Practice, Effectiveness and the Non-Treatment Paradigm.' *British Journal of Social Work 24*, 387–404.

Raynor, P. and Vanstone, M. (1997) *Straight Thinking On Probation (STOP): The Mid Glamorgan Experiment. Probation Studies Unit Report No. 4.* Oxford: University of Oxford Centre for Criminological Research.

Reid, W.J. and Epstein, L. (1972) *Task-Centred Casework.* New York: Columbia University Press.

Reid, W.J. and Shyne, A. (1969) *Brief and Extended Casework.* New York: Columbia University Press.

Robinson, G. (2001) 'Consultation on Reducing Re-Offending by Ex-Prisoners.' Unpublished Report to the Social Exclusion Unit.

Ross, R.R. and Fabiano, E.A. (1985) *Time to Think: A Cognitive Model of Delinquency Prevention and Offender Rehabilitation.* Johnson City, TN: Institute of Social Sciences and Arts.

Ross, R.R., Fabiano, E.A. and Ewles, C.D. (1988) 'Reasoning and rehabilitation'. *International Journal of Offender Therapy and Comparative Criminology 32*, 29–35.

Ross, R., Fabiano, E.A. and Ross, R.D. (1986) *Reasoning and Rehabilitation: A Handbook for Teaching Cognitive Skills.* Ottawa: AIR Training and Publications.

Shaw, M. (1974) *Social Work in Prison.* London: HMSO.

Shaw, R. (1987) *Children of Imprisoned Fathers.* London: Hodder and Stoughton.

Shaw, R. (ed.) (1992) *Prisoners' Children. What are the Issues?* London: Routledge.

Soothill, K. and Holmes, J. (1981) 'Finding Employment for Ex-prisoners: A Ten Year Follow-up Study.' *Howard Journal 21*, 1, 29–36.

Sykes, G.M. (1958) *The Society of Captives. A Study of a Maximum Security Prison.* New Jersey: Princetown University Press.

Trotter, C. (1993) *The Supervision of the Offenders – What Works? A Study Undertaken in Community – Based Corrections.* Melbourne: Victoria Department of Justice.

Truax, C.B. and Carkhuff, R.R. (1967) *Towards Effective Counselling and Psychotherapy: Training and Practice.* Chicago: Aldine.

Underdown, A. (1998) *Strategies for Effective Offender Supervision.* London: Home Office.

Vanstone, M. (1993) 'A "Missed Opportunity" Reassessed: The Influence of the Day Training Centre Experiment on the Criminal Justice System and Probation Practice.' *British Journal of Social Work 23*, 213 – 29.

Vanstone, M. (1995) 'Ethics in Social Work.' *VISTA 1*, 1, 49–58.

Vanstone, M. (2004) *Supervising Offenders in the Community: A History of Probation Practice.* Aldershot: Ashgate.

Vanstone, M., Lewis, S. and Raynor, P. (2004) 'Good Practice in the Resettlement of Short-Term Prisoners.' Unpublished report to the Home Office.

White, S. (1989) 'Mothers in Custody and the Punishment of Children.' *Probation Journal 36*, 106–9.

Williams, B. (1991) *Work with Prisoners.* Birmingham: Venture Press.

Zamble, E. and Quinsey, V. (1997) *The Criminal Recidivism Process.* Cambridge: Cambridge University Press.

CHAPTER 18

Postscript: Opportunities and Threats

Peter Raynor

This book has brought together an international group of contributors who have written about a wide range of approaches to social work with offenders, but who have in common a respect for evidence and a belief that those methods of work which are most likely to be beneficial to offenders and society should be preferred and encouraged. If only life were so simple! On the one hand, a comparison of this volume with its 1996 predecessor shows a far greater range of evidence-based approaches available to criminal justice agencies and practitioners, all of which are, to some degree, in current use in the UK. This should mean that the prospects for developing and delivering services in the criminal justice system which actually reduce re-offending are significantly better than in the past. On the other hand, we have to note that since the last edition of this book crime in the UK (as in most western industrialised countries) has been decreasing, but rates of imprisonment have increased (which several other countries have avoided) and the reconviction rates of those who pass through the criminal justice system have shown little change. In England and Wales in particular there is the additional prospect of further tough-on-crime legislation (see Chapter 4 in this volume), together with proposals to fragment and partially privatise the Probation Service (Home Office 2006). In order to understand these paradoxes a little better, it is instructive to focus initially on what has been happening in England and Wales, where the investment of both money and reputation in 'What Works' was greatest.

The history of this initiative has by now been thoroughly explored by a number of commentators and from a variety of perspectives (see, for example, Mair 2004; Raynor and Robinson 2005; Raynor and Vanstone 2002; Worrall and Hoy 2005), and readers interested in the full detail are referred to these sources. Briefly,

England and Wales (unlike Scotland) had retained a separate Probation Service following the welfare reforms of the late 1960s, and the Service came under political attack in 1993 when Michael Howard was appointed as Home Secretary and announced that 'Prison works'. Probation was attacked (quite unfairly) as a 'soft' service which saw offenders as victims of society, who should be helped rather than punished. An orchestrated press campaign (described by Aldridge and Eadie 1997) advocated the abolition of social work training for probation officers; for a while there was no training at all, and some newspapers and politicians pressed for the replacement of probation officers by retired or redundant army personnel. In reality this was best understood as a political phenomenon rather than the result of any serious thinking about criminal justice: a governing party which had been in power for a long time was becoming increasingly unpopular, and played a populist card in the vain hope of rescuing the next election. However, the threat to the Probation Service was real and pressing, and this is the main explanation for the urgency and enthusiasm with which the Service's leaders and the Home Office seized on new evidence about effective rehabilitation to create the 'What Works' movement in British probation. The election of the new Labour Government in 1997, with a public commitment to evidence-based policy, gave the Probation Service the opportunity to seek support and funding for new evidence-based approaches (mainly programmes). What has happened since, particularly when compared to the different development path in Scotland, requires us to learn some important lessons about implementation and about the fragility of political support.

First, implementation. The main funding for the innovations in England and Wales came through the Crime Reduction Programme, which set very demanding targets for the number of offenders completing accredited programmes: this was to be 30,000 per year, with another 30,000 to be achieved through Enhanced Community Punishment. These numbers were not evidence based, and in hindsight were much too high; the attempt to achieve them led to many of the wrong people being put on programmes, and contributed to very high failure rates (most people did not complete their programmes). The Service was subjected to a convulsive change process to try to achieve in three years what needed to take at least twice as long. Staff morale suffered, and the evaluation results, when they became available, reflected the implementation problems: the data came from the early stages of new projects when they were not well established, and the low completion rates of programmes meant that their evaluations were less informative than had been hoped (Harper and Chitty 2004; Hollin *et al.* 2004). The unrealistically high expectations of large reductions in recidivism raised by the Halliday Report (Halliday 2001) proved impossible to meet in practice, and the price has been a degree of reversion to official scepticism about effectiveness (Raynor 2004) and the re-emergence of political scepticism about probation.

Three particular problems of implementation appear to have contributed to these results (for a comprehensive independent critique see Goggin and Gendreau 2006). All three suggest that the problems lay not in the evidence-based approach itself, but in a failure to be evidence-based enough in some key areas. One, already mentioned above, was the rushed and centralised approach which left many of the staff behind: this ignored existing evidence, including UK evidence (Raynor and Vanstone 2001), that the introduction of effective innovations requires a substantial period of preparation and discussion. Professional staff will not adopt new methods with conviction and enthusiasm unless they believe that this can add value to their practice. A second, related problem was a failure to take into account existing evidence on how the quality and effectiveness of programmes can be reduced by over-hasty roll-out. For example, as early as 1999 a US meta-analysis compared 'demonstration' (i.e. pilot) programmes with 'practical' (i.e. rolled-out for widespread implementation) programmes. Better results were more commonly found among the 'demonstration' projects: in Lipsey's study the 196 'practical' programmes reviewed were on average half as effective as the 205 'demonstration' programmes. Even this level of effectiveness depended heavily on a few programmes, as 57 per cent of the 'practical' programmes had no appreciable effect. As he points out, 'rehabilitative programmes of a practical "real world" sort clearly can be effective; the challenge is to design and implement them so that they, in fact, are effective' (Lipsey 1999, p.641).

The third major problem lay in a failure to develop evidence-based case-management and supervision skills (see, for example, Chapters 10 and 11 in this volume) alongside the implementation of programmes. One of the clearest demonstrations of why this is important is provided by another meta-analysis (Dowden and Andrews 2004) which studied the contribution of certain staff skills to the effectiveness of rehabilitative work with offenders. The authors define these skills as 'Core Correctional Practices' or CCPs, which can be summarised briefly as effective use of authority; appropriate modelling and reinforcement; the use of a problem-solving approach, and the development of relationships characterised by openness, warmth, empathy, enthusiasm, directiveness and structure. The mean effect sizes of programmes were found to be higher when these were present, and significantly higher when other principles of programme effectiveness were also applied; staff skills and programme design complemented each other, rather than one being a substitute for the other. However, the authors point out that 'Clearly these CCPs were rarely used in the human service programs that were surveyed in this meta-analysis… These results suggest that the emphasis placed on developing and utilizing appropriate staff techniques has been sorely lacking within correctional treatment programmes' (p.209). Others might well define some or all of these 'Core Correctional Practices' as social work skills.

In addition to these questions of methods and implementation, the history of recent 'What Works' initiatives directs our attention to the politics of criminal justice. This is a huge topic in its own right (see, for example, Downes and Morgan 2002; Garland 2001) but a few points about its impact on evidence-based practice call for some comment here. From time to time the criminal justice system encounters a toxic mix of public anxiety, popular media which exploit crime in a sensationalist style for its entertainment value, and politicians who appear to accept and validate this presentation by the media. This leads to instability in policy-making and a plethora of new laws and initiatives which respond in a short-term way to perceived public concern rather than to evidence about the impact of previous or likely future policies. The intended outcome sometimes seems to be a positive newspaper headline rather than a real improvement. New Labour politicians in London have been particularly subject to these criticisms; a party which came to power promising to be 'tough on crime and tough on the causes of crime' has been very sensitive to the media, and has introduced an unprecedented amount of new policy and legislation about crime, often in haste and with very limited consultation. In Scotland the politicians' approach has, by contrast, been more consensual and consultative, perhaps reflecting the practical requirements of coalition government. These difference have been clearly shown in the contrasting approaches of the two governments to encouraging joined-up working in criminal justice – that is (mainly) a better connection between what is done in prisons and in the community in order to create more continuity in offender management, and better connections between criminal justice and the other agencies which are involved in providing services which may help people to avoid offending.

Taking England and Wales first, current discussions are dominated by the continuing process of trying to implement the 'Carter Report' (Carter 2003) and the resulting National Offender Management Service (NOMS: see Chapter 4 in this volume). Carter made three major recommendations: to limit the prison population, to introduce a period of supervision in the community to assist the resettlement of short-sentence prisoners and to introduce 'contestability' to open up the provision of probation services to the private and voluntary sectors. The first two of these have been effectively abandoned by the Home Secretary, John Reid, who was appointed in 2006. In addition to describing himself as 'the Enforcer' and his own Department as 'not fit for purpose', he announced the creation of 8000 new prison places while postponing plans for the 'custody plus' sentence which was designed to deliver resettlement services to short-sentence prisoners, on the grounds that it could not be afforded. The remaining priority is contestability, and on this topic the Home Office has ignored the majority of responses to its own consultation exercises. Instead it has, at the time of writing, just published an Offender Management Bill which will abolish the National Probation Service and replace it with local contractors chosen by the Home Office who may be 'probation trusts', voluntary organisations or private sector companies. Meanwhile, in speech after speech, including one to prisoners in Wormwood Scrubs prison, the Probation Service (which would be supervising many of the prisoners on release) has been condemned as unreliable or underperforming. Most recently, there have been two surprising announcements: from May 2007 responsibilities for prisons and probations will transfer to a new Ministry of Justice, and John Reed intends to step down as Home Secretary during the summer of 2007 at the same time as the Prime Minister Tony Blair. It is unclear what effects, if any, these changes will have on the current polices and proposed legislation.

There is, perhaps, some parallel with Michael Howard's arrival in the Home Office in 1993: common features include a governing Party which has been in power for a long time, is losing popularity and is very anxious about the next election: hence the perceived need for a display of 'toughness'. The current form of the NOMS proposals appears to be driven by politics: the process of shaping services by carefully considered change and thorough evaluation lacks media appeal, and instead the doctrine is that market forces and contestability will generate improvements more quickly – a belief which seems to owe more to private sector lobbying than to evidence. In Scotland, by contrast, the option of a single correctional service was considered, was subjected to a real consultative process (unlike NOMS), and was rejected. Instead, criminal justice social work remains with the local authorities, and the implementation and co-ordination of improvements are the responsibility of eight new Community Justice Authorities which bring together groups of local authorities, promote partnership with prisons and other relevant agencies, and handle the funding of community justice services. Change is incremental, with a focus on evidence and consultation. At the time of writing the Community Justice Authorities have produced their first Area Plans and these have been subject to a scrutiny process. Clearly the process of change will be complex and incremental, but it may benefit from being less subject to political panics than in England and Wales, and may be more capable of delivering durable and coherent improvements. Certainly the example of Scotland is attracting political interest in

Wales, where most services are devolved to the Wales Assembly Government but not, as yet, criminal justice.

Two final points are worth emphasising. First, rehabilitation is not simply the reduction of re-offending; it is also a relational process concerned with an offender's (or ex-offender's) membership of a society and a community (Raynor and Robinson 2005). The rehabilitation of offenders has found support in the past as part of a wider range of policies to improve welfare, reduce poverty and inequality, and promote what is now called social inclusion. Currently, countries which make a high proportionate investment in welfare provision tend to have lower rates of imprisonment (Downes and Hansen 2006). The Social Exclusion Unit's report on re-offending by ex-prisoners (Social Exclusion Unit 2002) began to articulate a link between recidivism and wider social exclusion, but there is a long way to go before the links between offender rehabilitation and wider social policy are adequately explored. Second, the commitment to evidence-based approaches cannot be pursued on a part-time basis: we cannot be evidence-based on Mondays and Tuesdays and purely political for the rest of the week. Experience in England and Wales has also shown a tendency to select from the evidence base those elements which lend themselves to a centralised and managerialist approach (such as programme manuals and audit) while neglecting those which needed to be developed in a more decentralised way (such as practitioner ownership and case management skills). The more devolved strategy which is being pursued in Scotland may provide a better model of how to promote ownership and involvement. Perhaps by the time the next edition of this book appears, enough research will have been done to show whether it can also deliver the improvements in rehabilitative impact across the system which have been difficult to deliver in England and Wales.

References

Aldridge, M. and Eadie, C. (1997) 'Manufacturing an Issue: the Case of Probation Officer Training.' *Critical Social Policy 17*, 111–124.

Carter, P. (2003) *Managing Offenders, Reducing Crime: A New Approach.* Correctional Services Review. London: Home Office.

Dowden, C. and Andrews, D. (2004) 'The Importance of Staff Practice in Delivering Effective Correctional Treatment: A Meta-analysis.' *International Journal of Offender Therapy and Comparative Criminology 48*, 203-214.

Downes, D. and Hansen, K. (2006) *Welfare and Punishment: The Relationship Between Welfare Spending and Imprisonment. Briefing 2.* London: Crime and Society Foundation.

Downes, D. and Morgan, R. (2002) 'The Skeletons in the Cupboard: the Politics of Law and Order at the Turn of the Millennium.' In M. Maguire, R. Morgan and R. Reiner (eds) *The Oxford Handbook of Criminology,* 3rd edn. Oxford: Oxford University Press.

Garland, D. (2001) *The Culture of Control.* Oxford: Oxford University Press.

Goggin, C. and Gendreau, P. (2006) 'The Implementation and Maintenance of Quality Services in Offender Rehabilitation Programmes'. In C. Hollin and E. Palmer (eds) *Offending Behaviour Programmes*. Chichester: Wiley.

Halliday, J. (2001) *Making Punishments Work: Report of a Review of the Sentencing Framework for England and Wales*. London: Home Office.

Harper, G. and Chitty, C. (2004) *The Impact of Corrections on Re-offending: A Review of 'What Works'*. Home Office Research Study 291. London: Home Office.

Hollin, C., Palmer, E., McGuire, J., Hounsome, J. *et al.* (2004) *Pathfinder Programmes in the Probation Service: A Retrospective Analysis*. Home Office Online Report 66/04. London: Home Office.

Home Office (2006) *Improving Prisons and Probation Services: Public Value Partnerships*. London: Home Office.

Lipsey, M. (1999) 'Can Rehabilitative Programs Reduce the Recidivism Of Juvenile Offenders? An Inquiry into the Effectiveness of Practical Programs.' *Virginia Journal of Social Policy and the Law 6*: 611–641.

Mair, G. (ed.) (2004) *What Matters in Probation*. Cullompton: Willan.

Raynor, P. (2004) 'The Probation Service "Pathfinders": Finding the Path and Losing the Way?' *Criminal Justice 4*, 309–25.

Raynor, P. and Robinson, G. (2005) *Rehabilitation, Crime and Justice*. Basingstoke: Palgrave Macmillan.

Raynor, P. and Vanstone, M. (2001) 'Straight Thinking On Probation: evidence-based practice and the culture of curiosity.' In G. Bernfeld, D. Farrington and A. Leschied (eds) *Offender Rehabilitation in Practice*. Chichester: Wiley.

Raynor, P. and Vanstone, M. (2002) *Understanding Community Penalties*. Buckingham: Open University Press.

Social Exclusion Unit (2002) *Reducing Re-offending by Ex-prisoners*. London: Office of the Deputy Prime Minister.

Worrall, A. and Hoy, C. (2005) *Punishment in the Community*. Cullompton: Willan.

The Contributors

James Bonta received his PhD in Clinical Psychology from the University of Ottawa in 1979. Upon graduating, Dr Bonta became Chief Psychologist at a maximum security remand centre for adults and young offenders. In 1990 Dr Bonta joined Public Safety and Emergency Preparedness Canada and he is presently Director of Corrections Research. Dr Bonta has been a member of the editorial advisory boards for the *Canadian Journal of Criminology* and *Criminal Justice and Behavior*. He is also a Fellow of the Canadian Psychological Association. Dr Bonta has published extensively in the areas of risk assessment and offender rehabilitation. His latest publications include a book co-authored with D.A. Andrews entitled the *Psychology of Criminal Conduct* (presently in its fourth edition). He is also a co-author of *The Level of Service Inventory – Revised* and *The Level of Service/Case Management Inventory*.

Tim Chapman worked with the Probation Board of Northern Ireland for 25 years. Since 1999 he has been an independent consultant in youth justice. He has supported the development of effective practice and restorative justice initiatives in Ireland, Scotland and England. He has published widely, including *Time to Grow*, a research-based approach to working with young people who offend.

Iain Crow has studied the social and psychological correlates of illegal drug use at the Institute of Psychiatry's Addiction Research Unit, and been head of research at the national offender rehabilitation and crime prevention organisation, Nacro, where he undertook studies on a range of community-based projects, including ones dealing with drug users. He is currently Reader in Research Methods at the University of Sheffield. He has published a text on the treatment and rehabilitation of offenders, and is working on a book on research in criminology.

Elizabeth Fabiano has an MA in criminology, is a certified MI practitioner and is recognised internationally for her programme development contributions in corrections. In the mid-1980s Elizabeth co-developed the R&R programme (*Reasoning and Rehabilitation*), the forerunner of the cognitive behavioural model as applied to offenders. Shortly thereafter, Elizabeth became Manager, Program Development and Implementation for the Correctional Service Canada, where she developed and introduced a core programming strategy throughout the federal correctional system in Canada. She went on to co-found T3 Associates Inc. with Frank Porporino and has continued her very active programme development and training work internationally in over 15 countries. Ms Fabiano has co-authored a number of monographs and journal articles in the area of effective correctional treatments and has two co-authored books to her credit (with R. Ross), *Correctional Afterthoughts: Programmes for Female Offenders* and *Time To Think*, the latter recently designated as one of the top ten influential books in the field of correctional education.

Loraine Gelsthorpe is Reader in Criminology and Criminal Justice at the Institute of Criminology, University of Cambridge. She has long-standing research interests in the conceptions and delivery of justice, with a particular focus on discretion and discrimination, the links between criminal justice and social justice, and community penalties. She has also published widely on youth justice issues and feminism and criminology. Current interests include psychoanalytic dimensions of criminal justice policy. Recent books include *Exercising Discretion* (edited with Nicky Padfield) and Community

Penalties: Change and Challenges (edited with Tony Bottoms and Sue Rex). She is currently completing a *Handbook of Probation.*

Barry Goldson is Professor of Criminology and Social Policy at the School of Sociology and Social Policy, University of Liverpool where he is also Director of Research. His books include: *Youth Justice: Contemporary Policy and Practice* (1999); *The New Youth Justice* (2000); *Children, Welfare and the State* (2002, with Lavalette and McKechnie); *Vulnerable Inside: Children in Secure and Penal Settings* (2002); *In the Care of the State? Child Deaths in Penal Custody in England and Wales* (2005, with Coles); *Youth Crime and Justice* (2006, with Muncie) and *Comparative Youth Justice* (2006, with Muncie). He is the founding editor of *Youth Justice*, the leading peer-reviewed journal in the UK specialising in youth crime and youth justice.

Sam Lewis is an RCUK Academic Research Fellow in the Centre for Criminal Justice Studies at the University of Leeds. In recent years she has undertaken research (with colleagues from other institutions) for the Home Office, local probation areas and youth offending services. Her research focuses on minority ethnic experiences of criminal justice, youth crime and justice, prisoner resettlement and Probation Service policy and practice. She is co-editor (with Raynor, Smith and Wardak) of *Race and Probation* (2005).

Shadd Maruna, PhD is a Reader in Criminology at Queen's University, Belfast. His book *Making Good: How Ex-Convicts Reform and Rebuild Their Lives* (2001) was named the Outstanding Contribution to Criminology by the American Society of Criminology in 2001. He has co-edited two recent books: *After Crime and Punishment* (2004) and *The Effects of Imprisonment* (2005). Most recently, he has co-authored the book *Rehabilitation* (2007) with Tony Ward.

James McGuire is Professor of Forensic Clinical Psychology at the University of Liverpool, where he is Director of Studies for the Doctorate in Clinical Psychology programme and also holds an honorary post as consultant clinical psychologist in Mersey Care NHS Trust. As a chartered forensic psychologist he has carried out psycho-legal work involving assessment of offenders for courts, mental health review tribunals and the Criminal Cases Review Commission. He worked for some years in a high security hospital and has conducted research in probation services, prisons and other settings on aspects of psychologically-based interventions with offenders, and has written or edited 13 books and numerous other publications on this and related issues. In addition he has been involved in a range of consultative work with criminal justice agencies in the UK, Sweden, Romania, Canada, Australia and Hong Kong.

Gill McIvor is Professor of Criminology at Lancaster University. Prior to that she was Director of the Social Work Research Centre at the University of Stirling and contributed to the establishment of the Scottish Centre for Crime and Justice Research. Her research has focused primarily on community penalties, with current interests in women in the criminal justice system, criminal justice responses to drug-related crime and specialist courts. Her books include: *Understanding Offending Among Young People* (1999 with Janet Jamieson and Cathy Murray); *Women who Offend* (2004, editor); *Managing Sex Offender Risk* (2004, co-editor with Hazel Kemshall) and *What Works with Women Offenders: International Perspectives* (forthcoming, co-editor with Rosemary Sheehan and Chris Trotter).

Fergus McNeill is a senior lecturer in the Glasgow School of Social Work (a joint venture of the Universities of Glasgow and Strathclyde) and a network leader in the Scottish Centre for Crime and Justice Research (at the University of Glasgow). Prior to becoming an academic in 1998, he worked for a number of years in residential drug rehabilitation and as a criminal justice social worker. His research interests and publications have addressed a range of criminal justice issues including sentencing, community penalties and youth justice.

David O'Mahony is a reader at the Department of Law, Durham University. He graduated in psychology and criminology from the University of Ottawa, Canada in 1984 and in 1987 was awarded the degree of MA in Criminology. In 1988 he was awarded an MPhil in Criminology at Cambridge University where he went on to work as a researcher and among other projects completed a national evaluation of the youth justice system in England and Wales. In 1995 he was appointed as lecturer in Youth Justice at the Institute of Criminology and Criminal Justice, at the School of Law, Queen's University, Belfast, and was promoted to senior lecturer in 2002. He has conducted research projects for the Department of Health, the Home Office, the Northern Ireland Office, the Probation Board for Northern Ireland and the British Council. David is presently directing a research study with colleagues from Queen's University, the University of Ulster, University of Sheffield and University of Wales examining restorative justice practices with young offenders. He was awarded a funded visiting research fellowship under the 'Gender, Sexuality and the Family' programme at Cornell Law School, New York in 2003. He is a member of the editorial board for the journal *Youth Justice*, and a member of the Northern Ireland Crime Prevention Panel and the Northern Ireland Restorative Justice Working Group.

Frank Porporino has a PhD in clinical psychology and has focused both his public and private sector careers for the last 33 years on promoting evidence-based correctional policy and practice. Frank was Director of Strategic Planning and Director General of Research and Development for the Correctional Service of Canada. In 1993, he co-founded T3 Associates in order to disseminate the cognitive model and provide other research-based training and technical assistance to correctional jurisdictions internationally. Frank is on his third term with the Correctional Services Accreditation Panel in England and Wales, and is on the Executive Boards of the International Association of Reentry and the International Corrections and Prisons Association. In 1998 he was awarded the ACA Lejins Award and in 2003 the ICCA Presidents Award for his career contributions to research and programme development in the field of corrections. He has authored numerous monographs and journal articles on the assessment and treatment of offenders, has developed a number of well-respected cognitive-behavioural programmes for both juvenile and adult offenders, and has also co-authored the book *Coping, Behaviour, and Adaptation in Prison Inmates* (1988, with E. Zamble).

Peter Raynor is Professor of Criminology and Criminal Justice at the University of Wales, Swansea. A former probation officer, his research over the last 30 years has included work on victims, drugs, youth justice, pre-sentence reports, through-care and resettlement of prisoners, risk and need assessment, the effectiveness of probation and programmes, and the impact of probation on minority ethnic offenders. He has published widely on criminal justice issues, including the recent books *Understanding Community Penalties* (with Maurice Vanstone), *Rehabilitation, Crime and Justice* (with Gwen Robinson) and *Race and Probation* (with Lewis, Smith and Wardak). He is a member of the Correctional Services Accreditation Panel for England and Wales, and the Scottish National Advisory Body on Offender Management.

Sue Rex spent over ten years at the Institute of Criminology, University of Cambridge, where she undertook wide-ranging research on the theory and practice of community penalties, including the evaluation of the accreditation panel. Having completed a fellowship with the Economic and Social Research Council, which enabled her to explore the role of communication in punishment and in community penalties, she returned to policy work in the Home Office in 2004 and is now working in the National Offender Management Service.

Gwen Robinson is Lecturer in Criminal Justice at the School of Law, University of Sheffield. Her primary research interests are offender rehabilitation and management; community penalties and restorative justice. Since 2002 she has been involved in a major evaluation of restorative justice schemes for the Home Office (led by Joanna Shapland at the University of Sheffield) which was completed in

2007. She is co-author (with Peter Raynor) of *Rehabilitation, Crime and Justice* (2005) and co-editor (with Tony Bottoms and Sue Rex) of *Alternatives to Prison: Options for an Insecure Society* (2004). In 1996 she obtained a Diploma in Social Work from the University of Oxford, specialising in social work with offenders.

Chris Trotter, PhD worked for 15 years as a probation officer and as a Regional Manager in Australia prior to his appointment to Monash University in 1991. He has undertaken more than ten research projects and published more than 50 books and articles during the past decade, focused primarily on what works in the supervision of offenders and on work with involuntary clients. Dr Trotter has developed a worldwide reputation for his work on pro-social modelling and has undertaken consultancies in Australia, Austria, UK and Ireland, Singapore and New Zealand to assist probation services to implement pro-social modelling. His book *Working with Involuntary Clients* has sold more than 10,000 copies and is available in German, Chinese and Japanese translation. The Cognitive Centre in the UK has full-time staff devoted to training probation officers in pro-social modelling and a considerable proportion of UK probation staff have undertaken the training.

Maurice Vanstone is Reader in Criminal Justice and Criminology at the Centre for Criminal Justice and Criminology, Swansea University. Previously, he worked for the probation service as a practitioner, manager, trainer and researcher. For the past 25 years he has been teaching, researching and writing on work with offenders. His publications include: *Effective Probation Practice* (1994, with Peter Raynor and David Smith); *Betrayal of Trust* (1996, with Matthew Colton); *Beyond Offending Behaviour* (1996, with Mark Drakeford); *Understanding Community Penalties* (2002, with Peter Raynor) and *Supervising Offenders in the Community: A History of Probation Theory and Practice* (2004), as well as numerous articles, chapters and reports.

Bill Whyte is Senior Lecturer in Social Work at the University of Edinburgh and Director of the Criminal Justice Social Work Development Centre for Scotland, Universities of Edinburgh and Stirling. Bill has worked as a social work manager and field social worker in the Lothians area, as a residential care worker in a (former) List D residential school, as an independent chair of child protection for a small local authority. His research has included adult sex offenders, young people involved in sexually harmful behaviour, community reparation orders, parenting orders, restorative justice, children's hearings, evaluation in youth justice, youth homelessness.

Stephen Wormith is Chair of Forensic Psychology, in the Psychology Department, University of Saskatchewan. Formerly he was Psychologist-in-Chief for the Ontario Ministry of Community Safety and Correctional Services and Deputy Superintendent (Treatment) at Rideau Correctional and Treatment Centre. He is the Canadian Psychological Association's representative on the National Associations Active in Criminal Justice (NAACJ). He is active in the voluntary sector as Vice-president of the Canadian Training Institute, and is on the board of directors of The International Institute on Special Needs Offenders and Policy Research (Canada). He is on the editorial board of *Psychological Services*. He is co-author of the *Level of Service/Case Management Inventory*.

Subject Index

Author Index